"Honey Fitz"

Also by JOHN HENRY CUTLER

PUT IT ON THE FRONT PAGE, PLEASE!

WHAT ABOUT WOMEN?

"Honey Fitz"

THREE STEPS TO THE WHITE HOUSE

The Life and Times of

John F. (Honey Fitz) Fitzgerald

by

JOHN HENRY CUTLER

THE **BOBBS-MERRILL** COMPANY, INC.
A SUBSIDIARY OF HOWARD W. SAMS & CO., INC.
Publishers • INDIANAPOLIS • NEW YORK

To my mother

CONTENTS

FOREWORD

"My boy, we do not talk of family in this country. It is enough for you to know that your grandfather is an honest man."

—Henry Cabot Lodge to his grandson.

SOME families are worth talking about, especially those who have brought honor and the cachet of public service to the names they bear, and who, despite foreign origins, are recognized as distinguished Americans.

President John Fitzgerald Kennedy, who has been called "the first Irish Brahmin," has fulfilled the expectation of his father, Joseph P. Kennedy. "The measure of a man's success in life," said Joseph Kennedy, "is not the money he has made. It's the kind of family he has raised. In that, I've been mighty lucky."

The President has also fulfilled a prophecy made almost a generation ago by his maternal grandfather, John F. Fitzgerald—the "Honey Fitz" of this story, in honor of whom the Presidential yacht is now named. In 1946, when young Kennedy, then a tall, slender war hero known to his torpedo boat squadron as "Shafty," was elected to Congress, Honey Fitz predicted that he would go on to be President of the United States.

The Fitzgeralds and the Kennedys thus have given the United States another political dynasty. They have brought to the American scene an eminent political family that has been likened to the Adamses, the Lodges, and the LaFollettes.

The Fitzgerald-Kennedy story began more than a century ago when economic pressures in Ireland forced Thomas Fitzgerald and Patrick Kennedy to seek new lives in new surroundings. Their progress led through the tumble of Boston politics in the most rowdy, brawling and florid era of American political history. It led through slums and tenement rookeries in alleyways, through Boston Latin School, Harvard College, the Boston City Hall, a State Capitol and the halls of Congress to the thirty-fifth Presidency of the United States. In John F. Kennedy, the first

9

Roman Catholic to occupy the White House, three generations have produced a statesman who has translated long-age dreams into reality.

When the results of the 1960 Presidential election reached the original homeland, there was a joyous celebration on the same stone quayside at New Ross, Ireland, from which Patrick Kennedy had sailed to America in 1849. Villagers danced and lighted bonfires, and Gaelic pipes rang out across the harbor, which more than a century ago was a scene of tearful departure. There were natives of County Wexford, too, who remembered that another great grandfather of the President—Thomas Fitzgerald— had left their sparse acres a few years before Pat Kennedy had waved his last good-by from the deck of a packet ship. County Wexford also sent congratulations to the new Chief Executive of the United States.

There had also been a great stirring of interest throughout the Emerald Isle in 1937, when President Franklin Delano Roosevelt named Joseph Patrick Kennedy, grandson of an Irish immigrant, to be United States Ambassador to the Court of St. James, the first time an American-Irish Catholic had been so honored. The folks back home were thrilled that their own Pat Kennedy's descendant had been elevated to a post once held by two Presidents of the United States—John Quincy Adams and James Monroe—and by such other distinguished Americans as John Jay, Edward Everett, Charles Francis Adams and James Russell Lowell.

There had been excitement, too, many years earlier in Irish villages when word came of the political success of a second Patrick Kennedy, son of Ireland-born Pat, who had been elected State Senator. It was still another triumph when John F. Fitzgerald, another son of a County Wexford native, became Mayor of Boston, which some Irishmen back home had heard called "the Athens of America" and even "the Hub of the Universe."

"We have always been a politically minded family," said Mrs. Rose Fitzgerald, mother of the President. "My father was in Congress fifty years ahead of Jack, and afterward he was Mayor of Boston." Her father, John Francis (Honey Fitz) Fitzgerald, was the first and one of the very few politicians ever to outfox Martin Lomasney, who ruled Boston political affairs as a czar for thirty-three years, beginning in the middle 1880s. Lomasney eventually had to make peace with Fitzgerald and support him in his campaigns for mayor.

President Kennedy was John F. Fitzgerald's favorite grandson. Even as a boy he often served as an audience of one when Grampa Fitzgerald was rehearsing one of his "impromptu" speeches. Honey Fitz used to marvel at what the boy had learned from his professors of government at Harvard, though Honey Fitz could have given these professors a practical insight into operational methods of politics, Boston style, of which they knew little. Later, when Jack Kennedy sought political advice, Grampa Fitzgerald gave him more than he needed. Even such a master politician as James Michael Curley, who is woven into the Fitzgerald story, soaked up political sagacity from Honey Fitz. The very methods Honey Fitz taught Jack on precinct, ward and city levels were later deftly used by the grandson on state and national levels. So, if the President has a touch of "Fitzblarney," is there any doubt where he got it?

John F. Fitzgerald, twice defeated for the United States Senate, died two years before his grandson achieved that honor. In one senatorial bid, John F. Fitzgerald lost to Henry Cabot Lodge, Senior, the gentleman from Nahant. In 1952, in a daring family rematch, John Fitzgerald Kennedy astounded political sharps across the nation by defeating Henry Cabot Lodge, Junior, in a gentlemanly contest for that same Senate seat. It was grandson against grandson.

"I recall that I was a freshman at Harvard," President Kennedy said years later, "when Henry Cabot Lodge, Junior, was elected to the Senate. I don't suppose I ever thought in those days I would some day defeat him for the Senate. I suppose there is some freshman in college today who isn't aware that he is probably going to end up by defeating me."

"Never a sentimentalist," wrote James MacGregor Burns in his biography of the President, "Kennedy would not think of his victory as vengeance for his grandfather's defeat by the earlier Henry Cabot Lodge thirty-six years before. But the day after the election, some old Irishmen sitting on a park bench in East Boston were sure they heard—from the place where Boston politicians go for their reward—the faint but happy rendering of "Sweet Adeline.""

"It was those damn teas that licked me," Lodge said, referring to the afternoon receptions for women voters held by the numerous Kennedy ladies. Those teas were symbols of the change that had transformed the uproarious years of Boston ward politics around the turn of the century when bricks were thrown and the air was heavy with insult and no tea was served at rough-and-tumble street-corner and ward rallies. That was the gaudy era of political high jinks when Irish chieftains squared off against their Yankee and Brahmin rulers.

The life of John Francis Fitzgerald encompasses the entire cycle of the change.

11

"Honey Fitz"

CHAPTER 1

Journey's End and a New Beginning

Give me your tired, your poor,
Your huddled masses yearning to breathe free,
The wretched refuse of your teeming shore,
Send these, the homeless, tempest-tossed, to me. . . .

—EMMA LAZARUS (*lines inscribed on the base of the Statue of Liberty*)

IN 1840, Boston was seven-eighths native-born American. By the time of the siege of Vicksburg in 1863, when John Francis Fitzgerald was born, the Fenian Brotherhood, an Irish organization which advocated violence when necessary, held its first national convention in Chicago.

Its Boston branch was flourishing. The Irish had begun to emerge as "a down-trodden majority," although the "nativists" were still in the saddle, socially, economically and politically. By 1875, New England itself had become predominantly Irish, and the Yankees and the Brahmins —its elite corps—were retreating in the face of the Irish invasion.

A courageous decision and a humble vegetable had combined to change the course of American history.

In 1839, after the Shawmut Bank of Boston had negotiated with Sir Samuel Cunard to make Boston the terminus of his Liverpool Line, the precise western terminal was fixed at Noddle's Island just across a narrow arm of Boston Harbor. In 1840, the first steam packets of the Cunard Company appeared in Boston Harbor: the *Unicorn* in June, the *Britannia* in July and the *Arcadia* in August. The first Atlantic steamship service to Boston had begun.

On July 4, when the *Britannia,* a tiny paddle-steamer, churned its way

15

from Liverpool to Boston to inaugurate a regular passenger and mail service between Europe and the United States, one of the one hundred and fifteen passengers who walked down the gangway was Sir Samuel Cunard, whose vision would change in short order the complexion of two continents. Also aboard to provide fresh milk for the trip was a cow.

From this modest and unheralded beginning, Boston was until 1848 the exclusive Cunard port in the United States, and even passengers bound for a distant port like New Orleans were advised by crooked agents to come by way of Boston, which was only a "short walk away." At least one Irish family—headed for St. John, New Brunswick—learned that their tickets were good only as far as St. John, Newfoundland. Many illiterate Irish immigrants were victimized in this manner.

Cunard Line rates enabled even the poor and "huddled masses yearning to breathe free" to cross the Atlantic. The line itself did not handle emigrant trade until 1863, but its low rates forced packet lines to traffic with the migrating Irish at reasonable rates. Around the turn of the century, the fare from Londonderry to New York ranged from $50 to $60, but by the 1840s the rates had dropped to a low of $12.50 and a high of $20. By the 1850s the fare from Liverpool or an Irish port to Boston was less than $20, plain food included. Over the years, passenger ships sailed from Dublin, Cork and Queenstown, but the packet lines, specializing in emigrant traffic, started from Liverpool.

Sir Samuel Cunard's bold move was one factor in quickening Irish immigration. What of the humble vegetable?

The vegetable was the potato which had at times reduced the Irish economy to a precarious level. One crop failure spelled ruin in 1822. By 1845, when four million of the nine million inhabitants of Ireland depended on potatoes for sustenance, the "spud" was to Ireland what rice is to China. "God bless it," said a housewife. "We had only to throw a few of them in the hot ashes and then turn them, and we had our supper." Sturdy Irish farmers might each consume seven or eight pounds of potatoes at every meal. Crews of packet ships, which ferried the emigrants to America, said steerage passengers often preferred potatoes to chocolate, cheese or plum pudding. Sick children in crowded holds of ships were heard wailing for their favorite food.

In 1845, Ireland lost a third of its crop, and the dreaded blight that rotted the crop in storehouse, as well as the tubers in the ground, returned the following year, doing even more damage. The blight, after slackening in 1847, returned in full force in 1848. By 1850, the disease had run its course, but the five-year famine was the end of the world for millions of Irish farmers.

When doom struck, a deeply religious people reeled under the blow, and their frantic priests, recoiling in horror, were powerless to help. One cleric on his way from Cork to Dublin saw potato patches in bloom and "rejoiced at the rich harvest in the making." On his way back a week later in that same year of 1846, he saw farmlands that had become "one wide waste of putrefying vegetation." He also saw weeping landholders wringing their hands in abandonment of hope. Panic and dread gave way to despair and resignation.

Ireland was suddenly a nation of nomads, who in their weary, dispirited wandering across rocky moors often left behind the old and infirm, all only weeks or days away from starvation. Cottiers awaited the end in mud cabins or thatched cottages as typhus came to deepen the gloom. Within two weeks, one family of eight was reduced to a twelve-year-old girl.

With cemeteries overcrowded and coffinmakers and gravediggers hard to come by, the dead were put into rude slab containers—some tarred inside—and lowered into hastily built graves. Many were buried in a communal pit and sprinkled with lime, and some of the "dead" were heard moaning in carts on the way to the graveyard.

Lucky ones turned their few possessions into passage money, and others begged for sovereigns enough to pay their way. Landlords sometimes gave passage fare in lieu of having on their hands tenants who, as paupers, might become perpetual charges on their estate. Certain landlords, alarmed by this possibility, even chartered ships and hired agents to supervise the trip, supplying provisions and pocket money.

Most of the uprooted took with them only such belongings as could be wrapped in a bandanna handkerchief. They left prayerfully, kneeling while their curates blessed them before taking the dusty road to the quay, knowing they were leaving behind loved ones who were sobbing, sick or dying. The more fortunate could wait in soup lines for slop which, said one observer, "would be refused by well-bred pigs."

The first big wave of immigration came in 1847 in packets soon to be known as "coffin ships." One in ten of the passengers, who were crowded like cattle in the vermin-ridden holds of ships, died during the rough crossing that took six to eight weeks under foul, unsanitary conditions. The "ship fever" which caused their death was commonly known as "famine fever" or "hunger typhus."

The Irish had come to America long before the Potato Famine, of course. As early as 1737, there were enough Irish in Boston to sponsor a formal celebration of St. Patrick's Day. And during the American struggle for freedom from England, no less a person than George Washington had written: "Patriots of Ireland! Champions of liberty in all lands—be strong in hope! Your cause is identical with mine!"

In 1846, when the population of Boston was about one hundred and twenty thousand, there were some twenty-four thousand Irish. The Boston Society for the Prevention of Pauperism, an employment agency, received job applications from fourteen thousand females in the four years ending in 1849. By 1850, an estimated thirty-five thousand Irish were in Boston, and five years later, when the total population of the city was three hundred and ten thousand, there were more than fifty thousand Irish—most of them from the southern and western counties of Ireland. By the turn of the century, the Irish had nearly taken over. There were two hundred and twenty-five thousand immigrants or their descendants, representing almost half of the population of Boston.

"They disembarked," wrote Lucius Beebe in *Boston and the Boston Legend,* "the clay pipes of tradition in the green felt hatbands, at the great piers of the Boston waterfront or at East Boston, as Noddle's Island was coming to be known, and they settled down, for the most part, within a stone's throw of the Cunard pierheads." Some brought picks and shovels with them, the main part of their baggage. Those who could afford it moved into boarding houses. Some moved in with friends or relatives until they could find jobs, and there were those hapless newcomers who were exploited by the "Intelligence Bureaus" or "Swindling Shops," organizations that, in a quest for cheap labor, traded in human misery. Their Irish foremen were called "padrones."

Overburdened Catholic priests and authentic benevolent and immigrant-aid societies could accommodate only a fraction of the load. During one two-month period in 1847, the House of Industry admitted four hundred newcomers, and temporary quarters for them were erected on Deer Island, where a few years later there was also an almshouse that never lacked tenants. Deer Island would one day become the site of a city jail.

The second wave of immigrants, seduced by Cunard Line posters and encouraged by word from cousins who had found work in the new land, was rudely jolted by the reception it received. Earlier immigrants had been welcome because of the labor shortage. Dependable Irish farm girls, working for low wages as domestics in boarding houses and in the palatial brownstone residences of wealthy Yankees, received as little as a dollar a week with room and board, while Irish laborers earned from seventy-five cents to $1.25 a day when they could find work. The colleens came to be known as biddies, pot wallopers, kitchen canaries or Bridgets.

Even these usually cheerful young ladies were rejected by some families who could not be bothered to send them to church on Sunday in their horse-drawn carriages. By 1850, over two thousand Irish girls worked as domestics in Boston.

The male newcomers were generally known as "greenhorns, clodhoppers, cattle Irish, Harps or Micks." Some became waiters but could not qualify as cooks or barbers. (In the nineteenth century, many barbers were Negroes.) Irishmen took menial jobs in grocery stores, factories or sweat shops if there were no NINA ("No Irish Need Apply") signs to cut them to the quick. In 1830, the *New York Evening Post,* mirroring a trend that had been established in the Empire City earlier than in Boston, ran this classified advertisement: "Wanted a cook or chambermaid. She must be American, Scotch, Swiss or African—no Irish." Even after the turn of the century, Boston Yankees who advertised for domestics in newspapers often specified "Only Protestants need apply." Posted on one bulletin board was this notice: "No Irish or Negroes Wanted."

Used to horses in the homeland, many Irishmen became blacksmiths, hostlers and stablers as well as coachmen. Others took jobs as coal heavers, stevedores or longshoremen, and those who dug ditches for sewers or canals were labeled "blacklegs" or "muckers." Brawny Irishmen were rounded up by the thousands to level the hills of Boston and— to create more living room—narrow its rivers and fill its canals, tidal inlets and marshlands, for Boston was water-locked during the early part of the last century. Some of its present streets were once canals, and much of the city we know lay under water and was wasteland at low tide. Boston, originally a narrow peninsula, was surrounded on all sides by water or marsh except at Roxbury Neck, and even here, in heavy storms, the water overflowed, making the city an island until sections were filled in. By the time of the Civil War, Boston was still snugly confined to the original peninsula with only two outlying areas: South Boston's point and East Boston's island. In 1833, the upbuilding of Noddle's Island— previously a place of large farms and a favorite with fishing parties—had begun; it was soon to become East Boston.

Boston's business sections were compact and close to residential neighborhoods, or within easy reach by horsecar or omnibus. Back Bay was, at this time, still a maze of ugly flats and open water, although its character had changed since the second decade of the century when it was a sheet of water at flood tide, spreading out from the town toward the Brookline hills which rose picturesquely beyond, with no dam, bridge or causeway to bar a view of rural Cambridge. The bay lapped the margin

HONEY FITZ

of what is now Washington Street at Boston Neck and the marsh at the bottom of the Common, which became the Public Garden. To the Board of Health, this Back Bay area was an "offensive nuisance," but in 1857, the "Back Bay Improvement" project led to the filling of the marshes and waterways, and the result became the most aristocratic rectangle in America—the heartland of Proper Bostonians.

The romantic story of the change had begun in Paul Revere's day, when what is considered the nation's first railroad was set upon the side of Beacon Hill, and laborers, digging away at the crest, dumped the earth into the sea. During the Civil War, the rest of Back Bay was filled in, adding more than a thousand acres to Boston proper and making its narrowest point the widest. Dump cars with opening sides brought in gravel from distant hills after all nearby promontories had been leveled. An excerpt from the November 12, 1961, issue of the *Boston Sunday Herald*, states:

While agitation grew in the South and the nation was on the brink of war, trains loaded with gravel from Needham made 25 trips around the clock for an entire year, dumping the fill into the muddy flats.

In their enthusiasm to build a bigger and better city, the workers covered a bit of ancient history that wasn't discovered until 1939. That year, the New England Mutual Life Insurance Co. razed the Rogers Building on Boylston Street that was constructed as the first building of Massachusetts Institute of Technology. On that site their present property now stands.

When workers went far below the old tidal marks seeking hard ground for the foundation, they discovered 65,000 stakes used for fish weirs by Indians. Carbon analyses showed the stone axe-sharpened poles to be placed in the sea about 2500 B.C.

Thus, the forebears of the Proper Bostonians were not the first inhabitants of Boston, after all.

One contemporary comment illumines the plight of the unskilled Irish proletariat who came to America in the last century: "Ferried over the Atlantic, and carted over America, despised, and robbed, downtrodden and poor, they made the railroads grow." Mayor John F. Fitzgerald told Lady Gregory in 1912: "If it were not for the Irishmen of fifty years ago we would not have our railroads in America. Irish immigrants of the 1840s and 1850s, working from sunrise to sundown for seventy cents a day, went out and built them while their wives and mothers stayed at home."

The Irish were exploited often by their own kind. Among the first Irish leaders in Boston were the padrones. Representing Yankee employers, they tapped the cheap, illiterate labor supply, forcing Irish laborers to work as many as fifteen hours a day, seven days a week, often at starvation wages. The padrones crowded contract laborers into sheds, barns, stables, low-ceilinged garrets, basements and cellars under the most unsanitary conditions imaginable. Cellars were often flooded by backed-up drains. Around the mid-nineteenth century as many as thirty-nine immigrants were known to "live" in one basement, and it was not unusual for fifteen or twenty to do so. One survey showed sixty-seven toilets in one hundred and eighteen houses inhabited by five hundred forty immigrants, and seventeen of the toilets were out of order.

One sink might serve a whole malodorous tenement; one outhouse, an entire neighborhood. Tuberculosis, cholera and smallpox were common in the overpopulated shanty neighborhoods. "Living in filth and hunger in their reeking Paddyville and Mick alleys and rookeries," wrote Francis Russell in *Heritage Magazine,* "they created the first urban mass slums of America. . . . Jeremiah O'Donovan-Rossa wrote of 'the wreck and ruin that came upon the Irish race in this foreign land.' "

It was not until 1906 that the padrone system of housing laborers in stables and cellars was prohibited.

Their homeland, with its pastoral pleasures and leisurely Sabbaths that might include family outings and games, had offered—before the potato blight, of course—far better living conditions than the squalid shacks and tenements of America. And farming even semibarren acres was preferable to the degrading work in sweatshops or with construction gangs. The squalor, discrimination and hunger bred in the Irish newcomers the same pessimism they had known in Ireland. Even if they had not swelled the city's population too quickly to be assimilated, they knew that the "original Americans," or nativists, would have loathed them. Few white minorities have ever been so harshly treated as these Irish, who were actually barred from some districts. Many, unable to find work, drifted. Around 1850, vagrant Irish paupers outnumbered the sum of all other nationalities, and parts of Boston had already become slums comparable to the worst sections of Harlem today. When Walt Whitman came to Boston in 1860, he found the Negroes better off than the Irish, who were on the lowest mudsill of society. The censuses of 1870 and 1880 still showed the Irish constituting two thirds of the laboring force in Boston.

By the century's turn, Irish settlements, rimming six miles of waterfront, had become slums. The immigrants had rapidly multiplied, and other waves were coming in numbers too great to be absorbed into the city's economy. As early as 1875, they had crowded Yankees out of some neighborhoods, driving them across town to the West End with its row of neat red-brick houses and tree-lined sidewalks. As the Irish prospered, they, too, demanded better accommodations and they pushed the Yankees even farther back. By the end of the century, the wealthier Yankees were still clinging to Beacon Hill and the Back Bay, while others had fanned out into such suburbs as Roxbury, Jamaica Plain and Cambridge.

From the beginning, isolated as they were in their Paddyvilles, the Irish had been forced to become even more clannish than was normal for them. Rejected by the Yankee-Protestant community, they created a society within a society, where their brogue, crude manners, religion, penury and congested living conditions were not derided. Historian Albert Bushnell Hart of Harvard wrote in their defense:

> They were said by unfriendly neighbors to be addicted to drunkenness, brawling and fighting, although in these respects, it would hardly seem that native Americans of that time were in a position to throw stones. Above all, the Irish were thought to be too clannish, flocking by themselves and cutting themselves off from the life of the community like an alien element; although one wonders what else could have been expected in view of the attitude of mingled dislike, distrust, and contempt which they so frequently encountered from the natives. In fact, they could usually find real friendliness and help only from people of "their own kind" and from their priests.

Actually, this clannishness, whether forced on them or not, had definite advantages. Irish storekeepers prospered because they were patronized by customers who found familiar food on their shelves. And it was comforting to hear the old country brogue, to feel the security of talking with countrymen who laughed with, not at them, when they came out with some such expression as, "Sure and begorry, 'tis a foine day, it is." It was reassuring to relax in warm friendly surroundings.

It was pleasant on Saturday nights, too, to get together with neighbors for a shindig in a kitchen or parlor and dance a jig, reel or hornpipe. As Lucius Beebe noted: "The North End, East and later South Boston, became shabby but joyous and at times riotous outposts of the Old Sod."

The Irish clans and the Yankee islands of homogenized culture had no basis for peaceful coexistence. "Resting on basically different premises," wrote Oscar Handlin, "developed in entirely different environments, two distinct cultures flourished in Boston with no more contact than if

3000 miles of ocean rather than a wall of ideas stood between them."

Henry Cabot Lodge, Senior, wandered afield when he said in the United States Senate: "The Irish spoke the same language as the people of the United States; they had the same traditions of government, and they had for centuries associated and intermarried with the people of Great Britain. . . . They presented no difficulties of assimilation."

In America, they did, indeed, present difficulties of assimilation, although not so many as Yankee Mayor Theodore Lyman implied late in the nineteenth century when he called the Irish "a race that will never be infused with our own, but on the contrary, will always remain distinct and hostile."

These were fighting words to the Irish, who had been oppressed in their native land for several centuries by the British. The Yankees of America themselves had rebelled successfully against British oppression, and they should have known that the new arrivals would seek independence in a land of freedom. They should have recognized that the same spirit of intolerance against which they had rebelled would not be tolerated by the Irish. Their cavalier and unyielding attitude was precisely the catalyst needed to spark a parochial revolution in a Boston that no longer exclusively belonged to the Lymans, the Eliots or the Adamses.

The clash between the two cultures would have far-reaching effects.

CHAPTER 2

Clash of Two Cultures

"Democracy equals groceries plus liberty."

— MAURY MAVERICK

"BOSTON was the most class-bound city in America when I picked up my political shillelagh," wrote James Michael Curley in his autobiography. "Its traditionally Republican government reflected banker and big-business control. It was almost as appropriate to say in those snobbish days that Boston was part of Beacon Hill and the Back Bay, as it was to say later, when the Irish assumed political control, that Boston was part of South Boston, stronghold of the refugees from the widely heralded potato famines of 1847 and 1867."

Boston had become a political powder keg soon after Ireland-born Hugh O'Brien jarred the Yankee-Protestants by his election as Mayor of Boston in 1885. From 1822, when the Town of Boston became a city, until the election of O'Brien, every mayor had been a Yankee, and if their administrations were for the most part mediocre, they were notably free from corruption. Martin Lomasney, who became the Czar of Boston Democratic politics and who is a principal in the Honey Fitz story, was not referring to Yankee mayors when he said, "None of these mayors are saints, gentlemen," and when the flamboyant Curley remarked that politics and holiness "are not always synonymous," he was not fingering the Yankees, either. In 1880, nobody challenged Mayor Frederick O. Prince when he said, "No allegation of municipal corruption has ever been made against any Boston official." Prince, however, was defeated for reelection in 1877 because he had been tolerant enough to appoint a few Irishmen to the police force. His rash action caused more angry comment than did Mayor Frederick W. Lincoln, Junior, who, when he sought to uniform the Boston police, was accused of copying the "liveried servants" of the old world.

Old Boston was stuffy. It was frigidly aloof, narrow and intolerant.

24

And Yankee mayors were not, until the time of the third Josiah Quincy, touched by the commonplace—unless one excepts Charles Wells, who had been elected in 1832 as a representative of the middle classes in protest against cavalier rule. The Irish accordingly rebelled, and since 1885 there have been only three Yankee mayors—Josiah Quincy, Andrew J. Peters and Malcolm E. Nichols. From that time till this, Boston politics has been Irish-oriented, and nowhere else in America has a single community so dominated a metropolis as has the Irish Catholic in Boston. It has added more than a dash of paprika to "cold roast" Boston.

Mayor Quincy, a true Democrat who could not do enough for the common man, was a transitional figure who got along so well with his Irish colleagues that no nationalistic arguments ever marred proceedings. One Irish leader he dealt with was Pat McGuire, the very man who taught Honey Fitz the political tricks which Honey in turn passed along to Jim Curley. Pat, Ireland-born, had a patrician eye for later immigrants.

"Each wave disliked and distrusted the next," Senator John F. Kennedy would say later, referring to Boston's immigrants. "The English said the Irish 'kept the Sabbath and everything else they could lay their hands on.' The English and the Irish distrusted the Germans, who 'worked too hard.' The English and the Irish and the Germans disliked the Italians; and the Italians joined their predecessors in disparaging the Slavs."

The story of John F. Fitzgerald must be told against the backdrop of the violent and at times acrimonious clash between the Yankees and the Irish during a turbulent era of social and economic upheaval. He clashed often with what James Michael Curley later called "the top homogenized members of the Yankee overlords." But without this Yankee-bred enmity and distrust of Roman Catholics, neither Fitzgerald nor Curley would have had the opportunity to climb the political ladder. The collision with bigotry made them strong Democratic tribunes of the lowly.

During the last two decades of the nineteenth century, the Irish won almost complete control of the city governmental machinery, partly because they spoke English and were able to adjust themselves quickly to American urban living, and partly because they had learned the mechanics of politics in Ireland where for centuries they had resisted British aggression. Yankee indifference was another reason. "The people here are a little aristocratical . . . but they don't trouble themselves much about politics as money and business is their aim," was one quaint appraisal of nineteenth-century Boston.

HONEY FITZ

The nativists who forced Irish immigrants into shanty Rivieras were caught in a net of their own weaving, for from the very solidarity of Irish clannishness stemmed Irish political power. It was logical for the Irish, barred from white-collar jobs, to turn to politics. Along with their natural affinity for the "great game," it was the quickest and easiest way out of the cellar.

Fitzgerald and Curley loudly identified themselves with the underdog, glorying (at times mawkishly) in the hardships of the underprivileged. Like other professional patriots, they sometimes overplayed the Machree motif. "Someone should let the Eire out of those windbags," Blake Ehrlich wrote in *The Boston Traveler,* referring to the purveyors of what he called "humbug Hibernianism and mawkish Machree sentiment." Both Fitzgerald and Curley on occasion were full of hot Eire.

In their fight for the down-and-outer, however, they developed a political strength which, as one writer put it, "washed the Colonial-descendant families behind their chaste, white Georgian doorways."

For centuries, the English had said that the Irish were incapable of ruling themselves, and the Brahmins and Yankees felt the same way.

The Irish, Lord Balfour had said, were "no more ready for home rule than the Hottentots," and what better grist could a demagogue grind in his mill than this! In Boston, the Yankees lost political control for the same reason their counterparts lost it in other big American cities. They did not understand that in America, democracy works from the bottom up, not from the top down. In the Boston of Honey Fitz's day, politics began on the precinct or grassroots level, and was in large measure built on personal and family contacts. The newcomers needed immediate help, and Irish leaders who could provide it were rewarded with votes, whereas the Yankees lost their leadership because they exploited, rather than helped, the common people.

In a reference to "the Puritan sons" in a speech made in 1912, Mayor John F. Fitzgerald said they (the Puritan sons) "cannot know . . . the personal memories that hallow this scene of our fathers' struggles. They, too, were Pilgrims, and we, as well as descendants of the Mayflower party, are the children of sacrifice and prayer. Our annals tell of villages emptied by famine, of crowded immigrant ships, of laborious lives in the new land, and the scanty reward of the laborers." Fitzgerald was more charitable than most of his political Irish brethren, whose resentment against their harsh Yankee "overlords" has taken some curious forms over the years.

James Jeffrey Roche, one of the most articulate spokesmen for the oppressed Irish, is said to have written only one good thing about the

English: "It is reported from London that Queen Victoria has written her autobiography and that it will not be published until a year after her death. Long live the Queen!" He felt the same way about the English descendants in America. Congressman James A. Gallivan, another troubadour in the Fitzgerald story, was a Harvard-educated politician always attuned to his Irish audiences, and they wildly applauded in 1921 when he introduced a bill into Congress to deport Admiral Sims to Canada as "an undesirable alien" because he said the Irish in Ireland could not be trusted during World War I.

When Michael J. Ward was chairman of the Boston School Committee, he teased Proper Bostonians—and even some who were Improper—by announcing that his committee was considering bringing Eamon De-Valera to Boston as superintendent of schools. "American citizenship is not a necessary qualification," he gravely said, "and I can't for the life of me think of a better man for the job."

He spurned Harvard's offer to help his committee find a suitable superintendent. "Harvard didn't consult me when the late A. Lawrence Lowell resigned and it was looking around for a new president," he said. "If it had, I would have recommended the appointment of James A. Farley to humanize the institution." He opposed permitting children to donate pennies for a Paul Revere bowl. "Paul's bowl was filled with rum, not pennies," he told the press. "He should have been arrested for drunken driving when he warned that the British were coming."

The delight in skewering Yankee pomposity was in retaliation for the cavalier treatment the Irish Micks had received and for the constant sneering at their low estate. "He is of the poor Irish, and there are touches of the cabin life of his ancestors in his plain homely ways," a Yankee said of Martin Lomasney, who, according to Lincoln Steffens, did so much to raise the status of the Irish. The Irish Mick answer was that it took courage for them to leave their native land in the mid-decades of the past century with all their possessions in one bundle. Illiterate? Native Bostonians would be, too, they said, had they lived in the "hedge school" era in Ireland when the common people—and were there many Irish who were not common?—were forced to depend for their little learning on the wandering schoolmasters who surreptitiously peered over the hedge to be sure no British agent caught them tutoring an Irishman. Hedge schoolmasters dated back to the days when it was a crime to teach an Irishman to read or write.

Referring to "nativist" agitation in the 1830s, which stemmed from Protestant alarm over the rising tide of Catholic immigration, Alfred Bushnell Hart noted that New Englanders of that period studied schoolbooks in which all Catholic nations were described in such terms as "ignorant," "lazy," "superstitious," "deceitful," "licentious" and "cruel." "Even a would-be generous writer like 'Peter Parley' would regale his readers with such statements about the Irish as that they set apart St. Patrick's Day for going to church, drinking whiskey, and breaking each others' heads with clubs. Hence when Irish immigrants then began to appear here in great numbers, people were prepared in advance to find their worse suspicions realized."

The Irish had come here to escape the poverty which absentee English landlords had bequeathed them in Ireland, and to escape racial and religious intolerance. But they ran into an even more virulent persecution —racial, social, economic and religious—from the native Americans. The story of the Catholic Church in Boston is full of persecution, ostracism and prejudice, for the colonists, like their descendants, had soon lost sight of the lofty ideals and liberty-loving maxims that had exiled them from their own land.

Long before the mass emigration to America, the Irish in the New World had been victimized. American history books glide over the practice of early English settlers of bringing in Irish indentured servants who were virtual slaves until they could buy or achieve their freedom. Captain John Vernon was hired in 1633 by the Cromwellian Commissioners in England to supply David Sellick, a Boston merchant, with two hundred and fifty Irish women between the ages of twelve and forty-five, and three hundred males ranging in age from twelve to fifty, to be found within twenty miles of specified localities in Ireland and transported to New England. Drake's *History of Antiquities of Boston* discloses Cotton Mather, in a writing dated 1654, requesting that Irish youths be brought over by England. There were many other historic grievances which Irish leaders would later dredge from old archives.

In 1688, Goody Glover was hanged as a witch on Boston Common for saying the Rosary in Gaelic while kneeling before a statue of the Virgin. She had also been charged with making the sign of the cross and of saying her prayers in Latin. As late as 1700, the penalty of hanging was prescribed for all Roman Catholic priests found in the Colony of Massachusetts. A law was enacted in 1704 that prohibited the opening of Catholic schools and fixed a fine of forty shillings a day for any father who hired any but a Protestant to teach his children.

The Revolution created still another crisis for Boston Catholics, as the Tories, enraged by Catholic France's offer of help to the revolutionists, stirred up strong anti-Catholic feeling.

In 1808, Pope Pius VII made Boston an Episcopal See, with the

Reverend John Cheverus as bishop. In 1823, his successor was the Right Reverend Joseph B. Fenwick, S.J. It was during his episcopate that Irish immigrants and Irish priests poured into Boston, and parochial schools and churches multiplied. Holy Cross College in Worcester was one fruit of Bishop Fenwick's zeal. And it was he who prevented violence during the riots and church-burnings of the 1830s.

A quarter of a million Irish had landed in America between 1830 and 1835, and the ten thousand who settled in Boston had displaced many native workmen. Demagogues, including Protestant ministers, were busy inflaming Yankee malcontents, and no one was surprised when the violent incitements flared into attack one summer evening in 1834.

On that evening, fifty good Bostonians descended on the Ursuline Convent in Charlestown. They had been intoxicated with wild rumors of nuns being locked in underground cells and Protestant pupils forced to become Catholics. These lurid stories had seemed to become creditable when it was reported that a demented nun had disappeared, and the Mother Superior had unwittingly fanned the rumors when she had refused to admit the Charlestown Selectmen who had come to investigate the allegation of dungeons and torture chambers.

The convent was, as a matter of fact, that rare institution, a school of high scholastic merit. As Albert Bushnell Hart writes, "The gentle sisters of St. Ursula were . . . highly cultivated women and accomplished teachers, and as such opportunities for the education of girls were rare enough in New England at that time, the school came to be largely frequented, mainly by the daughters of Protestant families."

But the fifty self-appointed vigilantes were indifferent to such facts. They set alight a huge bonfire, caroused around it, rang firebells and attracted spectators whom they roused to their own pitch and at length broke into the convent to sack it from roof to cellar. "Even tombs were desecrated," Hart wrote, "the sacred vessels stolen, the consecrated Host from the tabernacle profaned, and strewn about. Then the building went up in a roar of flames. . . . By a hair's breadth, the nuns and their pupils effected their escape, and made their way, pursued across the fields, to sheltering homes around Winter Hill." So ended what a Protestant historian has called "this most outrageous assault upon a house occupied solely by ten feeble women and fifty terror-stricken children." The historian added a comment: "Never, at least in New England, has there been a more cowardly performance."

On the following day, crowds of Irish laborers from Worcester, Lowell and Providence headed for Boston, and there might have been bloodshed but for Bishop Fenwick, who assembled his people in the cathedral and quieted them down. "Love your enemies," he admonished. "Do good to them that hate you, and pray for them that persecute and calumniate you."

The persecutions continued for another three years, falling most heavily on the Catholics of Massachusetts, who had to arm themselves to defend their churches from attack. The climax came on July 11, 1837, with the "Broad Street Riot." The trouble began when a Yankee fire company tried to cross an Irish parade, and fisticuffs followed. Whereupon a mob attacked an Irish section of Boston with such fury the neighborhood "would have been wiped out if Mayor Samuel A. Eliot hadn't called out the militia," according to Hart.

There was more trouble in September of that year when the "Montgomery Guards," a new Irish-American militia company, was taunted by other military units at a muster on Boston Common. As they marched back to their armory near Faneuil Hall, they were jeered and struck with missiles by crowds lining the streets. There was further commotion when the Boston Irish sent their Fighting Ninth Regiment to the Civil War, and the troops insisted on marching under the Irish rather than the American flag.

The growing antiforeign feeling culminated in the Know-Nothing agitation of 1852-1856. It was in opposition that the Fenian Brotherhood was formed and, despite the disapproval of the Catholic Church, expanded in secrecy until it held its first national convention in Chicago during the Civil War.

The Irish were subjected to many other indignities which would later provide themes for their demagogues. Irish had died in state hospitals without the benefit of last rites until, in the 1860s, a law was passed that permitted priests to enter such institutions. In Maine, fanatics tarred and feathered Father Bapst, a priest.

In 1884, the Know-Nothings had styled themselves the "American Protestant Association." Four years later, the APA movement centered about the activities of the Committee of One Hundred in Boston, which, besides sponsoring an antiparochial school bill in the General Court (as the state legislature of Massachusetts is called), attacked the Boston School Committee, then split evenly between twelve Protestants and twelve Catholics. Incensed at this situation and at the contents of certain medieval history textbooks used in Boston schools, the committee sent a flood of pamphlets to the voters of the city. The whole affair was laid at the door of the Jesuits, "that most infamous of religious sects." Despite the opposition of all Boston newspapers, the committee elected a Protestant majority to the School Committee for a brief period.

After 1880, the Yankee Protestants were further inflamed against the "foreigners" who threatened their place in society. The Irish had by then a powerful press in Boston, and it occasionally fanned the flames. *The Pilot,* a newspaper read primarily by Irish Catholics, told its readers that General Bragg, in nominating Grover Cleveland for President, had said that "the Irish might go to hell."

Meanwhile, the shanty Irish were climbing the social and economic, as well as the political, ladders. They became "lace curtain," "cut-glass," "suburban," "Venetian blind" or "F.I.F." (First Irish Families). These terms, incidentally, while used insultingly on occasion by the non-Irish, were whimsies originating among the Irish themselves and were repeated often enough in their own circles to achieve a broad currency. (One recent version classified Irish-Americans into the "clean lace-curtain Irish" and the "dirty Venetian-blind Irish.")

After long years of exposure to Yankees and Brahmins, the later-generation Irish would adopt many of their manners and customs to good advantage. John F. Fitzgerald and James Michael Curley, whose clashing careers were to shape the political destiny of Boston and, to some extent, the Commonwealth of Massachusetts, were born and raised in the era of the melting pot, when the cities of America were in a turmoil of expansion and growing pains with all the attending evils. Political bosses made themselves the symbol of this ferment, controlling and directing its force and making themselves powerful—and sometimes rich—in the process. It would be decades before old asperities were softened and old animosities mellowed by mutual understanding. Irish leaders might, like Oliver Goldsmith's *Squire Hardcastle,* enjoy old books, old wine and old friends, but richer dividends accrued from a calculated dislike of old Yankees, old Protestants and old Republicans.

Some of the early Irish leaders tried to bridge the gap that separated the two cultures in the Bay State. Said the courtly Patrick Collins, who became Mayor of Boston after President Cleveland had earlier named him consul general in London:

I . . . denounce any man or any body of men who seek to perpetuate divisions of races or religions in our midst . . . I love the land of my birth but in American politics I know neither race, color nor creed. Let me say now that there are no Irish voters among us. There are Irish-born citizens like myself and there will be many more of us, but the moment the seal of the court was impressed upon our papers we ceased to be foreigners and became Americans. Americans we are and Americans we will remain.

That was in 1876, when Collins tried to persuade his constituents to vote for Proper Bostonian Charles Francis Adams for Governor of Massachusetts. His Irish supporters, however, rejected Adams.

Others, like Fitzgerald and Curley, used the clash between the cultures as a springboard to success. The former, throughout his political career, lashed out against the "scions of the blue-blooded aristocracy of the Back Bay." His often repeated theme was that "New England is changing, and those who are most interested in its welfare should be willing to see that to the new elements that enter into it is given a proper share of the responsibility of its government."

He reminded audiences that the people of Massachusetts came "from the finest bloods in Europe, and these people who immigrated here, coming from all parts of the civilized world, have become staunch citizens, and their boys and girls rank high in our schools and colleges." But Boston Brahmins, he charged, were trustees of their own welfare. Their considerations were: "First, the safety of the trustee; second, the convenience of the trustee; third, the commissions of the trustee." He accused Beacon Street residents of avoiding legitimate taxes, and in his "Mort-main" (Dead-hand) speech delivered in 1911, he scored Boston financial interests for investing their money outside the Commonwealth and of tying up fortunes in trusts. "If Boston could disinherit about twenty-five men who have their hands clutched about the throat of commercial and industrial Boston, this city would attain a growth in the next ten years almost unbelievable."

Actually, there were fewer than twenty families in Massachusetts who comprised a tight oligarchy. For all their patrician manners and customs, they were autocrats whose ancestors, in the 1840s, had been the "lords of the loom" and the "lords of the long wharf" and leaders of the prosperous and conservative Whig party. They controlled nearly a fourth of all the nation's spindlage, according to Kurt Schriftgiesser, who writes of them in *The Gentleman from Massachusetts,* a biography of the first Henry Cabot Lodge. They also controlled at least half of the insurance capital of the Commonwealth, and forty per cent of the banking resources of Boston. Their money has been secure since the founding of the Boston Manufacturing Company in 1813 and the establishment of the Massachusetts Hospital Life Insurance Company five years later.

Schriftgiesser writes:

Known as the Boston Associates, these gentlemen controlled the very flow of the Merrimack and the Connecticut Rivers. Mill owners paid the rates they set. Manufacturers paid them for the use of the machines on which they held patents. The canals and the new railroads were under their ownership or control throughout the entire state. Their textile domain extended from Maine and New Hampshire to Rhode Island. They were the builders of cities, some of which, like Lowell and Lawrence, bore their names. They controlled the press and pulpit and politics of Massachusetts.

And they controlled the building of railroads and the cruel economy of the sweatshops and factories, all of which depended on exploited Irish labor.

Many of the early Irish political chieftains kept up a running attack on Boston's "feudal barons." "The big fortunes were made years ago, a good many of them by shady means—rum and slaves," said Martin Lomasney. "They made their money by fair means or foul. They left it to their descendants and their descendants are spending it all over the world. I believe State Street is run by Wall Street . . . Boston is asleep. I don't know what the cure is, but I know the basis: corporate interests . . ."

Irish demagogues accused the Brahmins of having ancestors who were Marblehead smugglers, Newport privateers or ruthless industrialists who made fortunes in the three-cornered trans-Atlantic trade—shipping Medford rum to Africa, picking up slaves there and transporting them to New Orleans, where they hauled aboard molasses to be delivered to Boston to make more rum.

Curley, who never worried whether his history was askew, got long mileage from the same theme: "You young Republicans," he told a rally in Springfield when he was running for the United States Senate against Henry Cabot Lodge, Junior, "have no more chance to join the Somerset Club than I have, if your ancestors didn't get rich in the first two or three generations by selling opium to the Chinese, rum to the Indians or getting it in the slave racket." He and Fitzgerald belabored the "purified Beaconese," the "blue-nosed bigots," the "snobocracy" and "the apostles of the royal purple." "The term 'codfish aristocracy,'" said Curley, "is a reflection of one of the most revered kinds of fish in the Commonwealth."

It was this gambit, used over and over by Fitzgerald and Curley, which, as one writer put it, "gave an outlet to the accumulated resentments and aggressions of the immigrant community." Irish politicians were richly rewarded for poking fun at the social set of the Back Bay and its Proper Bostonian values; at Republican reformers whom they labeled "Goo-Goos" (short for "Good Government Association"); at Harvard College, which in the Irish mind was the private preserve of Boston's affluent society; and at the conservative Yankees, who were blamed for everything that was wrong with Boston. They stepped up this offensive so successfully that no Protestant Republican office-holder or candidate dared to be seen on St. Patrick's Day without a green tie or green flower in his lapel. Leverett Saltonstall delighted his constituents in South Boston when he went through dusty genealogical records to dig up an Irish ancestor so he could join the Charitable Irish Society, which, by the way, is older than the Sons of the Revolution.

The clash between the two cultures produced some good clean fun, but there were moments of acrimony, too.

CHAPTER 3

Bare Feet and Patched Pants

"I love the North End. I have always loved the dear old
North End."

—JOHN F. FITZGERALD

"HISTORY seemed to come alive for me in those narrow old streets, where the American Revolution was planned and initiated," John F. Fitzgerald said on his fiftieth birthday anniversary. He was alluding to his "dear old North End" where, on February 11, 1863, he had been born in a four-story, eight-family, red-brick tenement within an anthem's ring of Old North Church.

The neighborhood is still full of historical reminders. A favorite tourist attraction is the Paul Revere house on North Square, the home of the patriot from about 1770 to 1800. It was built in 1676 on the site of Increase Mather's house, burned in the great fire of that year. It has been carefully restored to the style of that period, with diamond-paned and leaded windows, and is full of valuable relics. In the North End mall, almost within the shadow of Old North Church, is Cyrus Dallin's equestrian statue of Paul Revere, and it was a short walk for a nimble-gaited lad like Little Johnny Fitz, as the neighbors called him, to Faneuil Hall, the Cradle of Liberty. Near his home on Copp's Hill was the famed Burying-Ground, established in 1660. Here are buried Increase, Cotton and Samuel Mather, and Edmund Hartt, builder of the frigate *Constitution*. Fitzgerald's home on Ferry Street, long since wiped out in the march of progress, was two blocks from the shipyard where the *Constitution* was built, and he would remember this in congressional days, when he rescued that historic fighting vessel from oblivion. It was not far, either, to Griffin's Wharf, the scene of the "Boston Tea Party," where three ships were emptied of their cargoes.

HONEY FITZ

The North End is full of historic sites and old landmarks. Its central thoroughfare, Hanover Street, where the Fitzgerald family lived for a time, was named for the royal house of Hanover. It was near Green Dragon Lane (now Union Street) that the most famed of Boston's old inns stood—the Green Dragon Tavern. It contained the first lodge room of Freemasonry in America. Freemasonry played a great part in the secret councils of the Revolutionary Fathers, and they planned their strategy at the Green Dragon. The "North End Corcus," a patriot organization which originally included the numerous caulkers in the shipyards, met here and gave rise to the political term "caucus." The Green Dragon, established around 1680, existed until the widening of the street caused its demolition after 1820.

Long before the Irish immigrants came, the North End was dotted with fashionable as well as historic residences. Salem Street was once Green Lane, a street of elegant houses. Part of Prince Street was Black Horse Lane, which led to the Charlestown ferry. On North Square stood the original Old North Church, razed by the British for fuel during the siege. Here the three Mathers—Increase, Cotton and Samuel—successively were ministers. Garden Court Street nearby "perpetuates with its pleasant name the traditions of the beautiful garden where Gov. Thomas Hutchinson was born, and lived until his exile, in a stately house of brick," writes Edwin M. Bacon in *The Book of Boston*. "Here he wrote his *History of Massachusetts*." The house was mobbed and sacked in the Stamp Act riot on the night of August 26, 1765. On Garden Court Street also stood the Clark-Frankland mansion, celebrated in fiction by Cooper in *Lionel Lincoln* and by Bynner in *Agnes Surriage*. It was at 4 Garden Court Street, on the original site of Governor Hutchinson's mansion, that some of John F. Fitzgerald's children were born, including his daughter Rose.

When John Fitzgerald was born, Christ Church on Copp's Hill, built in 1723, was the oldest in Boston and was known as the "Old North," although the original "Old North," as noted, was in North Square. General Gage is said to have watched the battle of Bunker Hill from this belfry. There is some dispute among historians as to which Old North Church can claim the signal lanterns that warned Paul Revere on the night of his ride to Lexington and Concord.

With all these ghosts of the past haunting his memory, Little Johnny Fitz became an authority on the history of persons, places and events of his North End, of which he became the Number One Booster, just as he would later become the most articulate booster of Boston.

In his late teens, he was conducting a guided tour for a group of visitors who expressed an interest in Cotton Mather after being shown a Bible he had owned. Johnny Fitz saw a chance to practice a forensic skill he had been developing since he made his first political speech on Hanover Street when he was sixteen.

Mounting the pulpit, he gave an impromptu talk on Cotton Mather and his times, with no hesitation as to names and dates. He reminded the tourists of Macaulay's classic remark: "The Puritans objected to bear-baiting, not because it gave pain to the bear, but because it gave pleasure to the spectator." During that tour, the group visited the Old State House, built in 1713, from whose balcony the Declaration of Independence was read in 1776 to cheering crowds in the street. There was a lot to see in Boston, a lot of history to learn, for anyone with an inquisitive mind, and Johnny Fitz had an inquisitive mind.

One of the first Irish settlements after the Famine of 1847 was in the North End, and at the time of John's birth, this section had more immigrants than any other in the city. In 1863, the North End was solidly Irish, a series of hamlets crowded with red-brick tenements. There were Galway men on Copp's Hill, until it was renamed Connemara Hill. Donegal men lived west and north toward the Charles River in an enclave that came to be known as Donegal Square, and from the Old North Church to Faneuil Hall were colonies from Cork, Kerry and Limerick, all grouped along county lines, which Little Johnny Fitz early learned were strong. All of the North End was a Celtic island with a culture sharply contrasting with that of Yankeeland.

In this island, the newcomers—most of them not more than a generation removed from an Irish farmland—retained native customs. Many talked Gaelic and called one another by Celtic nicknames. Old-timers remember "Pat the Stag," who operated a pub where neighbors came with can or jug, the interiors of which were larded to keep down foam and increase content. Irish urchins delighted in dropping a stone or snowball into these open containers, which were also used to fetch milk or molasses —the poor man's syrup—from the grocery in days before convenient packaging. The practice of sending to a tavern for a container of beer was called "rushing the growler."

One contemporary of Pat the Stag was "The Black Mare's Foal." Another was "And Up She Rises." Such names were common, each with its significance, and if Yankees were puzzled by them, can they be blamed?

In this setting, John Francis Fitzgerald was born, the third of seven sons sired by Thomas Fitzgerald of County Wexford and Rose Mary

Murray, who, like her husband, had left that county in the 1840s and, after a tedious passage on an Irish Mayflower, settled in the North End. Thomas Fitzgerald was the son of John and Abigail Fitzgerald of County Wexford.

For a time, Tom Fitzgerald earned $6 a month working long hours on a farm in South Acton in the Nashoba Valley of Massachusetts, but he is better remembered as the genial proprietor of a grocery and liquor store in the North End near Paul Revere's house. Many of his customers were old salts—crewmen and skippers of fishing craft who brought their wriggling catch into the neighborhood piers for the convenience of the fish peddlers, whose tin horns provided background music for their honking about "fresh cod mackerel, haddock to fry, arrived this morning." For twenty cents, one could buy a whopping haddock which, when Ma stuffed it, provided enough food for a family of eight or nine, and such large families were common. Fish hawkers had constantly to keep an eye on street arabs who pilfered anything loose and edible, for excitement as well as hunger.

The oysterman carried a sack on his back, and during the evening, his haranguing of "Oys! Buy any Oys?" would lure a housewife to a front window. After success came, Honey Fitz liked to talk about the codfish he carried home by the gills and of his occasional yen for oysters, which Pa Fitzgerald did not always stock. Tipcart peddlers sold oysters, too, and sometimes Little Johnny Fitz would follow these yodeling vendors with their jouncing carts, and pick up from the cobblestones enough oysters for a stew.

It was a picturesque world of street-hawkers and clattering, horse-drawn wagons, whose drivers sold ice, fruit and vegetables, as well as bags of coal and bundles of kindling, from the tailboard. The air was full of the guttural chants of a cobblestone Caruso vocalizing on the virtues of "Fancy watermeloooooooooo," along with a cacophony of assorted cries, shouts and grunts.

The neighborhood rang with the "sweep o' sweep" chirpings of little chimney cleaners who warbled their trade from block to block, with their lampblacked brooms cocked across their shoulders and buckets to carry off the soot. Not all the soot went into the buckets. Some of it landed on their faces. In all this din and confusion you would be sure to find an early rising peddler, his pushcart loaded down with crabs and pyramids of oranges.

In the old North End, you could buy roasted peanuts or chestnuts from a street vendor, or raw fish, just as if you were in Rotterdam or Amsterdam.

Johnny grew up in this tight, bustling little community long before street lights were flicked on with the toss of a switch. He remembered the cool thrill of catching a chip of ice that flew out from under the iceman's pick. He romped with the neighborhood gang on rooftops, played baseball on the broad spaces of lower Hanover Street in the salt-tangy air and squealed with shuddery delight at the sight of a huge wharf rat scurrying into a dark corner or—more exciting still—up a ship's hawser.

"My playgrounds," he said later, "were the streets and wharves busy with ships from every port of the world." Watching the ships fired his imagination and reminded him later of the potential of the Port of Boston. The most vivid memory of his childhood? The terrible fire of 1872 that devastated sixty acres of downtown Boston—near enough for the smoke to make the Fitzgeralds cough.

When Little Johnny Fitz, known to his playmates as "Fitzie," was traipsing around the North End in bare feet and patched pants, horse cars were gaining favor as a common means of transportation, and the Belt Line horse cars ran from Roxbury around the West End and back. Travelers to East Boston got off the horse car at the foot of Battery Street, and while the car went onto a turntable, took a ferry that cost a penny across to a section where some of Boston's most distinguished citizens were born and raised. Fitzie didn't know any of the Boston nabobs in this category, but he got to know East Boston intimately when, years later, he ferried over to visit a political boss named Patrick Joseph Kennedy, whose father had also come from Ireland.

There were no electric lights, but some families were well enough off to discard candles and oil lamps in favor of gas light. There were no telephones, no subways or even such a simple convenience as a bathroom in most of the North End tenements—the Fitzgerald flat included. In his sixties, Fitzgerald told a reporter: "I remember the time when, if a man owned a horse, carriage or piano, he was considered wealthy. Today everyone has a car, radio and a hundred-and-one other marvelous conveniences we never dreamed of."

Since pink-cheeked Johnny Fitz's boyhood was not marred by the trammels of luxury, it gave him the time and freedom to walk down to Boston Common to watch the deer grazing. There were all kinds of improvised games to play, even at night under a flickering light.

And all the neighbors remembered that Johnny Fitz excelled in every game and sport from tag to polo. Anyone in the district would admit that "Little Johnny Fitz is the swiftest sprinter in the North End, the fastest swimmer, the best dancer, the most tuneful singer and the most eloquent speaker."

"As a boy I was proficient in athletics," he said. "In those days we used to run on the sidewalks and cobblestones on Hanover Street, and I could always beat any of the boys running, and was never beaten going around Fort Hill Square. They would bring boys in to run against me from all parts of the city. I won a half-mile championship in one New England track meet, but my forte was up to a quarter of a mile, and I preferred this distance, because I could run it so fast it scared the other boys off. However, I used to get so exhausted, I was barely able to lunge over the finish line."

Home was congenial. On Sunday nights, Mother Fitzgerald often made flapjacks, which Johnny especially liked, particularly when they were drowned in butter and syrup or molasses. Sometimes he couldn't wait for the garnishing, and the instant his mother turned her back, he would make a lightning stab for the platter and swipe one, whereupon she, with amused tolerance, would purse her lips and shake the spatula in his face. "Now, tell me, Johnny, was it you who did take that griddlecake?" By a skillful shifting of a look, Little Johnny, without coming right out and saying so, would imply that the culprit must have been Jimmy, Eddie, Mike or one of his other brothers. In any case, by the time Mother Fitzgerald had noticed that the flapjack was missing, the evidence was gone.

The entire family, all dressed in their Sunday best, filled a pew at the Catholic Church down the street, and the children stayed for Sunday School after Mass. Johnny, with his quick contagious smile and bright ways, was always a favorite with the parish priests at St. Stephen's Church, and it wasn't long before he was helping the priests run picnics, outings, minstrel shows, suppers, dances and fairs. In pastoral pursuits, Johnny Fitz also excelled, and he not only won the sprints but could boast, as an adult, that he had never been bested in a potato race. He had a drawerful of trophies to prove it.

A hard worker from this earliest days, he was still a teen-ager when he showed the bounce, energy and initiative that are among the marks of a leader. He was recognized as the most efficient and cooperative worker in any project that improved the lot of or gave pleasure to his North End neighbors. Always full of ideas, he originated novel entertainments to raise money for charities, as well as for his church.

Johnny Fitz took a long step forward when he was elected president of the Neptune Associates, the strongest social and athletic organization in the North End. Most members were old enough, but not smart enough, to be his father. Johnny kept moving, directing half a dozen youth groups.

He captained a polo team that competed in rinks in New England and New York. At Boston Latin School, which he attended after graduating from the local Eliot Grammar School, he managed and played right field on the baseball team, captained the football team for two years and was sports editor of the *Latin School Register,* the school magazine. He was proud of attending Ben Franklin's alma mater. Ben's boyhood home and the chandler shop of his father had also been razed for the widening of Hanover Street.

Fitzie did well in athletics at Boston Latin because he was strong and wiry and kept in shape by trotting to school, which in his day was in the South End beyond the Boston Public Library, where he often picked up books on his way home. Soon after graduation, he formed and became the first president of the Interscholastic Athletic Association.

He entered Harvard Medical School, but left before the end of the first year after his father died of pneumonia in 1881 at the age of thirty-three, only three years after "Mother Rosanna" had climbed the golden stair. A parish priest from St. Stephen's helped with funeral arrangements and was deeply concerned about the welfare of the boys who had so suddenly found themselves orphaned.

He drew Johnny aside, for he knew him best because of all he had done for the parish. "You lads have got to break up and live with friends," he said. "After all, you have no sisters or aunts to take care of you."

They had just returned from the funeral, and there was still rain in Johnny's eyes, but he was resolute. "No, no, no," he said. "We will never break up. I'll be father and mother to my brothers, just give me a chance. I'll keep the family together. No, no, no, I'll not allow our little home to be broken up." They were living at Merrimack Street at the time.

Honey Fitz, who was eighteen when his father died, retold this story so often that it came to be believed that he was the oldest of the brood, rather than the third in a line that ranged from four-year-old Henry to James, who was in his early twenties. "We were about two years apart, and in stature, like the steps of stairs," Honey Fitz recalled. "My father left us a few thousand dollars, not enough to educate me, and I thought my life belonged to my brothers, and that I could do better outside medical school, so I gave it up and took the examination for a position in the Custom House."

Over the years, he gave different versions of the story, but although

HONEY FITZ

they were finally able to afford a housekeeper, there is no question that Johnny Fitz kept the household together for many years, even after James left to be married and after brothers Thomas and William died. An old-timer recalls one version of the story, adapted for political rallies:

I was born on the top floor of a dingy brick tenement that had no bath-room or electric lights or any other conveniences—not even a humble accor-dion, let alone a harmonium or piano—and when my dear mother and father passed to their reward, I had to take care of all six of my brothers. I washed dishes, made beds, scrubbed floors, sifted ashes and brought up scut-tles of coal and firewood, climbing three flights of creaky stairs. For some reason or other it was my trust to boss the family. I even washed the faces of the older boys every day, and oftentimes dressed them. I remember that I used to accompany my mother when she bought her millinery from Kate Haley, or to Jordan Marsh Company when she bought socks and undercloth-ing for the family, and in that way I got experience which served me well. After feeding them and sending them off to school I would go out and earn money to keep the family together.

In another speech he said he organized his brothers into the "John F. Fitzgerald Marching and Singing Club," but there the history ends. The basic account of his "bringing up the kids" was unfailingly heart-warm-ing, as Honey Fitz unfolded the chokingly sentimental details with just the proper quaver of voice.

Johnny Fitz had come out near the top of the list on the civil service examination and was appointed a clerk at the Custom House under Lev-erett Saltonstall, Collector of Federal Customs, who was the grand-father of Senator Leverett Saltonstall. Johnny was then twenty. After three years on the job, he resigned to enter the insurance business, spe-cializing in fire insurance.

During all these years, despite family responsibilities, he still found time to chairman committees, make arrangements for St. Patrick's Day, lead a cheering section or umpire when the Charter Oak Baseball team played a visiting team in North End Park. And he was a joiner who could boast membership in more social, athletic and fraternal organizations than any other man in the North End. Over the years, he belonged to the Massachusetts Order of Foresters, the Ancient Order of Hibernians, the Knights of St. Rose, the Heptasophs, the Royal Arcanum, the Chari-table Irish Society, the Dorchester Catholic Club, the St. Alphonsus Asso-ciation, the Catholic Union of Boston, the Young Men's Catholic Asso-ciation of Boston College, the Franklin Typographical Society, the

Knights of Columbus, the Boston Press Club and half a dozen others, along with the Neptune Associates.

Johnny Fitz had a chiming, arms-around manner that enabled him to make friends easily. "He would make a good politician if there were such a thing," one neighbor predicted. If he had his sights raised on a career in politics, he was off to a good start, for he was not only well known to everyone in the North End, but himself knew by name every person important enough to vote, and he had a speaking acquaintance with most of the members of their families.

As he broadened his activities, he added to his list of friends, and once they met Johnny Fitz, they never forgot his vibrant personality. He could talk to you for ten or fifteen minutes at the rate of two hundred words a minute, without letting you cut in more than two or three times, then pat you on the back and tell you how much he had enjoyed the conversation. He spoke so frequently of the "Dear old North End," and with such rapture and relish, that the inhabitants came to be known as the "Dearos." There was an organization of "Dearos" who always had John F. Fitzgerald as the main attraction at their meetings.

In later life, when he traveled a great deal, he could scarcely appear in public without running into someone who knew him, and he had been photographed so often that even strangers who had never before laid eyes on him would call out, "Hello, Johnny Fitz." If the greeting was "Hello, there, dear old North End," he was especially pleased, for this was an acknowledgment of something he had contributed to the language.

A busy person like Johnny Fitz did not have all the time he wished to squire young ladies, although he met more than his share of girls at the dozens of socials he attended. There was one young lady, however, who made such an impression on him that, when he was seventy-nine years old, he could vividly recall their first meeting. Asked by a reporter for the happiest moment in his life he said: "When I got the girl I wanted— Mary Josephine Hannon. We've lived together now for fifty-two years. The first time I met her, I knew. I knew this was it." He smiled. "And, yes, yes, yes, I had plenty of competition, too, but I was the lucky one. We were married."

Now and then, Tom Fitzgerald would take his family to visit old friends in South Acton. They might take the cars to the end of the line and then hire a rig, or, while they were living in Concord, Tom might use his horse-drawn trap, if he took only one or two members of the family along, or the two-horse carry-all if a bigger vehicle was necessary. Tom Fitzgerald never forgot the pleasant smell of apple blossoms or the sight of tall corn in the Acton of his youth, and Honey Fitz named one of his sons Thomas Acton Fitzgerald, and returned to the town often in later life. On Patriots' Day in 1925, he officiated at the celebration of the one hundred and fiftieth anniversary of the town, pointing out that the first company to cross Old North Bridge in Concord on April 19, 1775, was an Acton unit, and that the only two men killed in the ensuing engagement with the British were Acton men.

Johnny Fitz was only fifteen when he first met the thirteen-year-old Mary Josephine Hannon. He walked into the kitchen, where she was washing dishes. "Hello, there," Johnny said. She turned and smiled, and he liked her shyness of manner. She had soft brown hair, blue eyes, a peachblow complexion and was slender and petite. Slight as she was, she had an erect bearing. After a moment, she found an excuse to leave the kitchen and went upstairs.

Johnny saw her again on other visits and got to know her a little better, although her shyness was always a barrier. One afternoon, he ran into her while berry-picking in Acton with friends from the North End, and she seemed friendlier in that rustic setting. And there came the day when Johnny Fitz really impressed her, along with all the farmers in the vicinity. He set what was called a local record when he picked twelve barrels of apples in one day. He didn't surprise his friends, who knew he had enough energy to do the work of two ordinary men.

John F. Fitzgerald was twenty-six when they were married in a simple church ceremony. They moved into his home in the North End, and some of his brothers lived with them for a while. Later, they moved to North Garden Street.

Johnny Fitz was doing well in the insurance business, for he had the kind of blarney a successful insurance salesman needs and so many friends he could always find a number who needed insurance protection. An East Boston neighbor of P. J. Kennedy, who insured his stable with Johnny Fitz, remembers how barren Fitzgerald's office was.

"There was a battered desk," in the tiny office, "and not one chair," he recalled.

"Fitzblarney" was all the young insurance man needed.

And Fitzblarney was also a valuable asset for a politician.

CHAPTER 4

The First Few Rungs

"I regard politics as among the highest and most helpful callings
open to American youth. It is my further opinion that there is no
line of endeavor more mobile, and by this I mean none in which
merit rises so quickly to its proper recognition. I believe that in the
long run, counting all factors and even hard luck, the better man
will win."

—JAMES A. FARLEY

JOHNNY FITZ burst into politics in the 1890s, when Boston was switching from Yankee to Irish political control. By the end of the century, the Irish were firmly in the saddle, although they by no means presented a solid front.

The Irish had long been known for their individualism. Over the centuries in the homeland, warring pastoral principalities, each with its own leader or "king," had torn Ireland apart. The Irish can be diffident about their champions. "They set a man up on a pedestal, and then say: 'There you are? Now, you big bum, make good!'" wrote James B. Connolly a generation ago in *Collier's* magazine in 1935. "And the Lord help him if he doesn't. Which is perhaps why they are a great race but a little nation."

Thus, by the late 1890s, embattled factions in Boston had produced scattered islands of power, each ruled by a petty boss. Neighborhood pride, Old Sod affiliations and fierce personal loyalties made the adhesion greater than the cohesion, thereby preventing a common front. No one powerful city boss emerged, as in other cities of America, but a few —in ever-changing uneasy alliances—could rule the city. For decades, the bosses of the twenty-five wards of Boston would play a fascinating, but sometimes confusing, game of political chess.

The power of the ward boss stemmed from contemporary conditions.

HONEY FITZ

Poor as they were, Irish immigrants were often too proud to beg, and in time of need, depended on their own kind for help, whenever possible. If, pending the next snow storm, Pat was out of work, his family did not starve if his neighbors could help it. Instead of cooking a pot of stew for her own family, Mrs. Flaherty across the alley, whose husband was employed, made a big batch of Irish stew in a washtub, and instead of the usual four or five loaves of bread, she baked fifteen or sixteen loaves in the oven of the coal stove. Pat and his wife and five children in their gratitude knew the time might come when they, too, might be called on to help. The Irish not only shunned the few charities that existed but were even reluctant to ask aid of the hard-pressed priests of the parish. It was up to the ward boss to see that such help as the generous Flahertys could not provide was given the needy.

Martin Lomasney gave a clear picture of the function of the ward boss: "Is somebody out of a job? We do our best to place him and not necessarily on the public payroll. Does the family run in arrears with the landlord or the butcher? We lend a helping hand. Do the kids need shoes or clothing, or the mother a doctor? We do what we can, and since, as the world is run, such things must be done, we keep old friends and make new ones." Another time, referring to the Irish, Hebrew and Italian residents of his ward, he said, they "are just my friends. I am right here with them all the time, and that's what counts. When you live with people three hundred and sixty-five days in the year, they get to know you and trust you. . . . Why, here's Jerry. He works in a grocery store and serves the people and gets acquainted with them. Through him and others who do the same thing, I get in touch with all the families of the West End." In Lomasney's opinion, there had "to be in every ward somebody that any bloke can come to—no matter what he's done—and get help."

The ward boss would be a key character in Boston politics until the Franklin Delano Roosevelt era of federal largesse. The *Boston Post* gave this picture of the ward boss in the 1940's, when Michael J. Ward sought reelection to the Boston School Committee:

Ward's political potency can be attributed at least in part to the amazing number of people he sees in a period of a single day. It's an experience to visit his office at school headquarters and observe the men and women waiting there to see him on some problem or other. Over a space of eight years he has made it a practice to serve as a trouble-shooter for parents looking for a School Committee member to whom they could go for advice and help. The number of persons he talks to in a day ranges from 30 to 150, and on some days the total might go well above this figure. Ward's No. 1 rule . . . is to be available for anyone who wants to talk to him about anything. From all indications the policy has paid political dividends, and there are few shrewder politicians in Boston—or anywhere else—than Michael J. Ward.

Ward put it this way: "I just sit in my office most of the time, and I do about twenty real favors a day. That's somewhere around one hundred and thirty favors a week, or about six or seven thousand favors a year. I make a lot of friends that way, and it adds up to votes." Some of the favors Ward did for his constituents are legendary.

"I'll never forget the fast one you pulled when you announced a free Fourth of July show for the kiddies at the old Dudley Theatre," wrote Harry Wasserman of the American Theatres Corporation in a letter to Ward. "We didn't know a thing about your pronouncement until I drove up Ruggles Street and saw a crowd of children in front of the Dudley waiting to get in. I tried to locate you at the Cabot Street bathhouse, but no luck. Then, knowing what a great guy you were, I got busy and put on a free show for the kids. When I sent you a bill, you practically had me in tears when you said, 'Harry, I spent all of my appropriation for ice cream, hot dogs and popcorn for those poor unfortunate children.' So after you wept on my shoulder, I tore up the bill, thinking what a terrific humanitarian you were."

While serving as secretary to Mayor James Curley (1921-1925), Ward added to his political potency by impersonating the boss. "Every lunchtime I became Mayor Curley," he explained. "When he went out the door I got busy. Speaking in his well-modulated tones I would call the Street Department and inform the superintendent that I, Curley, wanted to put some men to work. Then I would send over four or five buddies for the jobs. Curley didn't know it, but he made more telephone calls between noon and one P.M. than he made all day." By the time Curley became governor, Ward could do a perfect take-off on the big boss. He would pick up the telephone, call a top official in the Curley administration and in a perfect impersonation of that mellifluous delivery, say: "This is the governor. I am sending a gentleman over for some employment. His name is M. M. He comes to you with my finest recommendations. I'm sure you'll find a good position for him."

"Certainly, Your Excellency," the official would say. "I'll see to it personally."

Once he telephoned a department head and asked every consideration for his "first cousin." He did not know that his "first cousin" was a Negro. Another time, when two race track officials at Suffolk Downs refused to provide jobs for some of his supporters, Ward succeeded in having Sumner Tunnel closed on the day the track opened, on the grounds that it was "unsafe." As a result, many were late for the races.

Long before Mike Ward refined the art of bartering favors for votes, the ward boss was the neighborhood adviser, father confessor, foster parent, social service worker and court of personal appeal. Always on call for the little man, he made it unnecessary for the destitute or afflicted to subject themselves to the inquisitorial terrors of organized charity.

When "Pat" was jailed for gambling, getting drunk or cursing a cop, the ward boss talked to the probation officer or judge, and if bail was needed, he arranged for it. He provided wood and coal, coffins and burial plot, along with floral pieces. And at times he might ingeniously circumvent the law to do so. The role of big brother often gave the ward boss a chance to dramatize himself, as the relationship between Mike Ward and a Roxbury probation officer shows. Many of Ward's constituents or members of their families had been in the Roxbury Court from time to time, and they hated and feared a particular probation officer. One morning, Ward, then a State Senator, was in the courtroom when a chronic drunk stood before the judge. The judge, who had heard the case two weeks earlier, had promised the drunk that clemency would be shown him if he kept sober while his case was being continued. The probation officer told the court the drunk had not kept his pledge, whereupon Senator Ward jumped to his feet.

"Mr. Keene misinforms the court when he says this poor man should be sent to the State Farm," he said. "He's a goddamned liar."

The judge warned him he would be fined $10 for contempt of court if he did not apologize. Ward immediately turned to the probation officer and said: "Listen, you knucklehead, I wouldn't apologize to you if I was fined $100."

Just as he expected, he received front-page publicity for this scene, and he capitalized on it during rallies held in the next election. On the platform, he would pull out his watch and shout: "I will take the oath of office at eleven o'clock. At 11:05 I'll drive that probation officer out of Roxbury Court." That winter Ward arranged for a crew of men on welfare to shovel snow on the officer when he approached the court house. They chased him down the street, but they did not succeed in burying him.

At a time when death and unemployment coincide, it is not always easy to provide decent funerals, and this—until the coming of the welfare state—was often a problem for the ward boss or any other politician

appealed to for help. Although the names in the following story are fictitious, the incident actually happened in Boston:

The friendless Widow Murphy died and was headed for Potter's Field
if the sum of $200 was not raised immediately.

"I don't know where I'll get $200," Boss Mike said, "but I'll have it
by tomorrow night." He collared a State Senator and told him of his
dilemma.

"Be in the Senate chamber at eleven o'clock tomorrow morning," the
Senator said. "Just sit in the president's chair and be sure you have the
gavel."

"But the Senate isn't in session," Mike said. "And why the gavel?"

"Never mind. Just be there on time. And when I come in, don't say a
word until I raise my right arm. Then bang down the gavel hard."

On the following morning, Mike was on hand when the Senator
ushered two elderly Chinese into the Senate chamber. While Mike
watched, the Senator whispered to the two men, then his right arm
shot up.

"Two hundred dollars," Mike said, on a prearranged signal. He brought
the gavel down, whereupon each of the frightened "defendants" handed
him $100 and hurried out.

It was not some old Chinese custom. It was rather a case of illegal
entry into the country, and the two men were happy to get off with such
a small fine.

"I suppose there's no way I could find those poor fellows and return
their money," Mike solemnly said.

The Senator matched his dead-pan expression. "Impossible," he said.
"They are completely under cover by now."

"Well, I suppose what can't be helped can't be helped, and it is, after
all, for a good cause. I have enough now for a solemn high requiem
Mass."

Such unorthodox benevolence, colored by the peculiar whimsy developed by the Boston Irish politicians in their dealings with the Yankees, was by no means uncommon, although they were usually involved
more with Irish immigrants. Martin Lomasney and other ward bosses
were familiar figures at immigration centers. Lomasney used to meet
immigrants as they disembarked at the wharf, shepherd them to his club,
find jobs and living quarters for them and see that they became citizens.
Ward bosses gave them necessary instructions and helped them fill out
papers. One story involves Fitzgerald and Curley.

Curley, who used to conduct a class on naturalization at his Roxbury club, one night asked an immigrant how the laws of the nation were made.

"John F. Fitzgerald," he answered.

Curley asked how the laws of a state were made.

"John F. Fitzgerald."

"Well, you're consistent, anyway. Who is the President of the United States?"

"John F. Fitzgerald."

"And if I hadn't stopped the man there," Curley was quoted in the *Boston Post*, "I'm sure he would have gone on to tell me that John F. Fitzgerald drove the snakes out of Ireland and discovered America."

In days of insecurity and unfamiliarity with strange customs, the ward boss was a social security bureau.

Lomasney, whom Fitzgerald called "my political godfather," taught him that the "great mass of people are interested in only three things: food, clothing and shelter." Another Lomasney axiom that Fitzgerald remembered was: "The politician who thinks he can get away from the people who made him, usually gets what is coming to him—a swift kick in his political pants."

The son of an Irish immigrant tailor, Martin Lomasney bossed a powerful ward machine that was the envy and despair of other city bosses in Boston. He repeatedly showed his power by the astonishing ability to deliver an almost exact number of votes to defeat or support a candidate or a piece of legislation. He was upset when, in one election, thirteen of his constituents voted out of line.

"I know one is Jim Graham," he said. "I'd like to know who the other twelve are."

An orphan bootblack who became a city lamplighter, he was a realistic and ruthless politician in an era when Boston politics was synonymous with civic extravagance and various degrees of corruption. "The civic conscience of Boston, like a goboon in a Scollay Square saloon," said *Time* magazine, "is a battered vessel." Martin Lomasney, who dented the goboon on occasion, was more interested in results than in ethics and ideals.

"Successful politicians do not expect to be canonized or even achieve the state of blessedness to which persons of more polite and leisurely pursuits may aspire," Curley wrote. Lomasney was equally frank: "I have never posed as a political angel, and there is no place in politics for political saints and angels."

Lomasney was earning $1800 a year as City Health Inspector when he started building up the Hendricks Club, named for Vice-President Thomas A. Hendricks (who served with Grover Cleveland) in gratitude for a speech he had made defending the Irish. Every morning, Martin was in his private "throne room" by nine o'clock, sitting in shirt sleeves and wearing a battered yellow straw hat. He worked at a rolltop desk. In a corner safe were volumes of election statistics and confidential files that could be used when a political adversary needed to be cut down to size. Every ward boss of that period had something on every other, but none kept such systematic files as Lomasney.

Burly, jut-jawed, with glittering but appraising gray-blue eyes behind gold-rimmed glasses, Lomasney had a handlebar moustache (common in his day) that for luxuriance matched that of Pat Kennedy in East Boston, one of his colleagues. Martin could be blunt and, when ired, arrogant to a fault. He had always been a loner who was boastful of his power. To teach one ward politician a lesson, he told him: "Next time I will run a newsboy against you and beat you."

He did just that.

"We can trace through his biography," wrote Professor A. D. Van Nostrand of Brown University in *The New England Quarterly,* "the evolution of the emigrant nationalities into a powerful governing class; we can witness the political methods involved in their struggle; and we see the gradual disappearance of the boss once this class had achieved power." "Martin Lomasney," wrote Lincoln Steffens, "lifted the Boston Irish from agents to partners in the game, and they played it as Martin saw it played by his betters."

It was Martin Lomasney who put Honey Fitz into political orbit.

Fitzgerald's power stemmed from the influence he wielded over the strong Catholic population of Ward Six in the North End. With his gift for organizing, ubiquitous Johnny Fitz had the drive, outgoing personality and "gift of gab" his Irish electorate liked. His slogan was "Work harder than anyone else." Politics might be a business to Republicans, but to him it was a pleasure as well as a way of life.

He had no central organization at first, but he had the backing of the clubs and organizations to which he belonged, including the Red Berry Club, a political and social fraternity of old North Enders, who held many of their outings at Old Orchard Beach in Maine. The Neptune Associates, like all the boat clubs in the waterfront wards, was also important in local politics. In the winter of 1884, Proper Bostonians were jarred when this Irish club hired the staid Boston Music Hall for a dance, for it had almost invariably been used as an exclusive social and intellectual center.

Even the Neptune members worried about Fitzie's audacity, but the twenty-one-year-old president knew exactly what he was doing.

He persuaded city merchants to advertise in his program and politicians to buy tickets. He paid boys in various neighborhoods a few cents to carry his advertising transparencies at night and bang away on old washboilers, sounding a new kind of alarm in the domain of Paul Revere. As a result, Boston Music Hall was jammed on the night of the ball.

The affair was successful from a financial as well as social point of view, for Fitzie had turned off all the water in the building, thereby forcing his guests to buy soft drinks. A member of the entertainment committee, who had protested at the number of cases of soda pop Fitzie had ordered, was amazed when not one bottle was left. Never had the treasury received such a boost, and never before had the North Enders attended such a gala ball.

Fitzie kept staging Catholic socials, and introduced sunlight dances for the first time in Boston. In between his managing and leading his professional polo team, he found time to become a local authority on etiquette, consulted by boys on sartorial details and the kind of corsages or presents to buy for their girl friends. Even girls consulted him in matters of etiquette and dress, for Fitzie was the acknowledged social leader of a solid Irish district.

He caught the eye of Matthew Keany, the political boss of Ward Six who had helped him get the job in the Custom House in 1886. Johnny Fitz's breezy personality, added to Keany's support, won him a seat in the Common Council in 1892.

The seventy-five members of the Common Council met Thursday nights and debated every manner of bill. Most of the young Irish aspiring politicians entered by this gate, for the Council was dominantly Democratic.

"In the Council," Honey Fitz recalled later, "the first thing I did was to find time to speak for a playground down at the North End, and I got it on Commercial Street. It was the only place on the waterfront where folks could take their children. We voted $350,000 for the North End Park. I also put in a resolution calling for a committee to study the great Exposition in Chicago to see in what way Boston's commerce could be advanced."

He kept a card index of all men in his district who needed work, and hired a secretary to handle details. By this time, he had turned over most of his insurance business to his brother, Henry, who also helped him with patronage. Nobody had ever taken such good care of Ward Sixers.

Fitz favored men with large families, including the McColligans, whose sixty members voted as Fitz dictated. He formed the Jefferson Club, patterned after the Hendrick's Club, and the pewholders became voters who could also be counted on.

The average laborer at this time was usually only two weeks away from starvation, unless he had generous friends, and a steady job was prized. No gratitude was too warm for the ward boss who took care of the breadwinners. The politician who got the most jobs had the most loyal supporters. The Republican State Commissioners controlled the patronage of liquor licenses—a powerful political prop—but the Democratic ward bosses controlled most of the municipal jobs and were able to place their followers with contractors who did business with the city. Fitz hounded city contractors and public utility executives who in those days had more employees than the city itself.

At Thanksgiving and Christmas, he distributed food baskets and presents and made sure he was within camera focus when he handed a basket to a crippled child or a blind old man. He handed needy neighbors a few dollars for rent or coal and saw that none of his constituents was evicted for nonpayment of rent.

He had developed a sure-fire, vote-winning formula. Taking another page from the Lomasney book, he set up office hours at the Jefferson Club, where anyone could come in and talk to Mr. Fixit. He helped orphans and widows, provided food baskets for the poor at any time during the year, sent wedding gifts to benedicts and held picnics for hundreds of persons who had few recreational outlets. He would wander by during a school recess and order the driver of a Louis C. Merry pastry wagon to pull up by a playground, haul out his huge tray of "cat pies" and other goodies and treat every boy and girl in the school yard. Johnny Fitz was a decade ahead of Mayor Curley, who used to walk along the stalls of Faneuil Hall and, when he saw an old lady wistfully looking at a turkey she could not afford, hand a merchant $10 and tell him to wrap it up for her and give her the change.

It was always Johnny Fitz who took up a collection for a burial, and his "Wake-House Campaigns" set a pattern for other district politicians. Every morning, he bought a copy of the *Boston Globe,* which had the most complete death notices, and made assignments for his wake squad. Either he or one of his lieutenants visited every home in the ward where there was a death. Fitz was highly emotional and could weep as easily as he could smile, and it was a technique which helped him at political rallies. His Wake-House Campaigns were effective. And if a tearful widow ventured to say, "It was so good of you to come. I didn't know you knew Jim," he would never disillusion her by admitting that he didn't.

In the waning summer of 1892, Johnny Fitz told Keany he intended to run against incumbent George McGahey for a State Senate seat. Keany, who promised to wrap up the Ward Six vote for him, died before the election and received the biggest funeral in the memory of the North End. Every hack in the city was rented that day, the story went. Overnight, Johnny Fitz found himself the czar of Ward Six. A czar, but a benevolent despot.

Martin Lomasney backed Fitzgerald to everyone's surprise. "Johnny Fitz must have hypnotized Martin," a ward heeler said. Actually, Lomasney was still smarting over a rebuff to his friend Edward Donovan in 1890 when other ward leaders had denied him a nomination to the executive council of the Democratic City Committee. Lomasney also reasoned that, as the top man in a neighboring ward, Johnny Fitz might be useful in coalitions against other ward bosses who on occasion ganged up on him.

Fitzgerald spent two unspectacular years in the State Senate. In the Common Council, he had introduced an order that made October 12 (Columbus Day) a local holiday in Massachusetts, to the delight of his Italian constituents. As Senator, he was instrumental in changing the dour Fast Day of the Pilgrims into Patriots' Day (April 19), a legal state holiday commemorating the Revolutionary battles of Concord and Lexington.

"My principal achievement in the Senate, I suppose," he reminisced later, "was the work I did on the rapid transit committee. Nathan Matthews, Junior, was Mayor at the time, and he insisted that nothing be done in the line of legislation then, and wanted me to vote to refer the matter to the legislature of the next year. But I wanted something done, and I voted for the elevated road and the subways, taking the ground that Chicago and New York had rapid transit.

"The committee visited Detroit and Baltimore and saw tunnels underneath the rivers in both places, built and being built, and I came back red hot for action. I said Boston had waited long enough and told Mr. Matthews very strongly how I felt about it. I said my vote was the controlling one on the committee."

Like any successful municipal politician, Johnny Fitz knew the public would barter votes for convenient transit facilities at low cost. "I rode into office on a nickel fare," Mayor Jimmy Walker of New York quipped.

Even as a State Senator, Johnny Fitz had his eye on City Hall, as indicated by one conference he had with Mayor Matthews.

"I sat in the anteroom [at City Hall] for three hours, and he would not admit me. I finally made up my mind—and I was chairman of the Ward Six committee at the time, and had come to City Hall on some errand about a park appropriation—that I was responsible to my constituency, not to Mr. Matthews.

"I said this is a public office and I am going in, and when the Mayor's messenger got out of the way, I walked in and said good morning, adding that I had been waiting three hours to see him.

" 'I don't want to see you and I won't talk with you,' he said.

" 'You will talk with me,' I said. 'I am here for a public purpose and in the public interest.' "

Matthews threatened to have a police officer throw him out of the office, whereupon Fitzgerald drew a glass of water from the tank and drank to His Honor's health.

"I'll be sitting in that chair after you have gone out of office, and when I do, I'll be courteous always." Under the Mayor's glare he added: "Good day, Matthews. When you are out of that chair and you come in some day to see me, I will admit you."

Nathan Matthews, Junior, who lectured at Harvard on municipal government, was a frequent victim of the whiplash tongues of both Fitzgerald and Curley, whom he made a career of opposing when they became mayors. During one term at City Hall, Curley was walking past the City Club on Beacon Street when he saw Matthews chatting with a group of judges and lawyers. Matthews was carrying an old green cloth bag.

"I am delighted, Nathan," Curley said, bowing, "to see that you are still carrying your burglar tools in your Harvard bag."

The route to City Hall often led through the Halls of Congress in the early days of Irish political ascendancy. By the mid-1890s, the star of Johnny Fitz was rising, and he had gained stature locally as a second Napoleon. Actually, he was about as short and stocky as the Corsican and matched him in vivacity and energy. Even more striking was his facial resemblance. Cartoonists, by manipulating his features slightly and putting a tricorn hat on him, needed no caption. The delighted Ward Six boss read up on Napoleon, aped his mannerisms and openly adopted his slogan: "What I undertake I do." It would be more accurate to say he adapted the Napoleonic motto, for Johnny Fitz's version was "What I want, I get." The ward cigarmaker brought out a five-cent "Young Napoleon" cigar.

Johnny Fitz, ruddy, handsome, with piercing blue eyes, was by this time an acknowledged showman dowered with all the gifts a winning politician needs. More gracious and informal than ever, he made everyone he met feel like his next-door neighbor. Along with a shrewd common touch, his voice was a prime asset, despite a lisp. His handshake was a caress, and he was adept at the "Irish switch," which consisted of pumping one person's hand while talking to another. Johnny Fitz improved on this technique by gazing fondly at a third person during the handshake. Later he added a telephone technique that few other politicians could match. He would carry on two or three conversations at the same time, apt at any time to burst into song during one of them. He was always loquacious, and at times garrulous, but usually interesting.

Most of the time, Johnny Fitz was a kindly soul who wished all his friends had only one eye so he could dry its tears. In a querulous mood, he might complain of petty matters and let his tongue outrun his judgment or his imagination run away with his intelligence, but his dislikes were seldom more than verbal, except for his deep-seated animus against James Michael Curley who, like himself, was a child of audacity whom few could faze. Their personalities were otherwise markedly different. Fitzgerald was allegretto, Curley cantabile. Sometimes hot-tempered, Johnny Fitz was more often the Merry Andrew bubbling over with good nature, using his wit as a stiletto rather than bludgeon. Curley, on the contrary, took himself with a mock-portentous seriousness, and his humor was frequently cruel and sarcastic, as Fitzgerald knew so well.

While in the state senate Fitzgerald had consolidated his power in his home ward, for he controlled more job patronage than ever. The big public-service corporations who employed so many workers often needed favors, and one rule of political expediency was to trade to the benefit of loyal supporters. As senator and ward boss, Fitzgerald controlled three councilmen, two members of the state legislature and, with two other ward leaders, one alderman. Jobs poured into Ward Six.

No Tammany boss was more successful in putting friends, relatives and supporters in plush jobs. As congressman and later as mayor, he provided snug berths for several members of his family.

In 1894, the first nine wards of Boston formed the only Democratic congressional district in Massachusetts. By alliances with other ward leaders, Johnny Fitz was ready for his important political bid. And in his first major contest he proved himself a magnificent campaigner. The two leading Democratic politicians of Boston for two generations had the same arrows in their quiver. Fitzgerald and Curley had a typical Irish memory for apt literary quotations, a flair for the dramatic, no fear of ever making the bold move and an uncommon articulateness. Lines from "Municipal Ballad No. 79" shed light on Johnny Fitz:

"Honey Fitz can talk you blind
On any subject you can find.
Fish and fishing, motor boats,
Railroads, street cars, getting votes,
Proper way to open clams,
How to cure existing shams;
State Street, Goo-Goos, aeroplanes,
Malefactors, thieving gains,
Local transportation rates,
How to run the nearby States;
On all these things, and many more,
Honey Fitz is crammed with lore."

His articulateness was so well known, according to a *Boston Post* reporter, that if John F. Fitzgerald were wakened from slumber in the dead of night and asked to speak on any subject under the sun or elsewhere, "he will readily, not to say willingly, arise from his couch, slip his frock coat over his pajamas and speak eloquently for two hours and seventeen minutes on that subject." How could he miss? He had kissed the Blarney Stone even before Curley and, as the jingle says:

"This stone who kisses
Sure he never misses
To grow eloquent.
'Tis he may clamber
To a lady's chamber
Or be a member of Parliament."

To win votes in the mid-1890s, he had no need to reason when he could charm, no need to expound platitudes when he could pick up the votes of brothers, fathers and cousins by waltzing, as only Johnny Fitz could waltz, with the ladies.

"Where is your sister?" he would say. "She is the best dancer in the room." No ballroom ever contained so many best dancers as those Johnny Fitz frequented. And when he went to a ball, he let other young men monopolize the belles of the occasion, who, because they were accustomed to being danced off their feet, brought home no glowing reports of any individual male gallantry. Fitz sought out the wallflowers whom less thoughtful and less politically minded swains were neglecting. With each, he was the impeccable Prince Charming, faultlessly attired in immaculate linen. There were warm evenings when, to maintain his neat appearance, he had to change his celluloid collar two or three times and retire to the lavatory to comb his hair.

Fitzgerald's suspenders might dangle as he mapped strategy in back rooms with his lieutenants, but in public he was no less fastidious than Beau Nash. He knew when to wear evening clothes at political rallies, when not to look spiffy. In a taxi on his way from one function to another, he might change from tuxedo to business suit or vice versa, and before crossing the bridge into Charlestown, he never forgot to remove his fur coat during a chill November of campaigning. In Charlestown, as in Roxbury, the electorate was not impressed by "fancy duds." One earthy but authentic comment heard at a Roxbury rally suggests the indifference: "Look at Lazy Jack Nolan up there on the platform," a heckler yelled, "all dressed up in his brand-new jockstrap."

Johnny Fitz also knew when to swallow his r's, when to talk up or down. In Charlestown, he would tell all his grand old friends out there in the audience how happy he was, indeed, to be once again in dear old "Char-less-town," as the local burghers pronounced it.

Always smiling, dapper and debonair, he was never without his boutonniere, and he knew precisely when to be waggish, when to be tactful. "Never in my life have I asked any woman, even Mrs. Fitzgerald, to tell me her age," he said. "I should consider it the rankest discourtesy to do so."

Johnny Fitz threw out compliments with the happy abandon of the departing bride throwing her bouquet to the bridesmaids. In those days, before radio and television spoiled things by putting mass audiences within earshot of one speech, Johnny Fitz got away with no end of polite deception in the interests of making everyone feel good. At the ball of the County Mayo Men's Social and Benevolent Association at Paul Revere Hall, he told the guests how much he appreciated the opportunity "to look into the faces of the handsomest women I have ever seen in my life." Called on for a word or six hundred, he would express his regret that he had spent too little time in County Mayo during his last glorious trip to the Emerald Isle and would promise to do better next time. He glibly identified himself with any audience out of the purest of motives: He was seeking the votes of happy people.

In downtown Boston, over the Cobb, Bates and Yerxa grocery store, several Irish fraternal organizations had clubrooms. One Sunday noon, Fitzgerald dropped into the County Mayo meeting.

"I love County Mayo," he said during the course of his speech, "and I have always loved County Mayo because my dear mother was born in that fair county. All my life I have wanted to visit County Mayo, and if I am elected I will visit it." Later that day, he dropped into a few other club-rooms and assured the lovers of County Cork and County Sligo that his mother had been born in dear old County Cork or County Sligo, and that was why he felt so much at home in their midst. He knew the strong Irish affinity along county lines, and that the one thing which could divide the Irish of his voting population would be to arouse antagonisms between the men of Kerry, say, and those of Galway. One old-timer remembers Mrs. Donovan of Galway reminding her husband, a construction foreman, as he left for work: "Remember, Tim, don't put any Cork men to work today."

Less astute politicians who ran for office made the mistake of telling mixed assemblies they were proud of being Corkies, not realizing that their boastfulness was taken unkindly. Fitzgerald solved this problem by wearing a coat of many colors, and in days of poor communication, when clans divided the Irish electorate, he could usually get away with a hypocrisy that was considered acceptable politically. Just as it is almost impossible to utter libel in a political campaign, so the truth takes an awful beating.

Fitzgerald made any group feel proud of its native sons or traditions. In Lewiston, Maine, he was cheered when he told a crowd that Boston owed its world baseball championship to Lewiston's Bill Carrigan, who had piloted the Boston Red Sox to World Series' victories. At a banquet for shoe manufacturers in one city, he told a convention that he was wearing a pair of shoes that had been made in the city and was nothing fazed when told that only women's shoes were manufactured there at the time. He told a Pan-Hellenic meeting that "Boston is proud of its title of the 'Athens of America,'" and referred to ancient Athens as "the center of culture and civilization. While the Greeks of Boston have been few in number, many are already counted as typical Bostonians. It is a pleasure . . . to come to this hall tonight and meet a gathering of men whose ancestry is perhaps the most distinguished in the world."

In 1961, President Kennedy mentioned the affection his grandfather had for those of Italian birth, adding that in his Boston campaigns he became a descendant of the Giardini family of Venice. This statement irked the editor of an Italian newspaper which circulates in the North and West Ends of Boston.

"What Kennedy failed to say," he wrote in his weekly, "was that some

Boston dailies ridiculed his grandfather during his campaigns for telling French audiences that he came from the Geraldines of Paris—before Scotch rallies that he was a descendant of the McPhersons, and to German gatherings that his forebears were named Von Fritz."

Actually, at various times, John F. Fitzgerald did claim Greek, Roman, Norman, but always Irish, antecedents, and there is justification for all these claims. The ancient home of the Fitzgeralds in Waterford, Ireland, was for centuries occupied by the fighting Geraldines. It was a castle on over three hundred acres. The chronology of the Geraldines has been traced back to Greece, when they lived in that country and took part in Hellenic affairs, including wars. Later they migrated to Italy where they became "Gherardinis," not "Giardinis." The *Boston Post* picks up the story from there:

In Italy through a prosperous marriage to Lavinia, daughter of an Italian king by one of the Geraldines, their family became powerful and loyal Italians. When William the Conqueror needed help to battle the British, the Gherardinis gave up their opulent lives to give him aid. After the successful invasion William gave the Gherardinis castle Windsor and a lordship. In England the family dropped their Italian name for the more English Fitzgerald. "Fitz," which stems from the French word "fils" meaning son, indicates that the first of the modern line was a son of a Gerald.

From England, the Fitzgeralds moved to Ireland, where a Maurice Fitzgerald, according to the *Boston Post,* became a prominent citizen. The family, which had lived in Ireland for eight centuries before members migrated to the United States, can thus claim ancestry of Greek, Italian, English and Irish.

"Running back through genealogical history," John F. Fitzgerald told *Boston Post* readers, "I admit that I found we came from the Trojans via Italy; but also I found that after seven or eight centuries in Ireland we became real Irishmen, standing for Irish principles and freedom. . . ."

It took more than mellifluous blarney to win elections in the early days of Hibernian politics, when it was root, hog, or die. Votes that were cast were not always counted, and legal voters were not always permitted to exercise their prerogative.

In 1894, Johnny Fitz, alias the Napoleon of Ward Six, was opposed by Congressman Joseph H. O'Neil, who had already served three terms. Martin Lomasney had originated the "rotation in office" pattern, to "give the young men a chance." It was time for a change, he felt, and he fingered Johnny Fitz as O'Neil's successor. "He's smart and he's done more for this town than anyone else," Lomasney said. It did not occur to Lomasney that he was building up a political strong man who would cause him trouble later.

Fitzgerald would have refused to run against Congressman O'Neil but for the pushing insistence and confidence of Lomasney, for O'Neil was backed by three of the most powerful ward bosses in Boston—Pat Kennedy of East Boston, Jim Donovan of the South End and Joseph Corbett of Charlestown, all former State Senators and members of the "Big Four," who were otherwise known as the "Strategy Board" or "Mayor Makers." This trio was then bucking Lomasney for control of the Democratic city machine. Martin could speak Gaelic fluently, and his brother, Joseph, who was active in Boston's politics, had learned enough sign language to sway deaf mutes in Ward Eight. "What chance have you against the pair of them?" an outsider asked when he saw them both in operation in a precinct they controlled.

Johnny Fitz, hailed as the "boy candidate," was aided in this campaign by boyhood friends who arranged rallies and canvassed every ward, appealing to the voters of the dear old North End and others to give the young man a chance. Johnny Fitz called these youthful supporters his "volunteers."

"I had an army of young fellows who were friendly to me in different sections of the city," he recalled, going on to recount his activities as president of the Neptune Associates, and the friendships he had formed in other affiliations. "This gave me a large acquaintanceship. Then my athletic ability brought me into contact with boys and young men from all over the city. . . . So after service in the Senate, I became a candidate for Congress.

"These volunteers came to the polls early and took places in the line, and as the voters came along my friends would say, 'Are you going to vote for Fitzgerald?' and if they said yes, these young fellows would give up their places in the line and my friends, those who came to support me, did not get tired of waiting."

His theory was that grateful voters, given a place in the line so they would not have to wait long, would mark a cross beside his name on the ballot.

"I think that bit of strategy won that fight," he said.

But some of his volunteers were goon squads—one of his countermeasures for the strong-arm tactics used by candidates of the period. The unwritten rule, as Curley bluntly stated it later, was "Do others, or they will do you." Winning candidates had to "think ahead of the mob" and either outfox or outmuscle the opposition.

North End voters in the 1890s, and some from the West End, included rugged longshoremen, gashouse workers and fishermen, and it helped to have them on your side. One Fitzgerald lieutenant, Charles Ballem, was in charge of the less agreeable element of the volunteers. The most effective volunteers at the polling booths, indeed, were Ballem's "bull-pushers" or "cattle-pushers," as they were variously known— sturdy and burly men all, hired to feed the payload on the cattle ships that round-tripped from Charlestown to Liverpool. Some might be school teachers on vacation or sabbatical and among them were Shanghaied drunks, but the wrestlers in Ballem's elite corps were chosen on the basis of muscle. In his boyhood, Little Johnny Fitz, when he went down to the waterfront with the gang to dive off the coal wharf, used to see the eerie way the cattle ships pitched or rolled when the payload, under the goading of the pushers, shifted position. Little did he dream of the role the bull-pushers would play in his political career.

On election day, as on the day of the primaries, Ballem herded his pushers into a solid phalanx in front of the polling booths, and there they stood until the polls closed, permitting only Fitzgerald supporters to vote. Opposition voters who tried to crash the booths were shoved back. Fitzgerald men, according to an article in *Collier's* magazine in 1907, "were ready with their hands. One of them knocked over a Ward Seven man with a lead pipe, and thereby filed some nomination papers before him, whereupon Lomasney—oracle and professional silent man of Ward Eight—called the Fitzgerald Democrats the 'black-jack Democracy'—a name which lingers to this day."

Between 1894 and 1907, obviously, Fitzgerald and Lomasney had punctuated their ups with a few downs.

In 1894, it was, as in subsequent elections, a diamond-cut-diamond business. It was one kind of roughness against another. Fitzgerald, on the day of the primary, had lunched with two leaders in Donovan's Ward Seven, where O'Neil was strong.

"What are my chances in Ward Seven?" Fitzgerald asked. "Will I get the votes that will be cast for me?" He learned that the Marquess of Queensbury rules would, as usual, be dispensed with. "They told me with brutal frankness that they were bound to carry the ward for O'Neil by hook or by crook, and that there was no way of my winning it. This gives an example of the way politics was carried on in the city in the old days. Realizing that my time would be wasted in the South End, I took my volunteers to East Boston and Charlestown where they got in the line and helped me out."

The only Democratic Congressman from New England, Fitzgerald served for six years, winning reelection in 1896 and 1898. During his first term, he broke down, and his physicians, fearing tuberculosis was setting in, ordered him to rest. Boston friends bought him a horse and financed a trip to South Carolina, where he spent a few months riding in the open air, returning in good health.

In 1896, John A. Ryan, a Boston bookseller, opposed him in the primaries, basing his campaign on Fitzgerald's absentee record. The Congressman had spent his time galloping around the countryside, he charged, when he should have been tending the store in Washington, D.C. The bookseller gave Johnny Fitz less trouble, however, than a drunk at one South End rally. While Fitzgerald was talking, the heckler kept shouting, "I'm a Republican." Asked by the speaker how he had descended to so low an estate, he explained that his family had voted Republican for three generations.

"This is a reason, but not an excuse," Fitzgerald said. "Suppose your grandfather had been a jackass and your father was a jackass. What would that make you?"

"A Fitzgerald Democrat," the drunk shouted.

After his primary win, Johnny Fitz showed his voting strength by defeating the colorful Jesse Gove, a powerful Republican boss, on election day.

In 1898, in his win over Franz Hugo Krebs, he lowered the colors of another strong opponent. Even an orator of Curley's stature was in fear and trembling of Krebs's oratory. Mild-mannered, offstage, with close-cropped gray hair and handsomely dressed, he was burly with the erect posture of a West Pointer, but how he made the town rock at political rallies, a reporter noted: "For sheer power of denunciation, the ability to stir opponents to a frenzy, Krebs has never been surpassed in the city. Controversy, the more violent the better, was meat and drink to Krebs. There have been times when rallies in the South End were turbulent and tumultuous, when it seemed that one spark would blow the roof off. Then Krebs would appear and the air was filled with bloody murder. He loved to argue with a hostile audience. . . . Curley is an infant in arms compared to the explosive, hair-raising, utterly reckless Krebs of the old days in a political campaign."

One by one, Johnny Fitz was cutting giants down to size.

As the only Catholic in the lower house during the first session of

Congress, Fitzgerald had immediately become embroiled in a struggle to have federal funds allocated to Indian schools conducted by Catholic missionary fathers.

"I was licked on that issue, because it was then a rule that no federal money would be spent on sectarian purposes, but I did get an appropriation of $5,000 for a Catholic orphanage in the District of Columbia, because it was then the only orphanage there, and either had to have the money or close."

In twilight days, Honey Fitz recalled as his best speech a half-hour oration in the House of Representatives in opposition to the immigration bill with its literacy test. He felt that the immigration bill passed during that session, which required an immigrant to read the Constitution of the United States, was unfair to millions of people who would continue to strive to come to the United States and would help build it into a greater nation. In 1945, he recounted how, one Saturday afternoon, he influenced President Grover Cleveland to veto the bill.

"I went to President Grover Cleveland and protested through a whole afternoon against the bill, and he vetoed it. It is interesting to recall that on that afternoon I found the President alone. His only secretary, Robert Lincoln O'Brien (later editor of the *Boston Herald* and a Selectman of Abington, Massachusetts, who always maintained that any member of that town's Board of Selectmen was superior to Calvin Coolidge), was taking the afternoon off, and the President was answering some correspondence in longhand. Just look at the secretariat in the White House today and compare."

The effect of Cleveland's veto, he added, "was to bring millions of immigrants to these shores who would otherwise have been kept out."

He also told of an encounter with Senator Henry Cabot Lodge who "felt it was I who had prevailed on President Cleveland to veto the drastic bill, which would have put a complete stop to all the immigration. Senator Lodge accosted me in the Senate Chamber and said: 'You are an impudent young man. Do you think the Jews or Italians have any right in this country?' he demanded.

" 'As much right as your father or mine,' I said. "It was only a difference of a few ships."

It was largely through his drive that Charlestown Navy Yard, which had been closed for a quarter of a century, was reopened at a time when grass was growing on the docks and on the streets of the compound. "Boston Johnny," as he was called because of his persistent demands, succeeded in having appropriated $200,000 to reopen the machine shop, which had been virtually abandoned, and from that reopening grew the extensive Navy plant that would later have a payroll of $100,000,000 a year, a boon to Massachusetts. Fitzgerald also led the fight to purchase the frigate *Constitution* in 1897 when it lay rotting at a pier in Portsmouth, New Hampshire, and thus preserved it for posterity. He sparked the passage of a $6,000,000 appropriation for Boston Harbor and arranged for better living conditions and food for the Massachusetts Militia at the front during the Spanish-American conflict. He walked into President William McKinley's office at the White House and put on his desk a piece of what he called "embalmed beef."

"This is the food being served our boys who are out there dying on Montauk Point," he said, asking for an investigation of the War Department. "We are serving our boys embalmed beef." He had a point, as Mayor Fiorello La Guardia of New York City could later testify. His father, Achille La Guardia, died in Tampa, Florida, during the war, a victim of the putrefied army beef.

In 1898, Fitzgerald was invited by Lieutenant General Edward L. Logan of Massachusetts to visit his troops at Camp Alger. Congressman Fitzgerald entertained the servicemen with song, after providing them with thirty-eight barrels of beer.

In Congress, he wrote the report which defeated the ship subsidy bill and initiated another bill calling for an inland waterway from Beaufort, South Carolina, to Cape Cod. One result of this legislation was the construction of the Cape Cod Canal.

The Massachusetts congressman was rebuffed when he asked Speaker James A. Reed of Missouri to put him on the Committee on Naval Affairs. "You want to spend money on the Charlestown Navy Yard," Reed said. "I am not going to do it. I am going to put someone of the dominant party who is out of the district." Even this rebuff, however, did not keep "Boston Johnny" from wangling appropriations.

In Congress, he never missed a chance to make a speech and was always careful to go on record on the labor side of every question that had any bearing on the growing labor-capital struggle. During his six-year tenure, he talked at length on sundry topics, often getting his name into *The Congressional Record* by his frequent interruptions of speakers on the floor.

"Joe Cannon was then leader in the house," he recalled. "I remember he was speaking one day, and I was poking questions at him, when he turned to me and said: 'That little Irishman down on the front bench better wait until I get through with my speech. I want him to understand that I have a little Irish in me myself. If I let go my Irish, there will be something doing here.' The House laughed, and I let up.''

Less genial was caustic old Representative Grosvenor of Ohio. One afternoon, when Fitzgerald kept bobbing up, Grosvenor departed from his prepared text: "You are like a monkey on an organ-grinder's rope, always jumping around and chattering," he said. It was not impossible to freeze Fitzgerald as Grosvenor proved on that occasion. For once, "Boston Johnny" had no comeback.

While in Congress, he was a familiar face in the office of the Associated Press to be sure his speeches were well reported in New England. A Boston reporter who was taking a group from his city through the Capitol suggested a trip to the House to hear Congressman Fitzgerald.

"What, does he speak today?" one Bostonian asked.

"He will when he sees us," the reporter said.

A moment after they had taken their seats in the gallery, Fitzgerald rose, gave them a cheery wave and took the floor. After his speech, he went up to the gallery to greet his constituents, then rushed over to the Associated Press office.

Although he found President Cleveland "very cold," he described President William McKinley as "courtesy itself. If visitors came from Boston to see me, I could go with them to President McKinley. I took friends in there to see him when the Spanish-American War broke out and I arranged for innumerable releases of boys who went into the army and navy without their parents' consent. I was very fond of Mr. McKinley personally, and Mrs. McKinley was a woman of great graciousness."

Daughters Rose and Agnes accompanied him on one visit to the White House.

"I went to Washington as a little girl, and my sister and I were presented to the late President McKinley," Rose Kennedy remembered years after the incident. "He looked at us both, turned to my sister and said, 'You are the prettiest little girl who has entered the White House.' I thought this was a wonderful story until one of my children looked at me and said, 'Why didn't he say it to you, Mother?' "

Honey Fitz, in recounting the same interview, has a version that is only slightly different: "I remember taking my two little girls, Rose and Agnes, into the White House. The President, who always wore a boutonniere, took the flower from his lapel as I presented the young ladies and said to Agnes, who was five: 'I want to present this flower to the prettiest child I have ever seen.' "

Congressman Fitzgerald also became acquainted with Theodore Roosevelt, then Assistant Secretary of the Navy.

"He was very anxious that Charley Daly, who was finishing at Harvard in 1901, should be appointed to West Point. He tried to get President McKinley to do it, but there was no place, so I arranged for the appointment. Later, when he was being inaugurated Vice-President, he headed the line leading to the speaking stand. A terrific rainstorm came up and threw them back into the rotunda of the Capitol, and Mr. Roosevelt was forced back onto me. Recognizing me at once, he said: 'Mr. Fitzgerald, I want to thank you for what you did for Charley Daly in having him appointed to West Point. I appreciate it very greatly, as does every Harvard man.' "

Fitzgerald, irked because Daly had approved promotions in his department during Fitzgerald's absence, fired him from his post of Fire Commissioner when Fitzgerald became Mayor of Boston.

In 1895, Congressman Fitzgerald made a significant impression on Charles Schwab, a steelmaster then considered a "big Navy" man. Schwab had come a long way from the time he had groomed horses, polished harness and done other odd jobs around Andrew Carnegie's stable. Carnegie, impressed by his personality after hearing him singing in the stable one morning, had set him on an upward path and eventually named him president of the Bethlehem Steel Corporation. Congressman Fitzgerald, while in Washington, learned from Schwab ideas about investments and market values, yet managed to lose fairly heavily in the stock market on occasion.

During World War I, Charles Schwab chose Joseph P. Kennedy as the most competent executive to run Bethlehem's shipbuilding plant at Fore River.

While in Washington, Fitzgerald was in constant touch with his political lieutenants at home, permitting no grass to grow on the Boston-Washington trail. It was nothing for him to make a speech on the House floor at three o'clock in the afternoon, take the five o'clock train for New York, catch the midnight train for Boston, leave Boston that evening and be back in Washington on the following morning.

He kept a close watch on Ward Six, from which Irish voters and members of his Jefferson Club had moved as Jewish and Italian immigrants came in. He made sure that his political appointees retained a legal address in their old ward, just as he himself had done when he moved from the North End to Concord. He had won the 1898 congressional election despite the handicap of having moved from the neighborhood where he had been born and raised to a district twenty-five miles from the one he represented. Martin Lomasney, who had opposed Fitzgerald's candidacy that year in favor of ex-State Senator James A. Gallivan of South Boston, had used as a campaign slogan: "Defeat the Pretender from Concord Junction." The entire business of "mattress" voting would later be thoroughly aired, much to the embarrassment of Lomasney as well as Fitzgerald, who was called a carpetbagger by his Congressional opponent.

With racial and political realignments, the Congressman had to walk on eggshells as he planned his political future. In Ward Eight, according to the 1895 census, the Irish were being challenged, as they were in Ward Six also. The census listed forty-eight hundred "Americans," seventy-two hundred Irish, eleven hundred Italians, and sixty-three hundred Jews. Catholic youngsters found a new source of revenue in the neighborhood on Saturdays and Jewish holidays. Calling "Fire!" they would keep an attentive watch for opening windows and beckoning hands, as their Jewish neighbors invited them to tend the stoves and gaslights that ritual forbade the Jews to light on the Sabbath.

The Irish were still unchallenged as far as the Boston City Democratic machine was concerned. For a quarter of a century, Patrick Maguire had been the most powerful ward boss, and when he died in 1896, he left no single successor.

The situation led to more internecine warfare in the Democratic ranks.

CHAPTER 5

A New Century and New Problems

"In politics you don't have friends. You have allies."

— JOHN FITZGERALD KENNEDY

E DWIN U. CURTIS had been elected Mayor of Boston in 1894, and the confident Republicans, sure he would be reelected in the following year, went to the Republican Legislature and changed the mayoral term from a one- to a two-year term. Martin Lomasney and other Democratic leaders upset their plans by importing Josiah Quincy from Quincy, a direct descendant of the first Josiah Quincy, who was known as the "Boston Cicero." Defeating Curtis in 1895, he was the first Boston mayor to serve a two-year term and was reelected in 1897.

A contemporary remembered him as "the embodiment of humanness and Democracy." During his administration, political patronage was for the first time rampant. The only way he could repay political debts was to grant contracts and franchises and provide city jobs. He thereby hiked the city's operating cost a third and in four years doubled its already large debt, running it up from forty to eighty million dollars. In 1900, the year after he left office, over a third of all money raised by taxation went to pay its debt. Almost three fourths of the added cost of municipal government went to the big public works projects which furnished labor. It went, in short, to make city jobs.

Playgrounds, gymnasiums and bathing facilities were provided during his administration. "It was almost a fetish with him," wrote Albert Bushnell Hart, "that the poor should have as ample facilities for recreation as the rich."

During both terms, he was guided by a tribune which Martin Lomasney had labeled the "Strategy Board." It was a privy council of hard-headed Boston politicians who ruled the city and selected mayors. The Strategy Board had taken over after Pat Maguire died in 1896 and became the source of all important patronage. The pallbearers at Maguire's funeral were Mayor Quincy, John F. Dever (Maguire's chief lieutenant), General Charles H. Taylor, founder of the *Boston Globe,* and John F. Fitzgerald.

Born in Ireland in 1838, Maguire (known as "Pea-Jacket" because of the short sailor's jacket he used to wear) became a tailor who owned a clothing factory that supplied uniforms for the inmates of the city jail ("The Hotel") on Deer Island. One of the most conspiratorial politicians of his boisterous era, he, like Lomasney, used his knowledge of city politics to make money in real estate, and in 1882, he founded *The Republic,* a weekly newspaper which John F. Fitzgerald later acquired. Maguire had served for thirty years on the Boston Democratic Committee, but otherwise shunned office except for three years' service in the Governor's Council and as Boston Park Commissioner, a post which enhanced his power because of the patronage that went with it. Pat Maguire was not smart enough to be Governor and too smart to be Mayor.

For years, his machine had been the evergreen envy of Martin Lomasney and of Patrick J. Kennedy, the paternal grandfather of President John F. Kennedy.

During Mayor Quincy's administration, the Strategy Board voted to clip Lomasney's wings, knowing he wanted to succeed Maguire as Boston's Democratic boss. On the board at this time were Pat Kennedy, Joe Corbett and Jim Donovan—known as the "consuls." Mayor Quincy, who disliked Lomasney, worked closely and in secrecy with this trio, and, feeling that John F. Fitzgerald would be easier to get along with than Lomasney, they admitted Fitzgerald into their star chamber group. Once in, Fitzgerald joined the conspiracy against the West End czar.

While a frustrated and angry Lomasney lashed out against machine politics, the Big Four ignored him and parceled out plums to their supporters. They met in Room 8 of the Quincy House and dictated Democratic nominations all over the city. At this time, virtually all nominations for office were made in conventions by delegations elected from the wards. There was no counterpart anywhere in the nation that could match Boston Democracy of this period as a political unit.

"Smiling Jim" Donovan was the first of the Big Four or Mayor Makers to emerge as a powerful successor to Dictator Maguire. When Smiling Jim was a butcher boy, it was said that he could cut a chunk from behind the horns of a steer, smile at the customer and sell it for tenderloin. That smile carried him through a half century of stormy politics. From 1891 to 1895, he had already begun to step into the shoes of the aging Maguire, for, as chairman of the Democratic City Committee, he was the titular head of Boston politics.

Smiling Jim was a legend in his day. There was a saying that if Martin Lomasney had a million dollars, he would invest it in real estate, John F. Fitzgerald would save it for a rainy day, and James Michael Curley, according to the *Boston Post,* "would hand it out in bunches to every constituent who came along with a hard luck story on the theory that 'there's lots more millions where that one came from.' "

Donovan, who was dapper to the point of being foppish, took none of the money he made with him, but distributed it generously in the grand manner. The cigars he passed around were choice Havanas. To dine with him was a ceremony, with best-vintage champagne. "I can still see Jim walking into the bar of the Winter Palace Hotel or the Woodcock," was quoted in the *Boston Post* "and, with a sweeping gesture, ordering a round of drinks for everyone in sight." It was an insult for anyone to offer to pick up the check.

Curley would turn his largesse into a political advantage during the early part of the century, when he and Fitzgerald tried to wrest power from Donovan.

The brain on the Strategy Board was Joseph J. Corbett, a lawyer who became a Land Court judge. By the turn of the century, he had served in the State Senate and as Election Commissioner of Boston. The third powerful member of the board was Pat Kennedy, known to his colleagues as "P.J." He had entered politics in the 1880s and had served as State Representative and Senator. He was the son of the young Patrick Kennedy, born in Ireland in 1823, who had migrated from Ireland during the Potato Famine. The homestead he left still stands at Duganstown, Ballykelly, in County Wexford. In 1947, John F. Kennedy was greeted there by Mary Kennedy Ryan, a distant cousin.

"I'm John Kennedy from Massachusetts," he said. "I believe we are related."

Mary Ryan had heard the Congressman speak on the radio, "and he was a great talker, entirely," she told a reporter. Jack stayed for tea after she showed him the two-room cabin from which Patrick Kennedy had departed in 1849, when County Wexford was wilting in the grip of starvation, walking down the narrow dirt road to the Port of Cork with little more than passage money.

The granitic Kennedy homestead, basically unchanged except for a tin roof that replaced its straw thatch, is now used as a toolhouse. "They made very rough houses in those days," Mary Kennedy Ryan told Congressman John Kennedy.

Pat Kennedy had been rugged enough to survive the stifling passage in crowded steerage, and he walked down the gangway at Noddle's Island and settled in a congested, noisy neighborhood. It was a welcome noise, in some ways. The Cunard Line was building piers and warehouses and was hiring sturdy Irish immigrants as laborers and stevedores. Pat's shanty was near the terminus of the steam ferry that plowed across the harbor every five minutes, bringing in passengers for a two-cent fare.

Pat worked as a cooper, a trade which the Irish dominated since most of the barrels of liquor wound up in Irish saloons. His friends were servants, fellow laborers, longshoremen. He married a lovely colleen, Bridget Murphy, who had been born in Ireland in 1821. They had four children. Their first was a daughter, Mary, who married Lawrence M. Kane, and whose son, Joseph, figures prominently in the story of Honey Fitz and Joseph P. Kennedy. Then came Margaret, Johanna, and Patrick J. Kennedy, who was born in 1858 in mid-January. Patrick, Senior, died in November of that same year at the age of thirty-five. Bridget died in 1888 at the age of sixty-seven.

After her husband's death, Bridget supported her brood of four by running a small stationery and notions store on Border Street which led to the ferry. Later, she became chief hairdresser for Jordan Marsh. Her youngest child, Patrick, walked to a school taught by the Sisters of Notre Dame, and when he was old enough, helped his mother at the store. Later, after working as a stevedore and longshoreman, he took over a barroom in Haymarket Square and branched out into the retail liquor business, ultimately owning a half interest in three saloons. He prospered even more when he became a wholesale liquor distributor. One relic of those days is a wood-handled corkscrew on which is printed:

COMPLIMENTS OF
P. J. KENNEDY & CO.
IMPORTERS
15 and 17 High St.,
BOSTON, MASS.

P.J. had one pub in the Maverick House, another opposite an East Boston shipyard. The latter was popular with thirsty laborers who paused on their way home to exchange small talk with neighbors in the poor man's club. Who could blame Irish laborers for leaving their dingy shacks or tenements at night and crowding into Pat's bar, singing, telling jokes, carousing or just sitting and resting?

Pat Kennedy, blue-eyed with a curled moustache, rarely lifted a glass himself and would tolerate no tavern roistering. Brawlers were thrown out. Pat stood five feet ten and weighed around one hundred eighty-five pounds in those days, and his muscles rippled with authority. Although austere and reserved, he was good-natured, and usually serene and unassuming. Everyone respected him. He never cursed or raised his voice, but he might express extreme disapproval by calling a vagrant "a no-good loafer." Although he never finished grade school, he read widely and was especially fond of American history.

Pat, who belonged to the Elks and the Knights of Columbus, helped organize the Columbia Trust Company in 1895 and the Sumner Savings Bank two years later. He also had an interest in the Suffolk Coal Company which delivered coal in bags as well as in bulk to tenement dwellers. He eventually became president of the Columbia Trust in East Boston, which had a branch in downtown Boston. In 1887, he had married Mary Hickey. They had three children.

Since the Irish did much of their socializing at wakes and in pubs, undertakers and saloonkeepers developed a wide acquaintance. The saloon became a caucus room or campaign headquarters where conspiracies were hatched in a clay or corncob pipe smoke-filled atmosphere. There were eighty-eight saloons in old Ward Eight and an impressive number in other sections of town. The bartender, usually garrulous and with ample time for small talk, made friends easily, and a drink on the house meant firm votes. The undertaker was also a familiar figure in a neighborhood where tuberculosis, dysentery and smallpox took a heavy toll.

Pat Kennedy, as a pub keeper, attracted supporters who trusted his judgment, knowing his selection of candidates for office was based on merit. Nobody ever bribed Pat. The politicians he helped were rewarded for faithful service to the community, not for the size of their bankrolls. Pat told one barfly he would elect him alderman if he stopped drinking. He lost a customer, gained a political ally.

His power grew slowly during the early 1880s while he stayed in the background and worked with his lieutenants. Even during a campaign, he rarely made a speech. He did, however, enjoy discussing political issues in a calm, detached manner. When tempers flared, Pat's presence soothed. He was for compromise always, if it disturbed no principle. Corruption never touched him, which helps explain why never once was a single vote cast against his confirmation to any political office.

In 1888, Pat was district delegate to the Democratic National Convention that nominated Grover Cleveland, and he was also a delegate in 1896 and 1900. But his chief concern, as with other conspirators on the Strategy Board, was to wield power and control patronage rather than to hold office. In recognition of his power in East Boston—a boss who could deliver a significant bloc of votes—he was invited to join the Strategy Board which met whenever a conspiracy was to be hatched. In those days, all of Boston's political conspiracies began at Quincy House luncheons, where the board held their secret sessions. Some meetings, quite likely, were held on Kennedy's sixty-foot cabin cruiser, the *Eleanor,* during excursions to Peddock's Island in Boston Harbor, where Pat on warm Sundays often took friends on outings.

The Quincy House on the fringe of the North End, where the high echelon bosses usually convened, was one of the few hotels in the city which accepted city vouchers for meals and refreshments as well as for the carriage hire used by Boston politicians for weddings, funerals and official and unofficial trips about town, supposedly on city business.

Founded in 1860, it was the headquarters of the Democratic Party, and nearly every prominent Democrat—plus a few bold Republicans— who came to Boston stayed or dined there.

When the hotel was built in 1860, the owners sent two huge oxen drawing a large sign around the city. The sign announced that, when the Quincy House opened the next day, the two oxen would be served at the opening dinner. Its renown steadily increased from that spectacular beginning.

John Philip Sousa, the bandleader, lived there for years, and Sir Thomas Lipton was a guest of John F. Fitzgerald there in 1912. Fitzgerald, who had a passion for the historic hotel, said: "My whole political career is wrapped up in that hotel. I worked there on the Board of Strategy. I conferred there and ate there with some of the greatest men of our and other times. I can't remember how many times I've sung 'Sweet Adeline' in that hotel, but I'm sure it was more there than any other single place."

Honey Fitz was there to greet Babe Ruth and other members of the Boston Red Sox who stayed at the Quincy House during the World Series of 1914. But he was not present the night Bill Hogarty, a bartender, returned a hero after knocking out John L. Sullivan, heavyweight boxing champion of the world. On that day, when Sullivan was half-seas over, he met Hogarty on the street and insulted him. Stepping away from him, Hogarty lifted a water bottle he was carrying and threw it at the champion. It hit the fighter on the side of his head and knocked him unconscious. Hogarty was the first to help him come to, and they resumed their long friendship. A lightweight, Bill Hogarty had done in one second what Jake Kilrain had been unable to do in seventy-five rounds.

Another character who stayed at the Quincy House during the active political era of John F. Fitzgerald was "Lord" Asburton, better known to his contemporaries as "Jim the Penman." He was the original Jim, an international crook and forger. A great spender, he sometimes facetiously signed checks "C. Willet Work"!

The history of taxicabs is closely connected with the Quincy House. Bill Cummins, who owned the stand there for over twenty years, started when the horse-drawn vehicles were in vogue and was the daring pioneer who first parked a taxi at the front entrance. Hotel patrons gathered around to inspect the strange carriage and, for a lark, paid for rides in the quaint jalopy. Bill Cummins turned these experimental excursions into a lucrative business to add to Boston's history.

The noonday secret political sessions held in Room 8 of the Quincy House sometimes included alternate members of the Strategy Board. Although not regular members of the board, "Handsome" John A. Keliher and William T. A. (known as "William Talk A Lot") Fitzgerald, were occasionally invited to join the conspirators before John F. Fitzgerald became a regular member. William Fitzgerald was later Register of Deeds and figures less in the Honey Fitz story than does Keliher, who was considered by some political sharps to have been the cleverest member of Mayor Quincy's Strategy Board. Known as "the gray wolf of the Lomasney sheepfold," Keliher became a Congressman and Sheriff of Suffolk County and was another on-again, off-again colleague of John F. Fitzgerald.

Along with the secret meetings of the Mayor Makers were the political powwows held also in Room 8, starting at noon on Saturday and lasting well into the night. The Strategy Board inaugurated these sessions after learning this was the only way to guarantee a full attendance of ward chairmen, who enjoyed being wined and dined.

These monster banquets got out of hand in time, and Harry Nawn, treasurer of the Democratic City Committee, finally exploded when the beer bill for one Saturday fiesta was $600. The beer, of course, was champagne, the favorite tipple, and enough was consumed that day to float a swan boat. William Fitzgerald, chairman of the ward committee, was asked to take care of the bill which was never paid *in toto*. On the following Saturday the head waiter, Tom Ash, demanded cash on the line when he brought in the champagne.

Further trouble with the political gourmets developed after Pat Kennedy, Jim Donovan and Jeremiah J. McNamara returned from a junket to New Orleans. "Jerry Mac," well known to old-time Boston politicos, was the Democratic boss of South Boston, where he operated a saloon on Broadway. After being introduced to porterhouse steak *a la* Bordelaise in New Orleans, this trio taxed the culinary standards of the Quincy House. Their luncheon bill thenceforth included an item for "special sauce for three steaks," and this puzzled the treasurer. The headwaiter explained that two glasses of sparkling Burgundy were required for each portion of Bordelaise sauce, and the three bosses insisted that it be made precisely according to the New Orleans recipe.

Honey Fitz, John Keliher and Joe Corbett were among the gourmets who attended these powwows, which had their effect in shaping the political history of the Athens of America.

Smiling Jim Donovan also incurred the ire of the treasurer when he ordered Tom Ash to pass around thirty-cent Havana cigars, instead of the dime cheroots that had previously found favor. Young Jim Curley, who was getting his first hurrahs, was most impressed. Trouble brewed another time when Jerry Mac ordered fried onions along with his steak *a la* Bordelaise, whereupon Billy McClellan, another Irish political leader, drove him from the room by ordering a limburger and onion sandwich. Most of the ward bosses—John F. Fitzgerald and Patrick J. Kennedy excepted—had one thing in common: they enjoyed the glow of the grape.

By the turn of the century, the Young Napoleon from the North End, thanks to syndicate arrangements he had made with some of these convivial ward chieftains, was eyeing Smiling Jim's crown.

Of the Big Four, Fitzgerald was the most insistent on patronage. For years, he had controlled all public jobs in his own district, and as a Congressman he had branched out. "A street contractor who fought him found the city no longer needed his teams," wrote a contemporary historian. "The custodian of Copp's Hill burying-ground who said he was 'against Johnny Fitz,' was fired the following day." Young Napoleon kept his troops in line.

Since there were never enough jobs to go around, there was always a frantic scramble for any openings. Like most politicians, Fitzgerald knew that for every appointment he made, he created one ingrate and a thousand enemies. Depending on his army of doorbell-ringers, he had to repay them with favors, and while he commanded a well-disciplined group of workers, he was always badgered by greedy underlings who could bring him ruin.

Just before the end of the century, Patrick A. Collins, fresh from triumphs as consul general in London, had returned to Boston.

"What's the matter, Martin?" he asked Lomasney. "I come back here and find the Democratic party torn into shreds."

Lomasney told him how, after Pat Maguire's death in 1896, the control of the Democratic City Committee had come up for grabs, and how Donovan, Kennedy, Corbett and Fitzgerald had taken over.

In 1899, Collins ran for Mayor against Thomas N. Hart, an Irish Republican backed by the old Maguire-Dever machine. It was Corbett who had brought Collins into the fight. He depended on the General's record as Congressman and as the right-hand man of President Cleveland, whose friendship he had won by a famous Albany speech which stopped a Democratic defection toward James G. Blaine. He had also made a good record as consul general in London.

It was evident that Lomasney was beginning to nettle the Big Four. While he gained no victories himself, he was making it uncomfortable for them because of his repeated blasts at their cosy coalition. When Mayor Quincy finished his second term, therefore, they sought a candidate whose personal repute and prominence could weather any attacks by Czar Martin, and Collins, a person of kingly bearing and nationally known, was available.

Pat Kennedy had been an intimate friend and adviser to Collins, who was four years old when he came to Boston from Ireland with his mother. At fourteen, he was a coal miner in Ohio. Four years later, he was working his way through Harvard, and while in college was elected to the State Senate, then, after graduating from Harvard Law School and passing the bar, he went to Congress. No Democrat in New England had the following of General Collins who, although a former Fenian, Land Leaguer and Irish Nationalist, was not objected to by the Gladstone ministry when President Cleveland had sent him to London. He was easily the most distinguished Irishman of his day, yet genuinely American in every way, and for a quarter of a century had been considered one of the big Democrats of the nation, a man whose counsel was sought by party leaders at every level. Hating sham and meanness, he never engaged in rancorous interchanges or vicious mudslinging. A monument to his memory was erected in the Fenway in Boston, near the statue of his friend, John Boyle O'Reilly.

But Pat Collins received shabby treatment from some of Boston's Democratic chiefs.

Lomasney persuaded John R. Murphy of Charlestown, who was at odds with his townsman, Joe Corbett, to run against Collins. The city rocked under the thunder of factional warfare at its vituperative worst, although Collins personally had no part in the character assassination. When the polls closed, the two candidates were believed to be neck and neck. Then word was passed that the returns from two wards—one in Roxbury, the other in South Boston—were missing. Long after midnight, the returns came in, and Collins carried them.

The Murphy camp shouted fraud.

As a result, Murphy's supporters, to avenge the alleged chicanery, knifed Pat Collins. Murphy publicly announced his support for Hart, and although Lomasney declared for Collins, Hart, who won because of a division in Democratic ranks, was one of the earthiest of men who thoroughly enjoyed being Mayor.

By 1901, the Big Four were strong enough to elect Collins, who named Donovan superintendent of streets, a job Smiling Jim coveted, since it offered the most patronage. Thus Donovan became the most powerful adviser of a triumvirate that included Corbett and Kennedy.

After six years in Congress, Fitzgerald was out of a job in 1901, and trouble was brewing between him and the Mayor Makers, who had temporarily dwindled to the Big Three.

Johnny Fitz was uncertain about his political future.

CHAPTER 6

John F. Fitzgerald, Editor and Publisher

"You can't believe half the lies they tell about the Irish."

—*An anonymous Irish politician*

A NEW century brought abrupt changes. The horse car gave way to the electric trolley, and guests at The American House, off Scollay Square, timidly stepped into its new electric elevator, hoping they wouldn't be stranded between floors. Electric light was challenging oil and gas lamps, and the telephone and typewriter were coming into general use. In this age of five-cent beer, the Turkey Trot was competing with the waltz, and skirts inched up to permit a daring glimpse of ladies' ankles, which were still encased in high boots.

Congressman Fitzgerald, who had been supporting five children on a salary of $5000, had left Washington in March 1901 and was planning to revive *The Republic,* the weekly he had bought for use as a political pamphlet during his next campaign for office.

"It had been the practice for years," he explained, "to send a copy of *The Republic* to every Democratic voter in Boston. The paper was filled with political information favorable to Democratic candidates, and it was with this object in mind that Collins' friends had picked up the paper when the Maguire family was ready to release control."

When Collins was elected Mayor in 1901, *The Republic* was again put on the market.

"I knew there was not any too friendly a feeling for me in the organization camp," Fitzgerald said, "and that if the party leaders knew I was after the paper I wouldn't be able to get it." Its circulation was down to a trickle when Fitzgerald, through a straw buyer, paid $500 for it in 1901. Its assets were a few battered desks and run-down equipment in a dingy, old-fashioned printing office. Nobody but a man of imagination like Fitzgerald would have recognized its potential.

"I knew the success of a newspaper depended on its advertising revenue," he said, "and that advertisers look to women, who spend most of the money in the big stores that did most of the advertising. I accordingly made the paper more readable to women by publishing society notes." In his "Society and Clubdom" notices, he cleverly intermingled the social doings of Catholic women with those of the more patrician matrons of the Back Bay in the manner of an Irish Cholly Knickerbocker, who knew that names make news. If thirty per cent of all the prose in a weekly consists of names of persons in the community served by the paper, it is all to the good.

Fitzgerald had been currying favor with editors and reporters down on "Newspaper Row" for years, and it was easy for him to find help for his new venture. "I recall my first experience in printing *The Republic*," he said later. "William F. Kenney, a make-up expert from the *Boston Globe,* and I went down to my printing office on Pearl Street and started working on the first issue. We worked until three o'clock in the morning, and the night watchman, thinking everyone had gone home, locked us in. We called down to a policeman and made our way down a fire escape."

Fitzgerald, doubling as publisher and advertising manager, had advantages other weekly editors lacked. He was leader of Ward Six, he was still the boss of the North End, his political prestige had increased when he engineered the election of his brother Henry to the State Senate in 1903 and 1904. He was now in a position to ask heavy advertisers, including public service corporations, to run advertisements in his Irish weekly.

"Considering the favors at the disposal of city bosses it should not seem strange that the majority have close corporate connections," wrote Harold Zink in his book, *City Bosses in the United States*. "Public service companies of all kinds desire franchises, banks crave public monies, and certain industries require dock, street, and switch privileges. Many of them approach the boss and offer a substantial return for his good-will." Bankers especially are pleased when they can influence the appointment of the City Treasurer and Corporation Counsel, since they have an understandably curious interest in bond issues.

Fitzgerald was not yet a fully accredited city boss, but he was well on his way to that goal, and now he bent his persuasive talent to the selling of ads.

"Sixty per cent of the shoppers of Boston are Catholic, and my paper is the only effective medium for reaching them," he told George J. Raymond, one of Boston's biggest advertisers. According to *Collier's* magazine, he added: "Besides, if you should want anything in the Massachusetts Legislature or at City Hall, I can get it for you."

Many of Boston's department stores, along with public service corporations, ran half- or full-page ads in *The Republic*. Meanwhile, Fitzgerald had arranged with Nathan Sodekson, president of the Newsboy Union, to have newsboys posted outside every Catholic church on Sundays to peddle the weekly to parishioners at every service. His energetic promotion built a dying enterprise into a business that reportedly netted him a profit of $25,000 a year. As far as Publisher Fitzgerald was concerned, however, *The Republic* was an instrument to be used to advance his political career.

Mayor Collins, who had been reelected to another two-year term in 1903, was bucking the growing tendency of State interference in the city's affairs, and he irked ward bosses by keeping patronage down to a minimum. He and Fitzgerald were at daggers drawn, and the latter was now also at hot odds with the Big Three who had elected Collins after blocking Fitzgerald's return to Congress for a fourth term. There were also increasing signs of distrust between Fitzgerald and Lomasney who, in a letter he wrote his Ward Six rival, included this cryptic remark: "That woman you have been going with here wants to know when she'll see you again."

Fitzgerald rushed over to the Hendricks Club and demanded an explanation.

"Did you destroy the letter?" Lomasney asked.

"Of course I did. Do you think I would want anyone to see something like that?"

"Well, that's why I put it in there. I wanted to make sure you would destroy the letter."

"Never write when you can talk," Lomasney advised. "Never talk when you can nod your head." He would talk freely only with a single listener, for then, he explained, his "word is as good as the other fellow's in case of a showdown." He agreed with Senator Borah, who told Senator Styles Bridges: "A man running for office should think of ten words and say two."

In his newspaper, Fitzgerald kept needling the Collins administration, and the disenchanted ward bosses cut off from patronage added their nagging complaints. In his campaign to make himself the next Mayor of Boston, Fitzgerald promised his followers everything but beer in park fountains. One story had him dangling the same job in front of sixteen supporters. He would build playgrounds, bathhouses, libraries—even churches, he told newly arrived immigrants in Ward Six. When he failed to build a church, an immigrant admitted to his family: "True, but he got us our branch post office."

"But most effective of all," wrote George Kibbe Turner in *Collier's* magazine, "Johnny Fitz hitched his political chariot most ingeniously to a great movement of the population of Boston. Beginning with the swarthy hordes sent westward by the Russian massacres of the early 80's, the Jews, and then the Italians, had finally driven the Irish out of Ward Six. The old North Church and Copp's Hill were surrounded by still another wave of immigration. The Irish boys, who had deferred to 'Honey Fitz' when he first brought sunlight dances into Boston, were now scattered in more comfortable homes clear across the town. For fifteen years, while this scattering had taken place, Johnny Fitz had been playing louder and louder upon one familiar chord—'the dear old North End.' "

Turner errs only when he uses the term "Honey Fitz" in a magazine article he wrote in 1907. In 1916, a *Boston Post* writer, using the byline the "Observant Citizen," noted: "The surest way for a speaker to prove his ignorance of Boston politics is to refer to 'Honey Fitz.' Friends and enemies called him 'Fitzie' and 'Little Johnny Fitz.' The Honey nickname is a silly fake, meaningless to anybody who knows Boston's political history." According to the Observant Citizen, the error originated when a journalist came to Boston to write a political story. He was told that in the North End the older folks affectionately referred to their star politician as "Little Johnny Fitz." Adds the Observant Citizen: "That journalist either couldn't read his own notes or his stenographer transcribed her notes wrong, but the word Johnny got twisted into Honey in the manuscript before the article got into print. Fitz never had any such nickname, as a matter of fact." The "journalist" referred to could well have been George Kibbe Turner.

Despite this disclaimer, in later life Fitzgerald was widely known as "Honey Fitz," and there were interesting theories in connection with the origin of the term. According to one explanation, he acquired the name as a boy when he used to dip into the sugar barrel in his father's grocery store. Another explanation is that the "Honey" refers to the "hearts and flowers" delivery for which Fitzgerald was noted.

Depending on time and circumstance, Fitzgerald was variously known. After winning the hard congressional fight in 1894, he was dubbed "The Little General" and "Young Napoleon." In later life he was generally known as "John F.," "Fitz," "Fitzie," or "Honey Fitz."

During the fifteen years the Dearos had been moving to choicer addresses, Fitzgerald had been organizing church socials to keep his old friends together. His sentimental references to the grand old times they had drew this parody from Turner:

"As I came up old Hanover Street this morning—up the dear old North End—every man and child had a smile for me. It seemed as if the very paving stones rose up and greeted me. I met old Johnny Doolan on the corner. 'God bless ye, little Johnny Fitz,' he said to me, 'you deserve to win. Who sold the most tickets for the St. Stephen's Fair? Little Johnny Fitz! God bless ye, Johnny, I hope you'll win this day.' "

Some anonymous wag, taking up Johnny Fitz's favorite name for his former neighbors, called them "The Dearos," and by the time of the 1905 mayoral contest, there were Dearos in most of the wards of Boston. In that year Boston had more persons of Irish extraction than Dublin, and it was estimated that sixty per cent of Boston's total vote was Irish. Boston had also become one of the most foreign cities in America—slightly less so than Chicago and on about a par with New York City.

"New England is more Irish today than any part of the world outside Ireland," said Fitzgerald. "More than a dozen cities in Massachusetts and as many more in the remaining five states have chief magistrates of Irish blood. Boston is an Irish city, and the vast majority of us are still the hewers of wood and the drawers of water, but we can point with substantial pride to a record of progress and thrift in many directions."

Including all races, the total Catholic vote was close to seventy-five per cent. By 1905, the North End, with 60,000 residents crowded into its tenements, was known as "Little Italy," and had become one of the most picturesque foreign settlements in Boston, with "the proud Genoese" lording it over other Italian immigrants.

While maintaining his reputation as the Number One "uninvited guest" in Boston, Fitzgerald was constantly on the move. As Henry Cabot Lodge, Senior, remarked, there was not a more resourceful or adaptable political leader in Massachusetts than the King of the Dearos in making social and society functions important aids in political campaigns. He got further publicity not only through his *Republic,* but through the billboards advertising his weekly. Opposite a large picture of himself on one side of the billboard were the bold words: PUBLISHER OF THE NEW REPUBLIC.

Meeting him one day in 1905 in Thompson's Spa, Mayor Collins said: "I hear you are a candidate for Mayor. Is that why your picture is on all those billboards?"

"I'm just trying to promote *The Republic,"* Fitzgerald smiled. "I want to make it a paper for the Irish."

They walked to the cigar counter. "Well, after being Mayor for almost four years," Collins said, "I don't know why anyone would want the job. Too many demands are made on you."

City Hall had become "agony corner" for Collins, but it was an address that appealed to Fitzgerald. And now that he had built up a personal following that no other Boston politician could match, he was confident of getting there. Almost everywhere he went he heard the chant: "Little Johnny Fitz, the next Mayor of Boston."

He had strong support, not only in the North and West Ends, but in Charlestown, East Boston and Dorchester, where he had moved in 1903 on the theory that this sprawling suburb of the city was a better operational base than Concord Junction. Although not quite manorial, his Dorchester house was far more elegant than any North End tenement. In his "refitted mansion of the towered grandeur of the architecture of the 70s," as Turner described it, he had installed a stained-glass window that bore the coats of arms of the many families of the Fitzgeralds. Above the shield he chose for the center of the mullioned window was the motto: "Shawn A Boo"—John the Bold. It was a proper coat of arms for Johnny Fitz.

Boston newspapers had been hinting that ex-Congressman Fitzgerald might run for Mayor, noting that the machine leaders feared his strength. He was in Palm Beach in February 1905 when the *Boston Post* announced his definite candidacy. He was then a spruce forty. In July, James Michael Curley assembled twelve thousand of his faithful Ward Seventeen followers at Caledonian Grove, where his Tammany Club (a counterpart of the Hendricks and Jefferson clubs) held its powwows. Mayor Edward F. Dunne of Chicago was guest of honor, and he brought some of the Chicago wind with him. In his speech, Fitzgerald urged Boston to look to progressive Chicago if it wanted to become "bigger, brainier, and better, instead of retrograding as she has for ten years."

Mayor Collins, ailing, had gone to Hot Springs, Virginia, for a rest. When he died suddenly in mid-September, Daniel A. Whelton, one of Lomasney's lieutenants who was president of the board of aldermen at the time, became Mayor. The revised political situation left Jim Donovan in control of the machine at City Hall, and this led to a curious situation, as Fitzgerald explained years later.

"Lomasney and Donovan had been politically unfriendly for years, but Edward J. Donovan, the City Clerk (no relation to Jim) with whom Martin had lived for a long time, and Jim Donovan, had been close friends. It had been understood right along, though Martin and I had made no agreement on the matter, that he would support me for Mayor. Jim Donovan, who was unfriendly to my candidacy, thought the best way to defeat me was to get Lomasney's support, and with that in mind, put forth Edward Donovan, whom Lomasney was willing to accept."

Smiling Jim knew the Strategy Board would not be able to handle Fitzgerald. He went to Lomasney, who had made Whelton president of the board of aldermen, and said: "Put up a guy to beat Fitz." Henry Cabot Lodge, Senior, also feared Fitzgerald, who, he suspected would make trouble later. Lodge, who liked Lomasney, persuaded Louis Frothingham, a Republican, to give up his bid for the Lieutenant-Governorship, and run for Mayor.

"My friends considered this combination too powerful for me," Fitz recalled. "Jim Donovan, boss of the machine, and superintendent of streets, with Lomasney—who had been the most powerful enemy of the machine—and his friend, Daniel Whelton, who was in the Mayor's chair for the unexpired term, were aligned against me."

Fitzgerald's prospects looked dim. Mayor Whelton, who with Jim Donovan controlled all patronage, raised salaries of city employees and appointed new officials to hold the regulars in line. Fitzgerald was also opposed by the Good Government Association, which had been organized in 1903. The main impetus for reform came from the business community. In 1903, the Chamber of Commerce joined with the Merchants Association, Associated Board of Trade, Fruit and Produce Exchange and the Bar Association to form the GGA.

Its aim was to "inform the citizens of Boston, to awaken their civic pride, and to secure the election of honest and capable men to office, regardless of party affiliations." In 1903, it began work on what was to be the heart of its program for nearly twenty years—the annual published *Records and Recommendations* of candidates for municipal election.

"Men, not Measures" was its slogan. Candidates, if willing, were interviewed, and their public record and private lives were scrutinized. Every registered voter received a pamphlet. Alderman James Michael Curley in 1903 was rejected by the Good Government Association with the comment: "His record should make his election impossible."

There was much for the "Goo-Goos," as they were called by their enemies, to probe. There was the matter, for instance, of a Confederate flag captured by a Massachusetts regiment during the Civil War. As a gesture of good will, Boston's aldermen voted to return it, in person, at city expense. Only the disclosure that they had the wrong flag, plus the disapproval of the Common Council, kept the motion from being passed.

The Good Government Association was not only concerned with waste and graft, but also with the number of city employees on the payroll. Boston hired well over thirteen thousand people at a time when no more than forty thousand were needed to swing an election. Most of them worked for the street department.

Since 1895, Boston's population had increased by only twenty-three per cent, while city employees had increased by sixty per cent. The State Civil Service law was easily evaded through "provisional" appointments and through the granting of titles to "specialists," such as "Tea Warmers," "Tree Climbers," "Wipers" and "Rubber-boot Repairers." In ten districts, 144 of 579 workers were classified as "Watchmen," a job category that was a catchall. Here is a typical note written years later by James Michael Curley to Michael J. Ward:

Dear Senator:
The bearer, Mr. O'Brien of Roxbury, who is the father of a large family, is very much in need of some sort of work to provide for them. Will you use your good offices with some one of the contractors doing work for the city who might be able to put him to work as a watchman?

Some watchmen needed watching. One senator appointed a former deputy sheriff, appropriately named "Nipper," to the job of night watchman in the supply room of the Boston School Department. Several years later they met at a race track.

"Say, Joe," the "watchman" said. "Where in hell is the school supply department, anyway? I've often wondered."

"We didn't dare give Nipper the key," Senator Joe said. "If we had, he would have stolen every book and eraser in the joint."

This same state senator, one of the most ingenious politicians of his generation, accommodated another city worker who volunteered that he could make brooms when there was no Civil Service category for which he qualified.

"Okay," Joe said. "We'll create a job of broom inspector."

"Look, Joe," the Public Works Commissioner said when approached. "We don't need a broom inspector. When brooms wear out, we throw them away."

"Well, how about a broom repairer?"

The Commissioner shook his head, but a sudden rash of broken broom handles made him see the light.

"What irony," Joe said. "When my friend became a broom repairer, no more brooms were broken."

Curley went Joe one better. Some of the bathhouse attendants he appointed were listed as lifeguards.

The Good Government Association hit a snag when it tried to cut the quota of municipal workers, as these instances suggest. The political amateurs who vied with the professionals were at a further disadvantage when they directed their fire against trivia rather than real abuses.

In 1905, Fitzgerald was less concerned with the GGA than with the potent opposition of his own party, although he counted on the traditional factions among the ward bosses to aid him. There was no such thing in Boston as a Democratic party in the sense of such a party in other cities. Rather, there were Democratic leaders with their own supporters. "The tradition," one political observer wrote, "has been for a man to start by controlling a petty local fiefdom in a Boston ward and then to make deals with other leaders to move on to larger fields."

State leaders tried to arbitrate the intramural battle. William Gaston, a banker, warned that the party strife might cost the Governorship. But neither side would yield. Weathervane Martin Lomasney predicted the city's worst administration if Fitzgerald were elected. Congressman William S. McNary accused the Ward Six boss of blackmail and bribery while serving in Congress. Outsiders, not used to the heated exchange of epithets by Boston politicians, recoiled. The Reverend Dr. Leon Broughton of Atlanta, Georgia, used to southern courtesy, held a revival meeting in Tremont Temple late in November 1905, a few days after the primary, and forecast that the world was nearing its end in Boston—a phenomenon which some Brahmins would have deemed appropriate for the Hub of the Universe.

"Boston is hell," he thundered from the pulpit. "Put a school on every corner, a university on every square, Boston would still be hell, because it is without the blood of Christ. If half of what you politicians said about each other is true, then the devil might as well remove headquarters and establish himself in Boston. . . . Within the last few weeks Boston has shown up many hideous, dirty, hellish, immoral sidelights that any city or center of this great Union would not be willing to father. . . . I say, again, Boston is hell."

Dr. Broughton left Boston with an evangelical assurance that Boston politicians—if they could not be bought—could certainly be rented, and there was a fund of anecdotal material to cause him further dismay. One story concerned a contractor who had the indelicacy to drop into City Hall and offer a Boston mayor some money, whereupon His Honor leaped to his feet.

"Don't you ever dare offer me a bribe in this office."

"I understand, I understand," the contractor said. "I'll be at your house tonight."

Another contractor, according to legend, left an envelope containing $10,000 on a mayor's desk. The mayor put on his hat and hurried over to a hotel near City Hall and collared a loan shark who was conveniently waiting in the lobby.

"I'm a little short of cash," he said. "Can you let me have $500 for a month?"

Any implication of graft, of course, would be spiked by gossip of his financial difficulties.

Mayors of every American city since the turn of the century have had to take the rap for corrupt department heads, and although they are not generally so bitterly assailed as were George Washington and Abraham Lincoln, say, they are inevitable targets of criticism.

"In the hurly-burly of politics," writes Ed Flynn in his autobiography, *You're the Boss,* "you must be prepared to have leveled against you charges that you know are unfair and untrue. That is something men in the public eye have to reckon with: although they are personally cleared of charges, the persons making the charges, whether officials or newspapers, seldom have the decency to withdraw them when they find they are not true. From the partisan viewpoint the legend of guilt must be carefully preserved for future campaigns and elections."

And such charges, even though without foundation, have the tendency to convict.

In this campaign, Martin Lomasney, who had already raised a campaign fund of $60,000 for his candidate, might have further sweetened the kitty had he shown more finesse. When a Beacon Street maid answered a front doorbell and told him the master of the house could not be disturbed, Martin put his foot in the door. "He can't stall me," he said.

He received no campaign contribution from that Beacon Streeter!

Jaunty- Johnny Fitz taunted Martin every time they met. "Martin," he said, "keep cool."

But the Mahatma, as Lomasney was also known, was certain of victory. He predicted that the majority his Ward Eight would give Edward Donovan would more than compensate for the Fitzgerald plurality in the first ten wards of the city.

Nobody in Boston had ever seen such a bustling campaign. It featured a snorting procession of speeding automobiles—the first time a fleet of horseless carriages had been mobilized in a Boston mayoral contest. Johnny Fitz and six supporters led the parade in a big red car, followed by two more containing stenographers and reporters. Squads of "Dearos" and Jefferson Club members rushed on electric trolleys from ward to ward to greet The Little General, and, cheering wildly, they carried him on their shoulders into auditoriums where rallies were scheduled.

Young Napoleon's "lancers," as they were called by the reporters, were always waiting, and were as carefully trained as a stage chorus. The squads of lancers knew their exit and entrance lines and had been trained to respond to signals. When Fitzgerald stretched out his hand, as if protesting against the unrestrained acclaim, they shouted all the louder, and when he turned thumbs up, they lapsed into silence, only to shriek again when he hesitated and rubbed his hands. Fitzgerald flashed as many "signs," it was noted, as a major league baseball manager. He was like Napoleon, who said: "I need five million people to love me."

He plastered the town with posters with his portrait in the center circled by screaming type that proclaimed: "The people, not the bosses, must rule. Bigger, Better, Busier Boston." His fundamental slogan was "Down with the bosses!"

Both candidates were fluent speakers who knew where to bury the knife of sarcasm. When Fitzgerald said his opponent had not made a speech for the Democratic party in fifteen years prior to the contest, Donovan, who was smooth and educated, snapped back that Fitzgerald had done nothing else for fifteen years but talk. At a noon-day rally, Fitzgerald hurled a series of challenges. When asked to comment, Donovan pointed to a newspaper photo. "I have read what he says, but I compliment the photographer. He has caught Fitzgerald in his favorite pose, one with his mouth open."

Fitzgerald even used the originally derisive label of "Napoleon" to advantage, featuring it on buttons and posters. When a local cigarmaker brought out a "Napoleon" cigar, everyone knew who the Little Corporal was. If Mayor Collins had been Boston's most revered politician, Fitzgerald was easily the most colorful. He whipped crowds into a frenzy of delight as he shouted: "I am making my contest single-handed against the machine, the bosses and the corporations."

He drummed on the theme that Donovan was a puppet put in the race by the West End czar who had his eye on what some contemporary reporters referred to as the "City Hall Klondike." John A. Sullivan, who intruded into the Fitzgerald story at this point, had earlier said that neither candidate was fit to be Mayor, but suddenly he turned on Lomasney: "Today," he said, "we are engaged in holding the funeral services of the most degraded type of political boss in the U.S.—Mr. Martin Lomasney."

With no radio, television or loudspeakers, rallies were held on crowded street corners, where the rostrum might be the back seat of an automobile or a wagon tail-gate. Heckling—not all of it planted—might disturb a candidate's train of thought, and a thrown half-brick or rusty doorknob might be distracting.

The *Boston Post*'s "Observant Citizen" in 1932 took a backward look:

At one rally, the late James A. Gallivan was running for Congress when a brick was thrown at him, missing my own head by about two feet. I recall a plot to pour a tub of soapy water from overhead onto a candidate in another campaign. John F. Fitzgerald, who was a political opponent of the speaker, blocked that scheme by appearing beside him so they would have to drench him if they poured the water on his opponent. And I can recall a campaign where a candidate used to 'plant' somebody in the crowd to hurl insulting questions at him, to give him an opportunity to make replies that would delight his hearers. I have also seen rallies where opponents of the candidate tried to smuggle ripe eggs, vegetables and other things into a hall, while friends of the speaker guarded the doors to keep the vandals out.

The ripe tomato or vegetable barrage was especially popular in Curley's domain in Roxbury. One minor aspirant for office known as "Pimp" opened his speech thus: "I am your servant come to give an account of my stewardship." That was as far as he got. When he sat down and wiped off his face, his opponent's only comment was: "Pimp * * * *, small of stature and small of principle."

In 1908, Emmett McGrath, a Roxbury tailor only ten years out of Ireland, bucked the local ward machine. Warned by members of The Vernon Club to call off a rally, he hired a wagon and started his speech on schedule. While he was standing on the tail-gate, a beer barrel struck him on the back of his head. In City Hospital, he received flowers from the rowdies who injured him: "Best of luck. Get well soon. The Vernon Club."

"Every once in a while," the *Boston Post* commented, "when old-timers have been eating red meat or something equally potent, they get to sighing for the good old days when campaigns were battles; when fists were meant to land solid 'socks' on the jaw and when paving blocks and alley roses filled the air until the sun could scarcely be seen."

Conventions would be in a turmoil while inkwells, clubs and chairs were thrown about. Fighting their way to the center of wild meetings, riot squads themselves were often thrown out of the halls. "Voters entered the rallies dressed up in their Sunday best and looking neat and tidy," said the *Post*. "Usually they left with coats split up the back, eyes closing and knuckles bleeding."

At a rally in Roxbury's Vine Street Church (Ward Seventeen's headquarters, and scene of many a brawl), a free-for-all fist fight marred proceedings during the Fitzgerald-Donovan primary. At another raucous rally in a jammed auditorium, a candidate on the ticket heard his character assailed. Refused admission, he knocked down the "doorman," fought his way past three policemen, landed blows on several ward workers who tried to keep him off the platform and finally, panting, mounted the platform only to find that the speaker had fled through a rear entrance. When *The New York Times* noted that "Boston demands dignity in her candidates," it slightly exaggerated, for decorum has rarely been an integral part of most Democratic Donnybrooks—and most of the early-century Boston campaigns were indeed Donnybrooks.

As the contest sped to a climax, the city throbbed with excitement, newspaper advertisement broadsides added another new touch to political campaigning, and Fitzgerald increased his tempo. Donovan, not in the best of health, could manage only three or four speeches a night, but Fitzgerald, who had been averaging ten speeches nightly, addressed crowded rallies in each of the twenty-five wards of the city on the night before the November 15 primary, thus making a total of thirty speeches in one night for some kind of record.

Carrying all but four wards, he defeated Donovan by 3927 votes, giving the Democratic machine its worst drubbing. He had had to carry twelve wards to overcome the two thousand lead Lomasney's ward had given his opponent.

On the night he was nominated, he went to the East Boston headquarters of Pat Kennedy. As Pat watched him shake hands with local precinct workers, he shook his head in wonder.

"He knows them all," he said. "I don't know half of them, even though they are in my district." Pat had been amazed when Fitzgerald carried his ward.

"Now that the fight is over, Pat," Fitzgerald said, "let's get together." And the two members of the once again intact Big Four shook hands.

How had Fitzgerald engineered his miracle? The answer came later. A secret meeting held at the Somerset Hotel in Boston had turned the tide in Fitzgerald's favor. Amid all the bickering among machine bosses, ambitious young leaders like Curley and discredited bosses like James A. Doyle (soon to be a thorn in Fitzgerald's side), saw with the election of a new leader a chance for quick political advancement. Curley and Doyle, as well as Corbett, Keliher and other bosses, attended the secret session. The strategy paid off, for the home wards of the bosses present gave Fitzgerald a total of 8694 votes to 6587 for Donovan. It was a lead the City Clerk could not overcome.

The Goo-Goos and other reform elements had in the meantime persuaded Louis Frothingham, Republican Speaker of the State House of Representatives, to resign and enter the race. Frothingham was the first capable candidate the GGA had selected in its brief history.

The local Republican machine, however, sensing victory for the first time in years, wanted to win the contest with a candidate of its own choosing—that is, one whom they could control. Its primary candidates had been Judge Henry S. Dewey and Representative Edward B. Callender. Callender, ignoring the reformers, considered Dewey his only real opponent. The GGA backed its candidates with an intensive door-to-door canvass through its ward volunteers, and Frothingham's victory—by fewer than two hundred votes—brought a fierce blast from Dewey, who accused the GGA of misrepresentation in pinning a defeat on him. He charged fraudulent voting—especially in his home ward, where he had trailed Frothingham—and, encouraged by clever underground divide-and-conquer maneuvers (à la Napoleon) by the Fitzgerald camp, he took out nomination papers and ran his own campaign, which was highlighted by bitter diatribes against machine Republicans who had stymied his regular nomination. All this helped Fitzgerald in the three-week interval between primaries and election.

Now Fitzgerald's rumor mill swung into action. He had long ago developed the technique of submitting one speech to newspapers and delivering another behind closed doors in friendly territory. The *Sacred Heart Review* charged that when soliciting advertisements for his newspaper, "Fitzgerald makes a business of trading on the Catholic name. He has the effrontery to appeal to the businessmen of Boston . . . as the accredited representative of the Catholic people. He has the hardihood to pretend that he represents Catholic interests, and speaks for the Catholic clergy." As in business, so in politics. A typical underground story accused Frothingham, when outgoing captain of the Harvard baseball team, of blocking the election of an Irishman—David Scannell—to that honor. Scannell, a member of the Public School Association, publicly denied the rumor, pointing out that the candidate had graduated four years before him, and testifying to his personal religious tolerance.

Actually, like other politicians of the period, Fitzgerald was subscribing to the kind of Machiavellian philosophy of politics later enunciated by Thomas G. Corcoran, Franklin Delano Roosevelt's White House assistant: "The President," said Tommy the Cork, "must deceive, misrepresent, leave false impressions, even, sometimes, lie . . . and trust to charm, loyalty, and the result to make up for it. . . . A great man cannot be a good man."

In some respects, the Goo-Goos had been vulnerable to Fitzgerald's attack. They had been anti-Semitic in their endorsement of candidates for aldermen. One of the two Republican aldermen they had refused to endorse was a Jew who became known locally as "a Fitzgerald Republican." He blamed Louis Brandeis, a leading member of the GGA, who, he said, "is, or was, a co-religionist of mine." Brandeis, later to go to the United States Supreme Court, was at this time a crusader for the public interest.

Most of the Democratic leaders patched up their differences and fell into line behind Fitzgerald. Whelton now used the same tactics in support which he had used in opposition, appointing twenty-six new firemen by shortening the hours of the fire department. He temporarily created thirty-three new city officials and granted wage increases totaling $70,000 to almost three hundred other workers. This put more votes in Fitzgerald's pocket.

At the last moment, the irascible Martin Lomasney bolted, although it was usual for Democratic primary enemies to form a solid front against the Republicans. He summoned members of his Hendricks Club (of which Edward Donovan was president) and said: "I'm backing Frothingham. I know Fitzgerald can't lose, but I won't lie down and be with that gang that has done such a job on us. I'm going to put out the lights for two minutes. If anybody doesn't want to go through with me on this, he can just slide out in the dark." There would be no penalties attached to any person who left, he added.

During those two minutes in the dark, when the czar was gambling on a machine that had taken him twenty years to build, not one person left.

What prompted Lomasney to back Frothingham, a Back Bay Yankee who was a symbol of the hated aristocracy to the Irish way of thinking? It was partly because of the acrimonious attacks that had been made against Donovan by stump speakers during the campaign. The incident that triggered his revolt, however, came on primary day when, without consulting Fitzgerald, "volunteers" invaded Ward Eight and started a scuffle during which a gun was pulled. "That gun play, on top of all the stuff they had been springing on the stump, made me determined to fight," the Mahatma said.

A record ninety-two thousand voters turned out on December 12 to give Fitzgerald a comfortable plurality of eight thousand. Had two candidates not split the Republican vote, however, he would have lost by several thousand in a city where the normal Democratic majority was at least fifteen thousand votes. This meant that many of his once loyal Irish supporters had failed to vote for him.

Fitzgerald had not slept for forty-two hours before the election. "The night before election I made a whirlwind campaign, touching every ward in the city, and after the speaking I stayed up with my friends until the opening of the polls at six o'clock in the morning, when I cast the first vote in my ward." He had done the same thing in the Donovan fight, and would repeat the procedure in later campaigns.

A chastened Martin Lomasney admitted that his Ward Six rival had brought him "to the lowest position in my career."

It was also a crushing blow for the Good Government Association, for they knew that Fitzgerald shared Lomasney's view of reformers.

"One of the strongest human cravings is to be let alone," Lomasney said, "and an uplifter is never liked. Even the most decent and law-abiding citizens are leery of the reformer." Other politicians have put it in other ways. "Tammany is the sea and reform is only a wave," is one version. Another New York axiom is: "No reform Mayor ever served two terms." The basic reason for the bumbling of most reform elements was the inability of reform to identify itself with the masses of people. The rich, said one observer, "never had any basic interest in reform, for while each ward heeler was taking his, they were able, under Tammany, to make the really big grabs on subways, buses, etc."

"I shall be the Mayor of the whole people," Fitzgerald told the press, "and no man's individual interest shall prevail."

The campaign cost him $120,000—twice as much as it did Frothingham. "But it was not money which won the campaign," wrote Turner in *Collier's,* "it was action, ingenuity, and boundless, cheerful effrontery. For thirteen years Johnny Fitz had held Ward Six obedient and cheerful by public jobs. He extended that one basic system of ward politics over all the city. He set up an employment bureau for applicants for public work, keeping a card catalogue system of filing the names, desires and qualifications of every applicant, with a clerk in charge to take care of it."

Certain innovations Fitzgerald used in the campaign have been mentioned. There were others. He visited department stores and introduced himself to the salesmen and saleswomen. He introduced a "soda-water campaign," in which he treated women in important wards to ice-cream sodas or other light refreshments.

"He got me through the women," one ward leader reported. "Every time I went into their houses, and tried to tell the men the truth, the women would pipe up and 'Johnny Fitz this and Johnny Fitz that' until they simply talked me down and out." The Catholic clergy also helped Fitzgerald in this campaign.

On election night, he was unable to get into his own party in the dining room of the Quincy House, where a throng awaited him. Outside, the lines of admirers stretched for blocks to Faneuil Hall, all anxious to catch a glimpse of the new Mayor.

Fitzgerald got out of his car and pushed his way to the front entrance. "Let me in there! Let me in there!" he shouted to one of the policemen on duty.

"Sorry, buddy, but there isn't even space for a sardine in that dining room," the officer said.

"But, man alive, I've just been elected Mayor and they're all waiting for me! I'm John F. Fitzgerald!"

"If you were Sir Thomas Lipton you couldn't get in," the officer said. "I'm sorry, Fitzy, you can see for yourself that another person couldn't squeeze in there."

A moment later, with the aid of willing hands, Fitzgerald was lifted ten feet to the iron awning over the entrance of the dining room as the mob cheered. The roar of the crowd was immediately taken up by the men inside the hotel. From his precarious perch, looking down on faces he could see in the light cast by flickering flares, the new Mayor thanked the voters of the city for their support. The crowd cheered itself hoarse.

In 1906 he was inaugurated into an office which, in the days of Mayor Nathan Matthews, he had been ordered to leave because of his persistence in seeking favors for his constituents.

"It is to be hoped," noted the *Boston Post,* "that there will never be another political campaign in Boston descending to the low plane of the one just closed. . . . The attacks on Mr. Fitzgerald, who especially was made the target of all sorts of allegations, proved a fatal boomerang."

Fitzgerald, unlike Lomasney who was invariably adamant and unyielding, was always willing to compromise with political enemies, for he considered it good politics to pacify enemies and to be ready to greet a foe as kindly as a friend. When the smoke cleared, he beckoned to the dove to bring peace.

Lomasney, then in the state legislature, and fearing that his Hendricks Club men holding city offices would be sacked, rushed a bill through the House that would not only provide a hearing for all men discharged and removed from public employment, but also securing for such men the right of appeal to local justices. The bill applied to the entire state, but its primary aim was to block "the new headsman at City Hall."

When Fitzgerald assured Lomasney that his men would be left alone, he was satisfied when his bill was defeated.

When the original Napoleon was crowned Emperor, he turned to his brother and whispered: "Joseph, if father could only see me now." The North End Napoleon felt the same way. His one regret was that his parents had not lived to see him become Mayor of Boston. "It would have been a great delight to them, for they were natives of a country where democracy could not be exercised freely due to English dominion." He added: "I am the first son of foreign parents to become Mayor of Boston, thus my parents were the first persons of immigrant stock to have a son a Mayor." He was also the first Boston Mayor without a beard or mustache, and the first to dispense with overt forms of dignity.

"The old conception of His Honor as a republicanized copy of His Lordship has disappeared," he said. "We no longer require that the functionary should be an elderly gentleman of the old school, with a pretty gift for oratory, correct in pedigree, faultlessly attired, and a member of learned societies and exclusive clubs. A less formal and decorative personage seems to satisfy the requirements of the heart of a great business corporation. . . . Real dignity, of course, is never out of place, but once for all, the 'honorary' conception of the office has disappeared beyond resurrection."

John F. Fitzgerald had achieved a primary ambition, but now he had to pay the piper. For, in the form of patronage, he had many promises to keep, and in fulfilling his pledges he was bound to court disaster.

CHAPTER 7

Burglars in the House

"I don't think anyone can buy a mayor, but almost anyone
can sell him."

—JIMMY WALKER

M AYOR FITZGERALD came to City Hall in January, 1906 with a
far-reaching program for the development of Boston, and although he was no businessman, he had a broad background of
city affairs through a term in the Common Council, of state affairs through
service in the Massachusetts Legislature, and of national issues through
his three congressional terms. He condensed his plan into a "Bigger, Better, and Busier Boston."

And how he loved his native city! "The history of the city is noble, its
monuments are stately," he wrote in *The New England Magazine*. "Its
merchants have been adventurous and brought back wealth from many
climes; but they have used it for the larger development of their city.
Where else can such burghers be found, combining private enterprise
and public spirit, so free from ostentation, so sanely generous, as the
old Bostonians whose names are stamped upon all our liberal institutions.

"Its aristocratic section fronts on the Public Garden with an air so high-
bred, immaculate and harmonious that I believe there is not another such
residential unit in the world. Every dweller in the oblong between Beacon
and Boylston streets, Arlington Street and Massachusetts Avenue, seems
to have passed an entrance examination and proved himself a cousin of
all the others through the Mayflower, the Revolution, the First Church,
or the China trade.

"One feels that he is not merely the heir of a great tradition, but its
special custodian. If he could preserve the old principles which made
Boston rich, cultured and charitable, and adapt them to modern

conditions, if he could unify the whole city as what remains of the Puritan Boston is unified in its Back Bay citadel, he might feel that the future would take care of itself and all its problems find easy solutions."

In the following years, such fulsome praise would change into harsh criticism.

The most energetic Mayor Boston ever had was also, according to a contemporary newspaper account, "the most interesting personality in Massachusetts today. He is a bundle of dynamos that never seem to run down. Tireless? Why in the first two years of his first term he averaged two dinners and three dances a night, to say nothing of six speeches. In all, he attended 1200 dinners, 1500 dances, 200 picnics, and a thousand meetings. He made 3000 speeches and gave some 5000 girls the proud recollection of a dance apiece with Fitzy."

Requiring only five or six hours' sleep, he rarely went to bed before one or two o'clock in the morning, often topping off a packed schedule by browsing around newspaper offices chatting with editors and occasionally waiting for a glimpse of first editions as they came off the press.

"As Mayor of Boston," he said, "I have never declined to work any number of hours a day to further the city's interest, and have never declined to go anywhere or do anything because of fatigue." In one evening, after a full day's work at City Hall, as catalogued by a reporter who trailed him, he attended six banquets, speaking at each, seven dances and socials, and visited, just before the dawn killed the moon, a humble tenement where a wake was in progress. At eight that morning, he was back at his desk. Public office for him was an all-out personal dedication with no work-day limit. During his first administration, he rarely took dinner at home except on Sundays and holidays.

He was the head of all city departments except the school and three-man board of police. He was the superintendent of all superintendents, the chief executive, and the court of last appeal. Along with the multiplicity of his "housekeeping" duties, he was subject to pressure every waking moment, for tremendous personal demands are made on the mayor of any large city. Citizens write in to seek "tidings of some missing relative, and other curious epistles now and then enliven his correspondence," Fitzgerald said. "He is the official host of the city. He has public and social responsibilities limited only by his good nature and the physical law which forbids one body to be in two places at the same time. In his leisure moments he may be called upon to draw jurors, forward a letter of sympathy, present bouquets to school graduates, order a display of flags, or forbid an unseemly public performance."

While heading a complicated corporation which spent $100,000 a day, affecting the interests of 600,000 persons, and supervising the activities of thousands of municipal employees, he had to be accessible to a steady stream of visitors—domestic and foreign—as well as to favor-seekers and pompous individuals who complained if they were kept waiting for five minutes. "I had seventy-five Councilmen and thirteen Aldermen, and all eighty-eight of them were in my office practically every day trying to get jobs for somebody. I lived on crackers and milk as a result."

A mayor of a large city is cursed when snow clogs traffic, when garbage collections lag, or when fire engines arrive late at a fire. Fitzgerald himself was rarely late for a fire, and was once publicly rebuked by his fire chief for meddling while a blaze in a downtown furniture store was being extinguished. When he received news in April 1906 of the devastating fire in San Francisco, he immediately dispatched a trainload of food to the stricken city—another example of a mayor's "extracurricular" duties.

Teachers and city workers castigate a mayor for their low salaries, and taxpayers berate him for raising them. A mayor is expected to waste hours on fripperies and social amenities, greeting an unending procession of visitors. He must attend weddings, funerals, breakfasts, luncheons, dinners. He must settle squabbles, root out incompetence and graft, avert strikes, meet unforeseen crises.

After lunching with Prince Wilhelm of Sweden one August day in 1906, Fitzgerald drove to Cambridge for a tour of Harvard that consumed most of the afternoon. Another day he greeted Tom Longboat, the Canadian-Indian who had just won the Boston Marathon when a slow freight train crossing the road in Framingham held up the rest of the field. Fitzgerald was always available when a celebrity came to town, even if the rendezvous was the bar at the Adams House, where he sipped a soft drink while chatting with Teddy Roosevelt or some other dignitary. He delighted cameramen by sitting in a box at a "Red Socks" game (the "Red Sox" was a later name) with the widely acclaimed Mrs. Jack Gardner, who could outshine even Johnny Fitz in doing the unusual. She not only strolled down Beacon Hill with a lion cub on leash, but on occasion welcomed guests while sitting in a tree near the entrance to her palace in the Fenway.

There were out-of-town trips for His Honor, too. Fitzgerald led the Boston delegation that greeted William Jennings Bryan in 1906, when the perennial Presidential aspirant returned from Europe, and the Mayor managed to squeeze into the open carriage that took Bryan down Broadway on a parade.

Even in his absence from City Hall, there were worries. When he returned from one holiday at Palm Beach, he discovered that Acting Mayor Walter Collins had appointed or promoted ninety firemen in his absence. The Fire Commissioner who had approved these actions was the same Charles Daly for whom Congressman Fitzgerald had procured an appointment to West Point. Mayor Fitzgerald fired him from his post.

He established himself as Boston's leading booster and promoter by staging "Old Home Week," ostensibly planned to bring back former residents to help boom Boston. By the sheer force of his personality, Mayor Fitzgerald made the seven-day affair a mammoth public holiday, even though Puritan Boston held aloof, and the "old homers" failed to appear in impressive numbers. During this noisy festival, the Mayor made fifty speeches with the aid of a ghostwriter, and in the presence of his biggest public, recounted his achievements. He explained why he peppered his talks with poetical quotations: "They give tone, and the people like tone."

During seven days of continuous promotion, he provided trade and merchandise shows for businessmen, put tourists in sightseeing busses that took them to local battlegrounds and shrines, and staged parades, banquets, concerts, organ recitals, swimming races, track events, baseball games, horse and yacht races, as well as bonfires. Two big features were the industrial exhibits in cavernous Mechanics Hall and a big parade in which Governor Curtis Guild led 6000 militia.

"It has been a great celebration handsomely carried out," reported the *Boston Post*. John B. Hynes, later mayor but at this time a student at Boston Latin School, remembers his class being urged to take part in the celebration. Fitzgerald spared no detail to put Boston on the map. He named Julia Ward Howe poet of Old Home Week, and invited Vice-President Charles W. Fairbanks to be his special guest throughout the week. Fairbanks, he remarked to reporters, taught him something about the "art of popularity." "During a big parade we rode down through Washington Street in a carriage together, both seated, and of course there were cheers and applause at different points. Mr. Fairbanks said to me suddenly: 'Stand up, Mr. Mayor.' Up we both jumped. The result was an instantaneous demonstration of applause and cheers. Mr. Fairbanks had mastered down to perfection the psychology of receiving popular approval."

One diversion was provided by Houdini the Great, to the embarrassment of the Police Commissioners. Police Superintendent William H. Pierce, anxious to impress the escape-artist with Boston's "escape-proof" prison, clamped handcuffs and leg irons on Houdini, bolted the door and returned to his office. Half an hour later, Houdini walked in.

"Hello, Inspector," he said.

All was not levity, however. There were those promises Fitzgerald had made during the Somerset conference, and it was at this point that the cat lay down with the pepper.

"Contracts, just like offices," the *Boston Post* explained, "are a part of the spoils of office—the most valuable part. The raising of money for campaigns and the rounding up of votes calls for the liberal use of patronage. Contracts and offices are the only lures that can be used, and they are used."

Patronage elects—and defeats—mayors. Every district leader wants a job for himself and lesser jobs for his party hacks. A garbage-truck driver who delivered votes would like to be appointed Deputy Commissioner of Sanitation. Every mayor is familiar with the leech who moves in fast when he hears of a vacancy caused by the death of an official, and there is the classic pat answer when His Honor is asked: "Can I take his place?"

"I'm on my way to the undertaker's parlor now," His Honor says in all these stories. "I'll see if it can be arranged."

In big American cities, where democracy operates at the precinct level, the dregs of society expect their share of patronage if they have brought in a bloc of votes. One Boston mayor—not John F. Fitzgerald—got a hack a job at the Grafton State Hospital. The Mayor had cited the hack's abstemious qualities.

"And he was right," the new hospital attendant said. "I haven't taken a drink or loafed in twenty years. Like I told the Mayor, I just finished a twenty-year stretch at Dannemora Prison."

Even if that party worker were mythical, the brother of a Massachusetts governor was not. A customer on whom he waited in a leading Boston grocery store asked him why he didn't get a better job from his brother, who at the time was governor of Massachusetts. That very afternoon he went to the State House to see his brother—wearing his white market coat.

A constable appointed during the contemporary Mayor's term by a department head is a fair example of the patronage process as it was practiced in Boston. Told he had to sign his name on a report each morning, he bristled: "What the hell do you have to be to hold this job," he said, "A Harvard graduate?"

In Boston the situation was particularly complicated, as Mayor Josiah Quincy noted in 1897 when he complained that the executive authority conferred on the Mayor of Boston was distributed among thirty-three different executive departments, of which twenty-two had been created

102

HONEY FITZ

by state laws and only eleven by city ordinances. Nineteen departments were under the control of individuals, which made them fertile grounds for the growth of corruption.

Fitzgerald cut a switch with which to whip himself when he exchanged promises for support, even though it was the only way he could be sure of getting elected. He was caught between the sword and a wall. One politician whose support had given him hundreds of votes in a ward where he needed them, was a pub-keeper who had been expelled from the Legislature for election frauds. Two weeks after he had been rejected as City Street Commissioner, the new Mayor named him superintendent of streets. Under his direction, Boston's streets were dirty and ill-kept. Worse still, this official hired extra men who did little real work. Louis Brandeis denounced them as members of "the huge leisure class employed by the street department."

When the State Civil Service Commission decreed that deputy superintendents were covered by its rules, the Mayor, commenting that the street department was too cumbersome for one man to handle, split it into six parts, each headed by his own appointee. (This ordinance was repealed two years later.) A new Department of Supply was created and staffed with an undertaker who was in charge of buying all the city's goods and materials. He was cross-examined by the Finance Commission in connection with the purchase of coal.

"Did you know anything about coal?" he was asked.

"Not a thing."

"Did you know how to test it?"

"No."

"Did you know whether a test could be made?"

"No."

"Did you ever see a Bill of Lading?"

"No," he said.

In two years, the city lost $200,000 in dealings with one coal company, whose manager fled the state when an investigation was opened. In 1907, false bills of lading in such coal contracts brought about a grand jury investigation.

Gift contracts were a specialty of conniving department heads. Thomas F. Curley told the Finance Commission how he was rewarded for his campaign support. He and Jim Curley, having convinced Fitzgerald that their Ward 17 support was vital to his election, felt they were entitled to the second most important position to be given out.

"What position was regarded as the most important?" the Finance Commission asked.

"Superintendent of Streets," Tom Curley said without hesitation.

"What was the next most important?"

"Water Commissionership. . . . We were to name a man and I expected to be named."

Because of his jail record he was given instead a contract for crushing stone. "I obtained it from Mr. Fitzgerald for the support we tendered him in the primaries of 1905," he told the Finance Commission.

Dennis O'Neil, a protege of Pat Kennedy, can testify to the pressure to which Mayor Fitzgerald was subjected during one term of office. One morning O'Neil, leaving City Hall after persuading the Mayor to provide jobs in a bathhouse for three campaign workers, ran into Chris McCaffrey, an undertaker, and told him how pleased he was with the result of his mission.

"Good," McCaffrey said. "I'm on my way to City Hall now. I hear John F. hasn't yet appointed the Acting Superintendent of Public Buildings." At this point Joseph Lomasney, who had been named School House Commissioner, joined them.

"What's new, boys?" he said.

"Chris and I were just talking about the vacancy in Public Buildings," O'Neil said. "He's going to tap Fitzy for the job. If you see Fitz, put in a good word for Chris."

"Sure, you bet," Joe Lomasney said. "Well, see you later, boys."

On his way into City Hall, McCaffrey brushed past Lomasney. A few minutes later, the Mayor gave him a chirpy greeting. But his face clouded when McCaffrey asked about the vacancy.

"Damn it, Chris, why didn't you get here five minutes earlier? I just gave that job to Joe Lomasney."

The evils of the spoils system were soon apparent. The Superintendent of Sewers was a whitewasher and furniture polisher, but he had delivered votes. A saloon-keeper displaced a physician on the Board of Health, and the Superintendent of Public Buildings and the Wire Commissioner were liquor dealers. These appointments drew fire from the Reverend W. H. Bustard, a Baptist minister in Roxbury, who suggested that a more appropriate slogan for Boston might be "Boston for the Bosses and Boozers."

"Our present Mayor," he said, "has the distinction of appointing more saloonkeepers and bartenders to public office than any previous mayor." (He should have added undertakers to this category.) Then, prophetically, he added: "From James Curley's criminal record, I expect the Democrats of Boston to sometime elect him mayor."

Fitzgerald could not entirely be blamed. If florists and scoutmasters delivered votes, they, too, would have received their just rewards under the spoils system.

Irish politicians were not only impervious to such attacks from alien pulpits, but actually turned them to their own advantage. An attack by a Protestant clergyman engendered sympathy for Catholic politicians. Ward bosses instilled in the minds of their guileless constituents a burning hatred of "Black Baptists" and other Protestant sects. When a Baptist church in Roxbury caught fire, Irish Catholic firemen were slow in answering the alarm, and a ward leader who passed a group on a street-corner in the neighborhood, called out to them: "What kind of Catholics are you, anyway? Why aren't you down the street enjoying the fire?" The Catholic parishioners were incensed because the name of the minister of the Baptist church was The Reverend Gabriel Maguire.

Fitzgerald created the office of City Dermatologist that paid a salary of $4000-a-year, and gave it to a Dearo who was the son of the old leader of Ward Six. When he learned that a veterinarian received a generous salary for ministering to city horses, he split the revenue among five other loyal subjects. He added eleven new deputy tax collectors to the payroll, many of them bartenders and undertakers. He obtained valuable liquor licenses for three brothers, one of whom was his oldest brother, Jim, whose greeting to friends was often: "No hard feelings."

Jim owned the Bunker Hill House, a hotel with a pub, and the Alfred Tap. In 1933, he was appointed supervisor of industrial alcohol and intoxicating liquors for all New England. Edward Fitzgerald had a tavern on Atlantic Avenue. Brother George, who died in 1914 after ailing for four years, was a brewery salesman, and like Jim and Ed, was a ward manager. Henry, who had received the first license from the Republican State Commission, was elected president of the Total Abstinence Society of Ward Six, an honor that did not quench the thirst of his barroom customers. Johnny Fitz, who was accosted on the street constantly by job-seekers, would usually say, "See Henry," for it was this brother who handled patronage for him. Henry later became co-owner of the firm that manufactured the Elcho cigar, and saw to it that every license-conscious saloonkeeper in town stocked his cigars.

Johnny Fitz had another brother, Michael, who was a policeman in Charlestown. Better known was Joseph Fitzgerald who, thanks to Mayor

Fitzgerald, received an annual salary of $1100 for delivering the daily traffic report from the Warren Avenue Bridge to City Hall, a service that could more conveniently have been handled by the United States Mails. Joe achieved local notoriety as the "Human Postage Stamp." Later, when he was named superintendent of ferries, he became unpopular with certain city employees when he moved cots out of their offices.

The small embarrassments these fraternal appointments caused Fitzgerald over the years were nothing compared with the headaches awaiting him when he became Mayor. Patronage kept him in water that kept getting hotter.

Reformers uncovered corruption in the Department of Weights and Measures, which had prosecuted only one case in four years. The Good Government Association investigation, which had been prompted by the appointment of eight additional Deputy Sealers, revealed graft all the way from the peddlers to large public service corporations.

"Beginning at the bottom," wrote Lincoln Steffens, "where peddlers are allowed to use short weights because of political pull, laborers and clerks are given jobs for political reasons, coming up to contracts by city officials to themselves, it extends to the public service corporation which uses city officials to do its private work, and up finally into the region of big business."

Mayor Fitzgerald could do little about the wasteful mismanagement of the street, sewer, and water departments, the most dangerous source of patronage. Many laborers of that era considered these departments social security and unemployment compensation in one. In 1906, the Mayor tried to put through a pension plan for city employees sixty-two years old and over. The Good Government Association, opposing the move, cited figures showing that a third of all street department workers were over fifty, eleven per cent were over sixty, and fifteen men were over eighty-nine. (One was ninety!) The same figures might have been used against the GGA.

There were other charges of graft and corruption among the numerous department heads. It was charged that in the purchase of a swamp for a playground the city had paid three times its value. Another accusation was that the city paid for both sides of a shipment of paving blocks, and other padded bills were cited. A *Boston Post* cartoon of 1906, showing Boston tied down by graft, was captioned, "The Awakening of the Giant." There was a growing revolt against graft, jobbery, inefficiency and general financial recklessness on the part of the mercenary department heads.

The Mayor was personally attacked when his weekly newspaper prospered to the extent of being capitalized for $300,000. During his regime at City Hall, the American Telephone and Telegraph Company took two pages of the paper to advertise $40,000,000 worth of convertible four per cent bonds, scarcely the kind of information that would enthrall the two to four thousand readers of *The Republic*. Even the Boston Elevated was a customer, the first time this company felt obliged to announce it was running a railway service through the streets of Boston. In the first seventy-eight issues after Fitzgerald's election, the New England Telegraph and Telephone Company ran sixteen full-page advertisements and thirty-four others of varying sizes. The Edison Electric Illumination Company carried five full pages and fourteen smaller. Other public utility companies which placed large advertisements were The New England Gas and Coke Company, the Boston Consolidated Gas Company, and the Boston and Maine Railroad. City contractors, along with the banks and department stores, which had been among the first advertisers after Fitzgerald took over *The Republic,* continued to use that weekly as an advertising vehicle. In one special issue, city banks ran fourteen pages of ads at a time when rates were as high as $300 a page.

The Good Government Association, which had gained stature in 1905 when it exposed the "Fenway Scandal" of Mayor Collins' administration showing flagrant graft in connection with a state-sponsored plan to widen the Charles River and improve its banks, urged the creation of a special state-wide body to investigate city affairs.

Just as the Watch and Ward Society had been devised to police Boston's morals, the Finance Commission was proposed by rural Republicans to launder politics and prevent city officials from dipping into the till, as Tammany grafters did during the "cash register administrations" of some mayors. The Finance Commission was devised as a check on the city treasury.

"During the year 1906," wrote Albert Bushnell Hart, "the financial condition of the city and the methods employed in the administration of the city's business called for reform. Protests to the chief executive of the city brought no results. Hence the Good Government Association appealed to the Legislature to institute a complete investigation of city finances, to be used as a basis for administrative reform."

Financial problems were not peculiar to Boston. "There is no denying," wrote Lord Bryce, "that the government of cities has been the one conspicuous failure of the United States."

The post-Civil War years have been called the "Dark Ages" of municipal politics. The number of city dwellers rose from roughly five to over eighteen million in the three decades following 1860. This population explosion generated gigantic pressures which neither governments nor citizens could handle, creating appalling administrative problems for municipalities. Increasing costs of expanding local services and functions, which rose geometrically in proportion to the already staggering growth of population, spawned graft, as well as inefficiency. Urban dwellers demanded a better water supply, garbage disposal, public health measures, property protection, education and public transportation.

Mayor Fitzgerald felt some of these pressures the moment he took office. In 1907, he appointed one commission to study garbage disposal, another to report on needed improvements for the Port of Boston. These were but two of many city-wide problems that demanded his attention. In his first inaugural address in 1906, he had mentioned the financial burdens of the city, along with the escape of substantial personal property from taxation.

Reform had been in the air for decades. One result of a National Conference for Good City Government held in 1893 was the National Municipal League, and at the close of the century, the League became more active. In 1902, it met in Boston and called the city "the best governed of any of our larger cities." Boston, it reported, was the "best ordered," the "most settled," and the "least corrupt." The League could find no redlight district or any organized corruption. Times had changed since the 1880s, when policemen from the Joy Street Station used to rout pimps with billyclubs. The League further noted that Boston had no political boss like Cox of Cincinnati or Croker of New York. Instead of a single overlord, there were twenty-five bickering ward bosses.

In days when Boston mayors had no population explosion to contend with, there were fewer headaches at City Hall. In 1836, Mayor Samuel T. Armstrong might boast of "the erection of an iron fence for the enclosure of three sides of the Common, and the extension of the mall through the burial grounds of Boylston Street," but there were no accomplishments that would satisfy taxpayers of the twentieth century. Otis Norcross, Mayor of Boston in 1867, was one of the few who could say that during his administration he never spent a dollar of city money for his own use, never sold the city a dollar's worth of merchandise, never made a contract with the city, directly or indirectly, and never put a relative or friend into office. Nevertheless, he was considered a do-nothing mayor and lost his bid for reelection. Nathan Matthews, a self-conscious, lonely man in politics, and a Democrat who was Mayor of Boston from 1890 to 1894, was a respected Harvard graduate who later lectured at his alma mater on municipal administration, but he left few monuments to his terms of office.

His protege, the Republican Edwin Curtis, endeared himself to reformers by practicing municipal economy, yet after one term he was defeated for reelection. Harvard graduate Josiah Quincy, known as the "philanthropic mayor," during his four years at City Hall built so many bathhouses and playgrounds for tenement dwellers that he was accused of gross extravagance by the reformers. Then came the usual pendulum swing. Thomas N. Hart was limited to one term because of his rigid economy. Then came Mayor Collins, who ran a tight fiscal policy, causing ward bosses, now more powerful than ever, to grumble about lean pickings. He fell into disfavor because he was incorruptible. It was Collins who welcomed the delegates of the National Municipal League and told them to report to him if they found anything shady in his administration.

The same political morality prevailed elsewhere. Dorothy McCullough Lee lost her bid for reelection as Mayor of Portland, Oregon, because of her successful crusade against vice and gambling. "Dorothy just went too damned far," one of her former supporters said. The mayor who does not bow to the will of those who put him in office is often doomed.

Irish politicians did not, as Lincoln Steffens stated in his book, *The Shame of the Cities,* invent corruption. Before the Irish took over Boston, Yankee Democrats had channeled city revenue into their pockets, and Yankee Republicans, with all the resources of the state behind them, were able, by controlling the Legislature, to make profitable deals with the business community, according to Steffens.

Boston's Democrats could offer their supporters either local improvements like parks, bathhouses and playgrounds, or jobs. And it was the desire to create more employment that got Boston mayors into trouble. The seventy-five members of the Boston Common Council, who constantly needled Mayor Fitzgerald for jobs, became known as the "Boston City Scoundrels," just as the State Legislature was later dubbed "The Den of Forty Thieves."

By 1905, nearly seventy per cent of the population of Boston was of foreign birth or parentage. The Jews and Italians, next in numerical line to the Irish, tended to be Republican, for with Irish-Americans controlling the Democratic party, a deep bitterness had developed between them and other racial elements who were kept out of office and out of jobs. The Irish, still dominant in twenty-three of the twenty-five wards of the city, monopolized city jobs. It was still an immigrant era when voters considered themselves as members of a racial bloc that had to protect its own. If an overdeveloped racial consciousness was one separatist element, an overdeveloped religious consciousness was another. The latter intensified the bitter struggle between reformers and Irish politicians.

Most of the reformers were righteous, aggressive Protestants who, according to Irish bosses, were natural enemies of the Irish. Errors were made on both sides. The *Boston Herald* referred to the supposedly low intelligence quotient of immigrants, while Harvard's Professor William B. Munro lauded the superior "political ingenuity of the Anglo-Saxon." Frederick A. Bushee, "a sociologist, said of the Irish: "Our whole social system suffers from their weak personal characteristics." Fighting words to Irish editors!

Not all reformers were chaste, as Mayor Carter Harrison of Chicago later indicated. "I'll take my criticism from the people, but not from men who made their millions out of franchises for which they paid the city nothing. The so-called reformers are mostly millionaires who loot the people while they criticize me." Mayor Harrison saved Chicago $46,000,-000 by preventing a traction baron from getting a long-term streetcar franchise at terms unfavorable to the city.

In Boston, Laurence Minot was the first president of the Good Government Association. He was a banker and real estate trustee and speculator whose interest in municipal economy was not beyond reproach. While president of the GGA, he used information gained on the Board of Estimates to engineer several shady political land deals. Some of his colleagues were "captains of industry" who made public business a lucrative private business for themselves. In the first decade of this century, the Finance Commission found some of these men captaining some of the nation's largest corporations, yet they stooped to defraud the city of sums as low as $150. District Attorney Arthur Dehon Hill of Boston secured the indictment of thirteen big steel firms engaged in a conspiracy to rob the city. Five pleaded guilty and paid fines aggregating $6,000. Other big businessmen were just as guilty, but the only group brought to trial were these parties to the "Boston Agreement," a conspiracy of structural steel firms involved in high-level, non-competitive bidding.

The difference between politicians and reformers, according to one skeptic, is that the politicians pull out a gun and say, "Your money or your life. The reformers say nothing, and take both."

In any case, soon after Mayor Fitzgerald took office, reform was in the saddle. At the 1906 Republican convention, Walter Webster, a lawyer, proposed an official commission to investigate all phases of Boston's municipal affairs, and Mayor Fitzgerald endorsed the idea in his opening address of 1907. In November 1906, he had asked for a Finance Commission to investigate graft in the office of the Sealer of Weights and Measures.

"What is required," he said in January 1907, "is a business examination of the subject by a body of such representative, able, and impartial citizens of Boston that our taxpayers will have full confidence in the soundness of any conclusions which they may reach. . . . I fully realize that in order to accomplish the objects of the proposed inquiry by a Finance Commission constituted by the City Government must not only be, in fact, wholly free from partisan bias, but must be known to be so constituted that it cannot be affected by any personal or political influences. . . . My whole object is to make the proposed inquiry as searching and thorough as possible, and the constitution of the proposed commission should be enough to convince any fair-minded man that the mayor would be wholly unable to control the action of such a body, even if he were disposed to do so."

He appointed the Finance Commission in July, 1907, and a special Act of the Legislature empowered it to summon witnesses, compel the production of books and papers and take testimony. There was to be one member from five commercial groups, one from the United Improvement Associations, and one from the Central Labor Union. Nathan Matthews, representing the Real Estate Exchange, was elected chairman. John A. Sullivan was chosen by the Associated Board of Trade; John F. Moors represented the Merchants' Association, Randall Morris, the Boston Chamber of Commerce, George U. Crocker, the Clearing House Committee. George A. O. Ernst was selected by the United Improvement Associations, John F. Kennedy by the Central Labor Union. Kennedy was the only member friendly to Mayor Fitzgerald. Five of the Finance Commission's seven members were reformers, and four were GGA men.

It was said that Mayor Fitzgerald's initial proposal to form a Finance Commission was an attempt to avoid interference from the State House. Even he could not have conceived what the Commission would dredge up from the hidden sewers of municipal government. During its seventeen months of activity, this first Commission made what experts agreed was the most sensational and thorough investigation of any city government in history. A historian of the day called it "unexcelled in breadth and thoroughness in the field of American municipal finance," and it "proved beyond doubt the existence of inefficiency and corruption," he said.

Two hired civil engineers probed the street and sewer departments, and all criminal evidence was turned over to the district attorney. The Finance Commission turned a white light on shady operations in the Common Council and the Board of Aldermen. In 1875, the city's aldermen had assets of $769,000. In 1902, thirteen aldermen and seventy-five councilors in toto accounted for assets worth only $87,000. These statistics were eloquently damning, for at this time aldermen received an annual salary of $1500, while councilors were paid only $300 (but often claimed up to $2000 each in carriage expenses alone).

The City Council passed orders that conflicted with legal procedure, and their weekly sessions were attended by a "small army of high-salaried clerks, stenographers, messengers, and assistants," each receiving wages higher than state, federal or private business employee counterparts. The Finance Commission branded them "useless employees, generally politicians, maintained to aid the City Council in the non-discharge of its duties."

The Commission reported that the trend toward extravagance and corruption had been evident since 1895—the last year of Chairman Matthews' own term of office. It called for experts to enter municipal service in place of politicians, while recommending salary cuts—no inducement for superior personnel. Since 1895, the Commission reported, a trend toward "leaf raking" had added to general inefficiency. Each worker turned in only half of the man-day delivered in Matthews' administration. Masons working for the Metropolitan Water and Sewerage Board, under the Metropolitan District Commission, laid an average of 224 bricks an hour, while those working for the City Sewer Department, laid fifty. It cost up to three times as much to lay pipe in Boston as it did in other cities of Massachusetts, and its pavements, not counting materials, cost two and a half times as much as the sidewalks of New York. In five of the city's departments, which had mushroomed to fifty, the city lost an estimated $2,000,000 to avaricious contractors.

Said the Finance Commission: "The position of the head of a department under the present form of government, subject to intimidation from one man who has the power to remove him, from thirteen men who may refuse to confirm his reappointment, and from seventy-five others who have the power officially and publicly to abuse him, without opportunity for reply, is intolerable."

Arthur Dehon Hill of the Back Bay had succeeded John B. Moran as the District Attorney of Suffolk County. Moran, an enemy of Fitzgerald, had glossed over the case of the GGA during the "Fenway Scandal," for he was a friend of Mayor Collins. When Hill succeeded him, an observer said: "The grafter is not afraid of the Finance Commission. What makes him shiver is the little man in the big courthouse on Beacon Hill."

Moran had presented some of the Finance Commission's evidence to the Grand Jury, where it died. Democratic politicians of Boston had learned how to gain control of the Grand Jury and "nol-pros" charges brought in by a hostile attorney general. Dehon was more persistent.

One of his victims was Aldermen Frank Linehan, who gained stature among his colleagues by landing a punch on a fellow Alderman, James Michael Curley, and by actually punching Mayor Fitzgerald in the nose.

Linehan had swung contracts—actually his own—to William J. Hallion, who lived at his address. Linehan was seen in shirtsleeves directing one of "Contractor" Hallion's projects, and even his business correspondence was in Linehan's handwriting. The Finance Commission sent the evidence to Hill, and Linehan went to jail for buying stolen lumber that was used in the construction of a prison wall at Deer Island, where he was confined. After a story circulated that he sat on it, it became known as "Linehan's Wall."

Linehan, who accused his fellow aldermen of wholesale graft, was a small fish compared to the big ones that escaped the net.

George H. Battis, a former Republican Alderman, got three years after being convicted for stealing $300, which he drew for prizes for July Fourth athletic winners. Leo F. McCullough of the Common Council was sentenced to two years for filching $200. While president of the Council, he drew the money to buy a set of official books, then put it in his pocket.

Attorney Hill gave jury-fixers short shrifts, assigning two detectives to watch each juror. He watched the detectives.

His most sensational exposure came when Michael J. Mitchell, purchasing agent for the city, took the stand. Mitchell was a pleasant puppet who knew little about his job. He and Thomas F. Maher, a contractor, were indicted on a charge of stealing $13,000 from the city in a flagstone contract. Maher furnished the stone. Found guilty of conspiracy to rob the city, they went to prison for a year.

Mayor Fitzgerald was the star witness, and Hill blasted his testimony, "There is just one thing I want to say about that testimony, and that is, that it was not honest testimony, and that Mr. Fitzgerald when he came here did not come here with the purpose of telling the truth to the jury, and that his object was to throw the government's case, because he probably thinks we rely on him." He said later: "I don't know whether we have got all the conspirators or not, but I know we have proved a conspiracy. I promise you that if it ever comes out that any other man or men are in this thing, whether their names are Pat or John or Henry, or whatever their names are, I will put them where these two defendants are."

The judge in the case was told by the jury that a man not "charged" was deeper in the theft allegation than Mitchell, and the question was asked: "Whom did he mean?"

Fitzgerald's enemies pointed to him.

"The judge did not refer to me," he said. "Of that you can make sure. I am no crook." He added: "If Hill really meant what he said, he will present his evidence before the grand jury and ask for an indictment for perjury. I dare him to do it."

That was the end of the matter.

Although the Finance Commission harassed the Mayor, it did prove a useful device for getting rid of unwanted job-seekers. If a worker on the patronage list had a criminal record, he might get the usual warm greeting when he collared His Honor.

"What can I do for you, Joe? You want a job in the Public Works Department? Why, of course."

Later, after referring the man's record to the Finance Commission, he could "get off the hook" by saying: "Sorry, Joe, but they have something on you, and they would make an awful ruckus if I gave you the job."

During the last month of the Fitzgerald administration, the startling revelations of the Finance Commission were widely publicized, especially in reference to certain improper municipal contracts and to the "present alarming indebtedness of the city."

The Commission reported: "The politicians who had charge of the city finances in these two years did not invent all the schemes of misgovernment, but they took advantage of, improved upon, and added to those which they found in operation." The Commission, in attacking the concentration in the hands of the Mayor, added: "For the first time a man was elected to the office of mayor whose aim was not merely to use or perfect the political machine then in existence, but to become the machine itself."

The general extravagance and corruption resulting from the spoils system was thoroughly aired. "In the belief that they could not contract directly with the city, the practice has arisen of making contracts and selling goods under assumed names, or as silent partners with contractors or material men." Frank Linehan's case was a minor example.

Mayor Fitzgerald had inherited many problems, and was victimized by connivers slicker than any of their predecessors. He wove his own tangled web, however, when he created jobs under pressure. The Finance Commission found the executive business of the city "divided among too many departments, created in many instances for the purpose of furnishing high-salaried offices which could be filled without recourse to the civil service lists."

Even the cleverest mayors, like Fitzgerald and Curley, were frequently duped by their palace guard, who cut some incredible touches. Typical of such shenanigans was one incident that took place when Curley was Mayor. A ward boss wanted to furnish his clubhouse, and lacking the wherewithal, sent two squads of precinct workers out on separate errands. One overalled group went to the City Hospital, and, letting it be known that they were about to lay linoleum, moved the furniture out of the way. Just to be sure it wouldn't be in the way, they loaded it on a truck and deposited it in their clubhouse. The other work detail went to City Hall, which is a calm place on a Saturday afternoon. After assuring the custodian that new furniture had been ordered by the Superintendent of Public Buildings, the precinct workers drove off with several chairs, a horsehair divan, long conference table, desk and swivel chair, along with a few rugs for the barren rooms at the clubhouse.

The custodian helped them load the furniture on the truck. On the following Monday, the custodian asked the building superintendent when the new furniture was expected. Learning what happened, the superintendent angrily protested to the ward boss.

"So you're going to call in the police," the ward boss said. "Listen, you boob, it will make you the town's Number One laughingstock when the newspapers let out that you allowed part of City Hall to be stolen from right under your nose. It should be a lot easier to steal the gold off the dome of the State House than to steal City Hall." By this time, the building superintendent was nodding his agreement.

"Yeah. It would kind of put me on the spot, at that." He rubbed his chin. "Look, don't say anything to the Council about this. You know what a stink those guys can make."

"Okay, pal, but just one thing. Three of my boys need jobs. They have four or five kiddos. Think you can take care of them?"

"Sure, sure, send them right over."

A chairman of the Boston School Committee withheld an order to raze English High School until a new cafeteria was installed. Then he arranged for a parochial school to acquire the cafeteria at a negligible fee (the latter school was unaware of the withholding order). The chairman also sold excess city-owned chairs to certain institutions for twenty-five cents each.

The ward boss who acquired the City Hall furniture, like other bosses, depended on the old formula of the Christmas basket and ton of coal, but when the need was pressing, he occasionally had to improvise. The day he was elected senator, he was in the State House when two derelicts accosted him in a corridor and asked for a hand-out.

"I ain't eaten for two days," one said.

"I know. You two have been too busy drinking." The boss had a nickel and a $20 bill in his pocket—too little and too much to give them. He glanced speculatively at a heavy brass spittoon that belonged to the Commonwealth, and turned his back. The derelicts got the idea. On the following day, five more loafers from his district were ejected after being found loitering around the State House corridors. The boss had tipped off the police.

"I had to put a stop to the spittoon racket," he said. "After all, there is such a thing as moderation."

There is abundant evidence that Mayor Fitzgerald was sold by his palace guard, and the result, as the Finance Commission reported, was "a steady deterioration in the technical competency and moral strength of the heads of the executive departments, until at the time when the investigation was ordered, the administrative business of this great city was, so far at least as the salaried heads of departments went, with few notable exceptions, in the hands either of men without education, training, experience, or technical qualifications of any sort, or of men who had become so demoralized by the conditions which surrounded them as to be unwilling to protest against the most obvious extravagance and graft, if favored by the Mayor."

The citizens of Boston look to the Mayor for leadership, just as those of the state look to the Governor. The authority given both, however, is negligible compared with their responsibilities, and over the years, this even has never been corrected in Massachusetts. As late as 1961, Governor Richard Volpe said: "I have, for example, practically no control over department heads who are spending most of our money."

Even as he spoke, Representative Francis W. Perry, who had already exposed corrupt assessment practices and crooked parking deals, was getting headlines all over the state when he revealed the extent of "sweetheart deals" in the Division of Waterways. A Governor of Massachusetts lacks the authority to correct such abuses without the cooperation of other agencies.

In September, 1961, a political writer of the *Boston Herald* wrote: "Patronage which always has been a major headache for chief executives on Beacon Hill, is rapidly becoming one of the biggest problems of the

Volpe administration. The Governor, who is running a tight fiscal operation in the various state departments, is now being plagued by disgruntled
elements within the GOP and Italo-American circles. These supporters
of Volpe are interested in seeing the promises made to them by the Governor's associates materialize."

The "disgruntled elements" are the exact counterparts of the wolf pack
who turned on Mayor Collins when he denied them tax-hiking patronage.

In pushing for prosecution of the glaring scandals in his administration,
Governor Volpe was hamstrung by recalcitrant politicians, as well as by
outmoded regulations, and what *The New York Times* said in this connection is certainly applicable to the situation when Fitzgerald was
Mayor: "The 'in' group in politics here is still playing nineteenth-century
politics. The problem is how to divide the spoils, not how to manage
society. That matter didn't matter much in the old days, when the important decisions were made by private business. But as the public sector
grows in importance, corruption really begins to hurt."

Problems at City Hall are often more acute than those at the State
House. "The mayor of a great American city has more serious responsi-
bilities than the governor of any state or any individual senator," Mayor
Fitzgerald wrote in *The New England Magazine* in 1906.

As the following year waned, another city election was scheduled, and
although Mayor Fitzgerald was unopposed for the Democratic nomination, he could see clouds lowering.

CHAPTER 8

Napoleon Returns from Elba

> March, march on down the field,
> Fighting for FITZY;
> Break through Jim Storrow's line,
> His votes we do defy,
> Then we'll give a long cheer for FITZY'S men,
> We're out to win again;
> Storrow's men may fight to the end,
> But FITZ will win!
>
> —*Fitzgerald campaign song*

EARLY in 1907, the several John F. Fitzgeralds who hinted that they might run for Mayor included a junk dealer, an expressman, a stone cutter, a newsdealer, and a roofer who thought his honored namesake had "lost his grip."

"Vote for the original John F.," warned the Fitzgerald camp. "Beware of substitutes." It was possible to tell the authentic Fitzgerald by the slogan on his posters and in his ads: BIGGER, BETTER, BUSIER.

Anti-Fitzgerald Democrats, after the other Fitzgeralds had withdrawn their candidacy, put Representative John Coulthurst into the contest. Backed by Hearst's *Boston American,* Coulthurst was labeled "socialistic" by the *Boston Evening Transcript,* which could count as many readers among Proper Bostonians, certainly, as William Shakespeare.

Thomas J. Kenny of the Public School Association faded after failing to get the support of the Good Government Association, which in 1907 hoped to capture the Republican Party as it had in 1905 by running Police Commissioner Stephen O'Meara, a man of mighty moral muscle. This drew a snide comment from Fitzgerald on Columbus Day in 1907, when he was guest speaker at Carnegie Hall in New York.

"The Republicans," he said, "now recognize the Irish who fought the

117

Puritans. The Republicans want Stephen O'Meara . . . to run against me."

Back in Boston, Fitzgerald met George Albee Hibbard, whose candidacy had been mentioned. Hibbard said he had no plans for running. "I decline to be your undertaker," he added.

"Well," Fitzgerald answered, "I prefer to have a respectable undertaker."

Despite the GGA endorsement, the Republicans spurned O'Meara who, in any case, refused to run. The Republican City Committee finally chose Hibbard as their favorite son. Hibbard was Boston's postmaster and former head of the local Republican machine. The reformers, even though Hibbard was groomed as a reform candidate who would make City Hall a paradise of good government, refused to back a professional politician. The reformers were thus left without an official candidate in what might for them have been a moment of triumph. They also refused to endorse Coulthurst because of his "inexperience." Hibbard denounced Coulthurst's tie-up with Hearst, and Fitzgerald charged that he had voted against the "Overtime Bill" which would have prevented women and children from working before six in the morning or after six at night. This bill had already put the skids under other politicians.

"LODGE TO LEAD FIGHT AGAINST FITZGERALD," said a newspaper headline. Fitzgerald countered by exploiting "the Senator-Sage of Nahant's" stand on immigration. Foreign language circulars played up the issue for Jewish and Italian voters, and nothing was considered too remote from local affairs to be exploited. Down in Brownsville, Texas, shots had been exchanged between whites and Negro troops, and Lodge blamed the Negroes. Fitzgerald circulated his counter opinion among the city's colored voters. (Irish politicians over the years had used various strategems to woo the Negro vote. They had their pictures taken with colored celebrities, and one politician promised, if elected, to put up a statue of John Brown of Pottawatomie on Boston Common.)

Conservative Hibbard promised to serve only one term and to "clean up the mess," but most of the campaign was defensive and drab. Jewish leaders denounced Fitzgerald's Yiddish circulars, and Catholic leaders blasted him. John F. Kennedy of the Finance Commission was alone in his support of him. Martin Lomasney also lined up with Fitzgerald, whereupon the *Boston Post* ran a cartoon captioned "The Latest Affinity." The cut-line: "If you love me as I love you, nothing can cut our love in two." Boston politics!

Fitzgerald, again lacking machine support, was jeered at a rally in South Boston.

"Give us a song," the crowd yelled. "We'd rather hear you sing."

And that was in the pre-"Sweet Adeline" days.

When the smoke lifted, Coulthurst was seen with over fifteen thousand votes, enough to give Hibbard a plurality of more than two thousand. Fitzgerald was a frustrated second. Hibbard was elected "by the grace of God and the blunders of Fitzgerald," a reporter said. His racial innuendoes had backfired. Headlines told a sad story for the incumbent.

MAYOR'S MACHINE IS TORN TO SHREDS

and

DEMOCRATIC PARTY IN STATE DISRUPTED

After six years of Democratic rule, the Republicans were back in the saddle in a Democratic stronghold.

Although it was the worst defeat Fitzgerald had taken, he was as resilient as ever. On election night, when he knew he was beaten, a friend asked: "What of the future?"

"We held a conference a little while ago," he said, "and began our planning for the next election."

A few days later he met Hibbard. "Good luck to you, George," he smiled.

Hibbard, whose parrot-like nose was cruelly exploited by cartoonists, was a parsimonious Yankee who wanted his administration to be economical and efficient rather than popular. He succeeded notably, cutting down municipal expenses in departments under his control, and firing almost a thousand city workers. The Finance Commission nevertheless complained that some political appointments were still being made and that the labor force of 13,000 was cut by only seventy-four. In general, however, the Finance Commission commended his "businesslike administration," noting that he had effected a saving of about a million dollars in departmental efficiency, accompanied by an actual increase in service. Street maintenance costs were halved, and the city debt was sharply reduced.

Meanwhile, Fitzgerald, as chipper as ever, was shuffling the cards. Early in February of 1908, he wowed the members at the annual reunion of the John F. Fitzgerald Club, then left for his usual winter vacation in Palm Beach, where he was unofficial mayor in charge of all festivities-when-more-than-ten-persons-gathered.

HONEY FITZ

"Let them probe me as deeply as they want to," he said when the Finance Commission continued to badger him. "I welcome it." If Mayor Fitzgerald had been personally dishonest, the Finance Commission was unable to prove it.

The only member of the Strategy Board at the dock to see him off when he sailed for Europe on the *Cymric* in July was Pat Kennedy. Once on the high seas, he cabled the *Boston Post:* "Rakish craft has been following us since we left Boston Light. I suspect Finance Commission is on board. Am organizing passengers and crew to repel invaders. When I reach Ireland I will declare myself and secure the protection of the Irish parliamentary department."

From Ireland he wrote impressions for the *Boston Post* to give his constituents something to remember him by, and after a leisurely tour of Europe, he returned in September, leaving daughters Rose and Agnes in a European convent.

He gave more time to *The Republic,* which was still flourishing. He hoped to vindicate himself by returning to City Hall, and when the press noted that Young Napoleon was on his way back from Elba, he kept alive the metaphor. "My flag is nailed to the mast," he said in July, 1909. "I am like the old guard of Napoleon, who said, 'We die, but never surrender.' " He taunted other Democratic leaders: "I don't need the machine. I beat the machine in twenty-two out of twenty-five wards in my first fight. Anyone is welcome to the machine."

The Committee of One Hundred started something in 1907 when it persuaded Mayor Fitzgerald to name a Finance Commission. This led to the 1909 charter change by which nonpartisanship was introduced.

Before 1909, Boston had a weak mayoral, bicameral council government. A thirteen-member board of aldermen was elected at large under a system in which each voter might vote for seven of the positions. A common council was elected by wards—three members from each of twenty-five wards. Party designations appeared on the ballot. Before nonpartisanship was introduced, the voting strength of the Democrats was about twice that of the Republicans. The reformers wanted to join the Republican minority to the "better class" of Democrats who were voting Democratic on the local level because of state or national issues. Here are the basic changes made in the charter reform of 1909:

1. The Mayor was strengthened by eliminating the council's power to override his veto. His term was extended to four years.

2. A nine-member council was elected at large, three members each

year for three-year terms. This council replaced the board of aldermen and common council.

3. A permanent Finance Commission was created to serve as a "watchdog."

4. Provision was made for administration of departments by trained personnel appointed by the Mayor, but subject to approval of the state Civil Service Commission.

5. All nominations for municipal election were to be made by petition of not fewer than 5000 voters, without party label on the ballot.

The Democratic machine opposed these reforms. The requirement of Civil Service Commission approval would interfere with patronage, and at-large council elections would disrupt ward organizations. Democrats complained that the charter reform proposal was a Republican ruse to get a share in city government, and the Republicans agreed for the most part. In any case, Boston's voters adopted what was called the Plan Two Charter by a vote of 39,000 to 35,000, agreeing with experts who pointed out that the board of aldermen and common councilors had for seventy-seven years given an impressive demonstration of bicameral inefficiency and boondoggling, when they were not outrageously larcenous.

Fitzgerald, knowing he would have little chance of winning the regular Democratic nomination because of his defeat in 1907 by an obscure postmaster, welcomed Plan Two, for it gave him a chance to win the nomination by petition. It was the easiest way to bypass the Democratic City Committee.

His supporters, who had been collecting signatures weeks before the adoption of Plan Two, produced 20,000 names.

The Democratic machine, with no strong candidate, fretted. The reformers were again turned down by Police Commissioner O'Meara. One willing candidate nobody would heed was Miss Lillis D. Warden. "Boston needs a municipal housecleaning," she said, "and it may do the voters of this city good to get the ideas of a woman who has made a study of the subject. I don't see anything under Plan Two that prevents a woman from becoming a candidate."

Then came news which delighted reformers. James Jackson Storrow agreed to run. A few days earlier in his drawing room on the Merchants' Limited, he had asked Ernest J. Goulston, a close friend of Republican boss, Charles H. Innes, what his chances were.

"Well, for one thing," Goulston said, "you've got to overcome being a rich man."

"Do you think the religious issue will crop out?"

"Even though you are a man of unimpeachable integrity that's one thing that could hurt you," Goulston said.

"Another thing, E. J.—I don't want to spend so much money that I'd be accused of buying the election. I'd rather be defeated."

The Storrows were indeed unimpeachable. For three generations they had been Beacon Street Proper Bostonians, and the candidate could trace his line to pre-Revolutionary days. A tall, patrician and handsome banker, listed in the Twenties as the richest citizen of Boston, he had captained a Harvard crew which beat Yale, served as chairman of the Boston School Committee and was a former president of the Boy Scouts of America, a movement he had helped found. Although the outstanding banker of New England, he had a warm-hearted interest in such local needs as more playground space for tenement districts in the North and West Ends.

He founded the West End Club for newsboys, which lured even a few of Martin Lomasney's faithful sheep into his command. Later he gave Boston a quarter of a million dollars to turn the Charles River mudflats into a beautiful Esplanade, and his wife donated a boulevard years later that was named the Storrow Drive. A gentleman of the highest type, he had been friendly with Mayor Fitzgerald, and had occasionally stood by his side in the receiving line on reception days. A Yankee Democrat, he was proud of Boston's traditions, and felt it his duty to devote part of a busy life and his remarkable talents to city affairs. As Fitzgerald said of him later: "There were few men in the entire country who gave so much to maintain institutions of America as did Mr. Storrow."

He could count on Democratic votes in every ward of the city. To win, he estimated that he needed seventy-five per cent of the Republican vote, sixty per cent of the Independent, and twenty-five per cent of the Democratic. Bourbon Republicans would reject him because he voted on the Democratic ticket nationally.

At this time the Republicans had 26,000 votes in Boston, to 66,000 for the Democrats. While lacking votes, the Republican Party had wealth and influence. "In city elections," an observer noted, "it has money to spend. At such times, useful heelers and members of gangs belonging to the majority party often depart for a few weeks from their regular allegiance."

Two leading Democrats who departed from their regular allegiance for a handful of silver were Smiling Jim Donovan and Handsome Jack Keliher, and they were promptly dubbed the "Gold Dust Twins." According to Goulston, they each received $5000 in cash and would of course hold important posts in a Storrow administration, for both were talented and experienced.

The Gold Dust Twins convinced Storrow that successful elections cost money, and early in the campaign it became evident that Storrow would spend all the money his advisers considered necessary to win the election. It turned out to be the most extravagant campaign ever conducted in Boston, with estimates of each side's spending running to a quarter of a million for the Fitzgerald camp, and to twice that amount for Storrow.

There were constant rumors during the early part of the campaign of bribery. Big Bill Kelliher, a gambler with a jail record, was seen around town offering to bet any amount on Storrow in an effort to sway public opinion. Democrats said rolls of money were no small part of the great reform campaign.

With bulging wallets, the Gold Dust Twins collared every ward leader in the city. They came a cropper in four wards: Pat Kennedy's, Martin Lomasney's, James Curley's, and of course Fitzgerald's old Ward Six, where some of his more enthusiastic supporters still rated him with Paul Revere, if not with Cotton Mather.

"I am as certain now, as I was then," said William McMasters, who handled the Fitzgerald publicity in this campaign, "that Kennedy, Lomasney, or Curley could have named any price for their open support."

Reports had Curley being offered sums from $25,000 to $100,000. The correct amount, he told friends, was $60,000, and he added: "He was very persuasive in urging me to swing my support to him, but I stuck with Honey Fitz." He told one friend the amount offered was "the wealth of Croesus to me, but I can't sell out my people in this city. I don't intend to be a party to an exodus of city employees and let the Brahmins take over."

The word was passed around by Fitzgerald followers: "Take Storrow's money, but vote for Fitzgerald."

Pat Kennedy's personal preference as a candidate against Storrow had been Curley. More than the other members of the Strategy Board, Pat was impressed by the brash young political pitchman from Roxbury's Ward 17. Curley, the youngest candidate ever elected to the Board of Aldermen, had often been a nuisance as far as his colleagues were concerned, but by the end of his first term, they admitted the fiery, bumptious Alderman was dowered with logic and eloquence, and he was fearless and durable. Democratic leaders who had tried to defeat him at the polls could not counter the man's magnetic personality, which made him a natural vote-getter.

From Fitzgerald he had inherited an impish skill in gaining personal advantage by creating dissension, setting one ward leader against another. Even more than Fitzgerald, this son of a "mucker" was a transitional figure, a clear example of the common phenomenon of one class replacing another. He was by nature a "loner," although in the Storrow campaign he, Fitzgerald and Lomasney—as the leading proponents of Plan Two— marched shoulder to shoulder. Cartoonists pictured them as "The Three Musketeers."

Earlier in 1909, a mayoral boom had started for Curley, and although he laughed it off, he would certainly have accepted the nomination but for John F., whom at the time he idolized as a master politician.

"It's good advertising," he said, "but I have my eyes on the senatorial nomination. To tell the truth, I'm getting tired of the Board of Aldermen, and if Jim Doyle drops out this fall, you may see me giving the Senate a good time with my two-hour speeches." Then, in reference to Jim Dono- van and Doyle, he added: "I'm not looking for a fight, but I never run away from a fuss, and if they want a rough-house thing I'll go to it just as fast as any of them." Donovan and Doyle had been ganging up on him, realizing his potential.

Curley had developed a picturesque vocabulary that would soon chill Fitzgerald. One opponent was "King of the Crapshooters," and Donovan was "the smiling Jinker, the King Dodo of Ward 9. He has put his puppet, Jim Doyle, the Prince Popo of Ward 22 into the fight against our candi- date. But we are not afraid of Donovan's money, or Donovan's two hun- dred fifty suits or two hundred fifty pairs of shoes, or two hundred pairs of checked pants."

Throw mud and some will stick, was the Curley technique. "Of course, Jim Donovan didn't have the outfit I accused him of having," he said in an aside. "I remember one night telling a crowd about his valet. I said I had met him one day and asked how he was. He was all done in, he answered, and I asked why. His right arm was all gone, he said. 'You see, Mr. Donovan has two hundred fifty suits, and he has to have them all pressed every week. One man can't do that alone—and shine two hundred fifty pairs of shoes, too. So I've just been telling Mr. Donovan— either he gets an extra valet to spell me or I quit my job.' I told that to the crowd at a rally, adding: 'Do you know where Jim Donovan is now? Even though today is Friday, and he poses as a good Roman Catholic, he is down at Hotel Woodstock, and he is eating a big, succulent five-dollar steak with mushrooms.' I waited for this to sink in, then added: 'And he's got a bottle of Burgundy at his elbow. What do you think of that? Did you ever eat a big, succulent, five-dollar steak on Friday and wash it down with a bottle of Burgundy?' "

Pat Kennedy knew Curley was a rough-and-tumble fighter who swung hard in a pinch, and that he was superbly fitted for the "vaudeville" role that swayed voters at political rallies. He was a winner whom nobody could talk down. In the interests of harmony, however, Kennedy went along with Fitzgerald and Corbett, agreeing that Fitzgerald should run for mayor and Curley for congressman. All three for the moment at odds with Jim Donovan, still the Democratic king of Boston. It would not be long, however, before Fitzgerald and Curley would have him standing in a hammock.

Donovan earned $7500 as Superintendent of Streets, but made much more than that on graft, Curley charged, accusing him of accepting $50-a-week from the New England Sanitary Disposal Company, which had a contract with the city.

Donovan angrily denied the charge, but Curley knew his heated denials did not keep his power from waning. He was getting back at Donovan who, with Doyle, as early as 1908 had marked Curley for slaughter. "I accept the decree of these wolves who bite the hand that caressed them," Curley said, "and beg to announce that though they have killed others, they will not kill me." Curley, who in upswing days had referred to the bard of Stratford-on-Avon as "John Shakespeare" without any of his Tammany supporters having noticed his error, by the time of the Storrow contest, he had a choice Shakespearean repertory selected with the idea of demolishing a foe by ridicule.

"I found Shakespeare a great help," he said. "When I got into an argument, I generally could get something out of Shakespeare which I could put on an opponent to his disadvantage. He has helped me out of many a tight place."

He had a perfect line for Smiling Jim Donovan: "A man may smile and smile and be a villain."

As for Fitzgerald, Curley might have quoted that Shakespearean villain, Iago, who said of himself: "Oh, sir, content you, I follow him to serve my turn upon him." Curley and Honey Fitz had several Shakespearean duels later.

Without Curley support, Fitzgerald knew he would have little chance against Storrow, and again, even if he had to surrender choice patronage plums, Curley's support was worth it. He also needed the backing of Martin Lomasney who, in another shifting of the balance of power, obliged.

Hibbard, meanwhile, had complicated the situation by insisting on running, and an effort was made to push him out of the race. "I have received requests to put Mr. Hubbard out of the campaign," said Henry Cabot Lodge, "but I do not propose to meddle in the Boston city campaign in any way. I do not think I have any right to do so and I think I should do more harm than good if I tried to interfere."

It soon became apparent that the fine Italian hand of John F. could be seen in the maneuver. He and Lomasney put Hibbard in as a decoy candidate to cut into Storrow's Republican backing. But Hibbard, who was suffering from progressive tuberculosis of the throat, was a negligible factor. He was unable even to address rallies as the weeks passed.

Storrow, in a letter to A. Lawrence Lowell, then a professor of Government at Harvard, said Fitzgerald was "seriously discredited not only among those who believe in good government, but among those who believe in the spoils system, as they know that no promise he makes to them can be trusted; moreover, he has against him an aggressive section of his party which has actually obtained control of the city organization."

The *Boston Post* asked about Storrow's platform. "I don't want to pose as a reformer," Storrow said, "nor do I want to run as a 'businessman's candidate.' I am an ordinary citizen. I have made many mistakes in the course of my life. If I should be elected Mayor, I shall make some more. I only want it understood that I would try to treat everyone fairly, work hard, and do my level best."

He alienated some Republican reformers when he said, on accepting the nomination: "My efforts will be directed to a conservation of the city's resources for the purpose of putting them to the best possible use— not for the benefit of a few, but for the advancement of the city and the welfare of all its citizens." Republican malcontents were not interested in advancing the welfare of all citizens.

Former Mayor Josiah Quincy joined the Fitzgerald camp and assisted Joseph Corbett with campaign strategy, working out of Corbett's downtown law office. One move was to put City Controller Nathaniel H. Taylor into the race, along with Hibbard. Taylor, a Democrat and a clever journalist, had been Mayor Matthews' secretary, and was expected to take votes way from Storrow. The over-all strategy became clear as the battle was joined. Fitzgerald and Hibbard were "Johnny" and "George" to each other, and were friendly throughout the campaign. A member of the Finance Commission divulged that "Fitzgerald offered Hibbard the City Collector's job after the election." From then on, Hibbard was branded a Fitzgerald puppet, a theme expressed in cartoons with the caption, "Let George Do It."

All of Boston's newspapers except the *Boston American,* opposed John F. When his strategists, in their advertising copy, spelled his leading opponent's name "$torrow" to stress the difference in financial standing between them, one paper refused to run the ad until the dollar-bill sign was removed. Fitzgerald turned this refusal to good advantage, proclaiming that in its discrimination a Boston newspaper refused his advertising.

The Fitzgerald camp also blasted the tremendous newspaper and billboard advertising campaign for Storrow. Never had there been such a lavish display—another symptom of entrenched wealth, the cry rose. And the volume of advertising was indeed novel in days when many politicians used window-sheets, lantern slides and room-sized box kites trailing their names in huge lettering.

"My boyhood companions were barefooted and many of them sold newspapers in the streets," Fitzgerald told a rally at Faneuil Hall. "My opponent is so far out of touch with the common peole, he can't appreciate what the common people want." One of his first moves had been to suggest limiting each candidate's expenses to $10,000. Storrow, less known, and an inferior speaker, wisely rejected this pitch. Thenceforth it became "the rich man's candidate" versus the "poor man's friend."

Storrow could not match this demagoguery. In a room with a dozen friends, he was fluent and articulate, but he froze in the presence of a hostile or semi-hostile audience, and when he seemed to die on his feet, audiences thought he was a dull-wit. "I lose my confidence," he told a friend. "I can't spout the way Fitz does."

Audiences shrieked with glee when Fitzgerald told them how "Jack and Jim, the Gold Dust Twins," had sold out to Storrow. Asked what he was "getting" for favoring the multimillionaire, Jack Keliher said, "John F. Fitzgerald's goat." Fitzgerald shot back that Storrow had a $10,000 contract with every Boston newspaper, whereupon Editor Fahey of the *Boston Traveler* circulated an open letter in denial, adding that one of Fitzgerald's lieutenants, on the contrary, had tried to "fix" him.

Posing always as a friend of the poor, Fitzgerald said landlords were making it hard for him to hold rallies, since the Storrow forces were offering higher rentals. A later charge would be that his opponent's rich supporters had monopolized all the city's cars and other conveyances for their own use on election day.

The pervasive theme was summarized in a campaign poster showing a photograph of the Fitzgerald family captioned "MANHOOD AGAINST MONEY." Sensing a close contest as the weeks passed, Honey Fitz intensified his attack. "This is a fight of aristocracy against principle," he shouted. "The whole country is waiting to see whether J. P. Morgan can buy the Mayor's chair of Boston." His temporary friend, Congressman Joseph O'Connell, backed him up: "Never in the history of American politics has a candidate displayed so ostentatiously and offensively his intention to overwhelm his opponent by the brute force of the dollar."

Isaac Allen, a Negro ex-Republican, included the entire reform group in his denunciation: "They own many of the tenement houses that are reeking in filth, and they sit in their clubs eating canvasback ducks and drinking their wine and fattening their pocketbooks by the evils they do to the poor." And all the while, the Fitzgerald cannonading continued, holding up to ridicule the greedy venal partisans who sold their birthright for a mess of coin. "This," they proclaimed, "is not an election, but an auction." It was the struggle of a child of adversity and poverty against a scion of wealth. Fitzgerald got mileage out of every slip Storrow made. When the latter ignored his outstretched hand at a dinner in honor of the candidates at The American House, Fitzgerald shook his head sadly when he rose to speak.

"I was born of poor but honest parents," he said, "but I was always instinctively a gentleman."

In an era of trust-busting, Fitzgerald tried to identify the Boston philanthropist with the incorporated villains. Storrow had resigned from several directorships to devote full time to the contest, whereupon Fitzgerald accused him of being only a jump or two ahead of a lawsuit. He blamed the banker personally for the decline in Boston's industrial prosperity. "The Vanderbilts looked out for New York . . . the Goulds looked out for New York . . . Rockefeller looked out for New York . . . but James Storrow? He looks out for himself." This was the gist of his remarks in this area of attack.

Storrow, unused to the ruses of professional politicians, went for the bait, tricked into a logical but fruitless defense of old business transactions, a defense of all the corporations of which he had been director or for which he had worked. The *Boston Herald* headlined his rebuttal when United Fruit came under attack: "BANANAS CHEAPER, STORROW REPLIES."

What a theme of merriment for the next Fitzgeraldian barrage! Instead of pounding away at some issue of greater moment, Storrow became picayune on occasion. In one speech he charged the Fitzgerald administration of "dog-snatching" 6000 animals and selling them at a dollar each! And when charged with having soft hands, he awkwardly said: "I think I could wheel a wheelbarrow as far as he could, and I don't think I would be a bit ashamed of it, either." Actually, Storrow was a rugged person whose favorite hobby was chopping wood on his Lincoln, Massachusetts, estate.

Even editorialists of the *Boston Evening Transcript* were occasionally caught in Fitzgerald's tripwires. Neither Fitzgerald nor his associates, said one editorial, "would be selected by a private business house to take charge of its affairs." This reminded the electorate that Storrow was a businessman, not a politician, and had not President William Howard Taft said: "Nothing is more deceitful than the statements that what we need in politics is the businessman. Politics are a business—at least they are a field in which experience tells for usefulness and effectiveness— and a man who has devoted his entire life to the successful establishment of a business is generally not the man who will be useful to the public in the administration of public business."

Transcript editorial writers also gave the Little General a chance for more demagoguery when they noted that Storrow, far from being ill-at-ease among South Boston voters, "tactfully talked of athletics and other subjects of man-to-man interest," when his political views appeared unpopular. There it was again—the plebeian versus the patrician.

"I will cheerfully allow Mayor Hibbard and Mr. Storrow to divide between them the bulk of the Ward 11 vote," Fitzgerald said, referring to a fashionable ward he knew was against him. "They are entitled to it and ought to have it. But as an old resident of a community of wage-earners in the North End—Ward Six, I . . ." The words that followed depended on the nature and mood of his audience. If Samuel Adams was America's first rabble-rouser, John F. Fitzgerald was the second. In his lexicon, when an Irishman met a Brahmin, the former looked for a monocle, the latter for a brickbat.

Each candidate made outlandish charges, and their followers directed accusations up to and including murder. "I would like to ask Mr. Storrow, who is an overseer at Harvard College," Fitzgerald said, "if Harvard's continual refusal to pay taxes is in accord with the strictest code of ethics." If there was anything wrong with Harvard, it was Storrow's fault, he implied.

Martin Lomasney, picking up the theme, issued a pamphlet which stated that:

The Governor lives in Ward 11.
The Lieutenant Governor lives in Ward 11.
The Judge of the United States Court lives in Ward 11.
The Collector of the Port lives in Ward 11.
Four of the five members of the Transit Commission live in Ward 11.
Three of the five members of the School Committee live in Ward 11.
AND NOW WARD 11 WANTS TO GRAB THE OFFICE OF MAYOR!

Storrow, not fully comprehending Lomasney's dictum that the average voter was interested primarily in food, clothing and shelter, stiffly assured the populace that he would institute a pension system for municipal employees and would retain, not lower, the existing tax rate of $16 (the same rate as at the beginning and end of Mayor Fitzgerald's term). In all other respects, his program was that of a reformer, businessman, and progressive. He stressed honesty, civil service, "value for the dollar," extension of recreational and public health facilities, but he lacked the campaign largesse of Fitzgerald who guaranteed, among other benisons:

Better electric transit, including tunnels from the Common to South Boston and Dorchester.

Pressure toward the building of a new railroad to the West.

Establishment of a Public Utilities Commission.

Establishment in Boston of a free port like that of Hamburg, Germany.

Home rule.

An organized effort to attract business to the city.

An effort to promote closer commercial ties with Canada.

A city pension system.

More playgrounds and new streets.

And one final clincher: "The adoption of all practicable measures to prevent the larger taxpayer from dodging his just taxes."

While on this gambit, the platform warrior kept reminding audiences of Laurence Minot's land manipulations. "And this is the kind of gentleman of great wealth who was chosen by the reformers to be president of the Good Government Association."

Storrow's official campaign manager was Edmund Billings, who had been the brain of the GGA, and he was also advised by Nathan Matthews of the Finance Commission. They and the two "old pros," Donovan and Keliher, finally persuaded Storrow to rest his case on the revelations of the

Finance Commission. Sin or alleged sin, they knew, made a better issue than virtue. When Mayor Seth Low of New York, a reform candidate, was asked why his bid for reelection had failed, he said: "When I first ran, I attacked vice—and everybody is interested in vice. But when I ran again, I had to defend virtue. And who is interested in virtue?"

Sinister rumors crept into the contest. Never was character assassination more brutally practiced in a Boston campaign. And there were voters who were more interested in what was whispered about a candidate than in what was said about him.

Posters covered the streets and subways, and half-page ads suddenly appeared in newspapers, all with the headline FITZGERALDISM, which was denounced as if it were an advanced stage of leprosy. "The Fitzgerald ring, most corrupt and vicious to reign in City Hall."

The stone-crushing contracts, the coal contracts, the electric contracts, and the convictions of Mitchell and Maher and others were fully publicized. One of the most effective political cartoons ever used in a Boston campaign was paid for by Storrow. It showed Fitzgerald on the witness stand, perspiring as he kept repeating: "I don't remember," when pelted with questions.

Other Storrow advertisements were full of quotations from the Finance Commission report. At first, Fitzgerald almost wept with rage in the presence of newspaper friends because of the grief caused his family when these ads and cartoons picturing him with the word GRAFTER across his forehead. He charged a hostile press with wild exaggerations. He was far less sensitive, however, as the campaign picked up speed and he realized the effects of such accusations in three-quarter-inch type. It made the voters wonder how much the ads cost and how much Storrow was spending on all the subway and billboard splurging that flooded the city.

It was persecution, he charged, and John F. Kennedy of the Finance Commission was at his side some nights to testify that the sole aim of the other members of the Commission was to smear him. Fitzgerald blamed irregularities on subordinates over whom he had little control, asserting that the commission was guilty of foul play. Storrow, in one ill-advised moment, had dredged up damaging testimony of the late District Attorney John B. Moran, whereupon a pro-Fitzgerald ad berated the Finance Commission for dragging accusations from a "bewildered and dying witness."

Storrow's big front-page display advertisements with FITZGERALD-ISM in screaming type also boomeranged. Judge Joseph Corbett, former Mayor Josiah Quincy and William McMasters huddled and agreed that a counter-punch was needed. McMasters wrote out an ad, using exactly the same size type for the heading, and setting the copy in the same style as the Storrow display. After having proofs pulled by the *Boston Post,* McMasters took them to Corbett's office and handed them to Quincy.

"He let out a laugh that was entirely foreign to his conservative nature," McMasters said, recalling the incident in 1961. "Then, without a word, he handed the sheet to Corbett."

Corbett smiled in approval. "I wonder how Jim Storrow will feel when he sees this on the front page tomorrow," he said.

"Not tomorrow, if you will pardon me," McMasters said.

"Why not?" Josiah Quincy asked.

"I want them to run another ad, so everyone will know just what they are driving at. In that way, our advertising will be far more effective than it would be if we came back at them right away. They probably have a series to run every day. The day after tomorrow, we can run our ad right beside theirs. Everyone will be confused when they see both ads."

In Storrow's ads, Fitzgerald had been called everything that political invective could dream up. In the Fitzgerald counterparts, the copy began with an account of "Better Schools." On the second day, it called for "Better Streets." The aim was to induce newspaper readers to link the word FITZGERALDISM only with what was progressive and good in municipal administration. The Storrow FITZGERALDISM ads were withdrawn after running for four days.

Meanwhile, The Little General, encouraged, challenged Storrow to appear on the same platform with him and repeat, face to face, the charges he had made in his advertisements. To make it stick, he told Storrow he could bring along his attorney, if he feared advantage would be taken of him because of his inexperience in public debates. (Despite his legal training, Storrow was an inept speaker who, on occasion was almost tongue-tied.) When Storrow failed to appear, the crowd gave Fitzgerald the kind of tumultuous ovation usually reserved for a champion.

Fitzgerald stumped day and night, even on Sundays, when Storrow rested. Every noon hour and closing working day found him strumming on crowd sympathy, large and small, talking until two in the morning if there was anyone to listen. It wasn't what he said on his 2500-mile tour of Boston during five weeks of campaigning, it was rather the tricks of his delivery. One night in the friendly confines of his very own Tammany Club, James Michael Curley was greeted with the Tammany war-whoop when he likened the North End Demosthenes to Paul Revere, reminding the audience that "the awakening of the city today is like the awakening of 1775." Not since Grover Whalen called Mayor "Red" Hylan of New York "the greatest statesman since Abraham Lincoln," had there been such unrestrained praise of a public official. It was part of the game as it was then played.

Whenever he entered a crowded hall, Fitzgerald had to fight his way to the platform through a howling mob, as excitement hit a concert pitch. It depended on the kind of assembly whether he would act the role of The Little General, the product of the dear old North End, or the Honorable John F. Fitzgerald. In any guise, with his nimble wit and sense of timing, he gave a fine performance, telling audiences just what they wanted to hear. He filled the political life of Boston with brio and gusto, and as a platform warrior he was a picture, his ruddy face turned skyward, his full cheeks puffed out, sandy hair parted down the middle like a B. F. Keith's vaudeville actor, singing "Sweet Adeline" or indicting the malefactors of great wealth of State Street. The sparkle which comes to tipplers after the third or fourth goblet was natural to him.

And he left every auditorium amid pandemonium.

Some nights he drove fifty miles, never worrying about the itinerary. If he addressed an improvement association, which might wait in hostile silence for him to answer charges made against him by the Finance Commission, he would win them over by talking of transit improvements, garbage removal, and at the proper psychological moment, would tenderly refer to "the six at home."

In the tough atmosphere of Roughan's Hall in Charlestown, he would ask: "Do you want money power to control the city? Do you want the money-lenders to debauch the electorate and try to sneak into office by misleading the weak voter by the power of gold? But, no, no, no—a thousand times no. I know I can trust this intelligent audience to stand by the friend of the people—one of your own kind, to repudiate this grasping factor in the present election. Can't I, boys?" While waiting for the roar of approbation to subside he might spot the usual quota of panhandlers in the crowd, and be glad he was not of their kind. Pickpockets frequented crowded rallies, and when the bedlam was most unrestrained, they found it easy to dip for a wallet.

He made his rounds, addressing up to thirty-five rallies a night, while the enemy camp kept daring him to answer their accusations. He ignored them, waiting for a propitious moment to counterattack. It came.

The Storrow camp publicly accused him (in an advertisement) of a grafting deal which had occurred during the administration of Mayor Patrick Collins.

"Need I answer such charges as these?" he shouted, the very picture of injured innocence. "Need I answer such charges as these, when my desperate opponent resorts to such foul methods? I am accused of nefarious dealings which occurred in the time of our beloved Mayor Collins, the very quintessence of virtue, whom in his day no man dared charge with dishonesty." The script might vary, but the gist was always the same as he concentrated on this comforting theme from rally to rally, night after night. Anyone who would be so intemperate as to cast aspersions on a person of such integrity as Mayor Collins was scarcely a person to be believed. It was a touching text for a Fitzgeraldian sermon.

The Storrow camp was forced to apologize publicly, but John F. kept hammering away at that one charge, while ignoring all the others. He was masterful at exploiting a sense of fair play that existed in every voter's heart.

His caravan started at Young's Hotel downtown where, while taking supper he would dictate a speech for the newspapers. If the theme was the number of soak-the-poor corporations Storrow was affiliated with, somewhere in the text there would be his contrite admission that he could not cope with his opponent "if money were to be the decisive factor."

Some of the transactions he ascribed to the banker were mythical, but when he tried to disclaim them, doubts of his complicity would linger in the minds of the voters, Fitzgerald himself ignored the charge that as Mayor he had failed to protect the city against public utility corporations, while Storrow pledged, if elected, to give his "whole heart and energy to procuring cheaper light for the city and for the people of Boston." The Storrow camp finally charged the public utility corporations with secretly supporting Fitzgerald in the campaign, and tried to link him with State Street, in retaliation for Fitzgerald's threat early in the campaign to "take the lid off State Street."

Fitzgerald's hearts-and-flowers oration was reserved for special audiences.

"See what the Hibbard administration did," he told one audience on the eve of New Year's Day. "You remember the New Year's present those men got. Receiving $2.25 a day, if they were thrown out in the middle of winter, their entire yearly pay reached the munificent sum of $25 per year. And they had six or eight in the family. They were fired by the Hibbard administration. That is what the Finance Commission blamed me for not doing. Discharge these men in the dead of winter? Would I? No, no, no. I'd lose my right arm first."

By this time the crowd had sprung to its feet, shouting themselves hoarse. On the same night Jack Keliher might deride his claims to being "the working-man's friend," pointing out that in his claims of refusing to fire city workers and providing pay raises for others, he was stealing credit from the Central Labor Union, but who was interested in such academic hair-splitting? That kind of speech was soporific.

At other rallies Fitzgerald used entirely different tactics.

"The Finance Committee criticizes me for hiring labor that was incompetent and for not being able to get for the city a hundred cents for every dollar expended," he would plaintively say. "Do you know the way I was compelled to hire these men? The civil service commission had to be consulted. If I wanted ten men, they would be requisitioned and a list of twenty would be sent to me. Could I select the youngest and the most able-bodied? No, no, no. The man with sixteen in his family got first choice—that was the law—the man with fifteen got second choice, the man with twelve, ten, nine, and so on, was chosen according to the size of his family, and I had nothing whatever to do with the matter of their selection. And then I am criticized for not getting the same returns for the city as the private contractor, who can get the maximum of service from foreign labor with a minimum of expense." It was by such verbal legerdemain that Fitzgerald wrung applause from some audiences.

While Storrow was making his blunders, not once did Fitzgerald say anything for which he had to apologize, even though some of his charges were based on thin air. Even when he dove into one end of a sentence, and was on the point of stating something tactless, he collected his wits in time to emerge gracefully at the other end.

As the curtain dropped, his advisers told him to answer the charges that had daily appeared in the newspapers. Fitzgerald promised to answer them at a noon rally at Faneuil Hall. In the presence of an overflow crowd, he gave plausible answers to the charges and received a standing ovation as he left the platform.

He missed no opportunity to speak. As his caravan approached a lighted hall, he would send in a messenger to ask the guests whether they would like "the next mayor to meet the ladies and gentlemen." On such occasions he skirted politics, depending on his chime of manner to chalk up another batch of voters.

He barged into smoke talks, athletic events, even large cocktail parties. Included among other stops on one typical night were brief speeches at the Franklin Athletic Association in Dorchester, the Harbor View Yacht Club in East Boston, a Limerick Men's Club smoker, a Mayo Men's Club meeting and a jamboree given by the Cork Men's Association. On the way home he addressed a meeting of New Haven Railroad freight-handlers, the Ancient Order of Hibernians and the Galway Club in South Boston. He also dropped into seven or eight house parties every night, where forewarned hosts had convened from thirty to sixty guests. They forgot more momentous issues when Fitzy told them about the improved municipal services he had in mind for their neighborhoods, while patting children on the head and flashing his smile at the ladies. Beneath his genial tomfoolery was a coolly appraising mind.

In the closing days, the contest became more bitter than ever. In a bid for the votes of Italians in the ward where he no longer lived, Storrow charged that "Mr. Fitzgerald has a custom of going into outlying wards of the city and speaking behind the backs of citizens of other sections, calling them savages who live in huts, and then coming before them with honeyed words." The racial, religious warfare had at first been waged in private, behind the closed doors of ward and drawing rooms.

Jim Donovan had warned that the "introduction of racial and sectarian interests into the campaign would prove a boomerang," and Storrow had said on announcing his candidacy: "I am going to assume that the citizens of Boston cannot be fooled by claptrap political tricks; will resent appeals to prejudices, whether of class, creed, or race, and that they will see through them whether they are made openly or covertly and insidiously; are not interested in mud-throwing personalities; do want issues clearly set forth and honestly argued; expect me to publicly retract or modify any statement shown either to be mistaken or even exaggerated."

But his agents who attended Fitzgerald rallies discovered that Young Napoleon did not always follow the script of speeches as reported in newspapers, whereupon Storrow early in December accused him of "Continually blowing the bellows of religious, racial or social animosities." He referred particularly to stories charging him, Storrow, with being anti-Catholic, anti-labor, and anti-Negro. Fitzgerald admitted departing from his prepared text as reported in the papers, but otherwise denied the allegations.

Storrow boasted of having put Mark Stone, a Jew, on the aldermanic slate in substitution for a Protestant proposed, and called on Thomas B. Fitzpatrick, National Treasurer of the United Irish League, to vouch for him and decry Fitzgerald's tactics. This was the prelude to the most vicious phase of the contest.

In 1907, Fitzgerald in *The Republic* had described Storrow as "a man who acts from conscientious motives and is thoroughly earnest in all that he undertakes . . . and *The Republic* believes Mr. Storrow is not actuated by any motive that can be fairly viewed as hostile to those of Celtic blood."

Reminding audiences of this praise, Jack Keliher added: "Today the word is sent out through the slimy, underground political conduits that lead down from the Fitzgerald headquarters to the different distributing stations that Storrow is a bigot. I know, you know, and every unprejudiced citizen will know before very long that such a method of campaigning can but result in disaster for those so devoid of honor as to introduce such an issue in this twentieth century—the century of complete enlightenment."

The issue was relatively hush-hush, however, until the night of the Big Blunder.

Governor Eben Draper and ex-Governor Curtis Guild, Jr., had taken the stump for Storrow. One night Guild was advertised as the key speaker at a big rally staged by Storrow at Tremont Temple.

"Although it happened half a century ago," said William McMasters in 1961, "its impact on me was such that it seems as though it took place only yesterday. The huge auditorium was almost filled, and various speakers had tried to drive home the terrible danger the city would face if Fitzgerald returned to City Hall. It was a listless rally, however, until Governor Guild, who had just retired from the State House, took the platform. I shall never forget his dramatic stance. He was an eloquent speaker, but hardly had his opening sentence ended, and the wild applause begun, before I knew he had pulled a boner.

"Pointing to high heaven, he shouted: 'My fellow citizens of Boston, by what right does any candidate for high public office in this fair city dare to introduce the issue of religion into a political campaign?' He waited for the booming swell of applause, and it came. But I knew right there that the ex-Republican Governor had given wide publicity to the one issue that could be advantageous only to Fitzgerald, for sixty per cent of the voters of Boston were Catholic."

Once dragged into the open, Fitzgerald pounced on the religious issue, for it gave him precisely the chance he wanted to defend the Irish Catholics of Boston. The campaign became even more riotous and vituperative, and with feeling running high, voters not only argued the pros and cons of the contest, but knocked one another down. Fist fights interrupted every rally, and meetings of both candidates were scenes of wild disorder and tumult, with the police tripping over downed brawlers as they swung their clubs.

One night, just before eleven o'clock, cars carrying Storrow and his followers drove into South Boston, where a shrieking mob of two hundred men and boys armed with long torch sticks, red-fire torches and chunks of ice attacked the caravan. One ice chunk struck Storrow on the arm. There was bedlam another night in Clan-na-Gael Hall in the same section, when goon squads tried to disrupt a Storrow rally attended by some eight hundred partisans. Jim Donovan, unsmiling that night, shouted himself hoarse, but was drowned out by a hooting mob that ceased its frenzied screeching for only a moment when Storrow rose to speak. "I was a friend of Mayor Collins," he said. "I voted for him, and I made a subscription to his monument." Then he, too, was jeered off the platform.

On the following night, a Ward 17 rally was scheduled in the Vine Street Church in Roxbury, bailiwick of James Michael Curley. Twenty-five policemen brandished clubs as an estimated thousand males milled around the auditorium. Chairman Thomas F. Curley, a Storrow man because of the animosity that had sprung up between him and Jim Curley, ordered several hecklers ejected. McMasters, who was present, gives a graphic account of what happened.

"Emotion had taken over, and anything might happen, for the auditorium was jammed, and most of those present were loyal members of James Michael Curley's Tammany Club. I hoped Storrow wouldn't be heckled or booed, for newspaper reports of such rowdyism had already damaged our cause. Several speakers were given respectful attention when the audience quieted down. Then Tom Curley, who was proud of his oratorical ability, rose to speak. He had been known to rouse voters to wild emotional outbursts. That night, however, he was unable to finish his first sentence. Every time he opened his mouth or held up his hand for silence, he was jeered and shouted down. I feared Mr. Storrow would receive the same treatment.

"I need not have been disturbed. When Mr. Storrow stepped to the front of the platform, he was greeted by the most intense silence I had ever encountered. He was a very poor speaker, but he did the best he could, stumbling along for about twenty minutes. Not so much as one catcall or gesture of disapproval came from the audience. They just let him talk without interruption, and he continued in the embarrassing silence. No jeers, no applause. He completed his speech and walked out of the hall in the same funereal stillness. The hopes of the Storrow strategists to have free speech denied their candidate in one of the Fitzgerald strongholds were dashed."

It was a Curley ruse—one of the cleverest he pulled in the campaign. During the final ten days, the air was electric with excitement. Libel suits were filed, and campaign managers on both sides feared the explosive situation might get out of hand and lead to bloodshed. Storrow's partisans, meanwhile, radiated such confidence that Mayor Hibbard sarcastically suggested that his followers should hold "an acclamation meeting on Boston Common." The *Boston Evening Transcript* proclaimed that "Mr. Storrow's system of pre-election information is probably the most complete, the most unbiased and detailed, that any candidate ever had."

Even the cocky Honey Fitz thought he was beaten five days before the election. He knew political sharps were betting on Storrow, but he kept plugging. Those who saw him on the four days before election testified to his fighting qualities, but the outlook still seemed hopeless. On January 9, two days before election, the *Boston Post* picked Storrow by a margin of 4814, after conducting a poll, and on the same day its front-page ran the headline:

CITY IS ABLAZE WITH EXCITEMENT

Fitzgerald's biggest rally was held at Faneuil Hall on the Saturday night before election, when his forces hoped for a last-minute miracle. While background music was rare in those days, and had never been used in a political campaign, The Little General's advisers were well aware of the charm that music hath. McMasters gave the band leader a list of Irish songs to be interspersed with other melodies in his repertoire. When Candidate Fitzgerald arrived, he was greeted by "The Star Spangled Banner," immediately followed by "The Wearing of the Green."

"And then," recalled McMasters, "as if it were pure inspiration on the part of the band, came the song that Fitz was to attach to himself—'Sweet Adeline.' Everybody joined in the chorus, and it put the audience in a wonderfully receptive mood."

Years later Fitzgerald told how he came to adopt this melody as a campaign song. "It was during my campaign for Mayor against Storrow in 1910. I had driven over to South Boston and was delayed for fifteen minutes or so, because the place was mobbed. Hundreds of citizens dragged me all over the place, and my advisers got the idea I was exhausted, because the campaigning that night had been strenuous.

"We arrived at Faneuil Hall around midnight, and it was packed like a sardine can. The crowd had been listening to short speeches interspersed with songs by Representative Sorensen from Ward I, and someone in my party told me to rest while he sang one more number. I asked what the song was, and was told it was "Sweet Adeline."

" ' Now look here, boys,' " I said. " 'I'm all right and to show you I'm all right, I'll sing that song myself.' Well, I did, and it went over." Actually, he stood beside Sorensen and joined in the chorus before someone shouted: "Let the Mayor sing it himself." Fitzgerald added: "Only a few days before the rally, my daughter Rose had played the song on the piano and taught me the words, so I was familiar with the chorus. The song went well, and I have had to sing it in answer to popular request very often since."

Another feature of this gigantic rally were lantern-slides projected on a huge screen, intended to keep the audience in good humor until the speaking began. One quip flashed on the screen was: "You say CLEAN STREETS FOR BOSTON, Mr. Storrow. I agree, but first CLEAN UP STATE STREET." One of many cartoons included a picture of City Hall with the cut-line: NOT FOR SALE, MR. $TORROW.

The final demonstration at this rally lasted for fifteen minutes, while a horseshoe was passed from hand to hand to the platform where Honey Fitz waved it over his head.

It was past midnight on Sunday when McMasters checked Monday's advertising copy in the composing room of the *Boston Post*. McSweeney, foreman of the shop, showed him the Storrow ad which had Storrow booked for rallies in every ward making a total of thirty-six. After McMasters and he put their heads together, their advertisement was changed to announce forty speaking engagements. In localities where the voting was expected to be close, he felt the more energetic candidate might be favored. It would not do to let Jonathan Q. Public think Fitz had finally met his match in a dynamic ex-Harvard athlete. The Little General took great pride in his whirlwind tours.

"I was just about to take the revised copy back to the *Post*," McMasters wrote, "when Fitz, who had just returned to his Quincy House headquarters after a round of house parties and other meetings, lifted the phone for room service. He glanced around the room and asked his dozen lieutenants whether they would like a drink with their sandwiches. Nobody ordered anything stronger than coffee or ginger ale. I remember being impressed, having heard of the champagne parties that were common at Storrow's headquarters."

At the closing rally, Fitzgerald had to be passed over the heads of the crowd to get into Tremont Temple, while the band played "When Johnny Comes Marching Home Again." His howling supporters carried him out to his car on their shoulders. That last night's rallies drew a record attendance of more than 50,000 persons. The streets all over the downtown area were thronged well past midnight, and the excitement lasted all through the night, with some partisans staying up to join the "six o'clock Democrats" at the polls. Before retiring, Fitzgerald gave one speech from the top of a hack downtown, while a mob sang "Sweet Adeline" over and over between cheers for him.

"I never saw such an outpouring of men, women and children in the streets," he recalled. "They dragged my automobile along with ropes, and in the North End it was the same story. They dragged my car up from the ferries at two o'clock in the morning."

Both camps were wary on election day. For years it had been Martin Lomasney's custom to greet each voter by name at his own voting precinct, taking care to keep the legal distance from the booth. His lieutenants at each precinct had cards marked with his choice of candidates, and passed them out to the "sheep," who took the slate into the voting booth with them to "guide" them in the exercise of their franchise. When criticized for being Lomasney tools, one Hendricks Club member said: "If it is all right for a bunch of Harvard men in a Back Bay ward, or for Somerset Club members, to agree on a candidate, why isn't it just as honest for members of the Hendricks Club to stand by one another?"

Storrow, with two bodyguards, hunted in vain for Lomasney at his usual precinct on election day. Storrow accosted a Hendricks Club member, who had just been handed the slate for his precinct.

"I am Mr. Storrow. May I see that card?"

"Why should I show it to you?"

"I am a candidate for Mayor and have a right to protect my interests," Storrow said, as several persons gathered around. He explained the situation to the policeman who walked over.

"Any reason why the gentleman can't look at the card, Tom?" the officer asked.

"It's none of his business what's on the card, Larry. Besides, it's against the law for anyone to interfere with a voter within fifty feet of the polling booth."

"That's right, Mr. Storrow," the officer said. "Mr. Lomasney has always insisted that all election laws be obeyed."

At nine o'clock that morning, McMasters found Lomasney in his "throne room" at the Hendricks Club, and asked why he wasn't at his usual election-day post.

Lomasney swiveled around and grinned. "I figured it would be best for me to keep away. Jim Donovan is pretty smart, and I figured he might try to stir up a fuss so the papers could play it up in the evening editions.

It wouldn't help us any if the papers reported that Martin Lomasney had a brawl with Candidate Storrow."

Despite precautions, a brawl did mar the voting that day in Ward Eight. Robert Bottomly and Ernest Smith of the Good Government Association, after checking the voting list, tried to have the names of several voters deleted which they alleged were fraudulent. After an altercation with one of Lomasney's men, Smith was taken to the hospital with a broken nose.

January 11 was brisk and clear, and 95,000 voters—another record—went to the polls. Fitzgerald received 47,177 votes to 45,775 for Storrow, a slim plurality of 1402. Hibbard, who in the previous election had received over 38,000 votes, tallied only 1614, and Nathaniel Taylor trailed with 613.

"Our returns show that Mr. Fitzgerald won by only 291 votes," Storrow said after the tally. "We shall demand a recount."

A jubilant Fitzgerald called it the greatest triumph of his political career. "No man could ask for a greater victory," he said. "My family appreciated the triumph especially, because there had been so much injustice in the attacks made on me—so much misrepresentation and vilification. For the sake of my boys and girls I wanted to win the election as a vindication."

"It was racial and class feeling, and the consequent unwillingness to consider any of the questions involved with open mind, which defeated me," Storrow said.

Speculation over the cause of his defeat went on for days.

"GEORGE DID IT," said the cartoonists.

Significantly, only Jim Donovan's ward, of all the Democratic strongholds, went to Storrow, and by a mere 600 votes. Political swamis estimated that Fitzgerald's spectacular performance during the final strenuous four days had won him at least eight thousand votes. In Lomasney's ward, Storrow received a surprising 1271 votes, to 2013 for Fitzgerald.

The *Boston Globe* estimated that each camp had spent a quarter of a million dollars on the campaign.

Napoleon's return from Elba was greeted with mixed reactions. The hostile press did a turnabout, and with warm words of encouragement promised to support the new administration. The Speaker of the House of Representatives also pledged his support.

"Mayor Fitzgerald," said the *Boston Post,* "has the opportunity during the coming four years to give Boston an administration that will forever discredit the charges of graft and corruption that were so freely uttered during the campaign for his election. He is pledged to give the charter amendments a fair trial."

Fitzgerald said there were times during the campaign when he was "fairly mobbed by women." He felt they were "wrought up" because he had been so "unfairly maligned," and consequently they put pressure on their menfolk to vote for him, even though they themselves could not vote.

One of his first acts was to appoint ex-Mayor Hibbard City Collector, but the Civil Service Board refused to confirm him. This was the final blow for the ailing Hibbard. Repudiated by his own Republican Party during the campaign, penniless and gravely ill, he failed rapidly. After he died, Mayor Fitzgerald sent his family a personal check for a thousand dollars. In 1942, at the age of seventy-nine, Fitzgerald remembered him as his "noblest opponent."

"In 1910," he said, "Hibbard stood up in his boots and resented Storrow's nomination by the Good Government Association. That was very material in helping me win that fight. Hibbard, by his move, showed character because he acted himself for what he thought was right."

Fitzgerald was the first Mayor of Boston to serve a four-year term, thanks to the Good Government Association which, sure that Storrow would win, had strengthened the power of the Mayor and weakened that of the council. The outcome was ironic. Fitzgerald was elected, and the "Goo-Goos" had a majority on the council!

Years later, Rose Fitzgerald Kennedy would remember the similarity between her father's fight against Storrow and her son's battle against Richard Nixon:

Both campaigns were close.

The religious issue was introduced into both contests. Both Fitzgerald and Kennedy were staging comebacks after a political defeat (Fitzgerald had lost to Hibbard; Kennedy to Kefauver in the 1956 contest for Vice-President).

Kennedy, like Fitzgerald, challenged his opponent to meet him in open debate.

And, finally, both were tough campaigners noted for their energy.

CHAPTER 9

The King of Boston

"I love Boston. My whole life has been bound up in her welfare."
—JOHN F. FITZGERALD

I T WAS 1910. William Howard Taft was President. In New York City, following sensational disclosures of grinning depravity in the iron-breasted metropolis, William Gaynor was the new reform Mayor. Up in Albany Al Smith was guiding Jimmy Walker through the labyrinth of Empire State politics, and soon Jimmy and Honey Fitz—showmen both—would be warm friends. Another person in whose destiny the Boston Mayor would be involved was Franklin Delano Roosevelt who was making a name for himself in the New York Senate.

Life in Boston was still unhurried. Automobile traffic was light, but pedestrians were wary of horseless carriages, which went scorching down the street at speeds up to twenty miles an hour. But, noted Lawrence Mac-Kenzie in the *Boston Post,* there were "no strident horns nor canyon streets to step up noise and deckle the edge of human nerves." He gave a vivid picture of the times. "At home in the kitchen, mother cooked on a coal range, plush-cushioned uncomfortable furniture stood in the parlor, brass beds were all the rage, and gas-mantles gave a new and better light at night. Telephones were not yet a necessity, and electric vacuum cleaners, toasters and washing machines were unheard of. Dad wore a derby and probably a handle-bar mustache. He went to work on a swaying street car, fare five cents. He worked longer hours but not so nervously fast. In the winter he wore a paddock overcoat that fitted him like a corset and came to his ankles."

His Honor almost immediately found himself forced into the role of arbiter of entertainment. There had been capacity houses at the Park Theatre to see Ruth St. Denis give her weird and sometimes exotic dances which she had learned in India. The less aesthetic went to the Tremont to see bizarrely costumed Eva Tanguay cavorting on the stage, raucously singing "I Don't Care."

Boston clergymen, in an era when the ladies of The Hub still wore pleated skirts that swept the floor, condemned the shocking decline in local mores, pointing out that Boston society women, once the chaste arbiters of good taste, had so succumbed to the influence of Ruth St. Denis that they were dancing in bare feet. Mayor Fitzgerald was asked to check such objectionable dances and to ban certain forms of public entertainment.

"People have little appreciation of the manifold duties of the Mayor's office," he said. "For instance, the licenses for theatres and dance halls are given out here. Every time there is anything that tends to immorality in any of the theatres, or shows lack of proper supervision of the dance halls, the blame for it is placed at the Mayor's door."

In one day he was called on to consider whether a movie house and dance hall should be granted a license and whether a play should be censored.

"Society dances," he said, "eclipse in boldness anything attempted in public halls, and are mainly responsible for abuses developed in dance halls."

He finally banned the tango and Turkey Trot, and ruled that a police officer and matron had to be posted in every dance hall in Boston to prevent these shocking new steps. He suggested that dances and socials be held in public schools under proper supervision, rather than in the cheap, corrupting environment of honky-tonk dance pits.

"I think I can say without egotism," he later remarked, "that the dance halls are better conducted in Boston today than ever before. In fact, that is the substance of a report of a committee from Cleveland which has made investigations in about every big city of the country. And Boston's dance hall rules are copied in every city in the country."

When one of many rumors had him running for the United States Senate, he executed a step which, he explained, was the "Senatorial Skip."

His efforts to launder theatrical entertainment got him into unexpected difficulties. In 1911, when he banned "The Easiest Way," he remarked: "If the Hollis Theatre had engaged me to give a show in place of "The Easiest Way," it would not have had to close its doors, and the chances are it could have sold standing room at a premium." No violet by a mossy brook was Honey Fitz. His censorship drew fire from the pulpit.

"I would like to ask him," a Baptist minister fumed, "why he does not attack the dram shops, and the brothels of Boston, which in the guise of second class hotels are destroying so many men and women."

Later the Mayor prohibited the performance of "Salome" at Levitan's Theatre, much to the sophisticated amusement of Mme. Mimi Aguglia, the actress who had the title role. "For myself," she said, "I am glad that your Lord Mayor Fitzgerald will not let me play 'Salome.' I do not like the lady. She is a very bad woman. . . . But that is not what you Boston people say they want the play stopped for. They say it is sacrilegious. They say it is unchristian.

"Nice ladies come here to the theatre. They read the Bible to me. They say it is bad to have the head of John the Baptist on the stage in a play. They even give me little good books about the Bible. But they say nothing about the wicked women in the play. Salome herself they think nothing of."

Critics muttered that His Honor's Napoleonic complex was ruling him when in November 1913 he demanded that Harvard play Dartmouth within two weeks for the championship of the United States. "The present football season is an uncomplimentary commentary on the action of the Harvard football authorities in cutting Dartmouth off its schedule," he said.

He was drawn into other contentious areas of public interest, including socialistic meetings on Boston Common. There was mutinous muttering in radical circles when he denied permits to socialists and anarchists before a law against the Red Flag with its "No God! No Master!" emblazoned on it was passed. He would issue no permits to any parades carrying this banner of destruction. And Boston did have its share of anarchists in those changing times. One was a Boston barber who took a day off to go down to Washington with a revolver in his pocket with the idea of shooting President Taft. He never got past the gate at the White House.

The new Mayor had trouble with suffragettes. According to a 1906 definition, a suffragette was "one who has ceased to be a lady and not yet become a gentleman." Some of these embattled females became so aggressive they had to be reminded that gentlemen were present. By 1912, the equal-righters had become a booming voice wrathfully raised against men. Lida Stokes Adams in her blast at the chivalry shown by males as the *Titanic* sank, said: "I think the women should have insisted that the boats be filled with an equal number of men." In that same year,

1912, Mrs. Emmeline Pankhurst, a leading suffragette, told a big audience at Tremont Temple why women should be allowed vote, and Boston's most articulate spokesman for the ladies, Susan Walker Fitzgerald, toured the Commonwealth denouncing legislators who killed the suffragette bill. One night in Fitchburg, when some turned off the lights while Susan W. Fitzgerald was speaking, she kept talking in the dark for fifteen minutes.

"How would you like to have your mother or sister locked up all night in a room with eleven men?" she was asked, when she had commented on women's fitness to serve on juries.

"Any man decent enough to be selected for jury duty would be decent enough to behave in the presence of women," said Susan.

Women posted suffragette literature in Boston, and vandals tore them down, whereupon the militant ladies hired detectives to track down the culprits. In one demonstration that plagued Mayor Fitzgerald's administration, suffragettes, holding hands, formed a line across Washington Street in one of the busiest sections of the city and held up traffic for two hours. That traffic jam was as hard to cope with as another one, which occurred soon after the Mayor assumed office. A water main burst and sent a torrent of water (700 gallons a minute) into a downtown subway, delaying traffic for hours.

In 1913, and in the following year, the suffragettes stepped up their activities in Boston. One was jailed for heckling President Woodrow Wilson, and sixteen others were jailed for disorderly conduct. One, in angry protest, refused to be released, stripping off her clothes so the guards could not carry her out of her cell. Police matrons took care of her. By 1914, ten thousand equal-righters paraded through Boston streets, and Governor Walsh, the first Irish Catholic to attain the gubernatorial office, reviewed them from the State House balcony.

One day a suffragette came in to see Mayor Fitzgerald, and while waiting in an anteroom, struck up a conversation with Willie, the office boy.

"What do you suffragettes want, anyway?" Willie asked, leaning on his broom.

"Why, we want to sweep the country," she smiled.

"Do you?" Willie handed her the broom. "Well, suppose you take this broom and start right here while you are waiting."

And she did.

The Mayor himself was drawn into a controversy when his weekly criticized Mrs. Charlotte Perkins Gilman, one of the nation's leading suffragettes. Fitzgerald had puckishly taken issue with her statement,

HONEY FITZ

"The sins of the world have been blamed on women. Witness the story of Adam and Eve."

He was all on Eve's side. Adam, he said, was the first and worst sinner, and he quoted the Bible to prove it. But Mrs. Gilman preferred Eve as a martyr, and by the time the feud ended, Fitzgerald figured Adam wasn't so bad after all, and was beginning to feel like a martyr himself.

He had more pressing concerns. In his February inaugural in Faneuil Hall at the beginning of his term, he had stressed the wobbly financial foundation of the city caused by the heavy burden of debt and taxation imposed by the state, the increasing cost of maintaining public institutions, and took a slam at thousands of non-residents who accepted city services without paying for them. The city's government, he said, was not chiefly responsible for the extravagance so often mentioned by the Finance Commission. One sore spot was the devious escape from taxation by many wealthy residents. From one estate (the Quincy A. Shaw), he collected half a million dollars in back taxes.

During his administration, a Public Works Department absorbed the Street, Water and Engineering departments, and later the Department of Ferries and Bridges. As during his first term, he built playgrounds and recreational facilities, including the City Point Aquarium and the Franklin Park Zoo, to which he donated two bears and a leopard which had been presented to him, there being no room for them in his Victorian home.

He built a new Court House, City Hall Annex, libraries, police stations, and he eliminated horse-drawn fire engines in favor of motorized equipment against the opposition of the new City Council, which complained that Boston could burn down while the firemen tried to start the motors. You could depend on a horse, they said.

When he originated white lines to separate traffic lanes, he was accused of extravagance and of disfiguring the historic streets of Boston, many of them once cow paths. He turned his attention to city planning, garbage disposal, and carried out a campaign pledge to provide a retirement plan for municipal laborers. In January, 1914, a City Planning Board, consisting of five unpaid members, was established, and seven district buildings containing public halls, branch libraries and baths were in process of construction.

He held "town meetings" in city districts not represented by a councilor, and when Hyde Park was annexed in 1912—the first time since 1874 that the bounds of the city were enlarged—the residents were pleased when he attended the "town meeting" held there. At these sessions, usually attended by the Mayor and Council members, any citizen could air a grievance or voice a request. Following suggestions, he provided free rides on a ferry for the poor on hot nights and ordered the fire department to flush the streets at intervals during torrid weather. Feeling that if every resident swept in front of his own house the whole city would be clean, he kept a stretch of his Dorchester street clean at his own expense.

He inaugurated Mother's Day, the municipal picnic, and an official Christmas tree on Boston Common, around which a celebration was held. He did this in 1912, a year after he heard a derelict on Boston Common say: "This is Christmas Eve, but there is no Christmas tree for me." New York, Chicago, Philadelphia, and Washington followed Boston's example.

Wherever he went, he was informal and approachable. In 1913, his fourteen-year-old daughter, Eunice, accompanied him to New York City, and was surprised at the number of persons who recognized him. Every time they passed a cripple or blind person selling pencils or shoelaces, Eunice would press his arm and say, "Papa," and that was the signal for him to send his hand into his pocket.

It bothered him when he could not grant a favor. "One evening," he recalled, "I was caught in an animated conversation with a hack driver while I was shopping downtown. He begged me to order the automobiles that crowded Tremont Street to park on the opposite side of the Common, so the cab drivers would have a show. After he harangued me for twenty minutes, I told him there was nothing I could do about the situation. I not only lost time, but a vote as well."

His Honor was proud of the rapid development of the city, especially of the improvements which, as he said, "have forwarded the humane welfare of the thousands of citizens of this great city. There is the North End playground, the beach and all the bathhouses. We never had such advantages when I was a boy. There is the Consumptives' Hospital which I started in 1906. There is the High School of Commerce, where hundreds of boys are being taught the business principles which will mean so much to the future development of Boston. There are the aquarium and zoo, where today so many thousands of people seek pleasure and instruction."

He concentrated on education in non-academic fields. "Everyone can't be a scholar and a white-collar worker. Some have aptitudes for other things, and those aptitudes must be given a chance to develop." He wanted continuation schools that would teach a trade to those not qualified for professions, "so they will have an education of some kind to fit them for life, not only to make them good citizens, but for the sake of their own lives and their families, and for their usefulness to the community of Boston." His enthusiasm led to the creation of the Girls' High School of Practical Arts, the Trade School for Girls, and the School for Bookbinding and Printing.

In or out of office, Fitzgerald talked about extending Boston's trade by land or sea, along with developing new industries by investment of local capital, which, he said, would provide new job outlets. He constantly deplored the scattering of Boston capital in the Far West and South, and the more damaging dispersal of "Boston young manhood all over the land in quest of work which should be attainable at home." He was entranced by the Yankee captains who "a hundred years ago carried our merchandise around Cape Horn to the coast of China and founded business houses in Canton and Pekin." He saw no reason why graduates of the High School of Commerce should not recapture this trade and put the Western Hemisphere on a firmer foundation by adding customers from the yawning markets of South America.

Honey Fitz was a signpost who could tell you where to go, but not always how to get there.

He plumped for the teaching of Spanish. "There is going to be a great demand for Spanish," he said, "when the Panama Canal is opened. One of the most important features of doing business with the Latin-American countries is in knowing their language. Our students should be taught Spanish." Told that the language of Brazil, a South American Republic larger than continental United States and Alaska combined, was Portuguese, he said, "Don't change the subject." He had the same linguistic notions about South America as did Governor Thomas Dewey, who mentioned "our Spanish-speaking neighbors of Brazil." United States military personnel sent to Brazil during World War II often took along Spanish instead of Portuguese grammars.

He was particularly pleased with establishing a commercial high school, which was long in coming. "We had the first lighthouse in America," he said, "but we didn't have a High School of Commerce until 1911."

Fitzgerald increased the efficiency of the Board of Health by adding a corps of ten nurses under a medical inspector for the care of dangerous diseases. He inaugurated the Saturday half-holiday for city employees, raised the salary of laborers, built sewers and new streets, and opened a new subway to Cambridge, along with an underground transit. So as not to disrupt traffic, he had downtown streets wood-blocked by laborers who worked all night Saturday and all day Sunday for two consecutive weekends.

"I have not been content merely to fulfill the letter of my duties of the Mayor's office," he said, "but have endeavored by every means to make the city better and more prosperous."

No detail was too minute to escape his attention. He provided city laborers with iced oatmeal water or switchel on hot days when they were swinging a pick and shovel. Old-timers may remember switchel, an apparently friendly combination of water, molasses, ginger ale—and sometimes, oh horrors!—vinegar.

Fitzgerald took credit for creating the Finance Commission, that thankless child that was still a serpent's tooth to him, and boasted with reason of bringing to Boston to head the new Public Works Department, Louis K. Rourke, an engineer who had been employed by the Federal Government on the Panama Canal. It was also Fitzgerald's initiative which led to the organization of the Board of Directors of the Port.

In the summer of 1911, he had gone abroad with members of the Boston Chamber of Commerce to study the port of Hamburg and other European cities, and while in Germany he looked into its system of continuation schools. He made a good impression everywhere the group visited. Even Republicans admitted he was the best representative in Massachusetts to voice American ideals. He sang "Sweet Adeline" for Kaiser Wilhelm in Berlin after telling him the white race ought to unite against the Japanese. He sang and played the piano to the delight of numerous audiences in several European capitals.

"I am ashamed of myself," said the Burgonmaster of Hamburg. "Here is this man from America, which we think is the country of materialism, who not only sings, but plays the piano, while I, a member of a cultured, musical nation, can do neither."

Before his term ended, new lines were plying between the Port of Boston and German, English and Italian ports, with one line projected to Buenos Aires. Fitzgerald also took the Boston Chamber of Commerce down to the Canal Zone to stress the significance of the opening of the Panama Canal.

The permanent Finance Commission, established under the new City Charter, needled him constantly. Like other mayors after him, he felt he could have accomplished more if the Commission had cooperated with him, rather than wasting its time and the taxpayers' money in investigating trivialities. (The Commission was still firing away in 1961, accusing Mayor John Collins of Boston of spending more money on watchmen hired to keep an eye on equipment than the equipment was worth.) At a Chamber of Commerce gambol in 1913, Fitzgerald was "hailed" as the most expensive Mayor in the United States. He received a salary of $10,000, and the city paid John A. Sullivan $5000, Robert J. Bottomly $4000, and James E. Lee $3000, "to watch you, as representatives, respectively, of the Finance Commission, the Good Government Association, and the Public School Association, and that makes the total $22,000-a-year."

The Mayor called the GGA, "political hypocrites," and never tired of poking fun at the Finance Commission, which gave him no peace. "I think it's safe for me to take a drink of ginger ale," he said at a banquet, "for I see a member of the Finance Commission here."

Political enemies kept peppering him, too. On the eve of his trip to Europe on the *Franconia* in June, 1911, ex-Congressman Joseph F. O'Connell predicted his recall from office. In the city election, he said, "Mr. Fitzgerald will go to his Waterloo. They may applaud his singing and buffoonery, but they will never respect him enough to vote in his favor."

In November of that year, a Curley incident heightened the possibility of his recall. Eugene Foss was a candidate for reelection as Governor, and Mayor Fitzgerald not only campaigned for him, but at the last minute personally raised a fund of $3000 to help bring the voters to the polls. On election eve, Foss was billed as the featured speaker at a rally in old Armory Hall, East Boston. Dennis O'Neil, one of Pat Kennedy's lieutenants, was toastmaster at this wind-up rally. It was a foggy night, and the East Boston ferry which Foss took went off course and rammed under a Chelsea bridge. Meanwhile, the toastmaster introduced singers, musicians and other entertainers to keep the audience from leaving, but eleven o'clock struck without a word from Foss.

Congressman Curley, meanwhile, had left his automobile in Scollay Square and taken the trolley through the East Boston tunnel (fare, six cents) in the company of newspaper reporters.

"I had no idea," O'Neil said, "when I saw James Michael striding into the hall that he was coming. When he removed his coat I noticed that, as usual, he was wearing a cutaway and a gates-ajar collar. By this time, the audience was restless, and on the spur of the moment, I decided to perk them up.

" 'My fellow Democrats,' I said, 'if you will give me your attention . . .' I waited for silence. 'I am sorry that the Honorable Eugene Foss, our beloved Governor, is not with us tonight. However, we do have with us a distinguished statesman who is known to everyone in Boston—Congressman James Michael Curley, who represents the Tenth District. He was the right-hand man and guiding spirit of Speaker Champ Clark in Congress. Tonight, however, I am going to present to you, not the gentleman from the Tenth Congressional District. Tonight I am going to introduce to you the next Mayor of Boston. He is James Michael Curley, my great and good friend whom I have known over a great period of years.' "

Curley, who was not yet addicted to the squeaky shoes he later deliberately wore to make pewholders in churches turn to see him striding majestically down the nave, walked gravely to the platform.

"Tonight," he said, "I am here to help the Democratic Pahty (as he pronounced it) elect my dear and distinguished friend and colleague, Gene Foss. My friend Dennis has been most generous in introducing me as the next Mayor of Boston. I shall give you my comment in a very few words . . . I shall return to this very armory within two years as a candidate for the Mayoralty and—" he waited for the applause to subside, "and I say to you—I say to this most distinguished gathering—that I shall be elected."

Curley had had no inkling of the surprise O'Neil announcement, but like any good actor, he gave the performance expected of him.

The moment he made the announcement, reporters rushed to telephones, and a few of them accompanied Curley and O'Neil to Newspaper Row, where the politicians went first to the editorial offices of the *Boston Herald* to break the news. It was the first formal announcement of Curley's intention to run for Mayor, and it so irked the reformers they made a more determined effort to recall Fitzgerald.

It also upset Mayor Fitzgerald, for he knew that any pre-arranged plan for Curley to succeed him would stimulate the determination of his enemies to remove him from City Hall. He and Pat Kennedy exchanged telephone calls, and O'Neil, informed that the Mayor wanted to see him at City Hall, waited until the polls were closed before making an appearance.

"Do you realize that you have ruined me?" Fitzgerald said. "Right now the voters of Boston may be recalling me. Will you make an announcement that you spoke without any authority?"

"What good would it do now, John?" O'Neil asked. "The polls are closed. It's ten past four."

His Honor had reason to despair. The vote to recall him was 37,692 "yes" and 32,144 "no." He was relieved when the reformers and other enemies did not get the 54,194 votes (a majority) needed to unseat him, but it was painfully clear that his popularity had waned.

Foss, who was reelected, had in the meantime been accusing the Republicans of corruption. They had provided free transportation and luncheons in their "boodle campaign to debauch the voters," he had charged during the contest. Twelve electric trolleys, with placards advertising the candidacy of his opponent, Louis A. Frothingham, had taken voters to one mammoth outing near Fitchburg. Frothingham's big campaign fund, Foss charged, came from "special interests."

Mayor Fitzgerald, meanwhile, was repeatedly accused of extravagance, and no detail escaped the scrutiny of the Finance Commission. One charge was that he had installed electric light poles with harp-designed tops and orange lights for use in public squares and parks. His critics might have been interested in knowing that the harp, as a symbol of Ireland, was introduced by none other than King Henry VIII. His Honor was also spending too much on parades and celebrations of such events as the Battle of Bunker Hill and Evacuation Day, said the Commission. District leaders, on the other hand, said he was not spending enough. They demanded more municipal jobs than he could provide.

When Professor Emily Balch of Wellesley College told her economics class that the Fitzgerald regime was wasteful, Rose Fitzgerald's friend, Ruth Evans, demurred.

"I think you are mistaken," she said. "I know Mr. Fitzgerald very well, and I think his administration is very efficient."

"Very well," Professor Balch said. 'If you know more about this than I, you may take over this class next Tuesday and tell us about the mayoral administration."

Miss Evans obtained a mass of data from the Mayor, including information on big business corruption and the history of past enterprise and initiative in Boston. Fitzgerald was so pleased with her convincing defense of his administration that he later employed her in his office at City Hall. Her main function was to do research for his speeches.

"He usually recast what I wrote and put punch into it," she recalls.

One of his top admirers was his office boy, Willie Cronin, who considered him "the best there ever was in mayors." One Sunday night Willie went to his Dorchester home to borrow a book on stenography. The Mayor handed him the book, saying: "That reminds me of one of Mark Twain's stories, Willie. One day Mark Twain went to a neighbor's house, and seeing a book he wanted, asked if he might borrow it. The neighbor told him he could not, but said he could stay in his library as long as he wanted to read it. A couple of weeks later the neighbor came over to Twain's house and asked it he might borrow his lawn mower.

" 'Of course,' Twain said, 'as long as you use it on my lawn, you may have it as long as you want.' "

Willie recalled the morning he came into the Mayor's office at one minute of nine, "all out of breath for fear I was going to be late. The catch basins on my street weren't working, and the street was in pretty poor shape from a storm the day before.

"Mr. Mayor, I don't pretend to be a politician," he said, "and I ain't looking for favors, but it seems to me that the folks out my way ought to have a better street. I don't believe you know how bad it is."

"Willie, I'm much obliged," His Honor said. "Get me the Street Commissioner on the phone."

"That night," said Willie later, "Wrentham Street was in fine shape and has been since. Some day I may be running for Mayor myself, and if I do, I hope the people out my way will remember the good street I got for them."

Boston never had a more energetic Mayor. Fitzgerald told of one typical morning when he arrived at his office at City Hall at nine o'clock and found twenty-one men waiting to see him.

"The first man I saw wanted to know if I would shake hands with his six-year-old daughter if he brought her down that afternoon. I had to see her, no matter how pressed for time I was. If I hadn't, that man and his brother and father and his wife's father would have voted against me the next chance they had."

He took frequent holidays, however, usually accompanied by one or two members of his family. "I wouldn't enjoy a trip if I didn't have one of the girls or boys by my side." Rose had accompanied him on his trip to Panama on a United Fruit Company ship, as well as on his jaunt to Europe in the summer of 1911, when Agnes also went along. Ceremony, sometimes tinged with tomfoolery, marked every departure and arrival.

When he boarded the *Franconia* in 1911, he sang "Sweet Adeline" on the steamer's bridge, and the "Hurrah Johnny Cadets" saw him off as far as Boston Light. He took along giant firecrackers, sky rockets, Roman candles and red and green fire, and on July Fourth celebrated off the coast of Ireland, with song and pyrotechnic display. When the Irish Coast Guard saw the fireworks, they signaled the ship: "Do you need help?" In a clowning mood, Fitzgerald promised the Coast Guardsmen jobs as lifeguards on Boston Common and Public Garden. "Also," he said, "a few good swimmers are needed for the aquarium."

He was often the center of attention without trying. When a special train carrying Massachusetts members of the American Legion pulled into San Francisco for a national convention, the first query from a reporter was, "Where's John F.?" He was delighted when a friend, just back from London, said he ran into an Englishman in Piccadilly Square who asked: "Say, how is Bigger, Busier and Better John F.?"

"He did everything but make a balloon ascension," a contemporary reporter said. John F. did better than that.

In 1909, when aviation was still in swaddling clothes, Claude Grahame-White gave it a big lift when he flew out over Boston Harbor and clattered to Boston Light and back, receiving a $10,000 prize from the *Boston Globe* for his daring stunt. Fitzgerald was also crowded off the front pages when Eleonora Sears, who would later walk from Providence to Boston, was hailed as the first woman air passenger in New England.

In 1911, when Henry Arnold, a West Point graduate, joined the Air Corps, consisting of one plane and a few fliers, aviation again made headlines. The avaitor who was to achieve fame as General "Hap" Arnold, and who had been taught to fly by the Wright brothers, in that year carried the first United States airmail on a five-mile trip. At about the same time, the first national air meet was held in Squantum, just outside of Boston. The meet was sponsored by the Harvard University Flying Club. Glenn Martin, who had earlier stunted over the Brockton Fair, was present when Grahame-White took Mayor Fitzgerald on a "long sail high in the air" three times around the Squantum aviation field in his biplane. His Honor had had no intention of making this flight when he accepted the invitation to attend the aeronautical exhibition.

Adams Claflin, director of the meet, entered a box in the temporary grandstand where Hugh Nawn, vice-president of the Harvard flying club, was sitting with his father, Harry, a contractor and political power at the time in Boston.

"Hugh," Claflin said, "Grahame-White has just invited you to be a passenger on a plane flight to Boston Light as the representative of Harvard."

Harry Nawn nudged his son, who declined with thanks. Mayor Fitzgerald, sitting in a nearby box, heard the interchange.

"You ought to go up, Hugh," he said. "You have a chance to make history as the first civilian passenger. After all, Harry, when your number is up, it's up."

"I don't know why Hugh should go along if Claude Grahame-White's number happens to be up," Harry Nawn said. "No, I'd rather have him in this box than in that crate. If you want to make history, why don't you go along, John F.?"

"I wasn't invited." (This was a modest statement for a man known as "the Number One Uninvited Guest of America.")

"Would you go if you were asked?" Claflin cut in.

"Why, certainly, certainly, of course I would."

Grahame-White, whose name was confusing to bread lovers, was delighted, commenting after the flight that the publicity Fitzgerald had given him was worth a fortune.

It was always a relief for His Honor to get away from City Hall, where he was constantly besieged by starry-eyed starlets and crackpots of every description seeking publicity. There were always more invitations for breakfast, luncheon and dinner than he could handle. Generally, he could attend only three or four of the dozen evening functions to which he was invited. On his way in and out of City Hall, there were always panhandlers to block his path.

During his second administration at City Hall one memorable visitor was Gaby Deslys, a French actress who brought her own hen with her because she couldn't eat American eggs, she explained. She wanted His Honor to be photographed with her and the hen.

A visitor from Philadelphia made a snide comment about Boston's narrow, twisting streets. "I wish Boston were laid out in the same way as Philadelphia," he said.

"Well," said Mayor Fitzgerald, "when Boston is as dead as Philadelphia, we'll have her laid out the same way." Philadelphia was already known as "a cemetery with lights."

In 1912, he entertained Governor Woodrow Wilson of New Jersey at the Quincy House. That was the year Wilson changed a historic trend in Massachusetts which, since the 1850s, when the Republican Party had been formed, had always given her electoral vote to Republican candidates. In 1912, when the Bull Moose split the State and Wilson became the first Democrat to receive its electoral support, he made history that was not to be repeated until 1928, when the Bay State gave Al Smith its hurrahs.

Another visitor was William Jennings Bryan, who received a rousing reception when Mayor Fitzgerald introduced him to an assembly in the oak dining room of the Quincy House. Bryan got slightly mixed up that night, while making a speech in behalf of a friend.

"My candidate," he said, "is as honest a man as money can buy."

He waited for the laughter to fade and his timing was perfect as he took a sip of water, for he had made this part of his speech before.

"What I mean," he added, "is that he never stole a dollar in his life. All he asks is the chance."

158

HONEY FITZ

Teddy Roosevelt held his Rough Rider hat as he stood on a Boston Common platform to address a throng, after being introduced by Mayor Fitzgerald, and on another date (in April, 1912) some 50,000 persons tried to squeeze into the Boston Arena, which could accommodate only a fraction of that number, when Teddy arrived for a speech. In October of that year, when the Mayor visited President Taft at the summer White House in Beverly, Massachusetts, they posed for photographers after warbling "Sweet Adeline." Asked by a reporter what he thought of Teddy Roosevelt's Bull Moose platform, Fitzgerald said it was one-ninth moose and eight-ninths bull, unless he was "moosetaken." When Taft had become a candidate for reelection in 1912, Roosevelt led the Bull Moose revolt that divided the Republicans.

"Fitz, I see you have a new hat," Taft said.

The Mayor explained that he had doffed his old hat so much it had worn out.

Honey Fitz was always interested in politics on a national level, and in 1912 he attended the Jackson Day dinner on January 13 in Washington. In his book, *My First 83 Years in America,* James Gerard wrote, in reference to this annual dinner held in Washington, D.C., on the birthday anniversary of Andrew Jackson: "In a Presidential year this gathering affords an especially valuable opportunity for the exchange of views and for many intrigues. When the New York delegation arrived in Washington for the 1912 Jackson Day Dinner, Mr. Murphy (Charles Murphy was head of Tammany Hall of New York) and I were deep in conspiracy. 'You sit with me in my room at the Shoreham Hotel on the day of the dinner,' he said, 'and when people come in and talk to me, I will say that you have a candidate. Then you can spring your Roosevelt proposal and we'll see how they take it.'

"I think the first visitor was the popular Mayor Fitzgerald of Boston, widely known as 'Honey Fitz.'

" 'Mr. Murphy,' Honey began, 'we have a splendid candidate in our Governor Foss. You ought to consider him.'

"Murphy motioned towards Gerard: 'Well, Jim here has got a candidate. Go on, Jim, tell him about your candidate.'

"I then enlarged on the advantages of nominating Roosevelt on the Democratic ticket, but Fitzgerald was so nonplussed by what he heard that he seemed hardly to have strength to back gasping out of the room."

Gerard and Murphy tried the same routine on others who came into the room, with the same negative results, and Murphy concluded that his scheme was barren. Roosevelt was refused the nomination by the Old

Guard Republicans, who selected Taft. In the ensuing split of Republican ranks, Roosevelt ran on the Bull Moose ticket, making possible the election of Woodrow Wilson by the Democrats.

Another dignitary who came to Boston during Fitzgerald's second administration was Navy Secretary Josephus Daniels, but the most rousing reception was given to Archbishop John Williams in 1911, when Mayor Fitzgerald greeted him as "Boston's First Citizen." Seldom had such an enthusiastic welcome been given a native son. Boston's streets were ablaze with the color of American or Papal flags, or bunting of cardinal red. The Mayor, who escorted the Archbishop ashore in a government boat, presided at the city reception. Despite a driving snowstorm, some 100,000 cheering citizens lined the streets as a long procession, that included members of Catholic societies and the uniformed companies of the Ancient Order of Hibernians, filed past.

"Name" visitors were often persuaded to boost Boston. Thus the city, in the opinion of the Lord Mayors of Dublin and London, was "the best in the world." When Lady Gregory came to Boston, she told His Honor: "I always feel contented in Boston, because it is so homely." (She meant-"home-like," Fitzgerald explained.)

"You ought to," he said. "You live so much nearer Boston than any other American city. It is 182 miles closer to Ireland."

Lady Gregory, smiling, nodded her agreement. "Why, I know a girl who, when she came home from America, told me she was going back soon. When I asked her why, she said she had an appointment with her dentist in Boston."

Mayor Fitzgerald liked the convivial society of such a musical-comedy mayor as Jimmy Walker of New York whom he invited to an Army-Navy football game where Walker was dapper in a derby, Fitzgerald dashing in a Homburg. Both were first-nighters who enjoyed baseball games and prizefights. Both were supersalesmen and ideal good-will delegates for their city, and their camera smiles were always ready for photographers. Both kept up with the latest dance steps and were globe-trotters who expressed a wish to "drop in on" the King and Queen of England. Both said every big city they visited was the greatest they had ever seen. Jimmy Walker had his "I'll Love You in December" song to match Johnny Fitzgerald's "Sweet Adeline."

"I like the company of my fellow beings. I like the theater and I am devoted to sports." Jimmy said it, but those words might have rolled off Johnny's lips. There was one big difference, however: "This meal," quipped Walker, "is the best I've yet drunk." Fitzgerald abstained.

Mayor Fitzgerald was also fond of Sir Thomas Lipton, whom he entertained in his home in Dorchester, as he did Admiral Togo of Japan. Lipton also visited Mayor Fitzgerald at his summer residence in Hull on the South Shore of the Bay State, where his huge Victorian house commanded a clear view of Boston Harbor. Fitzgerald and Lipton were close friends whose personalities were strikingly similar. Delete the word "tall" (Fitzgerald in his prime stood five-feet-seven) in Alec Waugh's description of Sir Thomas in *The Lipton Story,* and the subject could be John F. Fitzgerald:

"He was tall, handsome, and ruddy-cheeked. He was somewhat vain of his appearance and never lost an opportunity of getting sunburned. He was a man who exuded geniality. He was always laughing, always making jokes, always telling stories. It was very hard to make him serious, to tie him down to anything. Even at a business conference he would behave as though he were at a party."

Both men, rarely in repose, dispensed the same blarney, and in both was a strong strain of buffoonery. In 1912, when Sir Thomas stayed at the newly opened Copley-Plaza Hotel (where Mayor Fitzgerald and his entire family were guests for a week at no charge immediately after the opening), they would take "walks" up and down the corridors. "Come on, John, we will have a race!" Lipton said during one stroll. "We will run back." And away they went like romping schoolboys.

If Fitzgerald was Boston's blue-ribbon flatterer, Sir Thomas was a mere half-step behind. After a banquet in his honor, Lipton said: "Now, John, remember, I want half a dozen of those menus, one for my town house and one for my country house and one for my boat. I want to have people coming aboard know my friend, John Fitzgerald of Boston."

Mayor Fitzgerald had a cook named Catherine Coffee who told a reporter in 1913, after she resigned to get married: "Corned beef and cabbage was good enough for him [Mayor Fitzgerald] when he didn't have Prince So-and-So or Duke Such-and-Such to dinner. For visiting royalty he had canvasback duck and pâté de foie gras." After one dinner, Sir Thomas told the press he "would exchange a couple of billion pounds of his tea for 130 pounds of Coffee."

Sir Thomas was a smash hit when Mayor Fitzgerald introduced him to an assembly at Dorchester High School. The old charmer told the boys and girls they were as fine looking as any he had ever seen; he did it in the convincing manner of Candidate Fitzgerald assuring a County Cork assembly that nowhere in his travels had he seen such handsome men and women.

"Good-bye, King," Sir Thomas said on one of his frequent departures from Boston. "I am leaving the finest city in the world and the finest people." His admiration for "the King of Boston" was genuine. "Among all my friends in America," he told reporters, "I rank Fitzy just about first. He is the finest personality I have met on my long travels."

Both thought work fun, but they liked sheer fun, too, and they despised snobbery in any form, agreeing with what former Attorney General Francis Biddle said in his autobiography, *A Casual Past*: "One need not be a snob to be a gentleman, or a fool to be an aristocrat." While a guest of Mayor Fitzgerald in 1912, Sir Thomas refused to attend a dinner given by the Boston Yacht Club unless his host was invited. During that visit, the Mayor's chauffeur drove them by the Somerset Club, that exclusive sanctum where firemen who clanged up to quell a blaze were reportedly told they would "have to use the service entrance."

"Sir Thomas," the Mayor said, waving toward the club, "that is considered one of the most exclusive clubs in America. Boys are put on the list for membership when they are born."

Lipton turned to Agnes Fitzgerald, who sat beside him. "Agnes, I wouldn't have much of a show in that club, do you think I would? When I was ten years old I was working for half a crown a week. Do you suppose that would qualify me for membership?"

"No, I don't know that it would," Agnes smiled, "but you are just as good a man as any of them."

Lipton returned her smile. "Ah," he said, "you are like your father."

Sir Thomas, who referred to Agnes as the only girl he would ever marry, once toasted her as "the most beautiful girl in the world."

He and Honey Fitz had much in common. Neither drank nor smoked. "Sir Thomas never lifted a cup, including a yachting cup," Fitzgerald teased, referring to Lipton's frequent, frustrating failures in sailing his yacht, the *Shamrock,* in international competition. The primary reason for his 1912 visit was to lift "America's Cup," or "the old mug," as he called the trophy.

"If I lift the cup I suppose I should take back an American lady to help me look out for it," Lipton said. It was the kind of remark that led to repeated rumors of his impending marriage to one or another American woman, including Rose and Agnes Fitzgerald. Even by 1910, when he was a jolly sixty, his name was linked with imminent romance, for it was always springtime and red roses when Sir Thomas was around. Wrote Alec Waugh: "It was also rumored that he had proposed to and had been rejected by the daughter of John Fitzgerald. The actual facts of this proposal are a reasonable indication of the measure of truth that ordinarily lies behind such rumours. At a party in the Fitzgerald house, a group of friends were teasing Sir Thomas about his sloth in marrying. 'Don't be so shy,' they said, 'who is going to be Lady Lipton?' He laughed and turned towards Miss Fitzgerald. 'Come along, Rose, stand up. We'd better let them into our secret.' Miss Fitzgerald entered into the spirit of the charade. 'Oh, no, Sir Thomas, I couldn't marry anyone so fickle.' That is the basis for the Fitzgerald rumour. There is no more solid basis of veritable fact for any of the other rumours."

Even Alec Waugh did not have his facts straight, according to Fitzgerald who gave this version: "After a banquet at the Copley-Plaza Hotel we met some personal friends and had a little sit-down, about twenty-five or thirty people, and there were fourteen or so very prominent ladies— I won't mention any names—some young girls and some married women, and they were pressing Sir Thomas in various ways to get him to commit himself as to the girls and women he had met, and particularly about his reported engagement out in Denver. They thought they had him pressed into a corner. Finally he said:

" 'If you want to know who Lady Lipton is going to be, she is right in this room. Stand up, Rose!' Rose is my daughter.

" 'I won't accept you, Sir Thomas,' said Rose. 'I think you are altogether too fickle.' They all howled—everybody in the place. Sir Thomas answered: 'Well, I know now how it feels to be jilted.' "

Lipton, who usually told American girls they were the best looking and best dressed in the world, advised against their seeking titles abroad, "since American husbands are the best."

During his December visit to Boston in 1912, he told how the King and Queen of England were kept waiting while Honey Fitz and friends took a cruise in the royal cutter. Mayor Fitzgerald, Rose and Agnes were traveling in Europe when they went to Cowes to watch a regatta. "Finally," Fitzgerald said, "Rose sighted Lipton's *Erin* in the distance and we went down to a wharf, hoping to find a motorboat that could take us out to the *Erin*. There was no boat there, but we noticed the King's launch and thought one of the members of the royal family was aboard. The launch came up to the wharf where we were, and the skipper looked around and was about to start away when the officer in charge came up to where I was and asked if he could be of any service, seeing that I was anxiously looking about. I told him I was a friend of Sir Thomas and was looking for a boat to carry us to the *Erin*. The officer graciously said the King's launch was at my service.

"As we approached the *Erin,* Sir Thomas saw us through his glass, and figuring it was some member of the royal party, possibly the King or Queen, he had all his crew brought forward on the deck to receive these eminent guests. Among his guests were some Americans, and they were all anxiously asking Sir Thomas as to the etiquette to be followed immediately upon the approach of the King or Queen. Sir Thomas was busily explaining when the boat arrived and as I popped my head over the rail he nearly fell on the deck, so great was his surprise. 'My heavens,' he said, 'it's my friend, John Fitzgerald of Boston, with Rose and Agnes.' "

Actually, the *Erin's* guest books included names of many royal personages in Europe and of illustrious persons in every walk of life on both sides of the Atlantic. Fitzgerald himself had previously been aboard with the Duke of Manchester, the King and Queen of Spain and princes of the royal blood, for all of whom he had sung "Sweet Adeline," but, he noted, "there was always an air of democracy all over the ship. Sir Thomas would talk to them just as to the rest. He once told me that one of the most pleasant things he ever did was the bringing together of the King and Queen of Spain.

" 'I made the match,' he told me, 'and it has resulted in a very pleasant home. The young people idolize each other and are as simple as children.' He was very happy over that. The Queen of Spain was the daughter of Princess Henry of Battenburg, the sister of King Edward. I was on Sir Thomas's boat one day when the Queen of Spain came up.

" 'Hello, Sir Thomas!' she called out. 'I am coming over to dinner tonight.'

" 'All right,' was his answering hail."

King Edward VII of England was fond of Lipton, an Irishman reared in Scotland, and he and his Queen Alexandra had been guests on the *Erin,* along with lesser royalty. (It was King Edward and Queen Alexandra whom Mayor Fitzgerald had inconvenienced during Cowes Yachting Week, highlight of the English sailing season.)

"I was entertaining several Americans when suddenly I observed the Royal launch making direct for my yacht," Lipton wrote in his autobiography. "I took this to mean that Their Majesties the King and Queen were about to pay the *Erin* a visit. At once my American visitors were agog with excitement. The ladies began, anxiously to practice their formal curtsies, while, in honour of Their Majesties, I ordered my crew to line up to attention. Finally the Royal Launch drew alongside. And who do you suppose jumped out of it? My old friend 'Honey Fitz,' otherwise Mr. John F. Fitzgerald, the Mayor of Boston, and his two young daughters.

HONEY FITZ

You could have knocked us all sideways with a feather, so great was our astonishment and bewilderment.

" 'My word, Fitz,' I exclaimed, 'but you have arrived in great style.'

" 'What do you mean?' he asked blandly. 'I took the best boat I could see available to bring me over to you.' Then he went on to say that being in London, he had decided to run down for the day and give me a call. Arriving at the seafront of Cowes he and his family had strolled along to 'that building over there,' pointing to the sacred steps of the Royal Yacht Squadron, and had 'hired the only launch he could see idle at the moment.'

Fitzgerald had addressed the launch skipper with such swaggering assurance, the latter inferred he had royal permission for the use of the launch, and promptly followed instructions. On boarding the launch, Fitzgerald said: 'Lipton, *Erin*,' and when the crew saluted, he added: 'Never mind saluting, take me to the *Erin*.' "

A few minutes later the King and Queen found the launch that was to take them to an offshore yacht, missing. "It was nowhere to be seen and came back, minutes late, after having carried the Mayor of Boston and his family out to the *Erin*. Fancy that extraordinary situation! The King and Queen waiting impatiently on the jetty while their launch was 'hired' by a genial American gentleman to pay a visit to his friend, Tom Lipton!"

Two nights later, Lipton, a dinner guest on the Royal yacht, explained the affair. "The king was highly amused with the whole story of 'Honey Fitz' and his unintentional effrontery, and finished up by saying that he would have to cancel the reprimand he had given to his boat's crew for being late!"

For years, Fitzgerald and Lipton exchanged visits. In 1923 they attended the Gloucester Tercentenary races, and a few years later Honey Fitz made a special trip to New York to visit the Irish yachtsman at the Waldorf-Astoria. "It's going to be a jolly old time and will probably wind up in Boston about Wednesday," Lipton said, in reference to an invitation Governor Alvan Fuller of Massachusetts had extended to him.

At various times during his administration, Fitzgerald was mentioned as a possible candidate for Governor, United States Senator, or Vice-President. As early as the summer of 1910, he had hinted he might seek the Governorship, but as he often did later, he changed his mind, unable to trim his winds to the prevailing breeze. A cartoonist, hailing him as "Caesar Fitz," compared him with Shakespeare's Julius Caesar: ". . . thrice presented him a kingly crown which he did thrice refuse."

The Reverend Cortland Myers at Tremont Temple said he would leave the state if a man were sent to the Senate because he could sing "Sweet Adeline."

"Why, they are talking of sending men to the United States Senate whose recommendation is that they are singers," he said in a burst of oversimplification. "I should think that the spirit of Sumner and Everett and Webster would arise and make protest."

By 1912, Mayor Fitzgerald, who had named his official car *Sweet Adeline II,* said he was "beginning to get tired of this *Sweet Adeline* business, although he found that his singing stunt was often more effective than speechmaking. "When I was Mayor of Boston and in other governmental posts," he recalled later, "I learned that everywhere a Mayor went he had to make a speech, and no one really wanted to hear a speech, so I sang."

Mark Sullivan called the ballad "the favorite carol of those who cannot sing," and Mayor Fitzgerald was told that in Flint, Michigan, it was a violation of the Volstead Act to sing the ballad. A Providence publisher told Fitzgerald: "Why, Mr. Mayor, whenever we hear of your singing 'Sweet Adeline' up in Boston, we always say 'Fitz is full again.'"

"Think of the reputation that song has given me," Fitzgerald said, when told he was the only person who could sing it sober and get away with it. He told the story of two drunks who were hauled into court.

"Your Honor," one said, "we was just up there in the park tonight singing a song, that's all."

"What song?"

"'Sweet Adeline,' Your Honor."

"Six months," the judge said.

After one rendition at Palm Beach, an elderly woman walked over.

"Mayor Fitzgerald, did you ever stop to think that 'Adeline' doesn't rhyme with 'pine' at all? The 'Adeline' is properly pronounced as if spelled 'Adeleen.'"

"I don't know that I've very often heard it pronounced that way," he said, "but since you say so, I'll sing it so as long as I am in Palm Beach." He didn't tell her he was leaving the following morning.

The ballad kept intruding into the Fitzgerald story like a prompter in a Sunday School play. On their way back from England, after their visit with Sir Thomas Lipton, the Fitzgeralds stopped in Ireland. Hugh Nawn, an old friend and neighbor of the family whose parents used to make peanut-butter sandwiches for Candidate Fitzgerald on those late evenings when he dropped in to see the Nawns, had been touring Europe with the Boston Chamber of Commerce group. He had joined up with the Fitzgeralds at Ostend, and returned with them to the United States. The night before they sailed from Queenstown, Nawn and Fitzgerald walked down to the waterfront.

"It was a beautiful moonlit evening," Nawn recalled. "As we passed a house we heard a lovely female voice singing 'Sweet Adeline.' "

Fitzgerald's most memorable rendition came on the 4th of July, 1920, when he was watching a baseball game in Hull. Suddenly a two-ton truck, out of control, veered toward the crowd of spectators. Fitzgerald, pushing several persons out of its path, was run down, the truck passing over both legs, badly lacerating one and tearing the muscles of the other. Smiling, Honey Fitz sat up.

"I'm not badly hurt," he calmly said. "Don't worry, I'll be all right. Don't be putting on such long faces." And sitting there, he sang "Sweet Adeline," and not until he finished would he leave for the hospital. It was six weeks before he could leave his home. He made his first public appearance at the Marshfield Fair, where his friend, Thomas Lawson of "Frenzied Finance" fame, led three cheers for Fitz, and the air was once more filled with the familiar melody.

Despite his size, Honey Fitz had plenty of courage. Present when some college students pelted the composers of "Sweet Adeline" with vegetables, Fitzgerald sailed into a group of them and swung from the hip.

Years before the Joseph P. Kennedys bought their winter home in Palm Beach, Mayor Fitzgerald was a familiar figure at the beach resorts, where he indulged his fancies and clowned. As Mayor of Boston, he was always dapper, though more conservatively dressed, but in the South he could wear the flashy sportswear that was more admissible in tropical climes.

Even in the Mayor's office, there were times when he was less than conservative. When Fitzgerald entertained Lady Gregory, he was smartly attired in a suit of black-and-brown checks, with a blue striped tie, blue stone scarfpin. He considered a straw hat ("Straw Kelly," he called it) seasonable until the snow flew.

"There is nothing of the baked bean about Boston's Mayor," wrote Henry N. Hall in the *New York World* in February, 1913. "He is all hot sand and ginger when awake, and never goes to bed without first singing the Hub to sleep. To the world at large he is 'Honey Fitz'; to the dear-o North End and to South Boston he is 'Fitzy,' or 'me darlin',' or just plain 'Fitz,' and to Harvard and the Back Bay, this bulwark of the Puritan fathers is affectionately known as 'the Pilgrim's pride.' "

When Hall interviewed him, he was wearing a "plain black cutaway coat and vest that fit like a glove, gray checkered trousers, a white shirt and green tie. No jewelry of any kind, except a very light and unobtrusive watch chain of platinum and gold." Hall said he "stood just under five feet eight inches and was a stocky 170 pounds with broad square shoulders thrown well back. Yet he was as nimble as a chipmunk. . . . His jaw is just as square as his shoulders, and it is so massive that the big, firm chin looks smaller than it really is. His face looks as if it were built from the bottom up, but the forehead is very broad, the laughing blue eyes are well apart, the large and well-shaped ears are on a level with the slightly hooked nose. The mouth is wonderfully firm, and the teeth come together with a snap like a steel trap, biting his long words off short. He speaks in snappy sentences, extremely fast, and with the faintest trace of brogue. The man simply radiates energy like a human dynamo and throws off new ideas at the rate of about one a minute. He loves Boston and is the greatest press agent the Hub ever had. He is a very live wire."

His ideas included using wireless by ships to report schools of fish at a time when wireless was relatively new. (The first wireless distress signal at sea, incidentally, was sent out in January, 1909, when the White Star liner *Republic* collided with the *Florida* off Nantucket.)

Other ideas were less practicable. In 1913, when gasoline was selling for twenty-five cents a gallon, he suggested that a huge tank be erected in a central part of the city where drivers could buy it wholesale. During World War I, he wanted aliens taxed a hundred dollars, and suggested they be drafted into a conscript Army. One idea would one day be carried to fuller flower by his grandson, President John F. Kennedy, when he activated the Peace Corps. Mayor Fitzgerald said it would be an excellent plan to require certain college students to travel to Europe, Asia and Africa as a prerequisite for a degree, to assure the United States of future leaders who would have more comprehensive knowledge that would qualify them for handling world problems.

He reached the half-century mark in 1913, and to show that his batteries had not run down, ran a hundred-yard dash at seven o'clock in the morning, a quarter of a mile at nine, wrestled at noon, and boxed at one o'clock. "I feel no older than I did twenty-five years ago," he told reporters, showing them a $1200 dinner set he had received from admirers.

The bathhouse keeper at Hull said he was the fastest swimmer ever seen at Pemberton Pool. He would walk into a locker room at six in the evening, dive into the water less than a minute later, take a quick swim, and be aboard the Nantasket boat for Boston at 6:10. He might take a cat nap on the way, for he could almost always drop into a chair and fall asleep. Not, however, if there was anyone to talk to.

He was proud of his versatility as an athlete. At a horseshow, he mounted a jumper and cleared the barrier, complaining afterward because the bar had been lowered from six to four feet. At a fair held at Rainsford Island, he milked a cow, to prove his further versatility. On his way past a playground, he might get out of his car to umpire a baseball game for an inning or two, and at an auction he could be expected to pick up the gavel and take over. Items moved, too, whether there were bidders or not. At a church fair he shouted, "Sold for five dollars to the Congressman," the first inkling the legislator had that he had just bought a piece of cake that was perhaps worth a nickel. Mayor Fitzgerald was completely unpredictable. One night, when he and his wife were guests of honor at the Dorchester Club, he added a touch by riding home with her in a siren-screaming fire engine.

Like Teddy Roosevelt, he had to be the bride at a wedding, the corpse at a funeral. In a matter of seconds, he usually took over any group, and was in as much demand as a referee of sporting events as he was as an orator. "Every twenty-second of February he officiates as manager of athletics at Hotel Royal Poinciana golf grounds," a friend wrote from Palm Beach. Honey Fitz said the only reason he took up golf was so he could challenge President Taft, whose wife wouldn't let him play with John D. Rockefeller, thinking it might dim his trust-busting reputation. Whether on the golf links or at a clambake, he was never still. In a clowning moment, he once slipped a folding straw hat under a person about to sit down at a picnic, and when the person apologized for ruining his hat, he snapped it back into shape.

He officiated at the openings of business establishments, inspected jails or hospitals, swore in officials, crowned beauty queens, attended outings for boy scouts and orphans. At Christmas he helped the Salvation Army donate food baskets, and if the recipient was a blind person, an appropriate speech would accompany the gift, as news photographers recorded the scene for a wider audience. He led grand marches, marched with high school cadets, addressed historical exercises and conventions, and laid cornerstones. When he dedicated a half-mile track at Franklin Field, he delighted the spectators by competing in and winning the first race. During one vacation at Old Orchard Beach, Maine, he replaced a baseball pitcher and in the remaining seven innings, struck out sixteen batters.

Nobody on his staff at City Hall could keep up with him. During holidays he gave them two months' work for every three weeks he was away. "It's no easy job being understudy to a man like Boston's Mayor," Colonel Richard Field, one of his personal secretaries once said, when the Mayor was in Palm Beach. "His Honor is expected back about March 17, and you just wager we'll all be glad when Johnny comes marching home again." Fitzgerald had to be back in Boston on March 17. It was St. Patrick's Day.

The Mayor could take a joshing as graciously as he could give one. At sessions of the Clover Club or gambols of the Chamber of Commerce, he often took a merciless ribbing. A member of the chamber, in reference to his good-will tour of the Canal Zone, mimicked him: "I think there may be some of those present here tonight who were present when we first landed under a foreign flag, and who remember the cheers that went up from the assembled multitude—'Three cheers for John F. Fitzgerald, our next President. Three times three for Fitz and his suite.' You see that they meant well. They knew and appreciated me, but they had taken a very small portion of one chamber for a suite. But the pilgrims became used to that, and before we parted it delighted them as much as it annoyed me to see my lithograph in every window, to see the papers carrying my name at the head of their editorial columns, to hear the school children singing *Sweet Adeline,* and to read that the Citizens Municipal League of Kingston, Jamaica, had recommended that Jamaica proclaim its independence in order to take advantage of the fact that a modern George Washington was on the spot."

Another tirade, signed Robert J. Bottomly, asked: "Is one John F. Fitzgerald in your midst? Beware of him! He is a menace to tropical vegetation and a promotor of discord. Restrain him! On second thought, turn him loose. If you keep him, he will be running your country and annexing others within a year. On third thought, don't turn him loose, as we want to keep him out of this country long enough to pull off and win an election without his presence. Maroon him."

Honey Fitz was a familiar figure in the office of the *Boston Herald* when his friend Robert Lincoln O'Brien was editor-in-chief. One night, in the absence of O'Brien, a friend dropped into his office and left a quart of gin, although the editor never drank until late in life, and then only penitentially and medicinally. The *Herald* reporters thought it a shame that liquid cheer should be wasted on an abstainer, so they carefully unsealed and uncorked the bottle, and when three drops were left, refilled the bottle with straight water, resealed it, and left it on O'Brien's desk.

Honey Fitz wandered in soon after O'Brien returned to his desk. The

Herald editor, expounding on the virtues of temperance, asked him to accept the bottle in behalf of some worthy moment of charity. John F. remarked later, after a party at his house, that while Robert Lincoln O'Brien was a great editor, he lacked good taste in stimulants, for his guests, heroically consuming the "gin," did so without noticeable banishment of the blues.

Parties at home were rare for the Mayor. "I have yet to spend a weekday night at home with my family since I have been Mayor," he said in May 1912. Weeks later, he felt his decision to spend one night at home called for a celebration, with the press represented. That night homework was forgotten, rugs rolled up, tables cleared, and music recordings sorted to find the catchiest tunes.

"I am to spend the evening with you, children, so proceed to make merry," he said. At this point his youngest son, Fred, made a running jump and landed in his lap.

"You must not mind what happens in this household tonight," Mrs. Fitzgerald told the *Boston Post* reporter. "You see, we don't have Mr. Fitzgerald often with us on a week-day evening, so it means a great deal to every member of the family."

Mary Josephine Fitzgerald was a slight, erect, brisk, slender little woman, with fair hair and luminous brown eyes that enhanced her serenity of expression and manner. She was youthful looking enough to be mistaken for her twenty-two-year-old daughter, Rose, or Agnes, who was twenty—seven years older than Eunice. At one reception, a reporter had asked Rose: "You are Miss Rose Fitzgerald, are you not?"

Smiling, she nodded.

"Thank you. And the young lady over there, in pink, is Miss Agnes, your sister?"

"Yes."

"And the very slim one in blue—which of the daughters is she?"

"Her name?" Rose's laugh was musical. "Why, don't you know? Her name is Mother!"

Mary Fitzgerald was the charming and gracious mother of three boys and three girls. She supervised their studies, clothes, games and social activities, stressing moderation and simplicity at all times. She frowned on jewelry or ostentation, and was the shy opposite of the dynamic Little General. Although active in club and social life, she shied away from publicity, devoting most of her attention to providing a stable home life for her children.

"I want my home to be a place of inspiration and encouragement to all my family," she told a magazine writer. "I am a home woman in every way, and my one ambition is to make the home the most happy and attractive place for my husband and children. I try to go about quite a bit with Mr. Fitzgerald. When I attend the theatre I always call for him after the performance and we ride home together. And I am not a stranger at his office in City Hall."

The Mayor appreciated her understanding. "Whatever my public duties have been, no matter how much they have taken me away from my fireside, she has never complained, realizing that when I accepted a career in public life, I had to fulfill my obligations, and although I have been away from home so much, we have a complete comradeship. My home life has always been very happy. My children have always been a source of inspiration to me, and whenever things have seemingly gone against me, I have invariably been given every encouragement at home by Mrs. Fitzgerald, who has been a model wife and mother."

Even Fred, aged eight, was impressed when his father spent a night at home. "I don't know about Dad," he said. "If he is sick, why doesn't he go to bed, and if he is well, why doesn't he go to work?"

According to Elizabeth Burt, the reporter who spent the evening with the family on this memorable occasion, His Honor was out of step with the rest of the Fitzgeralds. "If I were to meet him at a horse race," she said, "he would impress me as a Boston dandy of the smart set, a man who believes in keeping thoroughly in style."

Father Fitzgerald led a troop of happy youngsters into the library. Fred took one arm, Eunice, his next youngest child, the other. Tom, John, Jr., Agnes and Rose fell into line behind him while Mrs. Fitzgerald escorted Miss Burt into the large library.

"Turn on the phonograph, Rose," the Mayor said, "and we will liven things up a bit."

He danced an old-fashioned waltz with Eunice. Then Rose sat down at the piano and said she had a new song for him to try. Papa Fitzgerald, according to Miss Burt, "sang in a clear, well-paced voice the chorus of a new ballad. Then he sang 'Sweet Adeline.' "

Next on the program was a game called "Tom Jenkins Says Hands Down."

"It is a fine game," said the Mayor. "Clear the table and we will start it." He turned to the reporter. "In this game three persons sit on one side of the table opposite three on the other side. A coin is passed around under the table by members on one side. When the captain on the other side shouts 'Tom Jenkins Says Hands Down,' and three place their hands on the table. The captain is supposed to tell all hands to be raised but the hand covering the coin. This game, you see, trains the ears to catch the faintest sound."

After playing the game, he raised a window shade. "Out here," he said, "we have a playground for the children of the neighborhood." At one end of the clearing was a stable with most of its windows broken. "There isn't a whole window in it," he said, "but if it helps them to throw a ball any better, it is for a worthy cause." He waved toward the girls. "The girls are athletic, too, but they go in more for swimming and tennis. Eunice can turn a handspring as well as she can play the piano. All my girls dance, sing, and are fond of sports."

Rose, a pianist, and Agnes, who had an unusually lovely voice, had studied at The New England Conservatory of Music, and each was an artist in her line. Both had taken a special course in the study of grand opera, attending Saturday afternoon classes for three years. All three girls radiated charm and were pretty, and if Rose was the most animated and spirited, Eunice, whose physical resemblance to her father was striking, was especially witty and clever—"always ready with a bright retort," and curious about everything. At thirteen, she was visiting her father at City Hall when she saw the bronze heads on the wall.

"I can't see but one head of you, Papa. Why don't they hang two? Weren't you elected Mayor twice?"

Eunice was "father's own girl," with a special place in his affections.

Agnes, with her mother's hair and eyes, resembled her as well in manner.

"Each in her own individual way is a genuine beauty," wrote Angela Morgan in a contemporary article in *Cosmopolitan* magazine. "Miss Rose, with her dark hair and vivacious manner being a foil to her fair-haired sister." The writer further noted that Rose "displays depth and strength of mind rarely found in so young a woman. Undoubtedly her father's influence upon her life has broadened her outlook, so that she lives much more vividly than most girls of her age." All three girls, she said, "were endowed with personality, charm, tact, mental brilliance and some striking gift or talent."

On the night of Elizabeth's Burt's visit, Mayor Fitzgerald aired some of his ideas on bringing up a family. Mentioning a garden in the back yard, which his son Tom was cultivating, he said: "Tom wants to be a farmer, and I welcome such a desire with glee, for I think there are too many professional men trying hard and failing to earn a living now. We need producers, and it is the scientific farmer who is the most needed man of the day. I believe in having my sons working for what they get. I believe in letting them find out their own capabilities. Tom says he intends to work all this summer."

"What's the use of going into all that, Father?" Tom said.

"What's the use? Why, there is every use in the world, my dear boy. Don't you know that Miss Burt came out here to get just such information?"

Mrs. Fitzgerald smiled. "John, it does indeed seem refreshing to have you here. I am not sorry you are to have photographs taken to mark the evening. I am going to frame one and place a card over it on which I will write: 'Taken on his one evening at home.' "

The Mayor pulled down the shade. "Now you will make Miss Burt think I neglect my family if you keep on." He turned to the reporter. "I spend every Sunday with them, Miss Burt, and I have them each in town at least once a week. I am a family man. And the reason I am such is because I was one of many children. I took care of my brothers, did all the buying for the family, and was father and mother in one. This early training enabled me to shop wisely. Why, I think nothing of buying hats and coats for my girls. Just a little while ago I happened to see two coats I thought were quite attractive, so I bought them."

"And they were perfect fits," Agnes said.

"I'm never surprised when he brings me home a suit," Mrs. Fitzgerald cut in. "I will admit that although he doesn't spend many evenings at home with us during the week, he seems to have us on his mind a great deal."

Mrs. Fitzgerald never moved the furniture around or changed the wall paper without consulting the head of the house. "If I don't by any chance consult him, it is apt to turn out badly," she said. "He knows every little thing about the home. It is certainly nice to know you have someone to whom to turn."

Agreeing he had duties to perform at home, Mayor Fitzgerald added: "They stand in line here just as they do in town."

His frequent observation was that the best way to keep young was "to keep in step with his children. I play ball and tennis, swim, dance and mingle with them as though I was a pal, rather than a parent. I am up on the latest songs, even though I do dance old-fashioned waltzes rather than the Turkey Trot."

Even after turning fifty, he kept up an active interest in athletics, playing baseball, boxing and wrestling with his sons, and playing tennis with the girls. "We swim and dance together, too. It is the close association with my children, making myself one of them, which has materially served to keep me young." He admitted that wrestling with his older boys, Tom and John, was getting strenuous, for they were, by the time he reached fifty, "big enough to handle me pretty well."

Before escorting Miss Burt to the trolley, he showed her his chicken roost. "You must see our hens," he said. "I will show you some fine birds."

His quiet evening at home was featured in the *Boston Sunday Post*.

Honey Fitz was not the only member of the family often away from home. Since the glare of publicity was too much for Mrs. Fitzgerald, Rose became her father's official hostess, well qualified because of her tact, poise, personality, and looks. She accompanied her father to political rallies, dances, parties, banquets, and wakes, and all this helped build up his image as a devoted affectionate father. Rose, described at this time as "a very pretty girl of the brunette type," had her father's camera smile, and she also mixed well. One story that has gained currency had Rose meeting Pat Kennedy's son, Joseph, when she accompanied her father on one of his frequent visits to the elder Kennedy's home in East Boston. But actually, Rose and Joe first met at Old Orchard Beach in Maine.

Joe, like Rose, had been reared on politics. He has an early memory of two ward-heelers coming to his father's house. "Pat," one said, "we voted one hundred twenty eight times today."

As the lovely daughter of a popular Boston Mayor, Rose was considered a prime catch, especially in socially prominent Catholic circles. In the swirl of competition, young Joe Kennedy's chief competition came from Hugh Nawn, who more than once led the cotillion with Rose at the Somerset Hotel. Rose had everything, including a gracious background in which good taste had been stressed.

In January, 1911, she had made her debut, and in the flossy prose of a contemporary society column, she "emerged yesterday from the bud of girlhood into the blossom of society." It was an elaborate party, with 450 guests, including Hugh Nawn and Joseph Kennedy.

Rose had attended St. John's School, a parochial institution in the North End. When more Fitzgerald siblings arrived, the family moved from North Garden to Hanover Street, and was living in Concord Junction when Rose was graduated from a public grammar school.

In June 1906, Mayor Fitzgerald had presented a diploma to Rose, the youngest student ever to graduate from Dorchester High School. She not only graduated with honors at the age of fifteen, but was voted by her classmates as Boston's prettiest high school senior. Agnes received her diploma the following year from the Henry L. Pierce School in Dorchester, and both went on to the Sacred Heart Convent on Commonwealth Avenue in Boston. Rose continued her studies at Manhattanville, New York, while Agnes enrolled at Elhurst in Providence.

Mayor Fitzgerald had taught his children to put any talents they had to good use, and gave them full rein in their education. During their trip to Europe in 1911, he had looked for a suitable convent school.

"I wanted to go to one in France," Rose said later, "but all the convents in France were closed at the time on account of the trouble between the Church and the State. So, my sister and I spent a very wonderful year at Aix-la-Chapelle, the old capital of Charlemagne in the Middle Ages."

The Convent of the Sacred Heart, which she and Agnes attended, was a German school in Blumenthal, Prussia. It was an exclusive convent for the aristocrats of Europe. Here Rose mingled with frauleins with strange medieval-sounding titles. Nobody knew who the titled girls were.

In her book, *Life and the Dream,* Mary Colum, who was there at the same time as Rose, described the old-world training given at the Convent of the Sacred Heart. She wrote that "the only girl at the school ever to become a full-fledged ambassadress, as far as I know, was an American girl who seemed to be out of that life altogether—Rose Fitzgerald of Boston, later wife of the American ambassador to the Court of St. James. She was one of the few pretty and chic girls who were at the school."

The official language spoken at the convent was German, and French and music were required courses of study. An American classmate, Ruth Evans (later Mrs. Edward Scott O'Keefe), remembers the deep impression the German convent made on them.

"At home we had heard the worst music, and had attended the ugliest churches. Attending church and sunday school was a boring duty. We had to learn the catechism by heart, but had no deep religious feeling. Then, transported to a world physically austere, but so beautiful we both experienced a spiritual transformation, living in a world where the chief concern was 'to know, to love, and to serve God.' I remember the Convent of the Sacred Heart as a paradise of beauty and goodness—and gayety!"

While in Europe, Rose collected autographs of kings, queens, and lesser royalty, and, before she had completed this post-graduate course at the convent, had become a piano gold medalist.

She returned from Europe to resume her role in the social and political life of Boston, deftly handling the duties which her father assigned to her. Having presided over the launching of the *Bunker Hill* and broken a bottle of champagne over the bow when she was sixteen, she was by this time well versed in the role of official hostess. Her German was fluent enough to permit her to address a group of German students in their native language. "Rose Fitzgerald's speech was a big hit," the *Boston Post* reported. When the International Congress met in Boston, thanks to Mayor Fitzgerald's promotion, Rose and Agnes acted as interpreters, bringing their French and German into play. Their early training had not been wasted. From their earliest years, both girls had been taught the virtues of social service.

"I delight in my children, one and all," Fitzgerald said. "The girls are active. Both Agnes and Rose conduct catechism classes in the North End among the Italian children. They also teach in their sunday school." A former sunday school pupil remembers Rose as a "meticulous, punctilious person, but if she was serious it was not because she lacked a sense of humor. She simply insisted that we know our lessons."

The girls visited settlement houses and were active in other philanthropic work. They were also social favorites who belonged to several societies, including the Cecilian Guild, the Catholic equivalent of the Junior League, and the Travel Club, organized by Rose with the aim of continuing studies pursued abroad.

Rose organized and was first president of the Ace of Clubs. One requirement for the six charter members was study in Europe. The club discussed international affairs and staged an annual ball at the Somerset Hotel, where Rose and her escort usually led the grand march. In 1911, Rose was president of the Lenox Club. She would join only clubs with a purpose. "Pink teas bore me," she said. If she sought mere diversion, she played whist, bridge or tennis, or went swimming. Briskly vivacious, gingery and agile-minded, she had no time for gossip, although she, like Eunice, was curious about everything. "Exactly what do you mean by that?" she would say if a precise meaning eluded her.

In 1910, when she was twenty, Rose was chosen as the youngest member of the Boston Public Library examining committee, which determined books children should read.

On one trip with her father, they visited the White House in 1911 on their way to Palm Beach.

"Hello, Fitz," President Taft said when they entered his office.

"I'd like to present my daughter Rose, if you have a minute, Mr. President," Honey Fitz said.

"Oh, I'm never too busy to shake hands with such a pretty young lady," the President said, "as the crimson rushed into Miss Fitzgerald's face," the *Boston Post* reported.

President Taft wasn't the only gentleman who found the young lady pretty.

Joseph Patrick Kennedy, born in East Boston in 1888, was reared in a closely knit family of comfortable circumstances. He was the only son after a younger brother died in infancy. The Patrick Kennedys, like the John Fitzgeralds, thought their offspring should learn the value of a dollar and get into good work habits in preparation for a life of useful service. Young Joe sold newspapers, hawked peanuts and candy on an excursion steamer, worked as an office boy in a bank, and took tickets on a sightseeing boat when Admiral Dewey's fleet steamed into Boston Harbor after the Spanish-American War.

At the School of the Assumption, his teachers gave him special attention, for he was a gifted student with a particular affinity for mathematics.

After completing the seventh grade, he switched to Boston Latin School, arising early to catch the North Ferry. At Boston Latin he met boys from every walk of life, including a few Back Bay lads whose parents did not send them to Groton or St. Mark's. Joe developed a liking for Patrick Campbell, his mathematics teacher—who later became a famed headmaster—and often sought his counsel in later life.

Like his boyhood chums, Joe had played sandlot baseball, football, and shinny hockey on the mudflats or other improvised playgrounds, developing a highly competitive spirit which his father encouraged. At Latin School he was a top basketball and football player, and played first base on the baseball team, which he captained for two years. Ernest J. Goulston told him before the climactic game with English High School that if Latin won, the team would be Goulston's dinner guests at Young's Hotel. Boston Latin, which did not have to face the slants of Roy Green, English High's ace pitcher who had won seventeen straight games (he was ailing that day), won the game and enjoyed Goulston's hospitality. At the end of Joe's senior year, he won the John F. Fitzgerald Mayor's Cup (one of many trophies Mayor Fitzgerald donated to worthy, well-publicized causes) for compiling the highest batting average in Boston high schools. Joe's astounding average was two hits for every three times at bat!

Joe had several times met Mayor Fitzgerald (who personally presented the cup), for the Mayor had often visited his father, who, he recalls, stayed at home most of the time with his wife and family. Joe further distinguished himself by achieving the highest military rank in his school, and as colonel of his regiment, which won first prize in city-wide competition in 1908, he brought great honor to the school. He was graduated that year.

His mother, hoping he would go to Harvard, was pleased when he was accepted—one of the few East Boston boys who attended Harvard. He majored in money and banking, for he was already thinking in big, round numbers. "How can we make some money?" was a greeting he used often. Figuring it was easier to make a million dollars than a hundred thousand, he set his sights on that goal by the time he was thirty-five.

Although he did not make the elite Fly or Porcellian clubs (Franklin Delano Roosevelt didn't make Porcellian, but Teddy Roosevelt did), he was popular enough to be invited into the Dicky, Delta Upsilon, and Hasty Pudding-Institute of 1775.

He was regular first-baseman on the freshman baseball team, and made the varsity until he threw out his arm in the Navy game. He earned his letter in his junior year when he was sent in to play first-base in time to make the last put-out against Yale. In his senior year, he coached the freshman baseball team. His grades were gentlemanly, and when the baseball captain warned him that his average in economics was precarious, he switched to a music course.

Extracurricular activities included dramatics. He helped the D.U.'s stage "Ralph Roister Doister," a pre-Elizabethan play which starred his friend, Robert Benchley. A classmate, who recalls Joe's remarkable energy, said the big, tall, sandy-haired student was extremely popular, "but if anyone told me Joe would have a daughter who would become the Marchioness of Hartington, and a son who would become the President of the United States, I would have considered him crazy."

While in college, Joe Kennedy had heard Mayor Fitzgerald touting Boston as a great tourist city, and this gave him an idea. He and a classmate ran a sightseeing bus to historic shrines, operating from Faneuil Hall. He decided on this rubberneck idea while riding a bus from Boston to Lexington, when the driver told him the vehicle was for sale. Spieling glib history through a microphone, for three years he did the lecturing while his partner drove to such sites as the Old North Church and the battlegrounds of Concord and Lexington. "And now," Joe would say, "we come to the Paul Revere House, the oldest frame building in Boston, having been built around 1660. Paul Revere lived here from 1770 to 1800. It was from the doorway of this house that he set out on his famous midnight ride on April 18, 1774." This venture netted Joe $5000.

According to Robert Benchley, the Class of 1912 set some kind of record by producing "only one Bishop of Albania," "only one member who caught a Giant Panda," and "only one Village Clerk of Hewlett Harbor, Long Island." Benchley should have included in this select list "only one financial genius."

In her book, Mary Colum recalls that Bishop Spellman told her that Joe Kennedy, "the husband of a girl I had known for a brief space at a

German school, was a genius, and I ruminated on what sort of genius."
The answer was clearly a financial genius.

For several months after leaving Harvard, Joe worked in the counting
rooms of the Columbia Trust Company, later moving to the bank cashier's
office.

"After leaving college," he wrote in his twenty-fifth annual Harvard
report, "I entered the office of the Bank Commissioner of the State to
become State Bank Examiner at a salary of $125-a-month, traveling
around eastern Massachusetts. In 1914, I was elected president of the
Columbia Trust Company in East Boston, a small suburban institution."
His father, then a director of this bank, succeeded him as president.

When carrying a satchel of money on his travels, Joe kept it chained to
his wrist, in case any purse-snatcher got ideas. During his eighteen months
as Bank Examiner, he learned of the business practices of banks, and got
to know bankers. Later he raised $45,000 from his father and relatives
and bought stock in the Columbia Trust, just before the outbreak of
World War I. He then became the youngest bank president in the nation.
He was described as "a direct-action man who worked in rolled-up
sleeves, lunching on crackers and milk."

He was now in a position where he could think of providing for a family. He and the twenty-four-year-old Rose Fitzgerald were married in
October, 1914, in the private chapel of Cardinal O'Connell.

Agnes was her sister's maid of honor, and Joseph Donovan, who had
graduated from Harvard a year ahead of Joe, was best man. After a two-
week honeymoon, they settled in a $6500 house in a respectable, but
homespun, neighborhood in Brookline. Joe, in debt because of his investment in bank stock, borrowed money for the down payment.

Mayor Fitzgerald made his son-in-law director for the city of the Col-
lateral Loan Company, a position that gave Joe Kennedy his first headline.
Early in December, 1914, Boston newspapers reported that Joe Kennedy
was responsible for ferreting out a $150,000 theft web. One paper re-
ferred to the company as "the biggest pawnshop in the U. S."

Joe, who had grown up under the shadow of his father, had been known
as "Pat Kennedy's boy, Joe." Now he had acquired an even more celebrated father-in-law, a political thespian who made it hard for anyone to
follow him on the stage. But it wasn't long before his intimates were pre-
dicting that the Mayor of Boston would one day be known as "Joe Kennedy's father-in- law."

The house in Boston's "North End," where John F. Fitzgerald was born on February 11, 1863.

John F. Fitzgerald as a boy.

An outing of the Red Berry Club, a social and political organization of "North Enders" at Old Orchard Beach, Maine. An arrow indicates Fitzgerald.

A summer outing of the Neptune Associates in the early 1880s. Its president, Honey Fitz, is indicated by an arrow.

ENGRAVED BY LENOX ENGRAVING CO.

John F. Fitzgerald about the time he first entered politics.

Mayor John F. Fitzgerald, 1913.

Mrs. Fitzgerald and her daughters: Rose, Agnes, Eunice.

Honey Fitz's house in Dorchester, Massachusetts.

A fine horseman, Honey Fitz organized a polo team that competed in New York and New England.

President John F. Kennedy's two grandfathers, John F. Fitzgerald (*left*), then a Congressman, and Patrick J. Kennedy, at a fox hunt in Asheville, North Carolina, January 29, 1896.

City Hall, Boston, Massachusetts.

City Hall Annex, Boston, built during Mayor Fitzgerald's administration.

Honey Fitz singing "Sweet Adeline."

Mr. and Mrs. Joseph P. Kennedy and their family. At the far left in the second row is President John F. Kennedy, then seventeen years old.

U.S. Ambassador to Great Britain, Joseph P. Kennedy, welcomed home by his son, John F. Kennedy, a student at Harvard, December 1938.

Mrs. Joseph P. Kennedy, John F. Fitzgerald and Mrs. Fitzgerald in 1944.

The Elder Statesman. John F. Fitzgerald (*left*) presiding at a Massachusetts Electoral College meeting. In the center is Massachusetts Secretary of State Frederick W. Cook; at the far right, Archbishop Richard J. Cushing.

At Honey Fitz's seventy-seventh birthday anniversary in Palm Beach, Florida, Ambassador Joseph P. Kennedy serves him a piece of birthday cake.

Mrs. John F. Fitzgerald, widow of Honey Fitz and grandmother of President John F. Kennedy, at the age of ninety-five.

CHAPTER 10

Roxbury Magna Vox

"Hippodrome is useful in that it assembles and attracts
large gatherings, and gives the politician the opportunity
of explaining why he should be elected."

—JAMES MICHAEL CURLEY.

The eye of the storm that made Boston the most explosive and turbulent political community early in the century was James Michael Curley,
son of Irish immigrants.

Honey Fitz first met him in Pat Kennedy's house in East Boston, and
from that moment, like the predestined enemies of the Chinese proverb
who will inevitably meet in a narrow alley, these two most colorful showmen of a purple era of saints, scamps and reformers, knew they would
clash. For years they would rock on a political seesaw, lauding or knifing
each other as political expediency dictated. One moment Honey Fitz
called Curley a crook and a despised enemy. The next moment he was
"the greatest fighter known in Boston politics."

Curley was any one of a dozen different men, depending on whose interests he was serving, including his own. He was a gifted tribune of the
people, and he was at times venal. "He was either a thief who richly mer-
ited more than the two terms in jail he actually served, or he was a saint
who took from the rich to give to the poor," one observer said. Everything about James Michael Curley must be taken in proper context.

"He has one blind spot—he's a thief," a Boston journalist said of him.
Curley, accustomed to such talk, told one story on himself—one of the
many light touches of the 1913 campaign.

"Curley is a thief," said Benny Feldman of the North End. "Dun't vote
for him."

"Who told you that, Bennie?"

"Martin told me, dat's whom," said Benny.

Lomasney collared Benny later. "It's all right for me to call Curley a thief," he said, "but you cut it out."

Curley delighted in being called (as he was over the years) an old ham actor, political Barnum, Irish Mussolini, codfish edition of Huey Long, convict, jailbird, buccaneer, spellbinder and highbinder Sympathy Jim, James Myself, Ambassador to South Boston, the low-brow mayor of a high-brow city, and a combination of Santa Claus, Robin Hood, a Chinese warlord and John Barrymore. Indeed, there was truth in every description. His favorite descriptions of himself, however, were "the political kingpin of Massachusetts" and "the most unpredictable and colorful politician in American history." His eloquence was perhaps unmatched in America. "I heard one man say of him," wrote John Gunther, "with a kind of wistful affection, a man who certainly had no reason to be fond of him, 'I suppose that fellow is the damnedest single human being I ever met.' "

Curley dominated Boston politics for a generation. Like Honey Fitz, he was a key figure in the shifting alliances that were reshuffled in almost every election in the early decades of the century. While there were no antagonisms too deep to be reconciled, there was no political machine simply because there were not enough Boston Irishmen able to agree on a premise long enough to form one. The Irish are more critical of one another than they are of anyone else, Proper Bostonians included. "The Irish must be a fair race," said Dr. Samuel Johnson, "they never speak well of one another."

Curley had turned to politics for the same reason as his political tutor, John F. Fitzgerald—"because," as he put it, "industrial conditions were deplorable and prospects of getting anywhere seemed remote." When he followed Fitzgerald to the political stage, working hours for Irish Catholics were still long, wages still low, and working conditions wretched if not dangerous. Most avenues to greener pastures were still closed to the Irish. In those days before New Deal reforms, they achieved power through extensive use of patronage, after consolidating their power in their home wards by means of services provided for the indigent or ignorant.

Curley and Fitzgerald were alike in many ways. Their intelligence, drive and ambition compensated for opportunities denied them by the accident of birth, and neither was chastened by any disabilities he had. Both were symbols of revolt against Yankee Protestants. Witty and eloquent, the secret of their appeal was pure personality. Their aims were almost identical. Both aspired to the same political office, which in larger moments of their mystique, was the Governorship. Their careers were remarkably parallel in many ways, except that Fitzgerald attained each public office about a decade earlier. His followers often wondered what might have been the scope of his career had not an infant named James Michael Curley been born when Johnny Fitz was eleven years old.

While their talents were comparable, their personalities were markedly different. Honey Fitz was smiling, affable, informal. He was genial and gingery, and could dominate any group that did not include Curley. He was dwarfed by the imposing presence of Curley, who in his prime weighed about two hundred pounds and stood a broad-shouldered six feet. Although an effective orator, Fitzgerald was not in the same spellbinding class as the magna vox of Roxbury. Honey Fitz put punch into the jerky, three-quarter-time cadence of his rapid delivery, and could charm a bird down from a tree, but his range was limited. Curley could oratorically descend on an audience as gently as April rain. He could purr like a kitten, but he could also snarl like a wildcat. He could turn a jeering, hooting assembly into a wet-eyed or cheering audience, and any time he wished, while solemnly winking to a confederate in the wings, could make an audience laugh or weep. He was the one politician of his generation who dared call a crowd "you swine," as he did at the Marshfield Fair, and wind up his speech in a burst of applause. He once showed his platform magic by quieting a howling mob:

"Now you pickpockets and crapshooters, I'm going to make myself heard if it takes until six o'clock in the morning when you fellows are out at your occupation of stealing milk. I know these men. They are nothing but a pack of second-story workers, milk bottle robbers and doormat thieves. Now, you Tammanyites, mix in there with the crapshooters, and the first one that opens his face, plug him." He loosened his tie and took off his coat. "Here I am. Does any one of you bums want to step up here and make anything of it?"

This was the same orator who could impress a conclave of college presidents with his unctuous diction and grammatical niceties. The mere thought of opposing this man, whose voice was the finest instrument a political Pied Piper could wish for, gave even such a cocky campaigner as Honey Fitz the jitters.

Curley's sense of humor, which often took the form of deep-cutting sarcasm, and his sense of the dramatic and appeal to the heart, helped make him a great—not merely a good—orator. "When he talks," a contemporary reporter said, "everybody listens. If anyone, after listening to some previous, ordinary speaker has started away—he comes back as soon as his ears catch the sonorous voice of Curley."

It was primarily this rich, fluid intonation, which he could modulate from a musical whisper to a booming cadence, that made him the Cicero of his era. He had a "double" voice. One was deep and compelling, the other lighter and striking by contrast. He was not born with that voice—with those voices. It had taken him years to refine the shantytown inflection of his youth. He learned that a voice from the stomach goes to the heart. He disciplined himself to stand, shoulders back and hands at his sides, and put his paunch to good use, one secret of his beautiful delivery. There was a strong push-up of air from the depths of the lungs.

It was this voice that quickened his flair for the dramatic. Curley could greet a bootblack and make the occasion into a warm, tender experience, but could also, when the spirit moved him, with a blunt tongue strike terror into the hearts of his adversaries. "He touches his hat to some obscure and too much forgotten woman with a gallantry which would discount even the South," wrote the political editor of the *Boston Evening Transcript*. "He dynamites an adversary so that the fragments cannot be gathered together in as few as twelve baskets." Curley could be kindly and comforting. He was known to give a shivering newsboy five dollars for his papers and send him home, and to remove his own overcoat and hand it to a vagrant.

But in a slugging, roughneck mood, he could be ruthless and vindictively cruel. "You don't know how vindictive Jim is," one enemy said. "If I were blind and holding a tin cup, he would spit in it."

Fitzgerald was often so overcome by his own eloquence he wept on the platform, whereas James Michael turned on the jet of emotion deliberately, and his "golden baritone, touched with a faint Oxonian accent and garnished with classical allusions," as John Hutcheson wrote in the *New York Herald Tribune,* underscored any effect he wanted to achieve. He agreed with Ralph de Toledano: "The only time to lose your temper in politics is when it's deliberate."

He once showed his verbal magic by enchanting an audience while standing with his back to them as he addressed his own portrait. Fitzgerald, like his colleagues, admired the full orchestration of the Curley music, but at times he hated the lyrics.

Part of the community considered Curley humane, charitable, and the keenest student of government who ever sat in the Mayor's chair. "He is probably the last of the 'great men' type in municipal politics," one veteran political observer said. Thousands of others despised him as a cunning, contriving, cold-blooded charlatan, wholly unreliable and unscrupulous. Daniel H. Coakley once called him over the radio a "bully, bravo thug—a moral and physical coward, a blackleg and a jailbird."

He could turn the savagery of any such attack to his own advantage, thanks to his sense of public psychology. "Curley," said Robert Bottomly of the Good Government Association, "is an unconscious psychologist who always knows when to do the right thing at the right time."

Like Fitzgerald, he could be a buffoon when he chose. One Boston cartoonist had him referring to Fitzgerald as his "vaudevillian nemesis." But Curley was more than a buffoon. He could easily have been another John Barrymore. Producer Jack Warner called him "the greatest actor I have ever seen," and tried to sign him to a movie contract.

"I think I'd rather stay in politics," Curley said. He liked to write his own scripts.

Warner, in making "The Forgotten Man," a campaign film for Franklin Delano Roosevelt, gave Curley the leading role. Curley lost his script on the way to the studio, and everyone but he went into a tizzy.

"I don't need a script," he said. "I can ad lib."

"No man can ad lib for eleven minutes," Warner said. "My best actors can't do that for two minutes."

Curley, without a note, talked for eleven minutes, citing complicated statistics.

"That was the quickest film I ever made," Warner said.

"Eleven minutes?" Curley said. "I could have talked for eleven days."

He had only a grammar school education, but in his thirties he spent two evenings a week in the home of another political tutor, Charles H. Innes. Here he read books and reported on them like a schoolboy. He also studied "law" under Innes, who, he said, controlled "the royal purple vote," as well as the "vote of the redlight district of the South End." Innes was part of Boston's invisible government with a knack for anticipating bar examination questions. Many of his "law" students became jurists and politicians whom he controlled. As late as 1931, the *Boston Post*'s political writer said: "I doubt if there is any single Republican in the state who has so much power today." He had lieutenants planted everywhere in the city who "could deliver the goods," and was once characterized as the leader of the "crooks who run City Hall." His office, which included a battery of telephones on his desk, was soundproof.

Curley had been born and raised in tenement rookeries in Roxbury's Galway version of Paddyville. From boyhood he was taught to work hard, hate the arrogant rich, and to fight for what he wanted. He was less charitable than Fitzgerald, who, while sharing many of his prejudices, conceded that the Pilgrims and Puritans had been the first daring settlers, and he was as willing to praise the heroes of Lexington and Bunker Hill as he was to laud the Fighting Irish Ninth Regiment which fought valiantly in the Civil War. More brutal and callous, Curley won favor with his followers by smiting hip and thigh what he called the "Black Baptists," the "Brahmins," and the "State Street Hi-Jackers," whom he accused of robbing the little man.

"No man who ever ran for public office in Boston has excited such chilling, uncomfortable dread in the hearts of the opposition," wrote a Boston editor.

In the clawing political jungle of Boston, Curley was the most murderous puncher, and his best friends could never guess how low he might hit if he thought circumstances warranted. Even when Curley lost an election, the victor wound up dazed, bruised, and aching all over mentally. He might conduct one campaign bristling with slander and violence. In another he would smother an opponent with compassion, and pity him into political oblivion. He demolished one candidate, after being the target of his insults, merely by waggling a finger and intoning, with an admonitory shake of his head, "Naughty, naughty, Thomas." He gravely pleaded with his Charlestown supporters in another campaign to cast a few votes for a Proper Bostonian opponent, and knew from the Rabelaisian laughter that he had every vote in the hall.

In his early career, Curley aped his revered John F. Fitzgerald in many ways, patterning his Tammany Club on the latter's Jefferson Club. In the riotous confines of Tammany, Curley learned many an artful dodge, including an agility in ducking spittoons. More important, he learned to attune himself to the mood of an audience. He practiced techniques, which became neat formulas to be put to good use later. In a twinkling he could change the mood of a hostile audience by assuming a dramatic pose and thundering: "Geese honk, hens cackle, pigs grunt and boors booh. Ladies and gentlemen, on the other hand, express their feelings by applauding."

Like the Jefferson Club, his Tammany organization was a social agency that served his Roxbury parishioners as an employment agency, court of domestic relations, and loan shop.

Like Fitzgerald, Curley was a master of the personal touch in politics. As an alderman, he got headlines and won sympathy for the poor by spearheading programs for better working conditions. He concentrated on such vote-winning issues as fire-proofing hospitals and demands for more and better health centers.

Fitzgerald was quick to recognize Curley as his chief rival. Fitz had fought ward bosses on his way up, but it was Curley who ended ward-boss sway by creating an even more personal political organization than Fitzgerald's, based on the hard-core voters in his own Ward 17.

The Fitzgerald charm had less appeal than the Curley hippodrome with voters who were swayed by the flimsiest of excuses for supporting candidates. One candidate based his platform on the premise that he had "socked the Governor of the Commonwealth on the chin" at opening day in Fenway Park, and the main campaign issue of his opponent became an indignant denial that he had "connected." One notorious candidate was "Cyclone" Bonelli who won local acclaim by his toothless boasts that he had the longest police record of any candidate in the contest. "All you have to do is go down to the Roxbury District Court and see for yourself," he told one street-corner crowd. His campaign literature was limited to a circular on which was printed: "What has Gleason done for Ward Nine?" The inside of the circular was blank. Dick Gleason reassured the same electorate by an ungrammatical account of how he had beaten up two police officers on successive nights.

Fitzgerald, while he never operated like Curley, who boasted of the violence of his goon squads, used muscular volunteers in some elections. One member of Curley's violence-escadrille, after downing a heckler with a punch, solicitously leaned over him. "Oh, my," he said, "I think the poor man has fainted."

"The Irish have many fine qualities," Fitzgerald said, referring specifically to Curley, "but they lack finesse."

It was this very lack of finesse, however, that helped Curley. On street corners, speaking from a wagon to a raffish crowd that normally included a number of boors with throwable items in their pocket, a booming voice that could rise above catcalls was an asset, and a high premium was put on audacity. Mere dignity was often the signal for some kind of assault. Running for office in Roxbury was one way of risking life and limb. One politician spoke from a brick wall one night and was about to jump down in wild panic when two shots interrupted his flow of rhetoric. He quickly recovered his composure when a friend told him there was nothing to worry about. A heckler had just broken a couple of electric bulbs, that was all.

He recovered his poise, waving his arms wildly. "Go ahead and shoot, you craven cowards!" he shouted. "I'm not afraid of your lousy bullets."

After his speech he was shown two bullet holes on the wall behind him. He went home.

Political tricks practiced in Roxbury are legendary. Michael J. Ward, a former State Senator and Chairman of the Boston School Committee, and often consulted over the years by such professionals as Jim Farley, Leverett Saltonstall, Henry Cabot Lodge, and Joe Kennedy, tells of John "Wimpy" Hare, a candidate for the House of Representatives from Ward 9. "He was running against my candidate," Mike said, "but didn't know it. When he came to me for advice, I told him his weak spot was Ward 4. 'On election day station yourself at the Ira Allen School and pass out cards. Be sure to smile at everyone. Remember, no political candidate is fully dressed until he wears a smile.' "

"Wimpy" later discovered that the Ira Allen School was not in his district.

To estrange the Negro vote from an opponent, Daniel Curley, Ward gave a Negro supporter a fat roll of dollar bills with a ten-dollar bill on the outside and sent him into Daniel's home ward. This character, who let it be known he was looking for ward workers (who were paid $10 to help at the polls) kept insulting constituents. "Why, you don't control five votes, you phony," he would say to a block leader. "But drop over by Dan Curley's house the night before election and I'll see what I can do."

When Dan Curley saw the big crowd in front of his house, he decamped via the rear door, realizing they were all after money. Then Mike Ward drove up in a truck and addressed the crowd from the tail-gate.

"I'm not backed by the blackguards like Innes and Bottomly the way my opponent is," he shouted. "I don't have any more money than you do, but if elected I'll see that you get a square deal." He turned to a stooge in the crowd. "What time is Dan Curley scheduled to speak?"

"He took it on the lam," the stooge said. "When he saw these good people he put his tail between his legs and ran off as if they were lepers."

Many of Mike Ward's supporters were grateful for baskets of fruit he sent them from S. S. Pierce & Co. It was simple. Mike phoned in the order and asked that the bill be sent to him, giving the name of some affluent Republican opponent who, if he refused to honor the bill, lost a vote.

When Fitzgerald was elected Mayor in 1910, Curley was elected to the nine-man Council. In 1911, as part of the Strategy Board's plan, he ran for Congress against William McNary of South Boston and Joseph

O'Connell of Dorchester. "Joe O'Connell and Bill McNary were older and more experienced than I," wrote Curley in his autobiography, "and Mayor John F. Fitzgerald, who was supposed to be neutral, was passing the word around for O'Connell. I went into his office at City Hall one day and told him I'd knock his block off unless he came out publicly and declared his neutrality.

"Honey Fitz was most obliging in the matter."

Because of their squabbles over patronage, Curley and Fitzgerald were feuding at this time. Curley had been irked when Honey Fitz told reporters that O'Connell would whip both Curley and McNary.

Forced to split the Irish vote, Curley used another trick he had learned from Fitzgerald. Discovering that the Galway men outnumbered Corkies by more than two to one in South Boston, where he especially needed votes because of O'Connell's popularity in that area, Curley posed one question at every rally, after saying his ancestors came from County Galway.

"Who is the better man—one from Cork or one from Galway?"

The famed white-bearded gentleman with a bronze button in his lapel made his debut in this campaign. With old-world courtliness, he would rise at a Curley rally, and raising his cane for silence, enumerate the many kindnesses of James Michael Curley to members of the Grand Army of the Republic. A man of mystery who probably never got closer to the Confederate lines than South Boston, he added a dignified fillip to the showmanship of the many rallies at which he appeared, always rising at the proper psychological moment.

At one South Boston rally, McNary, threatened by a mob who mounted the platform, jumped up and grabbed a chandelier, clinging on tenaciously as goons tugged at his dangling legs. They pulled and pulled until the chandelier came out by the "roots," and when Bill was grounded, the chandelier landed on top of him.

McNary had harped on Curley's dishonesty. Curley dressed up a loafer in a rubber coat and hood, gave him an old lantern and told him to walk around South Boston with a sign pinned on his back: "I am Diogenes seeking the honest man, McNary." McNary was the butt of jokes during the rest of the campaign.

Curley also used the "little man" technique which Fitzgerald had taught him. On one occasion his opponent had bought up most of the available billboard space, and put up a McNary advertisement: SEND A BIG MAN TO DO A BIG JOB, and an O'Connell eulogy: ABLE, ACTIVE AND AGGRESSIVE.

Curley distributed small window sheets and attached a streamer to their billboard posters that proclaimed: ELECT A HUMBLE MAN, JAMES MICHAEL CURLEY.

After he won the election, and Speaker Champ Clark appointed him the Democratic "whip" of the House, he had a wider forum from which to attack old enemies. In one speech, he said the Boston Tea Party, traditionally considered a noble gesture by the Massachusetts aristocracy, was actually a "beer party." The tea-dumping plan, he added, was organized at Hancock's Tavern, which was owned by the Irish John Duggan, by patriots who met there to down their flip. This speech to his delight produced lively reactions from both "beer-partyites" and "tea-partyites," and Curley fanned the fire by saying John Hancock was of Irish descent.

He was reelected in 1912, and Mayor Fitzgerald hoped he would acquire a taste for Washington society. But during his second Congressional term, Curley found his thoughts wandering back again to the lush political environment of Boston, just as Fitzgerald's had more than a decade earlier.

And this, of course, posed a major problem for Honey Fitz.

CHAPTER 11

Two Vaudevillians on One Stage

"I have never been afraid to make the bold move. I think that
is why my life has been so much of an adventure."

—JAMES MICHAEL CURLEY

T HE STRATEGY BOARD had originally intended that Mayor Fitzgerald
would leave City Hall at the end of his second term to make way for
Curley, but His Honor insisted on running for a third time, and the
other members of the Big Four finally fell in line.

Curley fumed, yet he was riding high. Newspaper cartoonists portrayed
him on page one as a fearless David throwing rocks labeled "Ward 17
Control" and "Ward 17 Vote" at ten Democratic city bosses, including
the Mayor Makers. Curley made news when he told reporters about the
tinkle of hush money in aldermanic chambers and the financial sleight-of-
hand practiced by certain politicians. The inference was that he spurned
such boodle.

By 1912, he was openly hostile to Fitzgerald. "You are an old man,"
he told him. "Get your slippers and pipe and stretch out in your hammock
and read the *Ladies' Home Journal.*"

In that year, Mayor Fitzgerald gave a dinner for the City Council in
Room 8 of the Quincy House. Curley's presence did not shock him, for
the Roxbury politician was by this time another notable, uninvited guest.

It was Curley's turn to speak. "I am a candidate for Mayor in 1914,"
he said. "I shall run on a platform drawn up by the Finance Commission
and approved by Laurence Minot. I would like to announce in this connection also, that Robert J. Bottomly of the Good Government Association is to be my campaign manager."

Boston's City Councilors enjoyed the joke, knowing Curley was teasing when he boosted the Commission, sarcastic when he mentioned Minot, and joshing when he referred to Bottomly, the Phi Beta Kappa from Amherst College who figured it was always open season as far as Fitzgerald and Curley were concerned.

Came December 1912. The *Boston Post* reported: "The Roxbury Congressman and the Mayor have been developing a political coolness for some time. Their relations now are said to be such that a wide open break is regarded as likely to occur at any moment." The feud was blossoming into an entertaining comedy.

Mayor Fitzgerald, now convinced that Curley was the potential successor to himself as leader of Boston politics, had been encouraged earlier in 1912, when Curley told the press: "I will not be a candidate for the office of mayor if Mayor Fitzgerald will be a candidate for reelection."

Curley was conscious of his growing strength. "I fear no one," he told the Bridgetenders Union. "I stand by my record and reputation that I gained during the time I have been in public life."

Despite his statement at the Quincy House, Curley was not considered a serious candidate as late as mid-October of 1913.

During that year, according to Curley, he had often conferred with the Mayor, reminding him of the valuable aid he had given him against Storrow, when he jilted a bankroll to support him. Fitzgerald, he said, had agreed to back him before he reneged on his promise. In Curley's version of the interchange, Fitzgerald had told him that since he was eleven years younger, he could look forward to tenure at City Hall later. He further said that William Cardinal O'Connell sent for him and asked him to withdraw his candidacy in favor of the incumbent, and when he told His Eminence that he had promised his constituency he would run, he was asked what a word in politics meant.

"I consider a word in politics as sacred as a word in religion," I answered, "and he was not altogether pleased. This is the only personal altercation I ever had with the Cardinal, but I must admit that he never became one of my ardent supporters." (Curley found it expedient never to openly defy the Cardinal, unlike Martin Lomasney, who said when told the Cardinal disapproved of an action of his: "Tell His Eminence to mind his own business.")

There is a more likely version of this incident. Cardinal O'Connell was, by this time, disgusted with Curley's chicanery and three-ring-circus antics, for O'Connell wanted the emergent Irish recognized as respectable citizens. The Cardinal, whose parents had worked at looms in a Lowell textile mill, had himself come from a humble background, but he was rapidly gaining stature as one of the most respected leaders in New England.

As Archbishop of Boston and dean of the American Hierarchy, he was a power in the community and the political life of Boston. He was not only the spiritual leader of New England, but a powerful political figure whose wish usually became a command in the General Court of Massachusetts. Just as Cardinal Spellman's residence in New York City was later known as "the Power House," Cardinal O'Connell was referred to by state legislators as "Number One." He kept an eye on Boston politics from the moment he succeeded Archbishop John J. Williams, who had also won the respect of Yankees and Catholics alike. When Archbishop Williams became too ill to continue his heavy schedule, Bishop O'Connell had been transferred from Portland, Maine, to Boston as Coadjutor Archbishop. Williams died a year later and O'Connell succeeded him, becoming a Cardinal in 1911.

In 1908, the prelate had said: "Great dangers confront our Catholic men in public as well as in private life. What good is it for us to proclaim from the housetops that we are Catholics when our lives are a disgrace?"

It is true that Curley went to see Cardinal O'Connell. But, according to Edmund L. Dolan, later to become a secretary and colleague of Curley in matters in which larceny was involved, the encounter was quite different from Curley's autobiographical version. Dolan wrote: "Learning that Fitzgerald was spreading word that the Cardinal wanted him, not Curley, to run for Mayor, Curley started off to see His Eminence to ask for the facts. On his return, Mr. Curley related with rueful amusement that the Cardinal had given him the most beautiful dressing down, and had dismissed him with the warning: 'Don't ever again put your foot inside this door on a political mission.' "

Nor did the Cardinal's opinion of Curley mellow over the years. Finding themselves passengers on a boat bound for Nassau, Curley told reporters it was "an honor" to travel on the same ship as His Eminence. The reporters found the Cardinal reading in his stateroom as he sipped a glass of port. "I seem to have heard of him," he said curtly when they mentioned that Curley was aboard.

"If you do any business with that gang, I'll disown you," the Cardinal reportedly told a member of his family. He meant the Curley gang. And if there is any doubt about his opinion of the man, it can be dispelled by a remark he made at a meeting of the board of trustees of the Boston Public Library, when Curley's request to have his bust mounted in the main reading room was discussed.

His Eminence, noted for wry humor, settled the issue: "Is there any place in the cellar where we can put this abomination?" he asked.

The Cardinal, who often voted Republican, maintained his full prestige until his death. When a big insurance company in Boston forgot to put its American Flag at half mast on the day he died, it was so swamped with telephone calls that it stayed closed on the day of the prelate's funeral, as a belated mark of respect.

That was the kind of opposition Curley faced. The cards seemed stacked against his bid for the mayoralty. Joseph A. Maynard, chairman of the Democratic City Committee, was a Fitzgerald booster, and he brought Martin Lomasney into line. Most of the political leaders of Boston were against him, including the Strategy Board. The executive branch of the Republican City Committee vetoed him by twenty-four votes to two; the Democratic Committee twenty-five to one. "They told me I hadn't a chance," Curley said, referring to the Democratic committee. "I countered by classifying them as empty eggshells, and going over their heads to the people."

He spurned ward-boss support so he would owe no patronage. "There were those who rejoiced at first," he wrote in his autobiography, "sure that I was committing political suicide. Instead of soliciting their support, I warned them that when I became mayor I would put an abrupt end to ward bossism in the Athens of America." Actually, by this time this parochial form of social service had run its course, although ward bosses continued to splinter the Democratic party in Boston.

Curley counted on his mass appeal and the repute earned while he had toured New England as campaign manager for Presidential aspirant Champ Clark while in Congress. The migration of thousands of his upper middle class enemies from Boston to Cambridge, Dedham, Melrose, Newton and Brookline also conspired in his favor. The few Brahmins who still lived on Beacon Hill had negligible political power.

In November 1913, Curley announced that he would run, even if Honey Fitz sought reelection. Not until the latter part of the month did Fitzgerald formally announce his candidacy, adding that he would recall himself after two years. On the following day, Curley was quoted by the *Boston Post*: "Mr. Fitzgerald wants the same licking that Governor Foss received, and he will get it." Foss had lost his last bid for reelection.

As Curley stepped up his attack, ward bosses fretted, for as an alderman Curley had already forcibly shown that he would not hesitate to accuse them of graft or worse, nor would he stop short of making his charges more personal. For Curley, it was fish or cut bait: destroy all ward bossism or be destroyed.

During the early skirmishing, a South End flophouse was swept by a fire that took twenty-eight lives. One ugly rumor that came from a Curley supporter was that one victim was a brother of the Mayor—in the Arcadia flophouse "drying out." As usual, the false charge was more sensational than its refutation.

In the wake of the public's horror, Mayor Fitzgerald made a personal inspection of other crowded lodging houses in the area. On December 4, overcome by the nauseating odors and coal gas in the dingy Union lodging house in the South End, he swooned and fell headlong down a flight of stairs. He had been working night and day since the Arcadia (called by Curley "a 'scratch-house,' one of the rescue missions in the Skid Row section"), fire two nights before, and in his exhausted condition, the foul air and coal gas were too much for him. When Fitzgerald was hospitalized, the *Boston Post* suggested that the other candidates wait until he recovered before taking the stump again.

"I have been asked to stop campaigning because one of my opponents is ill," Curley answered. "It would be just as reasonable for Jordan Marsh to ask Filene's to close its store because the owner of Jordan's has a bellyache."

Instead of withdrawing, Curley turned his attack on the city officials who had allowed such conditions to exist, "where human derelicts were allowed to be roasted to death." Actually, the State Legislature in 1911 had defeated Mayor Fitzgerald's Fire Hazard bill, and he had made further vain appeals for better fire laws. He had demanded a law compelling the installation of hand fire extinguishers in certain types of buildings.

Under the withering Curley attack, which was also of a more personal nature, Fitzgerald withdrew from the race to the disgust of Martin Lomasney, who accused him of "quitting cold." Curley forced so many out of this contest that there was a little wheeze about a mythical voter who said: "Well, at first I thought I'd support my friend Mr. Smith, but he got out. Then I thought of John R. Murphy, but he got out, too. I was getting a bit discouraged when I remembered how much I like Jack Keliher, but he got out, also. After that, there was nothing to it. I said to myself, I'll support a man who can't get out." This man was convict Jesse Pomeroy, a lifer kept in a cell within a cell at the State Prison.

In some mysterious way, Curley had forced John R. Murphy out of the race. "If that distinguished gentleman from Charlestown," he said in reference to Murphy, "who committed political assassination on Patrick A. Collins, becomes a candidate for Mayor, and Fitzgerald is not, I welcome nothing better than giving him the best licking he ever got. And if John A. Keliher, general of the mud batteries in the last mayoralty campaign, is a candidate, I will lick both."

On the final day for withdrawals, according to Murphy's campaign manager, he met Curley in front of City Hall and told him that many of the signatures on the Curley petition were fraudulent and that he would be disqualified.

"By five o'clock this afternoon Murphy will withdraw and Governor Walsh will name him to the Finance Commission," Curley said.

Francis A. McLaughlin, the campaign manager who tells this story, said he rushed over to Murphy's office. "I just met Curley, and he told me a fantastic tale," McLaughlin said. "He said you were going to withdraw this afternoon."

"Frankie," said Murphy, "you and the boys can go out and bet every bottom dollar that I will stay in this contest until the votes are counted. Nothing will take me out."

"Around quarter past five that afternoon I received a wire from Murphy," McLaughlin recalls. "It read: 'Regret to announce owing to multiplicity of candidates and difficulty of raising funds am retiring.' "

McLaughlin never learned the exact reason for his eleventh hour withdrawal.

Martin Lomasney, at the last minute, switched to Curley. "I told reporters he waited until the fire was out before he arrived with his water bucket," Curley sneered. Lomasney took a different view. "I've declared for Jim, and it will put him over."

Fitzgerald joined the Strategy Board, which, for once, sided with the GGA in their support of Thomas J. Kenny, a City Councilman and a budget expert who had served on the School Committee and had practiced law. His speeches sounded like a treasurer's report as he cited forgeries of signatures and other irregularities in connection with Curley's nominating papers and conduct of municipal affairs.

Curley accused him of being backed by Brahmins, linked him to the wealthiest bankers, and added that he was "controlled entirely by the New Haven Railroad. . . . I invite the opposition of all corrupt ward leaders who have allied themselves with the downtown realty pirates," he told crowds, asking "every God-fearing citizen to save Boston from the banks and railroads."

Crowds at Curley's indoor rallies and outdoor meetings on freezing nights during the winter of 1913-1914 broke records for Boston. They were lured by his singers and entertainment acts and public theatre that included Punch and Judy routines. At one rally his followers were so eager to get into a school house where Curley was performing that they knocked down an iron fence. His supporters, meanwhile, stole rallies from the opposition by mounting a crate or barrel in the middle of an opponent's speech and carrying on a competitive discussion. When a Curley goon squad tried to break up a rally at Faneuil Hall, curses filled the air, and stones flew.

"Do you want this kind of man for Mayor?" the *Boston Post* asked next day.

On the platform, to laugh Kenny out of court, Curley acted out skits, and even before he arrived to speak, there was comedy. One night at Faneuil Hall a drunk walked shakily onto the platform and shouted: "Funnel Hull is full, Funnel Hull is full!"

"And so is Michael Dougherty," someone yelled.

Curley was about to address a capacity crowd when Honey Fitz, leading his Royal Rooters, paraded by in a high hat. Just as his arch enemy rose to speak, Fitzgerald raised his baton, started up the band and drowned out the oration. The crowd heard *Tessie,* not Curley.

Honey Fitz was a rabid baseball fan who occasionally accompanied the Boston Red Sox on their road trips. He and Mrs. Fitzgerald stopped at a New York hotel during one series between the Red Sox and Yankees. Melville Webb, a *Boston Globe* sportswriter who was one of the most enthusiastic Royal Rooters, was fond of practical jokes. When he saw in a New York newspaper a photograph of Mayor Fitzgerald with his arm around the shoulders of a beautiful unknown young lady, he sealed the picture in an envelope and put it in Fitzgerald's mail box. The photo, he felt, would shock Mrs. Fitzgerald if she chanced to see it first. "A couple of days later," Webb explained, "I got a letter from Mr. and Mrs. Fitzgerald thanking me for leaving the picture of their daughter, one of the best they had ever seen." Webb never revealed whether the daughter was Rose, Agnes, or Eunice.

Mayor-Elect Curley deliberately irked Back Bay and Beacon Hill residents by threatening to sell the Public Garden to pay the large debt left by Mayor Fitzgerald. His flamboyance also raised eyebrows. He borrowed officers from the Ninth Regiment, wearing glittering gold braid, to serve as his "staff." When the regiment left for the Mexican Border, Curley gave his staff officers wristwatches, and when the regiment returned he had commemorative "Mexican Border Service" medals struck off for the entire Second Brigade, including the Fifth, Eighth and Ninth Regiments.

A few years later, when the United States entered World War I and Marshal Joffre came to Boston to review local troops, Mayor Curley embarrassed Colonel Edward Logan of the Ninth Regiment by providing truck-loads of green ferns to be distributed to the troops to wear in their hats as a sign they were Irish. Curley had made no arrangements with

Logan, who was forced by Uniform Regulations to prohibit the wearing of the green.

In the closing days of the campaign, Fitzgerald and Pat Kennedy joined Lomasney's switch to Curley, the story went, but Honey Fitz later said he remained neutral, after supporting Kenny during the first part of the contest. Lomasney gave his flock cards with a cross indicating a vote for Curley, whom he supported only because he wanted to be on the side of a winner. His brother Joseph, who was strong for Curley, had told him of a tremendous turnout at a Curley rally in Symphony Hall. "Curley will win by twenty or twenty-five thousand votes," he added. "You better go along or you'll be backing a loser."

When Curley won by a plurality of only 5720, Lomasney was furious, feeling he could have beaten him by staying with Kenny. Actually, he couldn't be blamed for feeling the tide was running in favor of Curley in the closing hours. The climax of the campaign was a mass meeting held in Mechanics Building—the most crowded meeting in the political history of Boston. Curley had to climb a ladder and enter the hall through a window to greet his loyal subjects.

Curley had survived the most vicious of attacks. Then, strangely, on the eve of election he openly accused Fitzgerald of treachery, and there were signs of a complete break when they met in the barbershop of Young's Hotel after the polls closed. Honey Fitz, who was in a chair getting shaved when Curley came in, extended his hand.

"Come on over, Jim," he said. "I want to speak to you."

Curley drew away. "No, John, I don't care to."

Fitzgerald tried to sit up. "You've got me wrong, Jim."

"No, John, I have you dead right. You are the last man in the world who ought to desert me." He turned and left, refusing to return, until Fitzgerald had departed.

When told their feud was hurting them both, Honey Fitz said: "I want to make up with him, but he won't make up with me."

Later on the same night of the barbershop incident, Curley conceded at Faneuil Hall that his victory was "in a large measure typical of the victories achieved in the past by the fathers of the Republic, the men who made possible Faneuil Hall." And despite "the forces inimical to the welfare of the community that were arrayed against him," he promised he would be Mayor "for the entire people of Boston, responsible not merely to the 40,000 who elected him, but to the 700,000 Bostonians."

It sounded like the speech Honey Fitz made the first time he was elected Mayor.

The Mayor-Elect immediately served notice that he had no respect for

tradition. He refused to call at City Hall before the inauguration ceremony, as was customary. Normally the two mayors would lead a march
of all department heads, executives, secretaries, and invited guests to the
aldermanic chamber, where the oath of office was given. Curley said he
would enter City Hall as Mayor, so the ceremony was held in Tremont
Temple, in the presence of 2500 spectators.

Honey Fitz was sitting on the platform a few feet from Curley when
Curley lashed out at his predecessor for leaving him a treasury that was
down to a petty cash level. Under the shots of Curley, Fitzgerald's face
twitched and reddened. Curley had set the tone when they met on the
platform a few minutes earlier, coldly staring away from Honey Fitz as
they shook hands. Later that day Honey Fitz was interviewed by the press.

"In political circles," he said, "the feeling is that a battle to the [politi-
cal] death is on between this pair of chieftains."

Immediately following the inaugural ceremony, a police escort pulled
the new Mayor through crowded streets as he walked to City Hall where
he signed the oath book, called for the City Clerk and dictated a letter
firing the building commissioner, whom he had violently attacked because
of the Arcadia fire, holding him responsible for the lives lost. General
Charles Cole had been Fitzgerald's fire commissioner.

"In anticipation," said Curley, "General Cole brought along his resignation on his first official visit, and I appointed Chief John Grady in his
place. Charles Logue, Fitzgerald's man Friday, also 'anticipated' I would
want his scalp. Correctly, too. He went out."

It was a gray day for six hundred city employees and their families
when Curley took office. Seeming to know who his enemies were, he
fired them or demoted them to a pick-and-shovel detail. A few Kenny
adherents who had been working in the tropical environs of the Franklin
Park Zoo and the City Point Aquarium were sent to the cold quarters of
pumping stations. Curley also dropped all Fitzgerald contractors and replaced female secretaries at City Hall with male. Women could not vote.

"After I was elected," he said later, "Fitzgerald occasionally told me
off in his paper. Every time he did I would drop a friend of his from the
city payroll and substitute an equally competent citizen who had the
additional advantage of being a friend of mine. John F. had left in office
many men who were hostile to me. Not desiring to be ambushed in my
own camp, I removed them, and to trim down municipal expenditure, I
fired all superfluous payroll patriots and did not fill unnecessary jobs
vacated by death."

Where was that bigger, better and busier Boston? he asked. There were few municipal improvements to account for the empty treasury, he charged, "and the city was in desperate need for better school, hospital, transportation and recreational facilities." When he raised assessments, the bankers and industrialists who had at first lauded him, loudly protested, as did the ward bosses, who were stripped of their power.

Honey Fitz, he further charged, had left him a dole system. "I took people off welfare rolls and restored their self-respect by providing them with jobs, and while reducing the ranks of the unemployed, I launched a program of public works that had been so shamefully neglected by my predecessors in office. I extended tunnel and transit systems, expanded hospital facilities, replaced slum sections with parks and playgrounds and filled in swampy lowlands to provide beaches for the poor. . . . "

Honey Fitz was irked. "He is the most thoroughly selfish, conceited and cold-blooded character who has occupied public office in this country in the present generation," he wrote in *The Republic*. "When discharging men at City Hall, it was not enough to separate them from the payroll, but he sent special delivery letters to their homes after hours, so that the first news of the discharge would be known to the family. Chief John Mullen of the Fire Department was a notable example. Curley discharged this Fire Chief without a moment's notice, though he was America's foremost fire fighter at the time, and the chief, broken in heart and in mind, gradually went to pieces, winding up his days in a sanitarium in which he died years before his time by reason of the inhuman conduct of this man."

Reform groups dourly realized the significance of Curley's election, as did the ward bosses, for it ended the power of every boss in Boston except Martin Lomasney, whose tight little czardom remained intact. Honey Fitz and Pat Kennedy could no longer wield power as Mayor Makers. There was now a Big One to replace the Big Four. For the first time, Boston had one boss who had consolidated his power by handing out jobs and making himself personally accessible to everyone from dowager to ragtag and bobtail. Before he captured the City Hall Klondike, voters had received favors from ward bosses who worked through City Hall. Curley simply invited everyone to see him personally, and as many as 50,000 persons a year did so. A ward boss without favors to hand out was a clock without hands.

This puckered Honey Fitz, too. "His first move, even before taking oath," he said, "was a notice to ward committee leaders that they would be ostracized when he was Mayor." No language was too virulent to characterize them; they were the dregs of the universe, to hear him tell it.

"He behaved in similar manner toward those who were running the

State organization. There was no attempt at cooperation except a hypo-critical one with the G.G.A. to cover a secret business partnership. He let everybody understand that he was Mayor for four years, and those who did not show a disposition to stand for the Curley way of doing things at City Hall must be put out of business. He was too crude to under-stand that under the present city charter the best way to promote his party's welfare was by the conduct of the city's business in an honest and progressive spirit that would unite rather than divide the citizenship. One method employed by him was to serve notice on all those who wished the presence of the Mayor at any function, that nobody whose views crossed with his should be invited. He publicly gave notice that former Mayor Fitzgerald should be tabooed wherever he was expected."

The vendetta provided endless themes for editorial writers and cartoon-ists. One cartoon, captioned "The Curley-Fitz Feud Is Now On," showed the Mayor mounting a rostrum at a Democratic rally. "I see my vaude-villian nemesis has spouted here," he says. The second panel shows him walking off the platform in a huff. "I absolutely refuse to speak on the same spot as Fitzgerald," he remarks.

But Fitzgerald had his friends. "The Mayor is going out of public office," said Governor David I. Walsh. "He should have no regrets. He has earned contentment, peace, and happiness, which justly belong to him."

When Curley was not on his mind, Honey Fitz was as bouncy and self-contained as ever. "I take great satisfaction in what I have accomplished," he said, "and I expect greater things from myself, for I will not have to devote my time to the petty affairs of the Mayor's office, but will have an opportunity to range into the higher realms of business activity on larger lines of thought. I might take this occasion to say that I am deeply grate-ful to every citizen of Boston for the aid they have rendered me personally and the city. It gives me great satisfaction to be able to retire from the mayor's chair with so many expressions of good will as I have received in the past few days."

Shortly after leaving City Hall he sat down at the piano in the Boston City Club, and as the accompanist played the opening chords of "Sweet Adeline," he was smiling. "Mayors may come and mayors may go," he said, "but the municipal song will go on forever. We will now have the treat of the evening."

Whereupon Honey Fitz warbled his ballad.

The higher realms of business activity had hidden shoals, he discovered. In the summer of 1914, Honey Fitz bought the Oak Hill Clothing Company, against the advice of friends who warned that the store was flanked by Vorenberg's, which sold cheaper clothes, and by Leopold Morse, which sold better merchandise. Six months later the "John F. Fitzgerald Clothing Company" was taken over by the Kennedy Company, and Honey Fitz became president of the New England Securities Company, a loose assignment that did not interrupt his winter vacations in Palm Beach. Later he had desk-room with Laidlaw & Company on Franklin Street.

Just before his ill-advised clothing venture, he had another falling out with Mayor Curley at a spring gambol of the Boston Chamber of Commerce. Fitzgerald, impersonating Corporation Counsel John A. Sullivan, referred to the latter as the "Mayor de facto," whereupon Curley, who had been sitting next to J. Randolph Coolidge, president of the Chamber, rose and left, slamming the door behind him. It was their most open break.

After Fitzgerald sold the Oak Hill Company, Curley needled his business acumen. With a serene disregard of chronology, the Mayor chided his predecessor's claim of having created a bigger, better and busier Boston, and although his speech varied and was more inaccurate at one time than another, the gist of it was usually the same: "Here," he would tell assemblies, "was an illustrious establishment, which had endured the vicissitudes of the War of the Rebellion and the Panic of 1873—which with flying colors had survived the rigors of the Spanish-American War and the post-war depression. . . . And then, my friends, what happened to this glorious establishment? Within a few short months, this renowned enterprise was run into the ground—yes, completely ruined—by this same John F. Fitzgerald who dares speak of a bigger and better Boston. . . ."

One of many projected 1914 ventures was the purchase of the Boston Red Sox. But Honey Fitz gave up the idea of forming a syndicate to negotiate the transaction when Ben Johnson, president of the American League, turned thumbs down.

Meanwhile, Honey Fitz was studying the political picture. James A. Gallivan had replaced Curley in Congress, and Andrew J. Peters, who resigned his congressional seat to become Assistant Secretary of the Treasury under President Wilson, was replaced by George Holden Tinkham. Boston lost a third congressman when William F. Murray resigned to become postmaster and Peter Tague took his place.

Tague was another enemy Fitzgerald would meet in a narrow alley.

CHAPTER 12

Shamrock Turned Purple

"They get along like a couple of strange lions."

—*The* Boston Post, *referring to Fitzgerald and Curley*

THE enmity between Curley and Fitzgerald became a large-scale municipal diversion.

From his first moment in City Hall, the new Mayor went out of his way to make his predecessor the butt of ridicule. Two monuments of the Fitzgerald regime were the City Hall Annex, first occupied in 1914, and the newly installed high pressure water system. In testing the pressurized hydrants, Curley's fire officials turned them on full blast to raise a water screen around the polished new annex. They worked superbly. Four stories were flooded, and books and municipal documents floated down corridors. The flood did thousands of dollars' worth of damage. Everyone laughed when Mayor Curley called the annex a "mausoleum" —everyone, that is, but Honey Fitz.

Curley was at first hailed as a reform mayor, for he had expressed an interest in municipal economy and had made a political gesture in asking the distinguished Louis D. Brandeis to be City Auditor, a post Brandeis rejected. Curley had also assured citizens that he would cut expenses, clean out City Hall, discharge loafers, and get a full day's work from the goldbrickers on the city payroll.

Incensed by his criticism, Honey Fitz used his weekly to inveigh against Curley's tie-up with Marks Angell, president of the Roxbury Iron and Metal Company, who was given city contracts when buildings were to be razed or junk was to be turned into cash.

Although Curley tried to disavow Angell, referring to him as "a crony of Martin Lomasney," he had intimate dealings with him. One of his first acts in City Hall was to motorize the fire department, which entailed auctioning off horse-drawn fire engines and other obsolete equipment. Marks Angell bought all this and resold it to towns in the Commonwealth at substantial profit. Trying to make light of the charge that he had shared in the boodle, Curley called the GGA and Finance Commission sleuths "prevaricating Peeping Toms."

When Curley moved from Roxbury to more fashionable Jamaica Plain, Angell again entered the picture. Curley had built a seventeen-room neo-Georgian mansion on Jamaicaway which, wrote Francis Russell in *Heritage* Magazine, "was both a landmark of the rise of the immigrant Irish and a nose-thumbing in the direction of Beacon Hill." The move from Roxbury to Jamaica Plain became a *cause célèbre*.

In February 1915, the *Boston Post* noted that "Curley, actuated by the Post's 'Build Now' Movement, had secured an ideal site overlooking Jamaica Pond." The headline read:

MAYOR TO BUILD BEAUTIFUL
MANSION IN JAMAICA PLAIN

All the details came under a merciless spotlight. The red-brick Dutch colonial, which cost $27,600, had a massive, ornate, hand-carved mahogany stairway which Marks Angell had bought at an auction of the $200,000 showplace built by millionaire oil king Henry H. Rogers at Fairhaven, Massachusetts. Rogers had died in 1909, and a few years later a highway was projected which, according to Curley, was "on a line passing through the drawing room, which inclined its owners to believe that it would be less suitable for normal habitation." Fireplaces of Italian marble had also been acquired from the Fairhaven home, along with a crystal chandelier, with delicately carved Irish Waterford glass hung on silver chains, for the reception hall. Also in the mansion were gold-plated electric fixtures and mahogany china closets.

Probes were launched, and guesses at Curley's investment were in wild disagreement. The GGA and the Finance Commission, of which John R. Murphy was chairman, asked how a Mayor who received a salary of $10,000 a year as Mayor, and $7500 as Congressman, could build a $35,000 house on a lot costing $15,600. In *The Republic,* Honey Fitz asked how Curley could build a $60,000 house on a $15,000 lot on the same salary.

"A few years ago," he wrote, "James M. Curley was working as a corporation inspector for $3 a day. The year before he was elected Mayor, he paid nothing but a poll tax. Now he has a beautiful home on the Jamaicaway, with furnishings from the home of Henry H. Rogers, who died worth $100,000,000. [Mark Twain, when asked whether Rogers' money was "tainted," said, "It's twice tainted. 'Tain't yours and 'tain't mine."] He recently disposed of a fine summer residence at Hull, bought since he became Mayor."

"It did not occur to him," Curley recalled, ". . . that I disposed of one residence so I could purchase another." He added that Fitzgerald, after retiring from City Hall, "spent most of his time on his estate in Hull, and he owned another fine house in Concord." *The New York Times* had a comment: "Honey lives in a palace and is a plutocrat, according to the Spartan Curley." The Mayor's charge was prompted by Fitzgerald's comments about the "house with the shamrock shutters," known in political circles as "the house that junk built."

Curley had cleverly named an old enemy, ex-Congressman John A. Sullivan, his Corporation Counsel. Sullivan, who had been chairman of the Finance Commission, had a ready answer whenever a crushing report was issued on Curley's activities. The newspaper duels between the Finance Commission and the City Law Department produced some fiery literature.

Honey Fitz had challenged Curley and Sullivan to debate on the finances of Boston, and he and Curley had exchanged Shakespearean insults. Curley quoted *King John* in damaging context, and accused Fitzgerald of using city money to enrich his family. He charged that the city had bought land owned by Fitzgerald at padded figures. Sullivan finally sickened of the controversy, and was about to resign when Curley told the press: "Mr. Sullivan has joined hands with this Commission to frame the Mayor of Boston. He will not have the opportunity to resign. He is fired."

Sullivan, a gentleman of high integrity who later received an honorary degree from Harvard, had been annoyed by Curley's double talk in connection with money spent for his palatial home.

The Fitzgerald-Curley feud went beyond this episode. In January, 1915, Thomas Kenny, in a move calculated to embarrass Curley, invited Fitzgerald to a meeting of the City Council. There was such a hubbub in the council chamber that Curley's secretaries rushed out to see what was going on. Honey Fitz, in the presence of reporters, had charged that Curley had not put to use a sum between $500,000 and a million dollars that had been earmarked for public improvements. He denounced the new administration so eloquently that one of the scribes described his performance as "the most spectacular feat of Fitzgerald's career."

Where were the promised public improvements? Fitzgerald asked. "Conversation doesn't fill empty stomachs, and, gentlemen, I wish to state to you that I am glad I have not the present situation on my conscience." He turned to the reporters and councilors. "And now, boys, all join me in 'Tipperary.' "

Fitzgerald's aim was to keep on the front pages against the day of his next bid for public office. A month after this council blast, he was introduced to a large gathering in Lowell as "the most popular citizen in Massachusetts." He received additional publicity when Notre Dame University gave him an honorary Doctor of Laws degree at Commencement exercises in 1915. Thenceforth, to many, he was "Dr. Fitzgerald."

But the best way to tap the fount of acclaim was to hammer at Mayor Curley. Fitzgerald accused him of entering into "secret partnerships which involve the honor of the Mayor's office. Give up those secret partnerships. If you do," he wrote in his weekly, "I will be your strongest supporter." Some of his charges were crushing, and Boston newspapers printed them. "It fills the average citizen with disgust to read what His Honor says about conducting an honest administration when he realizes that everything is held up when possible. Insurance, banking, plumbing, junk, automobile supplies and other lines of business drain into a common treasury. No such barefaced exhibition of sordidness has been exhibited in the government of any other city in the world, and the facts are obtainable to prove the above, the Mayor knows it."

The *Boston Post* had a comment. "What chance has Curley when Fitzgerald has his whole family helping him? Look at Curley and Fitzgerald, once the best of friends, but now forever scrapping. They get along like a couple of strange lions. I guess one is sore because the other gets more space in the papers. Can't beat Fitz for getting on page one, top of column. When we thought he had gone into seclusion there comes a journalistic bombshell in the form of a report that he had ridden a goat."

In an October rally, 1915, for David I. Walsh in Tremont Temple, Fitzgerald and Curley found themselves on the same platform for the first time in a year. Curley was presiding when Congressman Gallivan rose and demanded "three cheers for Fitz." Curley took over.

"I would remind Congressman Gallivan that one chairman of this meeting is sufficient." When Francis Daly, his business partner who was sitting near him, saw that Curley was about to handle Gallivan roughly, he whispered: "Keep steady, Jim. Don't lose your head." Curley lowered his voice and turned to the audience. "Shakespeare's *Hamlet* without the melancholy Dane would not be *Hamlet* any more than a Democratic campaign without former Mayor Fitzgerald would be a Democratic campaign." In the burst of applause, Honey Fitz called out to his enemy: "Attaboy, Jim!"

In the mid-term city election in November, 1915, the GGA and other Curley enemies tried to recall him.

"John F. Fitzgerald rallied to my cause at the last moment," Curley said, "shortly after we met on the platform at a State Democratic convention over which I presided at Tremont Temple. John F. was the main speaker that day."

Over 35,000 votes were cast in favor of his recall, as against 47,000 in his favor, but again, as in the case of Fitzgerald in 1911, there was no majority. But the warning votes fired his dislike of the do-gooders, especially the Finance Commission which, during the last two years of his administration, would publish a damaging serial volume of reports of waste, extravagance, and fiscal legerdemain. The Commission charged that the bonding of city employees and officials was controlled by personal friends who were inexperienced in finance. One was Curley's plumbing ally, Francis Daly. Curley finally sold out his interests in the Daly concern in 1916, but the Finance Commission had enough ammunition if he sought reelection.

And he would do just that. "Fitzgerald used to be considered the perennial Mayor," he said, "until I convinced the public that only Curley could beat Curley."

That boast had a double-entendre which escaped Curley.

CHAPTER 13

Taking the Count

"A statesman makes the occasion, but the occasion
makes the politician."
                              —GEORGE S. HILLARD

T HE Irish insurgents had taken over in Boston, but the Yankee Protestants still controlled the state, even though the Governor of the
Commonwealth was David I. Walsh. Mrs. Fitzgerald and her daughters, Rose and Agnes, had been guests of Walsh's three sisters when he
was sworn in, and later, when he was elected United States Senator,
Honey Fitz wrote him: "I want you to know that it is your integrity that
made me your very warm friend and unshaken supporter throughout your
public career. I had dozens of rows about you, but nobody ever licked me
when the argument was over."

After Honey Fitz left City Hall, however, David I. Walsh stood in his
sun. The Yankee-Protestant domination of the Commonwealth interfered
with Fitzgerald's plan to be elected to the United States Senate, and in
1916 a more immediate obstacle was Walsh. In all his dreams, Walsh's
fair face beamed. Since 1914, when Fitzgerald had campaigned for Walsh
when he ran for Governor (while Curley refused even to appear on the
same platform as the candidate), the Governor had pursued an independent course. In 1915, he was defeated in a reelective bid by the Republican Samuel McCall in a sweep that made Calvin Coolidge the Lieutenant
Governor of Massachusetts. In 1916, the Democratic candidate for the
United States Senate would have to face Henry Cabot Lodge, who had
been a powerful national figure for eighteen years, ably filling the post
once held by John Quincy Adams, Daniel Webster, and Charles Sumner.

In one of his frequent trips to Washington, Honey Fitz sat in Senator
Lodge's seat in the Senate. "It feels natural," he said. When an attendant

told him that Daniel Webster had sat on the seat he smiled. "It feels natural," he repeated.

Walsh, feeling that Lodge was too formidable, decided to wait until 1918, when his chances of defeating Senator John W. Weeks were brighter. Meanwhile, Honey Fitz, in his opinion, would be soundly trounced by Lodge, and would fade from the Massachusetts picture. Dr. Fitzgerald's venture did indeed look cheerless, coming, as it did, in the year of a Presidential election, for he was not in the confidence of the Wilson Administration, and could not count on the national and state tickets helping each other.

Mayor Curley was another consideration. "One of the most attractive sideshows in Massachusetts politics," editorialized *The New York Times,* "is the fight between Mayor James M. Curley and ex-Mayor John F. Fitzgerald to determine who will rule in Boston. Governor Walsh has the distinction of having displeased both."

Curley was particularly browned off. "Jim Curley has about as much use for the Governor as a maiden lady for a shaving mug," noted the *Springfield Union* in October 1916.

In February of that year, Curley surprised the press. "Dr. Fitzgerald and I met at Palm Beach," he said, "and we buried all of our differences." Asked whether Fitzgerald would run for United States Senator, he remained deadpan. "Dr. Fitzgerald and I never once spoke of politics," he said. A month later he told his political organization, which he had renamed the Pro Bono Publico Club, that he would support the Fitzgerald candidacy. And by mid-summer Honey Fitz announced that he would be a candidate.

"I saw the Mayor on the Nantasket boat the other day," he said, "and he told me he thought I should run."

But by the time leaves were falling and Billy Sunday was in Boston wrestling with the devil at the arena, the two Irish chieftains were again on a Hatfield-McCoy basis, and Curley used language in private brawls with his foe that was remembered from gutter days. Furious because of the publicity given Honey Fitz in connection with the presentation of "Where Are My Children?" and "Is Any Girl Safe?" (Fitzgerald said Curley should have banned both plays), Curley, when he met Fitzgerald on the platform at a Democratic rally in Tremont Temple, threatened to "plug him on the jaw."

"It is needless to say," Fitzgerald wrote in his weekly, "that he did not carry out his threat. But this is a sample of Curleyism, which a few of the so-called leaders in Boston think it is dangerous to dislodge."

Such antics amused *The New York Times.* "If these amenities, so near the radiance of the Gilded Dome, distress the outlander, it should be remembered in Mr. Fitzgerald's justification that at a Democratic rally Mayor Curley threatened to 'plug' the former Mayor 'on the jaw.' Language like this from a Mayor of Boston is enough to make the statue of old Josiah Quincy in front of the City Hall drop into fragments or seek consolation in the arms of its fellow-effigy, Ben Franklin." *The Times* added that "Curley's genius for popularity was many diameters smaller than Fitzgerald's."

Curley was beginning to challenge this contention. Once, when they were bickering in the dining room of the Copley Square Hotel, Curley cut into a petulant remark made by Honey Fitz: "John," he said, "let's go out and see who the public believes, you or me." Another day, when Mayor Curley heard Fitzgerald singing "Sweet Adeline" in Young's Alley, he told a friend who was with him: "There goes John, again, disturbing the peace. He should be arrested."

"He's just jealous of my voice," Fitzgerald said angrily, when told of Curley's comment. "I can't understand him. He has a bitter feeling for me."

Curley, like Walsh, wanted to get rid of Fitzgerald, and other old feudists went along. "Ex-Governor Walsh," said Joe O'Connell, "has expressed to me his disgust that a man of Fitzgerald's type could be prominently suggested for such a high and honorable office as that of United States Senator." *The New York Times,* asking why the Democrats did not put up a candidate like David I. Walsh, accused the Massachusetts election of being "turned into a joke," referring to Honey Fitz as a "paragon of nonpolitical versatility. To this amiable kisser of the Blarney Stone, warbler of 'Sweet Adeline,' rider of Florida sharks, a butterfly flitting unconcerned around the solid men of Boston, famed in song, is given the uncontested honor of nomination for Senate in Congress." *The Times* lauded Henry Cabot Lodge's conspicuous fitness for a Senate "where he is among the few who linger as intellectual survivors of the days before it was being transformed into a second House."

The clowning that had endeared Honey Fitz to his Boston supporters did not find the same favor with Yankee Protestants, some of whom felt he lacked the dignity that belonged to a Senator. He was especially handicapped in running against conservative Henry Cabot Lodge, the "Duke of Nahant," who was almost the caricature of a statesman, and was of the purest Proper Bostonian lineage. Lodge was also a polished orator who could tell a good story. One involved the ineffectiveness of congressional investigating committees.

"Some of them," Lodge said, "remind me of Si Hoskins. Si got a job at shooting muskrats, for muskrats overran a mill-owner's dam. There, in the lovely spring weather, Si sat on the grassy bank, his gun on his knee. Finding him one morning, I said: 'What are you doing, Si?'

" 'I'm paid to shoot the muskrats, sir. They're undermining the dam.'

" 'There goes one now!' I said. 'Shoot, man! Why don't you shoot?'

" 'Do you think I want to lose my job?' Si said."

Henry Cabot Lodge had a grandson who was brought up "in an atmosphere of cigar smoke and inside talk on politics, accustomed to sit on the knees of men like Theodore Roosevelt and William Howard Taft." Honey Fitz, too, had a grandson reared in a similar atmosphere. And one day these two grandsons—Henry Cabot Lodge, Jr., and John Fitzgerald Kennedy, would also oppose each other in a contest for the United States Senate.

An aristocrat who remembered being pelted with snowballs by Irish "muckers" when he went coasting on Boston Common, Lodge was a shifting target for Honey Fitz, for even as a Brahmin he could count among his supporters Irishmen who saw him tip his hat in the St. Patrick's Day Parade. This general technique later became known as the George Holden Tinkham method of campaigning. Tinkham, a son of the Back Bay, in his original campaign went into every barroom in his congressional district and bought a round of drinks. Elated that such an aristocrat had honored their humble fathers, voters of the next generation remembered that their father had drunk a glass of whisky with a member of the affluent society. After his initial campaign, Tinkham let his opponents do most of the stumping.

The Irish also liked the way Lodge yanked the British lion's tail. Honey Fitz, although one of the most resourceful politicians in the state, ran the risk of losing votes if he was identified with Sinn Feiners or other aggressive Irish groups clamoring for the Irish Free State. It took a man with the dignity of Walsh to win the vote of liberals and reformers at odds with standpat Republicans who controlled State affairs.

Dr. Fitzgerald attacked Lodge's pedigree, telling rallies that in college his foe had "stumbled into a course in medieval history and had never emerged from that course. The robber baron is still his highest ideal and his dearest friend. His work at Washington has been for a very few, and they, let us be thankful, are not to name the United States Senator." This line of attack was meant to draw liberal votes.

Fitzgerald also attacked Lodge's stand on immigration, always a good text for a political sermon in Irish Boston. As chairman of the immigration committee, Lodge had sponsored many bills.

"The question of regulating and restricting immigration," Lodge had told the House of Representatives in 1891, "is one of the gravest which now confronts the country. . . . It has been said . . . that we are in no danger of being overcrowded by desirable immigrants, but we are at this moment overcrowded with undesirable immigrants."

In that year, Lodge had introduced a bill that would require all who sought entry to America to know how to read or write in their own language, a facility few citizens of the ghetto had had the opportunity to learn. "I do not want to see the quality of American citizenship decline beneath the effects of unrestricted immigration," he said, "and I am utterly opposed to a system which is continually dragging down the wages of American labor by the introduction of the importation of the cheapest, lowest, and most ignorant labor of other countries."

He found acceptable those who came from the United Kingdom, Germany and Scandinavian countries, but he frowned on the influx from Russia, Poland, Hungary, the Slavic countries and Italy. (Italy by this time was well represented. There is the story of a mayor in southern Italy who, in welcoming the King of Italy, said: "We welcome you in the name of our five thousand inhabitants, three thousand of whom are in America.")

Lodge also warned of the danger of "changing the quality of our race and citizenship through the wholesale infusion of races whose traditions and inheritance, whose thoughts and whose beliefs are wholly alien to ours and with whom we have never assimilated or even been associated in the past."

By 1916, the Italians had largely replaced the Irish in pick-and-shovel gangs, and Fitzgerald asked who would "do the crude labor" if Italians were denied entry. He pointed out that the Italians, like the Greeks, Jews and Poles, had produced great persons to whom the world was indebted. Some of the barred nations against which Lodge was trying to discriminate had produced great minds, and immigrants from those countries had helped build the United States into "the greatest and most powerful nation the world has ever known."

Honey Fitz made a better showing than was expected. *The New York Times* later recalled "the thrills and chills of the night in 1916 when he was alternately the winner and loser of the contest for Senator against Henry Cabot Lodge. That was the time the Senate convened with so many lame ducks." Lodge, surrounded by so many defeated colleagues, considered his narrow success a victory, but most of his Massachusetts followers set it down as a humiliating experience.

On November 8, while the country waited to hear the Presidential returns from California, and when Justice Charles Evans Hughes went to bed thinking he had been elected President over Woodrow Wilson, Lodge defeated Fitzgerald by only 33,000 votes. This loss enhanced Fitzgerald's state-wide stature, and he was thenceforth considered a political leader to watch. Fitzgerald, like Curley, was never glum in defeat, believing in the counsel of Cervantes: "Patience, and shuffle the cards."

On May 7, 1915, the Cunard Liner *Lusitania* sank off the southeast coast of Ireland with a loss of 1198 lives, including many Americans. The United States had been tooling up for war since 1915, and Charles Schwab was looking for a topflight executive for the Fore River shipyards of Bethlehem Steel. Honey Fitz, who had led the fight to persuade Schwab to bring the shipbuilding company to the Bay State, recommended his son-in-law, Joseph P. Kennedy, as did Guy Currier, the New England attorney for the Bethlehem Steel Corporation, who had been impressed by Kennedy's financial acumen in dealings they had had.

"I became assistant general manager of the Bethlehem Shipbuilding Corporation, where I remained through the war years," Kennedy wrote in his twenty-fifth Harvard report. "During this period the company built ships for the United States Government, and I came into frequent contact with the then young Assistant Secretary of the Navy, Franklin Delano Roosevelt."

The corporation had contracted with the United States and allied governments to build destroyers and repair warships. Kennedy supervised the activities of 50,000 workers, an inspiring source of patronage for Curley, but a frustrating one also, for Kennedy did no favors for the Mayor of Boston.

"After the war," Kennedy wrote in his Harvard report, "I became manager of Hayden Stone & Company, bankers and brokers, and continued in that capacity until 1924."

Honey Fitz puffed with pride at the success of his son-in-law, for he had long lamented that Boston banking had been barred to the Irish. Boston bankers had almost invariably come from Yankee Protestant families who owned Boston & Albany stock and confined their newspaper reading to the *Boston Evening Transcript,* known as the sturdy old lady of Milk Street.

"You have plenty of Irish depositors," Honey Fitz told one Boston banker. "Why don't you put some Irishmen on your board of directors?"

The banker shifted uneasily. "Well," he said, "a couple of the tellers are Irish Catholic."

"Yes," Fitzgerald said, "and I suppose the charwomen are, too."

This closed-ranks attitude drove good men from Boston, Honey Fitz often said. And one of them was Joseph P. Kennedy.

"Whether by accident or design," Honey Fitz once remarked, "the doors of our financial houses do not seem to open readily to applicants of Irish blood." Another time, when he complained to the witty Timothy Coakley, brother of Daniel, that the Irish could not get into banks in Boston, Coakley said: "No, the police are too vigilant."

In his aggressive manner, Honey Fitz as Mayor had tried to bridge the social chasm. "What this city needs," he said, "is a lunch club where the bluebloods will lunch with the rest of us." The result was the City Club, where Yankee Protestant bankers and lawyers broke bread with Irish Catholic leaders. There remained, of course, chaste enclaves in certain clubs, cotillions, and colleges beyond which the Brahmins would not retreat. They were like the stuffy dowager who was amazed at all the fuss made about Whistler's portrait of his mother. "After all, she was only a McNeill from North Carolina." The more modern Brahmin version was: "Jim Curley is the best orator in the country—too bad he's Irish."

Honey Fitz never wearied of assailing the money trust in Massachusetts. "It is not good for the city to have a small knot of men who control all the wealth and use it for their own schemes without any thought of the city in which they live," he told a New York reporter during his first mayoral term. "Many of the rich people in the Back Bay are not worthy. They have plenty of money, yet they invest little of it in their own city. They have not the brains to back up the reputations made by their fathers and forefathers. In too many instances old Boston sits at the tombs of its ancestors and fingers the withered leaves of laurel they won in bygone days. Old Boston is cold and proud, wrapped in the mantle of Puritanism, not progressive enough. It has been too long deaf to the aspirations of the young Irish, Italians, Jews, and Frenchmen in our midst who are eager to make their way in business here. The old Back Bay families try to keep them out. They are willing enough to hire their brains and use them, but they resent any attempt on the part of these men to get into business for themselves."

Charles Francis Adams, his friend, would remind him later of these sentiments.

Honey Fitz told of one Bostonian who had sponsored a candidate for the Exchange Club. "One day a member of the membership committee

came around and asked him to withdraw his friend's name because—
just listen to this—he had been seen working in his office in shirt sleeves!"

Honey Fitz, who was talking to Henry Hall of *The New York World,*
twirled a pair of tortoise shell-rimmed glasses. "Take Stone & Webster.
I know the partners in the firm. They are both Boston boys and fine fellows. Now in the last fifteen years they have taken more than $179,000,-
000 of Boston money and invested it in the West. They have floated all
their securities right here in Boston, and not a cent of all that Boston
money has gone to improve the city, to build up her commerce, add to
her industry, or give employment to a single one of her workers. There
are a dozen other firms that have done the same thing, but not on such a
big scale. Instead of promoting Boston's industries, they promote so-
called public utility schemes in new communities where they are allowed
to build the properties with the bonds." He had one final slap for Proper
Bostonians. "Now the people in the Back Bay . . . are a self-satisfied lot,
content to sit back and clip their coupons, but when it comes to doing
something for industry, they fail of their duty."

There were economic concepts and problems of distribution that Honey
Fitz did not fully understand. He would sit in a downtown restaurant and
point to a menu. "Only the other day," he would tell a luncheon compan-
ion, "as I drove through the Nashoba Valley, I saw fields full of squash.
Now, just look at this menu. Why isn't there any squash pie?" Another
time he would speak of the mounds of fish on Boston piers and ask why
fish chowder was not on the menu. He frequently pointed up a problem
without offering a practical solution, and when a waiter in one restaurant
gave him an answer, for once he was speechless.

"Our customers," the waiter said, "don't seem to like squash pie."

There were other questions for which Honey Fitz had no adequate
answer. The most pressing concern was the mayoral race of 1917.

CHAPTER 14

In Case of a Knockdown
Return to Your Corner

"The most successful politician is he who says
what everybody else is thinking, often and in
the loudest voice."

—THEODORE ROOSEVELT

IT was hinted that Honey Fitz might run for Mayor in 1917, but Curley,
who sought reelection, was now recognized as a tempestuous campaigner whose wit, gall, and vicious attack made it uncomfortable to
oppose him without risk of character assassination. In his weekly, Honey
Fitz accused him "of meanness and brutality unequalled in American
politics." When, in July 1917, Mayor Curley permitted an antiwar Social-
ist parade and meeting, Fitzgerald rebuked him publicly, whereupon a
fuming Curley pounced on him. In next morning's newspaper, Curley was
thus quoted:

"The only individual anxious to suppress the truth or to restrict free
speech is the one whose acts, public or private, will not permit thorough
scrutiny or exposure to the world.

"The frothing of a certain person on Boston Common last evening was
not directed against me personally because of anything said by me, but
was with a view to stifling free speech in general, as a measure of personal
protection from the truth, which in its nakedness is sometimes hideous
though necessary.

"I am preparing three addresses which, if necessary, I shall deliver in
the fall, and which, if a certain individual had the right to restrict free
speech, I would not be permitted to deliver.

"One of these addresses is entitled: 'Graft, Ancient and Modern,' an-

215

other, 'Great Lovers: From Cleopatra to Toodles,' and last, but not least interesting, 'Libertines: From Henry VIII to the Present Day.' "

Fitzgerald answered him effectively, but in a manner too dignified to rate headlines. He dropped out of the race, however.

According to the *Boston Post,* the city's leading political newspaper of the era, Curley looked like the man to beat. "John F. Fitzgerald is afraid of him. Mr. Storrow is not physically fit to make such a contest as will be necessary to displace him. Kenny can't talk. Ex-Congressman Peters permits such a man as Curley to invoke the very prejudices that alone enabled Mr. Fitzgerald to defeat Mr. Storrow."

Fitzgerald, whom Curley accused of having "a flexible support policy," stepped up the barrage of criticism in *The Republic.* "One of the disgusting contentions of those supporting Mayor Curley," he wrote, "is that his defeat would mean disaster to the Democratic party. Fortunately, this ground is taken by very few, and these men, if their careers are analyzed, will be shown to be beneficiaries of the Curley system at City Hall and its allied interests."

The Finance Commission had instructed its counsel, Henry F. Hurlburt, to present evidence of Curley dealings to the District Attorney, Joseph Pelletier. Martin Lomasney publicly charged: "Curley went in to Pelletier, got down almost on his knees, talked of his wife and family, and begged him to stay the execution of the law. 'Hold on, Joe, for God's sake, give me a chance. Think of my wife and family. Think of our party. Think of our people.' and Joseph Pelletier did."

Fitzgerald, meanwhile, charged that Curley was no friend of the "working class." "Although the cost of living steadily mounted during his administration, and he in the meantime built a palace for himself, he waited until a few months ago before giving the laborers any advance, and if it were not for the City Council, their pay would now be $2.75 a day instead of $3, whereas the ordinary laborer is now getting $4 a day." Honey Fitz told him to get out of the race and save himself "from an awful licking."

Mayor Curley compared Fitzgerald with other "renegade Democratic bosses," who put two puppets in the race—Congressman Peter Tague of Charlestown and James Gallivan of South Boston. Fitzgerald tried to swing Lomasney's support to Gallivan, but the Mahatma was for Peters, reasoning that he alone could defeat Curley. Lomasney, as usual, wanted to back a winner, and when Curley asked him to remove his decoys from the race, he said: "Why do you think I put them in the race? I put them in to lick you."

Mrs. Curley took an active part in this campaign. Writes Reinhard H.

Luthin in *American Demagogues Twentieth Century*: "At one rally this model husband placed his wife on one side of him and an American flag on wheels on the other. As the crowd applauded, he swayed toward her and the stars-and-stripes alternately and ended by embracing them simultaneously—a stirring, crowd-capturing demonstration of love for home and country."

Curley dismissed Andrew James Peters as a "Brookline squire endowed with three apostolic names," having discovered by this time that it amused his followers to tease Yankees about their vintage names. (When told that Endicott Peabody Saltonstall had been appointed a district attorney, he quipped: "What, all three of them?") Curley also called Peters, a graduate of fashionable St. Paul's School in Concord, New Hampshire, and of Harvard, an "abhorrent combination of Harvard and the slums," referring to the dowdy Eleventh congressional district which Peters represented.

Curley, however, who had received 47,000 votes the first time he ran for Mayor, collected only 28,848 to 37,923 for Peters. Gallivan tallied fewer than 20,000, and Tague was under 2000.

"The election of Peters for the four-year term from 1918-22," wrote Albert Bushnell Hart, "was a protest against the results of the personal and political influences which had too long been dominant at City Hall, and which tended to build up a personal and political machine. The mayoralty of Boston offers great opportunities for service, and carried with it responsibilities too great for thought of personal advancement. Both the letter and the spirit of the Charter of 1909 contemplated the choice of a municipal administrator rather than a political leader to preside over the work of this great city."

Curley, having granted wholesale increases to city employees, despite Fitzgerald's criticism in this regard, had also spent almost every cent of unappropriated cash in the City Treasury, and the election of Peters was a rebuke to his extravagance. While in office, Peters helped in the passage, by the legislature, of a charter amendment which made the Mayor of Boston ineligible for a second term immediately after the expiration of the four-year administration which he served.

His administration, because of his inability to cope with a rapacious palace guard who sold jobs and promotions flagrantly, proved to be one of the most graft-ridden in Boston's history. He was, said Curley, "an innocent dupe for a conscienceless corps of bandits."

Meanwhile, Curley, irked by Fitzgerald's support of Gallivan, lashed out at him more savagely than ever: "Fitzgerald's attitude was characteristic of his usual yellow tactics," he charged. "It was the same kind of tactics he used to break Patrick A. Collins' heart, the same kind that he cowardly pursued against David I. Walsh, the same kind of tactics and conduct which have become familiarly known as 'Fitzgerald tactics,' embracing all that is low, mean, contemptible and unmanly. I shall oppose Fitzgerald if he is a candidate for the United States Senate."

Honey Fitz had planned to run against Senator John W. Weeks, but David I. Walsh had strong backing, and Curley's enmity was no help. While Curley, in a mulish effort to get back at Gallivan, tried to unseat him in one congressional fight in 1918, and met another humiliating defeat, Honey Fitz went into the pit with "Weeping" Peter Tague in a battle for the seat in the tenth congressional district.

Curley was done, his enemies jubilantly agreed. When the votes were tallied, Gallivan had said: "Thank you, Mr. Voter, and good night, Curley." He added: "The only thing that Curley can get in Washington is the train back home." The Roxbury Demosthenes no longer had any patronage to give.

But Fitzgerald was far from done. The battle was joined in September, 1918, when Tague said: "The millionaire Bethlehem Steel candidate is beaten. He wants to go to Washington to get war contracts for friends."

Honey Fitz accused Tague of "playing rotten politics . . . with rotten money." But it was a drab contest. "I can't get any kick into this fight," Fitzgerald complained. One amusing incident stemmed from a false charge by the Tague forces that Fitzgerald's son, Tom, who was training for a commission, was trying to avoid combat duty. Bill Doyle, a friend who could speak in the Curley manner, mounted the platform at a rally in East Boston:

"There is no truth at all in these charges," he said. "Only last week I was in Hoboken, where I boarded the *Vaterland,* the biggest transport ship in the fleet. 'Is there anyone on this ship from Boston?' I shouted, never expecting to be answered, for there were thousands on the ship, getting ready to go to France to engage the enemy. Then suddenly I heard a voice come up from the hold: 'This is Tom Fitzgerald. Tell my Pa and Ma I was asking for them, and say a prayer for me.' "

Doyle raised his hand for silence. "And tonight," he said, "tonight Tom Fitzgerald lies in the mud in France, where—"

At this point Honey Fitz was on his feet, tears streaming down his face. "Stop it, Bill, stop it!" he shouted. "For God's sake, don't go any further. I can't stand it."

One of the most embarrassing incidents in the long career of Honey

Fitz occurred during this campaign. Although not a party to an alleged fraud engineered by Martin Lomasney, he was victimized by it. The incident stemmed from a falling-out Lomasney had had with Tague in connection with the anti-British feeling in Boston during World War I, when the Irish hatred of England was intense and bitter, partly because of remarks made by Admiral Sims and others. At the war's outbreak, Irish nationalism was so inflamed that Lomasney, among others, sympathized with German Imperialism and hoped for the defeat of Britain—the quickest way to independence for Ireland. Demagogues reminded the Boston Irish that after the Easter Week Rebellion in Ireland, the insurgents had been lined up behind barrack walls and shot down like dogs. Victor Herbert was elected president of the Friends of Irish Freedom in an Irish Race Convention held in New York, where Celtic resentment was also bitter. The death in a London jail, after a long, widely heralded hunger strike, of Terence MacSwiney, former Lord Mayor of Cork, was another incident that inflamed the Irish.

President Woodrow Wilson was caught between pressure groups. When asked to receive a group of Irish-American leaders who wanted to present a paper, he agreed, provided Daniel F. Cohalan did not accompany them. During the war, Cohalan had been a notorious rabble rouser. When the committee, headed by Cohalan, came to the White House, Joseph Tumulty, an aide, urged him to relent.

"Mr. President," Tumulty said, "this will make a terrible impression on his followers." Cohalan was a powerful political leader among a segment of Irish fanatics.

"That's just what I wanted it to do, Tumulty; but I think it will make a good impression on decent people," the President said. He knew Cohalan did not have the backing of many of his people.

In 1916, when England was fighting with her back to the wall, Martin Lomasney was a delegate to the Democratic National Convention in St. Louis. With the Easter Week's fighting in Dublin fresh in everyone's mind, the Irish question was the most sizzling issue at the convention. When Lomasney proposed a Freedom-for-Ireland plank in the Democratic National platform, he was shouted down, but it created a furor. Four years later at the San Francisco convention, Lomasney introduced the same plan, again to have it fail.

In 1915, Lomasney had engineered Tague's election to Congress with the express condition that Tague would do everything possible in the interests of Irish independence. President Wilson's war speech gave Tague his opportunity to strike a blow for freedom. Tague, according to Lomasney, had agreed to propose to the joint session that Ireland's independence be a condition to the entry of the United States into the war. Incensed because Tague had failed to do this, Lomasney threw his support to Honey Fitz in the 1918 contest, when Tague ran for reelection.

"Fitzgerald was brought into this contest because I refused to answer the beck and call of the notorious leader, Martin M. Lomasney," Tague told an investigating committee. "Only a short time ago, gentlemen of the Congress, you were called upon to make the momentous decision which resulted in putting this country into war.

"Lomasney served notice upon me that he would defeat me if I did not stand upon the floor of this House and insult the President of the United States when he arose to address you . . . He demanded that I get up on the floor of the House while the President was solemnly discussing the great question of the United States going to war and ask: 'Mr. President, what is going to be the attitude of England towards Ireland?'

"I refused to do that and that was why I was punished. Mr. Lomasney said to me: 'Don't you dare vote for war; don't you dare vote for conscription.' This man Lomasney was so strong in his pro-Germanism that he didn't want England to win the war."

The West End Boss, explaining how he had sent Tague to Congress, recalled his exact statement to Tague: "Peter, before you declare war in Congress, you stand up and ask what is England's attitude toward the freedom of Ireland." And Tague had agreed to do just that, he said. "It seems to me, Peter," he had added, "that if we in America are going to save England we owe it to our citizens and our constituents to see what England is going to do for Ireland."

Tague knew that with Lomasney against him, he faced a cheerless prospect in the congressional contest. Examples of the Czar's power were plentiful. In 1910, when the Massachusetts Civil Service Commission had rejected his brother Joseph's nomination as Health Commissioner, Martin confronted the commission personally and told them that he would elect a Democratic governor who would remove them from their posts. He chose Eugene N. Foss, a former Republican, and led the fight for his election as Governor in 1911, and his reelection in 1912.

In the bitter primary of the Fitzgerald-Tague fight, the Tague forces circulated a 'bona fide" birth certificate that "proved" Lomasney had been born in Nova Scotia, thus was a "Novey," not a son of Erin. In the primary, Fitzgerald had squeaked by with a margin of fifty votes. It was at this point that Tague decided to run on stickers.

He had his name printed on stickers for the convenience of voters, and was encouraged on election day to see dozens of workers show up at the polls to distribute these stickers to voters as they approached the booths. A less naive Tague would learn later that some of these workers were Fitzgerald men, and the stickers they handed out were ungummed. When they fell off the ballots, the blank ballots were, of course, void. A Fitzgerald supporter later told a friend, according to a congressional investigating committee, "that he had caused to be prepared and distributed stickers with no gum attached, in order that the persons seeking to vote for Tague would be thwarted in this by the falling off of the sticker after the ballot had been deposited in the box."

Tague protested shrilly, and when Fitzgerald took his seat in the House at the following session, his protests led to the investigation. In March, 1919, a congressional committee came to Boston to probe Tague's charges of fraud in the election, which he lost by 238 votes. One charge was that mattress workers had been used against him in the West End. He voiced this charge as if it were something new to Boston politics, whereas it was old hat in Boston politics at the time.

Chicanery was part of every Boston political campaign. Repeaters (persons who vote more than once) were as common as mattress voters. Ballot stuffing was as common as physical violence, bribery, blackmail, or whopping lies. From the moment a candidate filed his nomination papers, he was subject to trickery.

Miss Mary Meyer, who for a quarter of a century was executive secretary of the Democratic City Committee, on her retirement revealed how politicians would claw at one another in public or private. She filed all nomination papers for candidates, and as a result was always in hot water. Constantly charged with playing favorites, she was often the target of scurrilous tongue lashings, and was sometimes hauled into court, charged with juggling the names of candidates on ballots. She needed protection. "Every morning as I stepped from the street car at Washington and Milk streets, two police officers would hustle me through the waiting mob to my office."

Boston had its Damon Runyon characters like "Jo-Jo the Repeater," who, said the *Boston Traveler,* was "a knave with firm principles." One candidate won an election by stealing the ballot box before his opponents could vote. In another precinct, when voters caught tellers burning ballots in a stove, an election warden said: "Officer, clear the room," whereupon the cop on duty herded out the voters. The *Boston Traveler* also told the story of Big John, a district leader. During a fight for a party nomination, a ward-heeler rushed up to John, who was sitting in a caucus room.

"They're stealing the election from us," he said. "They're putting fraudulent ballots in the box."

John was unmoved.

"Aren't you going to do something about it?" the ward-heeler asked.

"Be calm, son," Big John said. "They're putting their ballots in the wrong box."

"Where's the right one?"

"I'm sitting on it."

In 1910, when Eugene N. Foss was running against Charles S. Hamlin, Herbert "Fingers" McGlinchy, a pickpocket, relieved several Hamlin delegates of the credentials which they needed to return to the political convention at Faneuil Hall. "They were all part of the spangled parade," said the *Boston Traveler,* "all part of the era of statesmen and scalawags that would dominate Boston politics for decades."

Repeaters were sometimes paid as high as five or ten dollars. One scheme was to steal a ballot and mark it up. The voter deposited his ballot and brought out from the polling booth another ballot which was deposited in return. In this way there was an accurate check on how the man voted. In some sections, ward leaders used to line up repeaters openly and pay them off. Even when honest Patrick Collins was elected Mayor of Boston in 1903, he was aided by such fervent supporters as Jimmy Walsh, who admitted to voting twenty-eight times in that election. One state senator, when a constituent was arrested for repeating, filed a bill that would give the judge the right to suspend a sentence if the offender did not repeat for a year.

"Of course, there was not another election for a year," he explained.

Politics in the early century was as devious as it was rough and dirty. Consider the maneuvers—freely and willingly confessed—of a former Massachusetts politician who shall be known here only as Senator Bill. One of the most popular politicians of his day, and a devoted tribune of the common man, he was dubbed by a Boston journalist "the Damon Runyon of Boston," and was referred to by no less a distinguished statesman as Henry Cabot Lodge, Jr., as "my fellow elder statesman."

"A machine politician who knew every imaginable manner and method of getting votes," said a *Boston Post* reporter, "he served ten successive years on the school board, then gave up his place to win a seat on the first Plan A Council. . . . His personal following is greater than that of any contemporary office holder in Massachusetts. He has maintained his vote getting strength for three decades."

When Senator Bill moved from Roxbury to another section of Boston, he unblushingly admits bringing along his mattress voters and repeaters. On January 1, 1936, there were 12,342 registered voters in his new district. On October 14 of the same year, there were 20,375—an abrupt increase of almost 8,000 voters. Warned by a friendly Attorney General that a detective agency had been engaged to investigate him, he further learned that the agency was hiring college students to help with the investigation.

"I went into Speaker Leverett Saltonstall's office and got some of his official stationery and envelopes. I wrote down a list of names of my supporters and used the stationery to inform the chief investigator that I would appreciate it if he could use some of my men on the enclosed list as checkers. I signed the letter, 'Sincerely, Lev.' When I was obliged in the matter, I sent around my supporters to ring doorbells in the district, telling them exactly where to go. Most of the 'suspects' they rounded up were Yankees who had lived at the same Republican address for years. These worthy citizens were, of course, furious when hauled before the ballot commission to find cause why their names should not be stricken from the voting list."

Senator Bill actually had WPA men assigned to him to be used as repeaters. "One told me he was registered under seven names. That was his WPA job."

Election laws before 1920 were loose enough to permit all this zany activity. Wardens at the polls were selected by election commissioners who usually heeded the recommendations of ward committees in making their appointments. Also, each party had unofficial checkers at the polls. It was easy to circumvent all these provisions, and circumvented they were!

To bottle up a precinct or ward, Senator Bill put in his own election officers and wardens, and since the law required two Democratic counters (tellers) and two Republicans to be assigned, he simply had supporters register as Republicans "to keep everything legal."

One of his wardens used lead from a precinct pencil, concealed under her thumbnail, to spoil ballots. "If a person voted for my opponent, she put a cross beside my name, and if the instructions were to mark a ballot with two crosses, she would pencil in a cross for a third candidate, thus invalidating the ballot." The "Republican" warden assigned to watch her, was another loyal subject. This sort of collusion, plus police cooperation, enabled repeaters to change their hats and coats and vote twice at the same booth.

Senator Bill's repeaters, he explained, registered from fictitious addresses, including boarding houses, vacant lots, warehouses, apartments, hotels, and cemeteries. In one election, a repeater impersonated Senator Bill's opponent who was not allowed to vote when he arrived.

"You have already voted once," he was told. "And that is the legal limit."

In another election two fifteen-year-old boys voted thirteen times each.

"You are my brother," a warden told one of them, permitting him to vote. The other lad forgot the name of the person he was impersonating. Another repeater was a Back Bay physician who said it was his hobby to vote once in each precinct. He would accept no compensation for his cooperation. (Curley tells of a man who in 1905 tried to vote in the name of Charles F. Lee, whereupon the warden said to a checker: "Phil, look at the miserable specimen of humanity who is trying to pass for the Reverend Charles Follen Lee.")

Senator Bill used to pay certain voters fifty cents not to vote (they were too "unreliable," he said), then send in repeaters to vote for them. "To offset opposing repeaters, we sent around monitors to get them drunk. Then our boys would drive them to some outlying district, so they wouldn't have time to return to vote. Even if they did get back, most of them were so drunk they couldn't remember the names of persons they were being paid to impersonate."

Senator Bill had a special strategy for unfavorable precincts. "Here, you usually had your own votes in by six in the evening, and figured that most of the voting after that was not to be trusted (*sic*). There were always long lines of voters from six until eight. To stall, in an effort to keep as many as possible from voting, our friendly wardens would keep breaking their pencils, and the cop on duty would take his time about sharpening them. Nobody dared challenge him, naturally. Around seven-thirty, we would send over our supporters who lived outside the district. They stood in line and stalled as much as possible. Their names weren't on the voting list, but it took time to check the regular and supplementary lists. Unless a person was in the building by eight, he was ineligible to vote, so our Fabian policy kept out a lot of legitimate voters."

The matter of closing time could be circumvented, too. In a mayoral election in the 1930s, Senator Joseph Langone of the North End kept his voting precincts open for an hour after the legal closing time, with no injury to the cause of his candidate.

Early in his career, in a Roxbury election, Senator Bill was opposed by a Negro candidate. Bill called the chairman of the Schoolhouse Commission. "If a school's doors can't be opened on election day, you are the only person who can order them broken down, right?"

That night, Senator Bill's men put mucilage and gum in the locks of the schoolhouse doors, where the voting booths for the precinct were. On election morning, the custodian was unable to open the doors, and Senator Bill, who had made sure that the cop on duty knew the regulations said: "Officers, these people have a right to vote. If the janitor can't open the door, break it down and let these folks exercise their privilege. The right to vote is sacred. Besides, some of these men are Pullman porters and they will be late for work if you don't do something."

"Sorry, Senator," the officer said. "It's against the rules and regulations. The only person who can issue such an order is the School Commission chairman, and—"

"Well, have someone get in touch with him. Call him and tell him to get over here."

It was past noon by the time the first vote was cast. The chairman had agreed to make himself unavailable that morning, but the custodian had finally succeeded in opening one of the doors.

Martin Lomasney knew all these tricks, but he preferred to keep everything legal, he said. One of his chief lieutenants was John I. Fitzgerald, no relation to John F. Asked whether Ward Eight voting was dishonest, he said: "No. The Ward was always too closely watched. Ballot boxes are never stuffed, unless it's absolutely necessary." Actually, Lomasney did not always keep everything legal.

He instructed illiterate voters to pretend to be without their glasses. Unable to read the names on the ballot without them, they were accompanied into the booths by Lomasney men to see that they voted properly. He arranged for youths under voting age to become naturalized American citizens, even though they were illiterate, for his influence extended even to the Federal Naturalization Bureau. Rounding up immigrants, he gave each a comb that fitted into a pocket. But it was no ordinary comb. Its teeth were cut in a pattern which, when laid on the ballot, covered all but the names of Lomasney's candidates. The practice became known as "going over the ballot with a fine-tooth comb."

At the time of the Tague-Fitzgerald controversy, the law provided that every voter be registered at his place of residence on the first of April before any given election. On every March 31, strangers trooping into the West End, many of them carrying a bedroll, were a familiar sight.

Several hotels and lodging houses in Ward Eight offered rooms for as little as twenty-five cents a night, and on this evening they were all overcrowded. A Harvard professor who studied the practice said the greatest colonization of voters in the history of the world could be found at certain addresses in the West End.

Martin Lomasney, arguing from the contention that a person is entitled to choose where he shall vote from, said the Supreme Judicial Court had ruled that if a man were a citizen of Boston and had no home, he could give the Boston Common as his home and vote from there. Governor Walsh, in recommending legislation to catch up with tax-dodgers, had singled out Massachusetts capitalists who claimed residence in small towns on Cape Cod, where they maintained summer homes, and where taxes might be extremely low. All that was required was a trip to the Cape so as to be in town as of January 1 to establish technical residence.

Lomasney thought he was within his rights as long as he had an honest address in the ward for every vote cast, even if that address meant sixty votes from a six-room rooming house. "Thomas W. Lawson had three homes, but he has his domicile in Egypt, and he votes there. It all comes down to a question of fact."

There had been one publicized charge of ballot-stuffing during the Tague-Fitzgerald balloting. Hammond R. Fletcher, a Republican precinct officer in one district, was so insistent on protecting the Fitzgerald interests during a ballot argument at his polling place, where he charged that the box was being stuffed, that he wrapped his arms around the box and refused to let go. The police, who took him to the station, had to take the ballot box along, too. That, too, was Boston politics.

The March hearings held in Boston were spectacular. Attorney John Feeney, a great trial lawyer, represented Honey Fitz, and Joseph O'Connell was counsel for Tague. O'Connell set off the first firecracker when he produced a newsclip from Fitzgerald's weekly newspaper which described Martin Lomasney as "a mere politician without visible means of support other than office holding and graft." Feeney finally convinced the Mahatma that any rebuttal would lend support to Tague.

"You say that you supported Fitzgerald in this contest because he is one of the big, broad men?" O'Connell asked.

"Yes."

"When you chose Fitzgerald because he is a big, broad man, did you recall what you said about him before?" The attorney picked up a copy of a speech Lomasney had made years before in which he had attacked Fitzgerald. The theme of Lomasney's reply was: "While the light holds out to burn, the humblest sinner may return." He was willing to take the repentant back into the fold, he said, pointing out that he had become reconciled with Fitzgerald when the latter ceased to be "a slippery eel."

Lomasney grinned when O'Connell read this part of his speech. "I was in pretty good form, then, wasn't I?" When the laughter died down, he went on: "Fitzgerald has broadened." Then Lomasney, who was wearing an old sweater as he sat in the witness chair, warmed up.

"Fitzgerald had his day of youth . . . when he had little regard for the rights of others less powerful, when he believed . . . that he could control everything and everybody. But neither he nor I believed in taking away a man's bread and butter. . . . He never removed a man because he was against us. I believe in gratitude, and I respect a man who fights me for the man who gave him his bread and butter. When Fitzgerald became Mayor, he had plenty of opportunity to discharge men who had fought against him. He had the power, but he used it with discretion. . . . When I saw that he was doomed to defeat in this fight, I said I'd stand by him, and that's why I am supporting him. I never forget a man who gives me a glass of water."

Even more than Tague or Fitzgerald, Lomasney was handed the hot end of the poker. Tague had dropped word that Martin was wealthy, and evidence in the case indicated that he had held stock in several trust companies, had a lease on a quarry and had been a partner in a construction company. Raging on the witness stand, Lomasney called Tague a liar, crook, quitter, grafter, and peanut politician, in a fiery effort to make the accuser stand accused. He punctuated many statements with a forward thrust of a lantern jaw that was likened to a "locomotive cow-catcher," and every newspaper in Boston reported his taunts and insults. Cartoonists caricatured him, lounging on the stand in an ermine robe with a crown on his head.

Attorney O'Connell asked him to define a mattress voter.

"You are, Mr. O'Connell. You are a mattress voter. You live in Brookline, but you still vote in Dorchester. I have the records here to prove it." He jerked his thumb in the direction of Tague. "Mr. Tague, over there, harbors a mattress voter in his own home in Charlestown—a man named Patrick Goggins. . . . Goggins has a respectable home in Somerville and lives there, but he votes from Tague's residence. I have the records here to prove it."

O'Connell denounced Fitzgerald for not taking the stand. The ex-Mayor, he charged, "by slippery, eel-like methods, after seeing Mr. Lomasney caught on the cross-examination hook, wiggled himself through a muddy coloring of newspaper interviews and boasts of defiance to a retreat where no attorney could examine him. If Mr. Fitzgeld could prove that election frauds were not resorted to, the witness stand was available to him for presentation of such defense as he could offer. It is apparent, however, he was afraid to face a severe and searching cross-examination."

Honey Fitz, who had taken the sun in Palm Beach, stayed in the background, but pointed out that the hearings had gone on for ninety days, during which time "I have been away sixteen days on my visit and return from the south." He adds: "I was too busy attending to the legitimate business of my congressional district to give time to the opera bouffe show being conducted at the Post Office building by Mr. Tague and his counsel."

It was the belligerent, menacing Lomasney posture reproduced in all Boston newspapers that proved his undoing. Joseph L. Kane, cousin of Fitzgerald's son-in-law, Joseph Kennedy, bought hundreds of newspapers, clipped out the photographs that showed Lomasney waggling his forefinger in the committee chairman's face as if he were a boss laying down the law to a committee of congress. Kane mounted the picture under the caption:

IS HE BIGGER THAN THE GOVERNMENT?

and sent a copy to every member of the National House of Representatives.

The report, signed by the majority of the committee recommending the unseating of Congressman Fitzgerald, branded Lomasney a Democrat who had no hesitancy when it suited his personal ends "in wielding his power to encompass the defeat of Democratic candidates. . . . He has built up his power through a number of years largely by means of the fraudulent votes of the liquor dealers, bartenders, and city job holders illegally registered in his ward, and in the padded returns of alleged residents in the cheap lodging houses."

The committee further charged that in the primary elections "the names of a number of young men who were absent from Boston in the military or naval service of the country were voted on. . . . In each case, where the name of the son was thus fraudulently voted on, the father was in charge of and present at the polling place at which such a vote was cast."

Tague claimed to know of seventeen soldiers whose votes had been misused in Lomasney's ward. He knew all the Lomasney tricks, having once been a party to them, when they conspired in his favor. "And one of these boys was lying dead on the battlefield of France when his name was voted upon," he added.

The committee agreed with the allegations of illegal registration and fraud in connection with votes cast in certain precincts, and while Lomasney came off without a scratch, Congressman Fitzgerald was unseated in October, 1919. Tague remained in Congress until Lomasney finally whipped him in 1922, despite the campaign circular Tague sent around, showing Lomasney wearing his cardigan sweater, with the comment: "Boss Lomasney appearing in the United States Court in a sweater. Is the Boss bigger than the law?" By 1922, that charge had lost its sting.

Honey Fitz, calm as always in adversity, maintained that hundreds of persons who had voted for him had been disfranchised "on the flimsy charges presented by Mr. Tague without any evidence to back up these charges."

On the day he was unseated, he said from Washington: "Tell my friends and supporters in Boston that I am not disturbed over the result in the House today. I would rather walk the streets of Boston a beggar than to gain office through the betrayal of those who had been my friends. Mr. Tague never would have been known in Washington were it not for the votes of men who today were disfranchised on his charges. . . . His conduct is despicable."

He accused Tague of "injecting the Irish issue to stir up the prejudice of the bigoted natures in the House. . . . I would sink into the ground before I would prostitute a cause that has struggled for centuries and is struggling now, and to which men and women of Irish blood have given their all."

Nor was he the only person of prominence to have been dismissed from the Halls of Congress: "Tell them also that the records of Congress show dozens of cases where members were treated unjustly by their seat being vacated. . . . There are half a dozen men in the Senate now who were unseated in recent years, while Mr. McKinley, who was unseated in the 48th Congress, was afterwards elected President."

Napoleon Fitz was not yet ready to retire to St. Helena.

CHAPTER 15

Ebb of Tide

"Boston demands a good deal of dignity in its candidates."

—*The New York Times*

EVEN out of office, Honey Fitz was a powerful figure. "The best known man in Boston is undoubtedly John F. Fitzgerald," the *Boston Post* noted in 1921. "He is more sure of a rousing reception at any gathering than any other Bostonian. His undoubted talents, his good fellowship and very fetching oratory are sure hits. He is able to cultivate popular favor as few people are. Yet has he the same power to turn his popularity into votes as he had ten years ago? It is very doubtful. Just at present, at least, he is on the shelf as an aspirant for political honors. He can get cheers easier than he can get votes."

And, like Jimmy Walker of New York, Honey Fitz knew that "cheers have short echoes."

He knew Curley was planning a return to City Hall. Mayor Peters, who "had had enough," was not up for reelection, but in John R. Murphy, Curley was tangling with an old campaigner known to contemporaries as a "superfighter." He had been chairman of the Finance Commission during the Curley administration and was Fire Commissioner when he ran for Mayor in 1921.

"Honeyboy Fitzgerald," as Curley sometimes called him, who had sparked Gallivan's campaign against Curley four years earlier, now swung his weight to Murphy. "Curley can't beat Murphy," he told a friend. "Tell him to be smart and move to New York where, with his ability, Tammany will make him Mayor in four or five years. In New York he can make as much money as he wants."

Curley gave Fitzgerald's friend a message to take back. "Tell that sonofabitch I'll chase him to New York."

"Whatever possessed Curley to start a war on Fitzgerald in the first

230

place!" said a *Boston Post* editor. "Had he Fitzgerald's support during the last eight years, political history would have been differently written. A very substantial citizen and a good man to have on your side is the energetic John F."

It looked like another Curley ebb of tide. The only newspaper with him was the *Telegram*. The Good Government Association, which at the time included substantial businessmen of Boston, worked feverishly to beat him, and political bosses on both sides strove their utmost against him. State Senator Donovan opposed him, along with ex-Mayors Fitzgerald and Peters.

Curley looked like a sheep for the shearing, but whenever he found himself the underdog, he swung hard. What was his sixty-six-year-old opponent, the venerable John R. Murphy? Why, "an old mustard plaster that has been stuck on the back of the people for fifty years." Old age and religion were the weapons he chose to use on his opponent, who told audiences over and over of his long years of experience in municipal government.

Invading a high school auditorium in a Murphy stronghold, Curley quieted an unfriendly assembly by mounting the platform and telling the audience he had just come from a rally where Murphy had been guest of honor.

"The toastmaster went on and on about John R. Murphy, and finally he turned to introduce 'the next Mayor of Boston.' " Curley shook his head sadly, as if the memory of some disaster had been rekindled in memory. "And there was the poor old man, fast asleep." He received a standing ovation as he left the hall.

At another rally, a tremolo crept into his accustomed resonance, as he shakily hunched over the lectern and shaded his eyes. "Peering closely about," he said feebly, "I see scarcely a face of those heroes I welcomed back from the Mexican War."

Honey Fitz unsuccessfully tried to ape one stunt Curley engineered during this vituperative campaign. Finding himself again in the presence of a hostile gathering, Curley turned his back to the audience and addressed his own portrait.

"Who built this magnificent building, with its fine library, its spacious gymnasium, and its hot and cold showers for the working man?" he intoned.

He tapped his portrait. "You did, Curley!"

"And who paved Dudley Street, once a cow path, and made it into a splendid modern thoroughfare?"

He tapped his likeness on the chest.

"You did, Curley."

"Who built the magnificent City Hospital down the street, a monument to medicine, and the envy of the world?"

"You did, Curley."

He wheeled, eyes ablaze, pointing a finger to an unknown character in the front row. "Finnegan, who put coal in your cellar last winter, when you were out of work and didn't have a thin dime?"

He pounded his chest. "Curley did!"

His finger found another anonymous target in the center of the hall. "McCarthy, who got your wife into the hospital and paid all the bills when you asked for help?" He paused until he joined in the chorus, in perfect unison. "Curley did!"

If this story has been told in various forms, it is a tribute to the old master, who knew when and how to alter his script.

Edward Murphy, whom Curley had earlier made an election commissioner, supported John R. (no relation) in the 1921 contest. One night his wife received an anonymous telephone call.

"Do you know where your husband is tonight, Mrs. Murphy? In a house of ill fame."

"Why don't you tell him that yourself?" Mrs. Murphy said. "Just a minute and I'll let you speak to Ed."

Fitzgerald could never match Curley as an actor, as was shown in one auditorium when he tried to use wall portraits as props.

"I have nothing special to say tonight," he said, "so I shall address the portraits on the wall and speak extemporaneously." He waved toward a likeness of George Washington. "There is the father of our country, the man who could not tell a lie, and there," he added, motioning towards a portrait of Abraham Lincoln, "is the Great Liberator, the beloved Emancipator, who laid his hand on the shoulder of the black man and said, 'You shall be free.'" Then Honey Fitz pointed to a likeness of Curley and removed his glasses. "How in the devil did that man's picture get there?"

"Why don't you pull in your ears, you bum?" a heckler shouted. "He's a damn sight better than them other two put together."

Long before this colorful campaign, Curley had been carefully preparing his strategy. His speaking schedule was full, and he missed no chance to advance a popular cause. He sided with the striking policemen in 1919, and kept reminding his electorate of Ireland's troubles. When the showdown came, however, the testy, honorable John R. Murphy proved to be a challenging opponent, a gentleman of moral muscle who appealed to the loyal sons of Kerry and Cork. He was, moreover, a brother-in-law of the beloved Irish poet, John Boyle O'Reilly, whom Curley put in the select company of Keats, Shelley, and Shakespeare.

Only one formula could effectively be used against Murphy—the formula of "vigorous assertion, repetition, contagion, and conviction." Curley "poison gas" squads swung into action, circulating the rumors that John R. Murphy had become a thirty-third degree Mason and was a disgracefully tight-fisted, hardhearted husband who was about to divorce his devoted wife so he could marry a sixteen-year-old girl. It was further alleged that he had become a director in the Loyal Coalition (a local anti-Catholic society), and that he had, alas, moved from his crude neighbors in Charlestown to the Westminster Hotel in Boston, so he wouldn't have far to walk to fashionable Trinity Church (Episcopalian) just across the way.

There were also reports of the pious talking Mr. Murphy being seen eating roast beef sandwiches on Fridays at Thompson's Spa. Reinhard Luthin, in his book *American Demagogues Twentieth Century*, cites the ending of one speech given before an Irish-American audience in South Boston: "And where was my esteemed opponent when all this was going on? He was in the Ritz Hotel in white tie and tails eating a steak dinner— and on a Friday!"

Curley supporters, attired in the clerical garb of Baptists, rang doorbells in Irish neighborhoods at unreasonable hours and asked irate Catholics to vote for their candidate, John R. Murphy. One plant at meetings was Francis McLaughlin (Murphy's campaign manager early in the 1913 campaign), who could use his sonorous voice to good advantage. The ritual ran thus: A stooge in the audience would rise. "Sir, may I ask you just one question?"

"Why, certainly. Proceed."

"We all know you know Murphy better than anyone else. Is it really true he has left our church?"

McLaughlin, pretending to be embarrassed, would bow his head and strike a meditative stance. "Brother, it grieves me to have to tell you and all you other wonderful citizens here tonight that this charge is true. Yes, brother, John Murphy has departed from our midst and has joined the infidel. He has become an Episcopalian."

While some of the stories circulated about Murphy were probably apocryphal, most of them were rooted in fact, despite Curley's sly disclaimers. "Enthusiastic supporters of mine," he wrote, "without consulting me, conducted a very excellent propaganda campaign in my behalf. They appeared in many places, where liquor was sold, in semiclerical garb with a prayerbook in their hand and a pious expression on their face, and discussed in a loud voice the sad fact that John R. Murphy had left the Catholic Church and joined a Masonic order. It was a form of propaganda never before attempted and was done without my consent, but was most effective."

One story had Candidate Murphy appealing to Cardinal O'Connell to set the record straight on the Sunday before election. This letter, according to Curley, was read from pulpits all over the city. When a certain Father Murphy read the document, he added a postscript: "I was born a Murphy and all my life I have been proud of the Murphys, but there is one Murphy I am not proud of. And remember, now, I am not talking politics."

Other political shenanigans highlighted this contest. In some Boston elections, candidates have supporters call opponents to offer them a fleet of cars to ferry voters to the polling booths, a hoax that is sometimes discovered too late. The Curley forces varied this technique, having learned that the Murphy camp had lined up a fleet of automobiles, which were scarce in those days. The opposition compiled a list of the car owners after calling the Registry of Motor Vehicles, and with these names Curley supporters kept telephone lines busy.

"This is Mr. Murphy's campaign headquarters," a voice would say. "We note that you have offered your car for our candidate in tomorrow's election. We appreciate your generosity, but find that we have a surplus of cars and won't need yours. Many thanks, now, and good night."

Curley, meanwhile, had tied up every available taxicab. Lack of transportation cut down the Murphy vote on election day.

Curley returned to City Hall, edging his way in with a plurality of only 2696 votes out of 157,000 cast for four candidates (including two "stalking horses"). Honey Fitz, who had lost several thousand dollars in a campaign wager, was unhappy, but as usual, he rebounded.

In mid-January 1922, he announced his candidacy for the United States Senate. He had been assured of the backing of the National Democratic organization, and even the mercurial Curley hopped onto his bandwagon. When they shook hands and sang duets of "Sweet Adeline" and "Tammany" in February at the Elks Club, it was the first time they had been civil to each other since 1916.

"John F. Fitzgerald," said Curley, "is a dynamic force for good, and for Boston's sake we are fortunate that he is available now that Henry

Cabot Lodge is growing too old to be senior senator from Massachusetts."

The picture abruptly changed when Attorney General J. Weston Allen entered the Republican Primary against the incumbent, Governor Channing Cox. Allen would not only defeat Cox, the Democratic swami calculated, but the expected bitter battle between them would leave the Republican Party shredded, with the defeated portion thirsting for revenge. With this in mind, Honey Fitz withdrew from the senatorial race and ran for Governor, opposing three Democrats in the primaries. He received more votes than their combined total, and newspaper headlines acknowledged that "Fitz Makes Great Run."

Meanwhile, Allen and Cox, as predicted, had clobbered each other in the primary. Allen called Governor Cox a sinister Charles Innes-mannikin and a tool of the invisible government—a back-stage group also known as the "Big Boodle." According to Thomas Lawson, the Big Boodle was a ruthless group of men who dominated Bay State politics. Early in the century, Lawson exposed "its open purchase of almost the entire Massachusetts Legislature," and boasted of driving "its organized bribers, headed by one of the state's leading citizens, into disgrace and obscurity." Allen accused Cox of having a tie-up with the Big Boodle and further charged him with laxness in prosecuting the principals in the Mishawum Manor scandal because his friend Innes was involved.

The Mishawum Manor scandal was a shakedown racket in which women, at best scantily clad, were hired to lure wealthy men into hotel rooms, where photographers hid in closets. Men of means were thus blackmailed by a "poison gas squad" led by Daniel Coakley, a former teamster, bartender and streetcar conductor who had been "discharged for neglect of duty," a notice he framed and hung on the wall of his office.

Coakley became a shady lawyer who was said to have known the price of every man whose help he needed. "A remarkable case of biological adaptation to environment," was one appraisal of this man, who was uncannily clever. When Godfrey Cabot, perhaps the most proper of Proper Bostonians, and guiding spirit of the Watch and Ward Society, tried to get data on the Mishawum Manor case, he hired a private detective whom Coakley had sent to him for that precise purpose.

After a dinner party given in honor of screen star Fatty Arbuckle at the Copley-Plaza Hotel in 1917, several motion picture magnates, including Hiram Abrams, Adolph Zukor and Jesse Lasky, went to Mishawum Manor in Woburn, Massachusetts, for more song and carousing. It was past eight on the following morning when the party ended. Retaining Coakley as counsel, the film executives raised $100,000 in the hope of quashing publicity. This amount covered Coakley's fee of $31,000, the $15,000 that went to three other lawyers representing the several women involved, and other incidental expenses.

Attorney General J. Weston Allen came into the spotlight when he led the court battle for the successful removal of District Attorney Nathan A. Tufts of Middlesex County. Tufts was refereeing a football game between Princeton and Swarthmore when notified, between the halves, that he had been ousted. Allen also caused the removal from office of Joseph C. Pelletier, who either died "of a broken heart" or committed suicide as a result of his disgrace, which included his disbarment. After the State Supreme Court investigated, both Tufts and Pelletier were accused of dropping criminal cases, some in connection with the Mishawum Manor scandal. Coakley and William J. Corcoran, Tufts' successor, were also disbarred for taking part in the conspiracy.

Governor Cox had been considered colorless until Allen unleashed his attack on the handling of the Mishawum Manor affair. This assault gave Cox a chance to demonstrate his real personality. Showing a surprising lack of political judgment, Allen had transformed the Governor from a mild, good-natured person into a raging lion, the press reported. In a climactic address at Faneuil Hall, Cox gave an address which the *Boston Post* called "the greatest single political speech ever delivered in this generation in Massachusetts." When it ended, the blindest observer knew Cox had Allen licked. Even if Allen had had time for a rebuttal, he could not have destroyed the image of righteousness which Cox had built around himself.

Cox, speaking from the platform of Faneuil Hall, patterned his technique after that of the late District Attorney, John B. Moran, who in his campaigns always spoke for himself. "I have no gang—no confederates to pay off," was his gambit. Cox, too, was alone on the rostrum, and the impression he created won over many of the independent or uncommitted votes he needed. He convinced the public that he had no political machine.

"There is still something uncanny about the complete defeat of Allen," said the *Post*. "Attorney-generals of the past, even those who did little or nothing, have been popular figures. But Allen, who performed the hardest and worthiest task of any man who ever sat in that office, got the cold shoulder when he sought his reward."

Cox suffered more unfavorable publicity when Ernest J. Goulston, a Boston advertising executive, held a dinner in his honor at the Quincy House. A prohibition agent raided the party, seizing several bottles of liquor. Even though Governor Cox left before the raid, he was embarrassed because of the raid.

The Cox-Fitzgerald campaign warmed up in October. Arguing that "present-day campaigning methods were obsolete," Honey Fitz challenged Cox to tour the state with him in a series of joint debates. Night after night at rallies, he challenged his opponent.

"If I listen," Cox quipped, "he may challenge me to sing."

Fitzgerald agreed. "Governor Cox said in a speech at North Adams last night he is afraid to meet me on the same platform because I might challenge him to sing."

Joe Kennedy, who had asked Walter Howey of the *Boston American* (later the prototype for the editor in the MacArthur-Hecht smash hit "The Front Page") to support his father-in-law, attended some of the rallies in his big chauffeur-driven Locomobile. Honey Fitz rode around the state in his own Locomobile. His supporters, who had rented a fleet of trucks to transport members of the faithful to a huge rally in Framingham pine grove, remembered at the last moment that there were no seats in the vehicles. They solved the dilemma by borrowing benches from Boston Common. Fitzgerald, who donated the milk for the outing, was jarred when the bill exceeded $1000. Some of the refreshments were stronger than milk.

Cox reminded crowds of the ungummed stickers and fraudulent voting in the 1918 congressional fight. Nevertheless, day after day, Fitzgerald, apparently the winner, kept cutting into the Cox strength, hurling pointed charges about Mishawum Manor and other shady dealings, and demanding answers to a series of embarrassing questions. Adopting the same technique Fitzgerald himself had used against Storrow, Cox blithely dismissed the charges, waiting for a break. And it came.

Just when it appeared that he was about to beat Curley to the State House, Honey Fitz pulled a boner with a carelessness that was not his custom. He made one false accusation in the closing days of the contest. The time-worn charges made by Cox had damaged his cause only slightly, especially because they had not been widely publicized over the state. Fitzgerald wrongly accused the Governor of having tried to repeal the five-cent fare on the Boston Elevated.

"This is exactly contrary to the truth," Cox said, and Honey Fitz was forced to apologize from the platform. That trifling detail changed the course of the contest.

Cox trapped him again. He launched such a powerful broadside at his opponent from the stage of Symphony Hall that he baited Fitzgerald into answering it. In Faneuil Hall, Honey Fitz defended his record, but the more he explained, the more he yielded the offensive to Cox, who knew the tide had turned just in time. Cox won by more than 60,000 votes.

"Channing H. Cox is Governor of Massachusetts again by the grace of J. Weston Allen," the *Boston Post* reported. "It was the Allen campaign against Cox that made a great political figure of the Governor. It was the woeful lack of tact and political management on the part of his primary opponent that gave Channing Cox a chance to demonstrate that he was a real personality." Fitzgerald's gallant fight did not pass unnoticed, however. "Yet it would be unfair not to pay tribute to the amazing campaign of the ex-Mayor. Nothing like it had been seen before in Massachusetts. He is the superman of campaigners and he is greater in defeat than he ever was in victory."

With him on some of his ward tours was his six-year-old grandson. But little Jack Kennedy was too young to realize that the active political career of his grandfather was over.

"I think the Republicans can thank the women for their victory," Fitzgerald said, "particularly the women's clubs, which though not supposed to be political, used their organizations, not only in registering, but at the election today, for the Republican Party."

In the best of humor, he had no thought of imminent tragedy. On election day, November 8, he left to visit his ailing daughter, Eunice, at Lake Saranac. Less than twenty-four hours after her return from the hospital, Eunice, who was twenty three, died of tuberculosis at her Dorchester home.

During World War I she had served as a Red Cross worker, giving "herself nightly to the entertainment of servicemen in the Red Cross Cottage on Boston Common while her brother, Tom, was a soldier in France," reported the *Boston Post*.

The loss deeply grieved the old campaigner, for Eunice had always been Papa's little girl, his favorite.

CHAPTER 16

Second Step to the White House

"Go you and try a democracy in your own house."

—Lycurgus

WHEN Curley ran for Governor in 1924, his hated rival, David I. Walsh, made the tongue-in-cheek observation that "the people were never offered a stronger, abler, more eloquent or more courageous candidate for governor than James Michael Curley."

In that contest, when Alvan Fuller topped Curley by 165,000 votes, Mrs. Fuller did "a Honey Fitz," adding to the interest of her husband's hard-hitting campaign by singing at rallies. She had been an opera singer before her marriage and was therefore not to be compared too closely with the tone-deaf John F., who could fluff the lyrics of "Sweet Adeline" in his seven-hundredth rendition.

There was less harmony in 1924 in Democratic ranks, for the tattered party was in even more disarray than usual, prompting Martin Lomasney to warn Fitzgerald and Curley that he would pour no oil on roiled political waters unless they "buried the hatchet and agreed on a strong wheelhorse to defeat the Republican mayoral candidate."

The wayward Curley defied the Mahatma by putting his amenable Fire Commissioner, Theodore Glynn, in the race, knowing well that he could not win. Curley wanted a weak Republican in City Hall against the day of his return to that address.

An old-timer recalls a scene in a room of the Quincy House where a strategy meeting was held, with Daniel Coakley present. It was a hot day, and Honey Fitz had loosened his collar and was pacing the room with his suspenders dangling.

"This is the time for us to forget our differences and save the city from

239

the Republicans," he said. The endorsement of the Democratic City Committee, for which Fitzgerald had the inside track, eventually went to the seventy-five-year-old Joseph H. O'Neil, whom he had defeated in the congressional race of 1894. O'Neil became the choice after Fitzgerald withdrew from the contest, much to the relief of his son-in-law, Joe Kennedy, who by 1924 had wearied of the charges that were always aired when Honey Fitz was a candidate. Some of the charges were of a private nature made during anonymous telephone calls to Mrs. John F. Fitzgerald.

In its early stage, the mayoral race was confusing. In August, *The New York Times* prophesied that forty candidates would run for the office, noting there were "no primaries, and party labels are not recognized." Curley, by a charter amendment put through by reformers, could not succeed himself, and nobody took this master of the tall story too seriously when he announced that Mrs. Curley (who was a better politician than he, in many respects) might run. He reminded the press, that Honey Fitz, a few months earlier, had suggested that Boston women should wake up and run for city offices.

Political bosses of Boston had long since shown how the city vote could be manipulated. By putting several Irishmen into a mayoral contest, the Irish vote could be disastrously split to the advantage of a Republican candidate. In 1924, Ernest Goulston had told Fitzgerald at the Lamb's Club in New York that he was raising a campaign fund to put Malcolm E. Nichols into office.

"It will be my job to divide the Democrats as much as possible, and Nichols will walk in," he said.

Goulston's apartment at 857 Beacon Street became a branch headquarters during the campaign, with mattresses spread on the floors of several rooms, and the fifty-odd men who had keys to the apartment were called the "apostles of Nichols." The apostles, not all of them anointed, arranged house parties and went into stores and barrooms soliciting votes.

Early in September, Fitzgerald had announced his candidacy and had set up campaign headquarters in Room 52 of the Quincy House.

"It is my job not to try to elect myself but to help stop Nichols," he said late in September, 1925.

"I have been convinced that my candidacy will keep Charlie Innes and his gang out of City Hall," he said in another interview. "It was Innes and his crowd who foisted the present city charter on Boston, leaving it the only city in the state where a primary for the selection of candidates to be voted for on election day is denied its citizens. Mr. Nichols, if elected, would be a willing tool of Mr. Innes and his Republican machine, and that would be a bad thing for Boston."

Four days later, in a move which one newspaper called a "tremendous surprise," he withdrew from the contest. "With John F. Fitzgerald sitting on the sidelines," the paper said, "the mayoralty campaign will lack a certain thrill only he can provide. Lovers of the spectacular may regret that this most colorful personality will not be seen charging up and down the municipal gridirons, going through for gains, being thrown for losses, smearing his opponents or being smeared. The battle will not be quite the same with the 'doctor' out."

At sixty-two, Honey Fitz still showed his old-time militant fire. He was in top physical condition, although gray-thatched, and could still fox-trot with the best of them. At his birthday party the year before, he had counseled: "Keep young. Mingle with young people. Go through life good-natured and friendly. . . . You will derive the greatest happiness from making others happy." Then he put his arms around his two Kennedy grandsons, Jack and Joe, Junior, and sang "Sweet Adeline." He sang it again over the radio that night.

On his sixty-second birthday party, he had more advice. "One of the most important missions in life is to make friends and keep them. Show kindness at all times."

After dropping out of the race, he warned voters of the importance of the mayoral election. "It will be the first time since the new charter went into effect that an attempt has been made by the Republican minority of the city to take possession of the city government. In four previous campaigns since the new charter, all the candidates have been Democrats." It would be a mistake to elect Nichols, he added, for even were he not a puppet of Innes, "he would be a minority mayor with a great majority against him in the City Council, and from the beginning of his administration until the end of his four years, constant turmoil would result."

When the candidates boiled down to six, Honey Fitz joined Martin Lomasney in backing O'Neil. "Boston is enjoying herself to the top of her bent," commented *The New York Times*. "Seldom has there been so lively a scramble for what some tribune of the people has called 'The City Hall Klondike.' " *The Times* further noted that "Fitzgerald, whose heart goes out to O'Neil, has been warbling 'Sweet Adeline' with all the ancient rapture, but amid so many Democratic feuds, caution seems to temper a little the vigor of his oratory."

At one O'Neil rally, the toastmaster, forgetting the candidate's age, remarked that Honey Fitz "could give life to a corpse." Interrupted by laughter, he quickly added that the O'Neil candidacy was not the cadaver in question.

O'Neil stole enough votes from Glynn to elect Nichols, and wound up a poor third.

Fitzgerald had been a good prophet. Nichols was indeed a puppet, as Governor Alvan Fuller indicated. "Bottomly is the morning mayor, Innes the afternoon mayor, and Goulston the night mayor." Innes was the day mayor and Nichols the nightmare, was another version.

It was the Republican turn to juggle assessments, among other municipal baubles, and "The Three Horsemen," as Fitzgerald labeled them, could claim that they were merely trying to put asunder what Curley had wrought. Nichols was also the pawn of a corrupt palace guard at City Hall to a degree unmatched since the days of Mayor John O'Brien of New York, a Tammany tool. Asked whom he would name Police Commissioner, O'Brien told the "wolf pack," as City Hall reporters were called: "I don't know. They haven't told me yet." As he read one speech—obviously for the first time—he laughed so hard at the opening joke his glasses fell onto the platform and broke, and an aide had to finish the speech. In addressing a school graduation, he said he had always loved the classics ever since he translated Horace from the original Greek.

With Fitzgerald and Curley retired, the new state boss was Senator David I. Walsh. The former mayors were not lightly to be dismissed, however. It was Fitzgerald's stand on Prohibition, for example, which enabled Walsh to defeat his Republican opponent in 1926.

"The campaign to elect Walsh to the Senate began when Fitzgerald demanded that the Democrats line up for modification of the Volstead law as the chief issue of the campaign. It threw a scare into the ranks of Republican leaders from which they never recovered," said the *Boston Post*. "The Republicans wanted no wet and dry issue. The *Post* editor also noted that "John F. Fitzgerald, who is about as shrewd a political observer as anyone in these parts, has started something by the demand that David I. Walsh and other Democratic candidates come out flatly for beer and wine as the chief issue in the fall campaign. The Fitzgerald blast will certainly compel the Democratic candidates to do some heavy thinking."

In this fight, Fitzgerald and Curley, in opposite camps, enlivened an otherwise drab primary by heaving verbal brickbats at each other.

In his leisure, Honey Fitz had more time for family associations, and saw a good deal of the Kennedys in Brookline. The two oldest of an eventual brood of nine children, Joe, Junior, and Jack lived with their family in a modest gray frame house in a neighborhood where similar dwellings were built close together on both sides of a tree-lined street. The Kennedys always chose a house near a good school and playground. As the tribe increased, the Kennedys moved to a larger and more luxurious gray home nearby, in a more fashionable neighborhood. When the Boston team was staging a rally at Braves Field off Commonwealth Avenue, the Kennedys could hear the cheering. Grampa Honey Fitz often took them to see the Braves or Red Sox play, for he never lost his enthusiasm for the Boston clubs, developed in days when they were champions and when he led his "Royal Rooters."

In 1926, Joe and Jack enrolled in the Dexter School in Brookline, a private academy which few Irish Catholics attended, although Joseph P. Kennedy, Sr., was a trustee. Joe, one grade ahead of Jack, told his classmates he would one day be President of the United States, an ambition transmitted to him from Honey Fitz and Pat Kennedy, by way of the former Rose Fitzgerald and her husband. Jack, who quarterbacked the unbeaten Dexter School football team in 1926, had a definite ambition, too. He wanted to be like big brother Joe, who usually bested him in their youthful scraps, for Joe was brawnier. Myra Fiske, one of Jack's teachers at Dexter, remembers him as a "very fine boy." Later she called him "a man whom I very much admire."

Sister Eunice (named for her aunt) remembers that "Joe had more personality than Jack, maybe, but Jack had more charm. Joe was physically bigger and stronger, but Jack perhaps had a higher I.Q. I remember when he was about seven, they gave Jack an I.Q. test and mother told me afterward how exceptionally high it was. I think he was brighter than the rest of us. Whenever we discussed things, he was always the one who looked things up."

Jack credited his mother for motivating him and encouraging his interest in books and his general intellectual curiosity. "She would talk about history, too, but I wouldn't say she was *au courant*. No, I wouldn't say that the germ of my interest in history came from her. I have an inquiring mind, and I like history. After all, if you're an engineer, you like to read about engineers."

Brookline neighbors still remember seeing Papa Kennedy pulling his children around snowy streets in a homemade soapbox sled. On one outing, Papa was so absorbed in dreams of further financial conquests that he continued padding along after Joe rolled off the sled while rounding a corner.

The Kennedy siblings got into their share of trouble. "I used to have a ruler around and paddle them occasionally, because when they're young, that's all they understand," Mrs. Kennedy recalls. Sometimes, when Joe or Jack was ordered to his room on a bread-and-water diet, he slipped down the backstairs to the kitchen, and if the cook or chauffeur caught him raiding the icebox, they would promise to keep mum. On rare occasions when their allowance was cut off, the boys could usually charm the price of a movie out of one of the domestics.

"You're spoiling them," Mrs. Kennedy told their chauffeur, Harry Pattison, when she caught wind of this.

Papa Kennedy was often away on business trips during those Brookline days. During one absence, he was so engrossed in operating in stocks while spending seven weeks in a suite at the Waldorf-Astoria that he did not see his daughter, Patricia, until she was a month old. When he was away, Mrs. Kennedy supervised the children's play, and kept a card-index file on all the children, "recording when each had measles, whooping cough, chickenpox or any of the children's diseases. I made a record of each physical examination and the result of each visit to the dentist." An intimate friend remembers that her children were always on her mind. "She would leave any party early to be home in time for a baby's feeding, and was always punctilious about her responsibilities as a mother."

There were always enough Kennedys on hand to form a quorum or to choose up sides for a game. "On pleasant days," Mrs. Kennedy recalls, "I took the children for walks. I wheeled one in a baby carriage and two or three toddled along with me. I made it a point each day to take them into church for a visit. I wanted them to form a habit of making God and religion a part of their daily lives, not something to be reserved for Sunday."

Grampa Fitzgerald might stop by to take two or three of the children for a ride on the swan boats in the Public Garden or to the zoo at Franklin Park. The Brookline Kennedys also visited the Fitzgeralds in their Dorchester home. John F. Fitzgerald, Jr., Jack's uncle, remembers him coming into their living room as a small boy. "You've got a grandfather clock and a baby grand piano," he said.

In her husband's absence, Mrs. Kennedy was the disciplinarian and character-builder. "She was the glue," said Jack years later. "She's not as forceful as my father, but she was the glue. She was highly devout."

Rose Fitzgerald Kennedy never forgot the deep feeling of religion she had absorbed at the Convent of the Sacred Heart in Germany. "You have to tend to the roots as well as the stems, and slowly and carefully plant ideas and concepts of right and wrong, religion and social implications and applications," she explained.

As familiar with shrines and historic pilgrimages as her husband, who had in his youth conducted guided tours, she took the children to such landmarks as Plymouth Rock, Concord Bridge, the Old North Church, and Bunker Hill.

On Sundays, the family crowded into their Model-T Ford and Joe, Senior, drove the ten mlies to Winthrop, where his parents lived their last years. Grampa Kennedy was remembered by the boys as a kindly, but more awesome and austere person than Grampa Fitzgerald. They could not relax so much with him. "On those Sunday afternoon visits, he wouldn't let us cut up or even wink in his presence," Jack said.

During their Cohasset summers, from 1919 to 1926, Grampa Kennedy used to take the paddlewheeler from Rowe's Wharf to Nantasket, where Harry Pattison met him with the Kennedy's Rolls Royce, acquired by the time the family had moved to their second address in Brookline in 1919. "Grandfather Kennedy always brought a bag of toys or some goodies for the kids," Pattison remembers. "He was a man of great dignity, Mr. Patrick Kennedy."

By 1919, the family was affluent enough to afford a governess for the older children and a nurse for the younger. "I did not want to move each time Joe changed business enterprises, because I thought it was wrong to interrupt school, their friendships, and the routine of the family," Mrs. Kennedy said. "I felt the same way when it became necessary to move to New York." Moving such a large family and domestic staff too often would have been a formidable problem of logistics.

Joseph P. Kennedy, by 1926, was fashioning his far-flung financial enterprises into a labyrinth that would have taxed the energies of three or four men of less acumen and perspicuity. Honey Fitz, who had given up his enthusiasm for manufacturing chocolate beverage which he had once hoped would give Coca-Cola some competition, came close to becoming a Hollywood executive on the payroll of his son-in-law. In February, 1926, the *Boston Post* ran a front-page headline:

JOHN F. FITZGERALD
IS LATEST MOVIE MAGNATE

"Former Mayor John F. Fitzgerald will be actively interested in the

$10,000,000 motion picture venture that will be headed by his son-in-law," reported the *Post*.

Honey Fitz, who never actually took the position, verified the transfer of the control of the Film Booking Offices of America from British control to Boston interests. "This is one of the biggest deals in the motion picture industry," he told the press. "My son-in-law has long been interested in motion picture distribution and production. He believes there is a big field for the future. He will take active part in the executive management of the concern, and both the production and distribution facilities of the organization will be increased with a view to making a profit of a million dollars a year."

"Every venture in which he [Joe Kennedy] participated was successful," the *Post* reported, "and by 1926 he was rated a millionaire, although he was only thirty-seven years old. He is the son of P. J. Kennedy of East Boston, who was Wire Commissioner of Boston during the first Fitzgerald administration."

Joe Kennedy's interest in motion pictures dated back to 1919, when, with a group of Bostonians, he had bought control of a chain of thirty-one small movie theaters scattered over New England. He also produced films for a short time. In 1926, when he acquired control of the Film Booking Offices of America, he made an average of one picture a week—mostly Westerns and melodramas. Stars under contract included Fred Thompson (whose horse, Silver King, was better known than the winner of the Kentucky Derby), Richard Talmadge, Evelyn Brent, and "Lefty" Flynn, the former Yale football star. One successful production was "Broken Laws."

During the mid-1920s, he took over several motion-picture companies, reshuffled them, and sold out at a handsome profit. Two films which he produced independently starred Gloria Swanson, who had become a friend of the Kennedy family. He refused to exhibit one of them because of a vivid seduction scene involving a convent girl. One film he backed —"The Miracle Man"—returned him $3,000,000 on a $120,000 investment.

In Hollywood circles, Joseph P. Kennedy was put in the same exclusive bracket of big-time producers as Jesse Lasky and Samuel Goldwyn. His Film Booking Officers of America, one of the world's leading producers and distributors of films, serviced seven hundred of the largest theaters in the nation. In 1929, it was bought by Radio Corporation of America, later known as RKO Pictures, one of many successful ventures.

"In 1928," Joe Kennedy wrote in his Harvard report, "I was elected chairman of the board of directors of the Keith-Albee-Orpheum Theatres Corporation, and in 1929 and 1930 I was president and chairman of the board of directors of the Pathé Exchange, Inc." He had made an estimated $5,000,000 by the time he quit the movies in 1930. Meanwhile, he had been speculating on Wall Street.

"Anyone can lose his shirt in Wall Street," he said, "if he has sufficient capital and inside information."

He did not lose, however. In August, 1929, he surprised the Street by clearing out of the stock market weeks ahead of the crash. Asked how he had the foresight to sell short for a reported $15,000,000 coup, he said: "I dropped in at a shoeshine parlor on Wall Street. The boy who shined my shoes did not know me. He wasn't fishing for information or looking for a market tip. He was the average wage earner or salaried employee playing the market like everybody else in that day. He looked up at me as he snapped the cloth over my shoes and told me what was going to happen to various stocks and offerings on the market that day. I listened as I looked down at him, and when I left the place I thought: 'When a time comes that a shoeshine boy knows as much as I do about what is going on in the stock market, tells me so and is entirely correct, there is something the matter either with me or with the market, and it's time for me to get out,' and I did."

Unlike most Wall Street plungers, Joe Kennedy protected his family by giving them an anchor to windward. In 1929, he gave each of his children a trust fund of a million dollars. "I fixed it so that any of my children, financially speaking, could look me in the eye and tell me to go to hell," he said. Earlier, Bernard Baruch, an old friend, had advised against the plan.

"It will make your children too independent," he said.

"They're already independent," Joe Kennedy countered.

According to Rose Kennedy, the children first learned of their legacy by reading the item in *Time* magazine. "I can remember telling Henry Luce at a dinner party how worried we were about the publicity," she said. "It was after the Lindbergh kidnaping, and we were afraid the publicity might give people ideas."

Jack Kennedy, apropos of some wild stories about the trust funds, said: "It's been made into a myth and I'd like to see the record set straight. The story goes that he put a million dollars in trust for each of us to be self-sufficient so that we could devote ourselves to public life, and that he did this when we were very young. Well, that was in 1929, and he was speculating. It was very risky business. He was speculating pretty hard, and his health was not too good at the time, and that was the reason he did it. There was no other reason for it."

Jack Kennedy was twelve when he became a millionaire.

At this time, the overworked Joe Kennedy had shed thirty-two pounds and was sent to a hospital for a check-up. The rest gave him an opportunity to clarify his "social views," he said.

"Kennedy's life has gone in the sections and jerks of a fast freight train," reported *Time* magazine in 1939. In his spectacular career he had earned separate fortunes by shrewd speculation in real estate, liquor importing, and dozens of other enterprises. He found it simpler by then to list himself in his annual Harvard class report as a "capitalist." He had previously referred to himself as a banker.

"The legend of Joe Kennedy made him at once the hero of a Frank Merriwell captain-of-the-nine adventure, a Horatio Alger success story, an E. Phillips Oppenheim tale of intrigue, and a John Dos Passos disillusioning report on the search for the big money," said *Fortune* magazine in a profile of Kennedy. "The truth makes him the central character of a picaresque novel of a sort not yet written."

Years after leaving Boston, Joe Kennedy remarked: "Boston is a good city to come from, but not a good city to go to. If you want to make money, go where the money is." That was not the only reason he left Boston, however.

In 1926, the Joseph Kennedys and their seven children were a cultured American family, and Joe had already shown symptoms of financial wizardry. He was still *persona non grata* to the inner banking circle, however. It was one thing for an "Irishman" to run a little East Boston bank and handle immigrants' remittances; it was another thing to be welcome in the sanctum of high finance.

Galen Stone, of Hayden, Stone & Company of Boston and New York, had given him a frosty reception at first. Unable to see him in New York City, Kennedy dropped into a seat beside him on a Boston-bound train and tried to interest him in ordering ships from Fore River. Two weeks later, Galen Stone named him manager of his Boston office, a position he held from 1919 until 1924. During those years, according to *Fortune* Magazine, Kennedy moved in the "intense, secretive circles of operators in the wildest stock market in history, with routine plots and pools, inside information and wild guesses," and he learned market operations thoroughly.

Soon the Kennedys were spending their summers in a huge, gray, wooden house overlooking a rock-bound beach at Cohasset. There the Kennedy children learned to become expert swimmers. The Kennedy chauffeur, Harry Pattison, drove the family Rolls Royce during those years. Edward Moore, who had been John F. Fitzgerald's secretary for years, lived in a tiny bungalow adjacent to the big house. Moore, according to *Time* magazine, was "Irish as a clay pipe," adding that he was "nurse, comforter, friend, stooge, package-bearer, adviser, who played games with Joe and the children, bought neckties and bonds for Joe, opened doors, wrote letters, investigated investments, saw to it Joe wore his rubbers."

As Joe Kennedy's financial empire expanded, it better suited his interests to settle his family near his New York headquarters. In 1927, when he was still managing the Stock Exchange department of Hayden Stone & Company, he put his family and domestics into a private railroad car and moved them out of Boston which, he said, "was no place to bring up Catholic children."

The family settled in a comfortable home in woodsy Riverdale, New York, and Joe Kennedy sold his summer house in Cohasset and bought a rambling, shingled, eighteen-room summer place in Hyannisport on Cape Cod, overlooking Nantucket Sound. Although frequently referred to as a "cottage," this three-gabled house with its wide porches where the children could romp, has more aptly been called the "big house."

As Kennedy prospered, the family spent winter vacations at Palm Beach, where the John Fitzgeralds were frequent guests, and summers at their home in Hyannisport, with its tennis court, spacious lawns for softball and touch football, swimming pool, Swedish bath, and private theatre. This home, like all the other Kennedy domiciles, has an extensive library and comfortable furniture in the best taste, with no suggestion of the ornate. Here visitors might find Joe, Senior, stretched out on the wide porch with a stockmarket ticker chattering away by his side, making further fortunes while reclining.

One of the family boats was christened *The Ten of Us,* and when Teddy, the ninth and youngest of the Kennedy children, was ready for the sea, it was renamed *One More.* Later boats included a sailboat, the *Victura,* a fifty-foot cruiser, the *Marlin,* and another sailer, the *Restovus.* Still another sailboat was named the *Rose Elizabeth,* in honor of Mrs. Kennedy.

In the summer of 1927, Joe, Junior, and Jack, champions both, had just won first prize in a race and were relaxing over books on the porch when they spotted an overturned sailboat a couple of miles offshore.

"Joe P. Kennedy, Jr., twelve, and Jack Fitzgerald Kennedy, ten, sons of Joseph P. Kennedy, motion picture magnate and banker, and grandsons of John F. Fitzgerald performed a daring rescue this afternoon in

Hyannis Harbor," reported the *Boston Post*. "After finishing the race in which their boat, the *Rose Elizabeth* . . . won first prize, their attention was called to one of the other boats which had filled with water and was in a sinking condition two miles from shore. The Kennedy boys took right out into the open sea just in time to rescue Ralph Russell, who was holding on for his life to the bottom of his boat. He was taken aboard the *Rose Elizabeth* in an exhausted condition."

Before that summer ended, Honey Fitz surprised a beach gathering by swimming more than half a mile in rough water off Craigville Beach. It was his last day at Hyannis, and some of his friends were joshing him about his wind, asking whether it was as good in the water as it was on the platform. He countered by saying he would swim to the Beach Club to show he was still long-winded in every way, despite his sixty-four years. William Martin, his chauffeur, followed in a rowboat, but his assistance was not needed.

"You're good for many more campaigns," a friend remarked when he came out of the water.

After that summer vacation, Jack returned to the Riverdale School, where he attended the fourth, fifth, and sixth grades. In September 1930, he enrolled at the Canterbury School in New Milford, Connecticut, the only Catholic school he ever attended. "I feel pretty homesick but it's O.K. now," he wrote his parents, adding that he would "be quite pious I guess when I get home," since attendance every morning and evening at chapel was compulsory. He found time, however, to play "baggamon" and went out for football "practite." Except for spelling and Latin, he did well in his studies.

During the Easter vacation, an appendectomy kept him out of school and he never returned to Canterbury.

When the family moved to Bronxville, he went through the seventh and eighth grades, and was ready for Choate School in Connecticut.

Back home, Honey Fitz told the editor of the *Boston Herald,* and anyone else who cared to listen, that Boston had lost his son-in-law because of Yankee hostility to Irish-Catholics. And in his 1936 book, *I'm for Roosevelt,* Joe Kennedy himself scored the snobocracy in such ringing Rooseveltian phrases as the "privileged aristocrats," the "ungrateful rich," and the "modern Bourbons," who, like the French Bourbons of the eighteenth century, never learned and never forgot.

As for Honey Fitz, he preferred such homespun men as Al Smith, whose brown derby would be the best known hat of 1928.

CHAPTER 17

Rough Talk in Massachusetts

"No human being ever paid me a cent, directly or indirectly, for services rendered."

—JOHN F. FITZGERALD

IT WAS 1927. Calvin Coolidge did not choose to run. Gene Tunney promised Jack Dempsey another shot at his heavyweight boxing championship. Gertrude Ederle swam the English Channel, and Charles Lindbergh, returning from his solo epic, received press notices that filled two freight cars. Dorothy Parker, who came to Boston to seek clemency for Sacco and Vanzetti, was fined $5 for "loitering and sauntering."

It was a sad day in Boston when the Adams House, whose bar made Teddy Roosevelt and John L. Sullivan seem to belong to the same biological species, closed, and customers wept at midnight when Honey Fitz sang "Sweet Adeline" there for the last time.

In May, 1927, however, the new Ritz-Carlton was ready for business, and Fitzgerald entertained Mayor Jimmy Walker of New York at the gala opening. It was the year Jack Sharkey knocked out Jim Maloney and put Boston on the fistic map. At a testimonial dinner for Sharkey at the Parker House, Charles Innes was toastmaster, but the life of the party was Boston's busiest booster—Dr. John F. Fitzgerald.

Earlier in the year, he had put on another good show for newsmen when they interviewed him on his birthday anniversary. By this time he and Mrs. Fitzgerald were living in a third-floor suite at the Bellevue Hotel, where all Boston politicians foregather in defeat or victory. After jumping over a few chairs to show how spry he was, he climbed through a window onto a ledge so that photographers could get outdoor shots of him.

He still stayed up until two or three o'clock in the morning, he told the press, and was still addicted to browsing around newspaper offices waiting for the first edition. To vary a weary routine, he warbled "Till We Meet Again." He broke tradition again on his following birthday anniversary by singing "Sweet Elaine" over Boston and New York radio stations. Though written by the authors of "Sweet Adeline," it never got into orbit.

The year passed uneventfully for Honey Fitz, but in 1928 he was again rally-deep in politics, stumping for Alfred Smith, popular Governor of New York.

Curley, in an effort to set himself up as the leader of the Smith forces in Massachusetts, presided at "bull-pen" sessions at Young's Hotel, and the rising wave of sentiment throughout the state restored the ex-Mayor's waning prestige. Smith's candidacy became the most moving political cause in the history of Massachusetts.

Among his sponsors were Senator Walsh and Joseph Buell Ely, the first Yankee rural Democrat to impress Boston voters. In the early part of the Smith boom, outcast Curley had been shunted to the sidelines, while the Walsh-Ely combine reaped the benefits of Smith's popularity. They and other Democratic leaders had marked Curley for political extinction.

But Curley saw in Smith just the springboard he needed. Smith, an Irish-Catholic from the sidewalks of the East Side, and a Democrat with mass appeal, was a forthright speaker with the outgoing personality Boston voters liked. He was a wet, and Boston was dripping. The situation invited Curley forensics.

Announcing that he would run for Mayor in 1929, he lauded Smith and opened a loft in Young's Hotel that came to be known as the bullpen. Young's Hotel, one of the oldest and most famous hotels in Boston, was rich in tradition and known the world over as an eating place. At one time, during its noon hour, more persons dined there than in any hotel in the world. Celebrated jurists, financiers, and politicians played pool or billiards there, after sampling "Old Mike" Bowen's broiled tripe masterpiece in the mirrored men's dining room, if they wished to bypass the choice prime beef, mutton, and turkey that weighed down the tables. One of Young's waiters was Horace Hemesley, who had been born a slave in Baltimore. He served Presidents and lesser dignitaries, always with the same greeting. He would ask in his mellow voice: "Is you gentlemens gittin' all you wants?"

But the hotel's splendored history was merely a memory when Curley began to attract crowds to it once more. He held forth at noon every weekday, extolling the Happy Warrior and lampooning his Republican opponent, Herbert Hoover. He came to be recognized as the most vocal and articulate of all Smith adherents.

It was a wise move for a mayoral candidate, for almost everyone wanted to hear about Smith, right down to election day. When handsome young Maurice Tobin, one of his lieutenants who was looming as a rival, asked permission to talk from the bull-pen, Curley graciously assigned him a date. Tobin was delighted until he realized his speaking engagement was on a Sunday.

Early in 1928, Fitzgerald and Curley had been snarling at each other. In April both were invited to the annual ladies' night meeting of an Improvement Association in Dorchester, a parochial setting for two political luminaries. With perfunctory greetings, they took seats at opposite ends of the guest table. In his speech, Fitzgerald, after lauding the work of the association, charged that Curley during his first administration had neglected Dorchester, particularly in the crucial matter of garbage removal. He then stepped to the center of the hall, sang a song, and left, amid loud applause.

It was Curley's turn to speak. "The gentleman who sings the drunkard's song," he began, "has been Mayor of this city and is qualified to discuss ashes and garbage, but I prefer to talk about more significant things." On other occasions, Curley embroidered on this speech, adding that in ancient Rome, of which he had a monumental ignorance, a certain tribune of the people, boasted of his efficiency in removing ashes and garbage though, at the same time, depriving the Romans of their freedom. This tribune met his just reward when the populace rose up and buried him in ashes and garbage. Audiences loved Curley's version of history.

Curley's bull-pen strategy had marshaled the Irish-Catholic vote so solidly behind him, and had attracted such state-wide attention, he could not, when Smith came to Boston, be denied a place of prominence at the Smith reception at the Boston Arena. Curley rode with Walsh and Smith from the railroad station through crowded streets in a shower of confetti and ticker tape, waving his hat, bowing and smiling, in a successful effort to make himself the center of attention. According to one newspaper, "It was a personal victory" for him.

In this setting, the two most fabulous Democrats of their generation passed the olive branch. In October they met at a wildly enthusiastic rally at Young's Hotel, where the crowd filled the oaken dining room and overflowed into the streets for blocks. *The New York Times,* noting that these two engaging campaigners had signed and sealed a pact of peace, added: "These two statesmen are not unlike in many of their qualities. Each has the gift of passionate, biting speech." They shook hands, patted each other on the back and smiled in a memorable reconciliation amid the happy and unrestrained howling of a surprised throng. Although they were still enemies, the Smith cause was too strong to permit their vendetta to endure. It was a stirring picture of united Democracy in the Bay State, where a disunited Democracy was more the rule.

"We are going to get together not for this alone," Honey Fitz shouted, "but for years to come and forever," and a crowd of 5000 cheered. They pledged themselves to battle for Smith, but political sharps guessed that the two ex-mayors would be clawing at each other again after the election. A *Boston Evening Traveler* caught them wearing brown derbies and smiling benignly as they shook hands, and often during the campaign they were seen arm-in-arm, sporting those same brown derbies.

Fitzgerald and Curley were powerful stumpers during the contest, although they were snubbed by some Smith leaders unaware of their influence with the electorate. At one South Boston rally for Smith, James Cheever heckled Fitzgerald, and when he started to badger the next speaker, Governor Ely, two men sitting near him punched him on the jaw. At another rally a Curley supporter, drunk, shouted, "It's a lie!" when Honey Fitz began his speech, whereupon willing hands dragged him out of the hall. The campaign was mild, however, compared with the good old days, and there were old-timers who voiced complaints, wondering what politics was coming to.

Even from Smith's defeat, Curley benefited, for he was identified with him, and the intense local resentment over the bigoted methods used against Smith nationally were translated into votes for Curley.

During the fight, Curley had promised Honey Fitz he would support him for Governor in 1930. When the time came to file papers, however, Fitzgerald again wavered between running for Governor or Senator. *The New York Times* predicted that "the lively Dr. Fitzgerald had his eye on Washington. He would be very comfortable in the seat now occupied by Senator Gillett. He would not actually need the assistance of Mayor Curley to obtain the nomination any more than Curley's election would depend exclusively on Fitzgerald's support, but with Curley's approval the road would be easier."

He would be a formidable candidate for Senator, experts agreed. "The Republicans might have a job on their hands to beat the redoubtable John F.," said the *Boston Post*. "He is well supplied with money, having made several millions in the past ten years as the result of shrewd investments."

The newspaper may have been deceived by Honey Fitz's chauffeur-driven Cadillac. Honey Fitz speculated heavily, but it is doubtful that he ever made or lost several millions, for he left a personal estate valued at only $105,956. (His wife, Mary, received approximately half of the adjusted gross estate, and two sons, Thomas A. Fitzgerald and John F. Fitzgerald, Jr., each received about $5,300. Rose, who was named executrix, was not provided for in her father's will, but a note for $58,415 from a 1947 loan was recorded paid to her from the estate on October 4, 1951.) Honey Fitz also left bequests ranging from $100 to $500 to Boston College's School of Business Administration, several North End churches, and St. Margaret's Hospital (where he was a patient), Beth Israel Hospital, and the Children's Hospital. Other than his wife and sons, he left nothing to relatives.

The *Boston Post* further noted that "a seat in the Senate would just about climax Fitzgerald's public career."

By mid-summer 1929, it was predicted that Curley would run for Mayor, Andrew J. Peters for Governor, and Honey Fitz for the United States Senate. (One veteran political observer maintains that Peters was bypassed because he was taking a nap and refused to come to the telephone when called by the chairman of the State Democratic Committee.)

Since Massachusetts was an independent rather than a strictly Republican State, Fitzgerald was given a fair chance of winning the election. "His name is as familiar throughout the state as that of any other citizen," reported *The New York Times,* "bar none. He is honored because he always has expounded the doctrine of a bigger and better Boston, and has never sounded the plaints of pessimism respecting the future of New England. He is a great campaigner, and 'Sweet Adeline' always hits the crowd. But he is older than he once was, which is not to say he is over the hilltop too far for formidable strife, and there are now conditions which have altered somewhat the favorable circumstances in which he made his great fight against Lodge."

During all this 1929 speculation, Curley waged another colorful campaign for the mayoralty. His principal opponent was Frederick Mansfield, a dignified lawyer who was unable to dent the Curley armor effectively. Another candidate was Dan Coakley, who always added spice to any contest. Night after night on the radio, Coakley pleaded with Curley: "Release me from my oath of secrecy as your lawyer, Jim, so that I can tell the people the truth about you."

"I never listen to Coakley," Curley commented. "He isn't sufficiently entertaining."

Curley taunted Mansfield. "Where were you, Freddy," he asked, "when Al Smith ran for President? You were home, with your little red slippers on, reading the *Ladies' Home Journal* while letting the big parade go by." He ridiculed him as the candidate of the Good Government Association which needed only a little ivy to make it resemble a perfect ruin. "The mountain labored," Curley said, "and brought forth a mouse."

Another person who squirmed under Curley's withering sarcasm was a former Curley supporter, "Billso" Hickey, who joined the Mansfield camp. By linking him with an aristocratic woman of the time, Curley made him a laughing stock.

"You can imagine my astonishment last Thursday afternoon," Curley told rallies, "to see Billso Hickey strolling down the street with Abigail Homans."

"I'll punch that so and so in the eye," Hickey said, when his sister rebuked him for consorting with Abigail. In the devious ways of Boston politics, however, Billso knew what he was doing. He wound up years later with a political post given him by Mansfield.

Such diversions as the Billso Hickey incident were no substitutes for the traditional Fitzgerald-Curley clashes, as one Boston newspaper noted in its complaint about the colorless campaign.

"He (Curley) would be in his element tearing the hide off John F. Fitzgerald, Martin Lomasney and others, but these former enemies are now his dear friends and he just can't slam them. Mansfield has no record in city politics for Curley to attack."

At one big rally over which Congressman John W. McCormack presided, Caledonian Club bagpipers enlivened proceedings. Honey Fitz was main speaker at this meeting, at which Curley predicted he would sweep into office.

When Mansfield mentioned his service during the Spanish-American War, Curley found an opening he needed. "Ferocious Freddy" sounded, he said, as if he had been "one of Colonel Teddy Roosevelt's Roughest Riders." His opponent, he teased, had never marched past Norfolk, Virginia, "where he had served with distinction as an apothecary clerk for a few months." He added that "the so-called blood stains on his uniform had been caused by a bottle of iodine he carelessly spilled," and said "the only powder he handled during that arduous conflict was talcum powder."

When Coakley said he wanted to become Mayor so that he could punish those who had destroyed Joseph Pelletier, Curley countered: "Dapper Dan, you know the person responsible for the ruin of Pelletier. It was you, Dapper Dan."

Martin Lomasney challenged Coakley to tell the truth about his black-mail squad. "Why don't he tell the story about Mishawum Manor?" he ungrammatically asked his Hendricks Club. Nobody has ever been told that full story.

On the Sunday before the election, more than twenty-five thousand persons packed Boston Garden as the band played "Tammany" and "The Sidewalks of New York." Honey Fitz, after singing "Sweet Adeline," cited Curley's previous mayoral administration as "the greatest in the history of all the mayors Boston ever had." Curley in turn promised Boston "the greatest administration any city ever had in the history of the American Republic."

He received more than one hundred sixteen thousand votes to less than ninety-seven thousand for Mansfield. Coakley trailed, as usual, with fewer than three thousand votes.

In victory, Curley ditched Smith, convinced it was not yet time to consider a Roman Catholic for the Presidency. Smith had lost the common touch since 1928, he said. "Having discarded his brown derby for a tall hat, he had wrapped himself up in DuPont cellophane and Morgan ticker tape." One Smith supporter violently disagreed, explaining that Smith still chatted amiably with the bootblack at a Tammany haunt—the Stevens House on Lake Placid, and added one unpublished anecdote to the Smith repertoire. When a waiter in the dining room of the Stevens House asked the Governor whether he wanted a cocktail, Smith pulled a flask from a hip pocket.

"No thanks," he said, "I'll drink my own."

Midway in Curley's administration, Republican Governor Frank G. Allen's term expired, and Joseph Ely of Westfield became the candidate of the Walsh-Smith machine. Honey Fitz, in another switch, changed his mind about running for the Senate and became a candidate for Governor, as did Captain John J. Cummings, who advised Fitzgerald to "retire to the pastoral pleasures of his home in the millionaires' colony at Ware-ham." (Fitzgerald's new summer home was not far from the Kennedy compound at Hyannisport.)

Fitzgerald in 1930 had served as chairman of Curley's Tercentenary Celebration Committee. During the many functions, Governor Allen and Mayor Curley had often appeared on the same platform and had treated each other with such deference that it was inferred by political sharps that a "deal" was in the making.

When Allen named Frank A. Goodwin, a Curley Republican, chairman of the Finance Commission, this feeling grew, even though Curley maintained that he persuaded Fitzgerald to run because Walsh and Ely were openly challenging his leadership. The wiseacres correctly surmised that he was planning to run for governor later, and if he decided to do so in 1932, it would be to his advantage if Allen remained in office for another two years. Ely, whose stature had grown because of his alliance with Al Smith, could count on a substantial Irish vote, and Curley feared he would become the core of a powerful state-wide machine. Ely—but not Fitzgerald—could beat Allen, Curley reasoned.

A futile effort was made at a Worcester convention to choose a candidate, as the contest was becoming acrimonious. Curley went out of his way, in his support of Honey Fitz, to ridicule Ely and Cummings. At one banquet Curley rose to speak.

"I am no enemy of Joe Ely," he said. "He is a good country boy." Then, turning to Ely, he added: "Joe, better you should be buried 20,000 leagues under the sea than be elected Governor of this great and glorious Commonwealth of Massachusetts. As I consider you, I am reminded of the Biblical story of the man who came down from Jericho and fell among thieves."

This observation was particularly embarrassing, since Ely was sitting next to Daniel Coakley at the time.

Curley also used Cummings for target practice. "Can you imagine John J. Cummings being elected Governor?" he asked crowds. "Of course, nobody would think of such a thing. Cummings is a nice fellow in many ways. If I were an employer I would not hesitate to hire him—as an elevator man." He waited for the laughter to end. "And I believe he would make a good one."

While Fitzgerald was assailing the opposition, Ely, considering him his only serious rival, lampooned him. "Think only of me, John F. Fitzgerald," he mimicked his opponent at a rally. "I am Boston. Boston is not hogging anything. All Boston wants is John F. Fitzgerald."

Former Governor Al Smith came to the Bay State during this campaign and devoted most of his eloquence to a plea for the election of his "friend and staunch supporter, Joe Ely." It was a strategic move to dispel any opposition created by Curley's charges that Ely "was no friend of the Irish."

The Mayor had launched his most vicious charge over the air on the twelfth of September, calling Ely an enemy of the Irish for whom "no one with a drop of Irish blood in his veins, no lover of liberty anywhere in the world," would vote. He charged that Ely had told Judge Daniel T. O'Connell, brother of the ex-Congressman, Joseph, that "if the Irish want to fight, let them go back to Ireland to fight." In his savage attack, Curley said Ely had slurred the Irish at the state convention in 1920, when he championed a plank in the platform favoring the League of Nations.

As early as July, Honey Fitz had said he preferred party harmony to the office of Governor. "Is it too much to expect that the Boston Democracy will take the lead in showing an unselfish spirit? That is my position, and I would rather be known in the future history of politics in the state as a leader in the movement for decent treatment and for my Democratic associations than be Governor of Massachusetts."

In his bid for the office, he had made the going lively, but he collapsed a fortnight before the primary, and during his convalescence in a hospital, he withdrew from the contest which he was favored to win. His name, however, remained on the ballot, and Mayor Curley proclaimed a big vote for him in the primary would do more for him than any medicine. In his determination to secure Fitzgerald the nomination despite his withdrawal, Curley became even more devastating, irked further because Honey Fitz had given him little advance knowledge of his decision to get out of the race. Night after night Curley, turning the campaign into a personal fight, spoke to huge crowds and talked over state-wide radio hook-ups.

Ely's frantic supporters chose Frank J. Donahue, chairman of the state organization, to return Curley's fire. Keen and eloquent, and a masterful politician, Donahue (later a Superior Court judge) informed the radio audience that as chairman of the Democratic State Committee in 1928 he had been well aware of all efforts made in support of Al Smith. He implied that Mayor Curley's interest in Smith was insincere, prompted only by a wish to use Smith to his own personal advantage. He accused Curley, on that final night of the campaign, of having refused to take the stump for Smith on certain nights.

During the campaign, Curley had stressed his efforts in behalf of Smith, emphasizing his bullpen activities. At his daily forum meetings, he had brought about such an increase in voting registration that Al Smith was able to carry the state. It was precisely because the Ely camp feared his success in capitalizing on the name of Smith that Donahue took to the air.

Mayor Curley, who was sitting with his son, James, listening to Donahue's speech, became progressively more enraged. When it came his turn to speak, his voice was charged with emotion. Without saying that his wife had been dying of cancer in 1928, Curley told the radio audience: "Mr. Donahue knows why I did not leave my home at night during that campaign," adding that he had at the time "a more important though sadder mission," of which Donahue and others were aware. Never did he think, he said in conclusion, that anyone would stoop so low as to bring such a sacred matter into a political campaign. It was a dramatic address, but not so dramatic as an incident that occurred just before Curley went on the air.

When Donahue had completed his radiocast, he walked into the reception room where Mayor Curley was sitting with his son and a few friends. The moment Donahue entered, Curley leaped to his feet and lunged at his frailer critic who made for the nearest exit as studio attendants and visitors stepped into the path of the Mayor. Contrary to an often told story, Curley never struck Donahue, for he was intercepted by his son, James. The Mayor was, however, accused of assaulting Gael Coakley, who had tried to curb him. Gael's father, Daniel, tried to capitalize on this incident.

All during the primary, Daniel Coakley had been the chief hatchet man against Curley. Their enmity had become deeper than ever during the previous mayoral campaign when a newspaper cartoon had shown Coakley as an octopus, with one tentacle clutching gangsters, and the others wrapped around the fire and other city departments. This cartoon, Curley had said, was "a slight caricature."

In his radiocasts, Coakley accused Curley of putting Fitzgerald in the race "as part of a scheme to reelect Governor Allen," adding that Curley would later "turn against him and slaughter him at the polls." In one broadcast, Coakley, who pronounced his adversary's name as "CURley," said: "When Jimmy finds things going against him, when the city-paid scouts tremblingly tell him part of the truth, when he learns there is revolution in the ranks, when the rebellion breaks out at City Hall, when the usually tractable near-leaders refuse to obey, then Jimmy reverts to type. The brass knuckles and the blackjack are taken from the safe. He bursts out in the language of the old Ward 17 days. His voice is raucous, and he takes the high road with the old cap and sweater."

In his final radiocast, Dan Coakley delivered what may be the most scathing political attack ever made over the air: "Since I last talked to you, two hours ago," he said in part, "my young son, Gael Coakley, a boy of 130 pounds, has been brutally assaulted by that masquerading son of a bitch who, God save the mark, is Mayor of Boston." He added that Curley, "surrounded by twenty blackguards, dashed into the broadcasting room. Chairman Frank Donahue had just finished a truthful talk about this . . . Mayor. In language unprintable, the guttersnipe language of his old . . . days, this . . . this blackleg Mayor, backed by his . . . rushed at Donahue. I'll get you, you son of a bitch, if it's the last thing I ever do.' My young son, alone with Donahue in the room, stepped before him. 'Don't, Mr. Mayor,' said he. 'Get out of the way, you little son of a bitch!' shrieked the Mayor. Grabbing him by the arm, he held him close and, lifting his leg, 'kneed' him in the groin. Then the . . . companions of the Mayor struck the boy twice from behind."

Coakley said Curley was enraged because Donahue had told the truth about Curley's relations with Governor Smith, and in another broadside he said the Mayor was politically dead.

Ely received over 117,000 votes to almost 85,000 for Fitzgerald and fewer than 13,000 for Cummings. It was obvious that Curley's introduction of bigotry in the closing hours of the campaign had boomeranged. Many Boston Irish showed their contempt for such tactics by voting for an "enemy."

The *Boston Herald* predicted a victory for Allen. "Curley Onslaught on Ely Makes Party Nomination for Governor Utterly Worthless," the political editor of the *Herald* said. Ely and Curley, meanwhile, made up in the interests of party harmony.

The Mayor presided at a rally in Tremont Temple toward the end of the campaign and introduced Ely as "the clean, able, brilliant leader of Democracy from Western Massachusetts." The assembly tittered. Ely in turn called His Honor "the great Mayor of Boston," noting that "a little fight was a good thing for the party." He had enjoyed being called "a hick from the sticks," he said. "Now they say I'm a tiger, masquerading in the garments of a Yankee Democrat."

Newspapers commented that the union of Curley, Fitzgerald, and Lomasney factions meant a solid Democratic vote in the city, adding that Curley and Ely gripped hands "while delegates shouted themselves hoarse."

Mayor Curley entered the meeting like a conquering hero while the band played "Hit the Line for Harvard." In the front row of the balcony stood Daniel H. Coakley, cheering as lustily as the rest. Asked why he was cheering for Curley, whom he had not long before called a blackleg and convict, he said: "Why not? We're all good Democrats out to win in November."

On the platform, Curley shook hands with everyone except Frank Donahue. One difficulty in holding the office of Mayor, he said in his harmony speech, was that "there is a certain element of dignity that goes with the office that prevents you from going back to the stone age and carrying out the dictates of your heart and mind with your strong right arm."

At another harmony meeting in Worcester, Curley was even more affable. The "pahty," he said, "has selected Joseph B. Ely, and as a token of my willingness to support Joe Ely for election, I am presenting him with a check for one thousand dollars to help defray the expenses of his campaign." In the pandemonium, Ely did not notice that the check was made out to the Boston Democratic Committee, Curley's own organization!

The Finance Commission, meanwhile, was tightening a net around Curley. One investigation led to the office of City Treasurer Edmund L. Dolan, who had organized the Mohawk Packing Company which sold inferior meat and provisions to hospitals of the city. This was easy to manage, for the hospital employees included tools of City Hall who took the vow of obedience. Some of the "boys" were assigned to the kitchen, which made it convenient for ward leaders to pick up a case of eggs or a carton of bread loaves for some family in need. Ward-heelers actually walked into the City Hospital and did more pilfering than its administrative officials ever dreamed. If challenged while leaving with a basket of provisions, the recipient could aim a grapefruit or any other fruit in season at a challenging employee.

The Finance Commission also discovered that the Mayor had approved the settlement of an insurance damage case against the city for $85,000, after the company had offered to settle for $35,000. Of the $85,000, the claimant received $20,000, Curley's lawyers took $20,000, and $15,000 was given to the agent of the company who brought the case to the lawyers. Nobody knew where the other $30,000 went.

Governor Ely further charged that the city had been bilked to the tune of hundreds of thousands of dollars in the settlement of land takings in connection with building the East Boston Tunnel. One Curley, the Finance Committee charged, received a profit of more than $100,000. Dolan was also accused of organizing the Legal Securities Company, which bought bonds in the open market and sold them to the city at inflated prices.

Dolan went to jail, and Curley was ordered to repay the money he allegedly received through crooked dealing.

On his birthday message in 1930, Honey Fitz had commented on the "grafting in public life." Politics, he said, had changed drastically since he first went into public life in 1891. "In those days there was very little graft. Men of those times as a rule liked to serve the people without price." Although politics had changed for the worse, he still would have chosen it as a career, but would have studied law on the side.

"All my life, since my eighteenth birthday," he added, "I have been doing things for others without compensation. No human being ever paid me a cent directly or indirectly for services rendered."

He was getting along in years now, looking back over his shoulder. One pleasant memory was waltzing to the strains of "The Blue Danube" with Mrs. Fitzgerald, as they cruised down the Danube River.

"Is 'Sweet Adeline' really your favorite?" a reported asked.

"No, not really. But everyone can join in and sing it. My favorite—and I raven't sung it for twenty years—is 'Marguerite.' " He sang it for the reporters as Mrs. Fitzgerald smiled her approval.

Honey Fitz had no immediate political ambitions for himself as he watched the behind-the-scenes struggle between the forces of Al Smith and Governor Franklin Delano Roosevelt of New York, who had succeeded Smith.

CHAPTER 18

A House Divided

"There is an old saying in Boston that we get our religion
from Rome and our politics at home, and that is the way most
Catholics feel about it."

—JOHN F. KENNEDY

JOSEPH PATRICK KENNEDY always had his eye on the main chance,
and as the son of Pat Kennedy, as the husband of Rose, and as the
son-in-law of John F., he had an insider's view of politics. Boston
politics, however, with its petty intrigues and shifting alliances, left him
cold. By 1930, having relinquished enough of his motion-picture and sundry activities to take an active role in politics, he looked for "a leader
who will lead." He found one, he thought, in Franklin Delano Roosevelt.

In 1932, he donated $15,000 to the Democratic campaign fund, loaned
it $50,000 more, and contributed a reported $100,000 indirectly. For Joe,
such sums were change dropped from the till while he totaled his receipts.

"I think I was the only man with more than $12 in the bank who
openly supported him," he said, referring to Roosevelt.

Honey Fitz, a bitter-ender for Al Smith, was in the opposite camp.
As an elector-at-large, with Jessie Woodrow Sayre of Cambridge, he told
the press in 1932 that the Bay State stood solid for Al Smith. "There will
be no betrayal of Governor Smith among the Massachusetts delegates.
Governor Ely will nominate him and be sure to make a speech that will
bring out all the great points in Governor Smith's career, and, in my
opinion, electrify the convention." Never was he more prophetic. Ely's
ringing nomination speech in behalf of Al Smith was, according to Herbert Bayard Swope, the greatest speech since Robert G. Ingersoll nominated James G. Blaine. Al Smith was so moved that he embraced Ely,
misty-eyed.

Curley, hoping to recoup his leadership, which was rudely jolted by

David I. Walsh when Ely went to the State House, had spearheaded the Roosevelt bid in the Bay State after jumping aboard the bandwagon in the spring of 1931. He estranged thousands of his once loyal rooters when he went around the state with Jimmy Roosevelt, bucking an Al Smith sentiment that was stronger than ever. Among societies that dropped him from membership was the Ancient Order of Hibernians, surely an ominous touch! At times, Curley found himself in the company of Joe Kennedy, who steered clear of him and refused even to be photographed with him. In 1932, Kennedy was a member of a strategy group known as "the Silent Six," who rode in Roosevelt's campaign train. Kennedy was the financial adviser of the Roosevelt team.

Roosevelt had ordered Curley to put up a slate of convention delegates, but his ticket was swamped by Smith followers, and to the delight of Walsh, Ely, and Fitzgerald, he failed to win a delegate's seat. Then, in a typical Curley coup, he showed up at the 1932 Democratic Convention when he took the floor as "Alcalde [Spanish for "Mayor"] Jaime Miguel Curleo, delegate from Puerto Rico."

When the time came for the island territory to cast its ballot, "Señor Curleo" rose and announced through a button-hole microphone that Puerto Rico's six votes were for "the next President of the United States, Franklin Delano Roosevelt." Insiders reported that a delegate from Puerto Rico was unable to attend. Another version is that it took several martinis to persuade her to capitulate to Curley, whose party had a hard time getting rid of her afterward. In any case, the delegation had the authority to fill the vacancy she created, with the approval of the convention.

Often told is the role of publisher William Randolph Hearst at the convention. When FDR's bandwagon was hub-deep in political mud, his strategists wooed a bloc of delegates who were backing John Nance Garner of Texas. In his autobiography, Curley wanders afield, according to some observers, when he takes credit for bringing Hearst into the Roosevelt fold, although James H. Guilfoyle in his book, *On the Trail of the Forgotten Man,* writes that Curley did get through to Hearst and told him that "Mr. Garner cannot be nominated for the presidency, but if you will throw your support to Mr. Roosevelt, I can guarantee that Mr. Garner will be nominated for Vice-President. In fact, I am ready to lead the fight for him." In his own book, Curley writes: "I called Hearst in San Simeon. I told him Garner didn't have a prayer, but that if he would swing to Roosevelt, Garner would become Vice-President."

Curley also said: "Joseph P. Kennedy had called Hearst and told him that Newton Baker, the Secretary of War, seemed to be a dark horse at the convention." That part of the statement, at least, seems to be correct. Joe Kennedy was one of several who reached Hearst by telephone that night, knowing that the publisher, a long-time friend, was a political power in pivotal California.

"Yes," Kennedy admitted later. "I did bring Hearst around for Roosevelt, but you can't find any mention of it in the history books. Hearst even sent his contribution to Roosevelt through me."

Curley, on the contrary, never reached Hearst on the telephone, according to a person who was with him that contentious night. After conferring with Jim Farley and other strategists, he returned to his room in Chicago's Congress Hotel and asked John B. Hynes, who later defeated him for Mayor of Boston, to get Hearst on the line.

"There were seven or eight calls in ahead of Curley's," Hynes recalls. "At about eleven o'clock that night Curley went to bed and asked me to wake him when I got the call through. I gave up at four in the morning when I learned that Hearst had gone to bed."

Hearst helped swing Garner into line, and Roosevelt chose him as his running-mate. When Roosevelt defeated Hoover, Joe Kennedy staged a mammoth celebration on two floors of the Waldorf-Astoria in New York.

Fitzgerald's efforts in behalf of Smith had caused another rift between him and Curley. At a rally at Boston Garden, during which he sat on the platform with Ely and Curley, he rose to sing.

"Get the sonofabitch a lamppost," Curley said. "He's going to sing the drunkard's song."

Honey Fitz soon realized that Roosevelt's victory was a boon to his son-in-law. Kennedy was in line for the job of Secretary of the Treasury until Louis McHenry Howe told Roosevelt it might be embarrassing for the White House to have a Wall Street speculator in the temple.

In 1933, Kennedy resumed operations on the Street and acquired Somerset Importers, a liquor combination. He also cleaned up on a stock pool when a false rumor made the rounds that a glass company was manufacturing bottles for the liquor industry. Kennedy's coup on Wall Street in 1933 were investigated by the Senate Banking and Currency Committee, which uncovered nothing illegal.

"In 1934," wrote Kennedy in his Harvard report, "Franklin Delano Roosevelt named me chairman of the Securities Exchange Commission." Putting a Wall Street plunger in charge of a reform commission created to protect the investor raised eyebrows in financial circles, and many wondered whether Wall Street had taken over the New Deal. Kennedy himself questioned the propriety of having a big-pool operator regulating his fellow sharks.

"You know how I've made most of my money," he told Roosevelt. "Right in the stock market. Well, think of the howl that will go up if you name a Wall Street man."

According to an SEC aide, "It was a very smart thing to do. If anybody knew the loopholes and dodges of Wall Street, it was Joe. He knew them all. What better man could clean up that mess?"

Even more impressive than Rose Kennedy's collection of more than two hundred costumed dolls from all over the world was Joe Kennedy's collection of homes and apartments owned or rented in the United States or abroad, in such scattered outposts as Hollywood, Washington, Palm Beach, Hyannisport and the Riviera. After accepting the SEC appointment, he rented a palatial thirty-three room house in Washington on a bluff overlooking the Potomac. It was more posh than his Hyannisport "cottage," with its private theatre, swimming pool and other sybaritic trappings. "Marwood" also had a pool, along with a dozen baths, and extensive stables. The master bedroom had gold-plated faucets, and the private theatre in the basement could accommodate a hundred guests.

His chief assistants on the Securities Exchange Commission were William O. Douglas, later a member of the United States Supreme Court, and James Landis, former dean of Harvard Law School. By the time he resigned from the SEC in the fall of 1935, it was purring smoothly, and the broad basic principles of its functioning had been laid. Roosevelt lauded his work, and although he had once been described by John T. Flynn as an "antisocial gambler, a blundering wrecker of corporations, a tool of other capitalists, and a conscienceless market manipulator to boot," the same writer and Roosevelt biographer later conceded that Kennedy was "the most useful member of the Commission."

"The most important thing I did was to write a law to stop selling short," Kennedy said. "They said I could never do that, but I knew how because I'd sold short myself and made a lot of money selling short and I knew how it worked."

Over the years, Joe Kennedy was a member of the Metropolitan, Burning Tree, National Press, Siwanoy Country, Oyster Harbor, Gulf Stream and Seminole clubs, along with the Bath and Tennis. He had little time for recreation in the 1930s, however. He busied himself in corporate reorganizational work until the spring of 1937, when Roosevelt named him chairman of the United States Maritime Commission. In this assignment, the President told him later, "You have maintained your justly earned reputation of being a two-fisted, hard-hitting executive." By this time, Kennedy had written *The Story of the Films,* and in 1936, his book, *I'm for Roosevelt,* boosted Roosevelt's bid for reelection.

The aim of the newly formed Maritime Commission was to create an American Merchant Marine and administer the United States Merchant Marine Act. In ten weeks Kennedy settled ship operators' claims against the government for a small fraction of the money demanded, and set up a scheme for subsidizing shipping companies to the extent of $25,000,000 a year, thereby inviting criticism that he was a lobbyist for ship-owners. The National Maritime Union, on the other hand, labeled him a "union-wrecker" because he favored legislation to outlaw strikes and make arbitration of labor disputes compulsory. In any case, it was a job well done and put Joe Kennedy in line for an even more important assignment.

Kennedy's fabulous career made him one of the most talked of members of the Harvard Class of 1912, especially when they gathered for their reunions. He had already hit pay dirt by the time of his tenth reunion, which was held at the Pilgrim Hotel in Plymouth. One highlight of the affair was the showing by Kennedy of exclusive films of the Jack Dempsey-Jess Willard and Dempsey-Georges Carpentier heavyweight championship fights, along with a more glamorous if less gory showing of "Kismet."

Robert Benchley, one of his old Delta Upsilon cronies, stole the spotlight at the twentieth reunion when he gave his classic "Treasurer's Report," but Joe Kennedy was back in stride by the time of the four-day twenty-fifth reunion, when his classmates ribbed him in a hilarious skit titled "In the Good Old Maritime," whose theme was "Local Boy Makes Good." A classmate, Edward Gallagher, once treasurer of the Boston and Maine Railroad, appeared in the role of the Commissioner of Maritime. In the opening scene, in the Maritime office of the United States, a stenographer was frantically trying to answer a dozen jingling telephones.

"It can't be nine o'clock," she kept telling callers. "Mr. Kennedy isn't here yet."

During the jingling confusion, Kennedy walked in, wearing spats. He hung up his cane, and while taking off his gloves, turned to his secretary.

"Get me Frank at the White House," he briskly said. When the call was put through, he picked up the phone. "I'm here, Frank," he said. "It's nine o'clock. Start the country."

As he hung up, bells clanged in the wings, horns honked and whistles blew. Joe, who was sitting in the audience at Rindge Technical High School in Cambridge, was delighted by the skit, as were members of his family.

The Kennedys, who received special permission to bring the children's governess to the reunion, presented a logistics problem at times. When, at a dinner held at Symphony Hall during the reunion, Joe Kennedy was unable to find a table large enough to accommodate his family, he took them to a restaurant two blocks down the street. Hearing about the incident, the class secretary set up a table and escorted the Kennedys back to Symphony Hall.

Meanwhile, Honey Fitz had still been sitting on the sidelines in the Bay State as Ely was reelected Governor and Frederick Mansfield succeeded Curley as Mayor. In 1934, Curley ran for Governor against Gaspar Griswold Bacon, a Proper Bostonian, and charged that while millions of Americans were on relief rolls, "J. P. Morgan, Jr." (Bacon) was on Morgan's preferred list.

"I have never had any banking connections," Bacon countered. "Can you say the same, Mr. Curley? Aren't you still president of a bank? What were your connections with the Industrial Bank & Trust Company, which failed and left thousands of depositors high and dry?" Bacon also asked about Curley's preferred list of contractors.

Curley chicanery spiced the contest. Black limousines pulled up to groups of WPA workers, and a genteel voice would admonish the men leaning on shovels. "You loafers ought to be ashamed of yourselves," a Curley supporter would say. "Get to work, you lazy bums." When the limousine sped off, the cursing laborers could read the sign on the rear:

GASPAR GRISWOLD BACON FOR GOVERNOR

Several days before the primary election, in which he defeated the Walsh-Ely candidate, Curley showed he had not lost his flair for hippodrome when he staged a rally at the Majestic Theatre in Boston, with stirring music, solos by popular singers, acts by vaudevillian comedians, and oratory by Curley. In the hinterlands, Curley varied his technique. At one rally in Amesbury, he introduced Judge Emil Fuchs, a major league baseball owner, and Rabbit Maranville, one of his stars. Sitting with a group of prizefighters was Roy Green, who bore a marked resemblance to Gene Tunney. When Curley realized that members of the audience mistook Green for Tunney, he rose to the occasion.

"And we also have with us here tonight," he said, "the former heavyweight boxing champion of the world, who is taking an active interest in my campaign. Gene Tunney, rise and take a bow!" Roy Green needed a police escort on his way out of the hall to fend off autograph-seekers.

Two squads of Curley workers solicited votes by telephone. The first made calls between six and ten at night. The second, posing as workers in the Bacon camp, made their solicitations after midnight, an old Curley tactic calculated to infuriate voters.

It was during this contest that a Curley rooter, preceding him at rallies, walked down the aisle at rallies shouting, "Up, up! Everybody up for the Governor." In his frenzied appeals he would sometimes froth at the mouth. "Danny the Coat Snatcher" had also been added to the strategy council. Sitting right behind Curley, he would tug his coattail when he showed signs of making a statement that might boomerang. Such were the tactics which Plato had never anticipated in his New Republic.

Curley was flown into office on the wings of New Deal largesse. He had finally defeated Honey Fitz in the twisting race to the State House.

Infuriated by last-minute appointments made by Ely in an effort to embarrass his administration, the Governor-Elect confronted the out-going Governor in the executive suite of the State House and in crude language told him off. It was an unparalleled scene in the annals of Bay State politics when these foes confronted each other at that meeting. Curley, who chased Ely around the table, never quite caught up with him.

Ely joined Honey Fitz in the ranks of elder statesmen.

CHAPTER 19

Dawn of the Golden Years

"Tonight is a big night in Boston politics as the Honorable
John F. Fitzgerald is making a speech for his good friend,
James Michael. Politics makes strange bedfellows."

—JOHN F. KENNEDY

B Y 1936, Honey Fitz was the Little General only in his dreams. In
that year, perhaps to remind him of former grandeur when he was
the most glamorous political figure in Boston, if not the Commonwealth of Massachusetts, he was elected president of the Clover Club, a
socio-political fraternity where political celebrities are not only insulted,
but on occasion pelted with rolls, as Curley once was.

At the "swearing in" ceremonies, Honey Fitz was resplendent in the
attire of Emperor Napoleon, wearing a powder-blue coat, great coat and
black tricorn. He was attended by Marshal Nay and Marshal Yea. The
toastmaster at this ceremony, held at the Parker House, hailed the new
president as "the best Mayor Boston ever had." Honey Fitz contested
this. He stepped onto the floor and led three rousing cheers for himself
as "Boston's greatest Mayor and the only known rival to Caruso," after
singing his old theme song.

At another such banquet, the aging warrior who had filled the political
life of Boston with excitement, was given even more credit than he sought.
"Fitzie," the master of ceremonies said, "discovered Niagara Falls, conceived the High School of Commerce, built City Hall Annex, invented
political ether, put an end to the Spanish-American and the First World
Wars, planned the Chamber of Commerce, freed Ireland, and invented
the Ku Klux Klan to save the Irish from being bored in America."

Although Honey Fitz was still years from admitting he was on the
shady side of the hill, he must have felt a bit old in 1936, when his pet

271

abomination, James Michael Curley, opposed Henry Cabot Lodge, Jr., in the wheel-spin of politics, in a contest for the United States Senate. Honey Fitz, after all, had run against the young aristocrat's grandfather. This contest was the first of four from 1936 until 1942 that warned of the decline of that era during which personal political machines had flourished, nourished by the turbulence of swift urban and industrial growth and based on a spoils system that carried the seeds of its own decay.

In 1936, Curley tried to keep the political vaudeville circuit operating. He called Lodge "a boy sent on a man's errand" and "Little Boy Blue," and tried to palm him off as "a sweet boy with an illustrious name." He set class against class. Jeered while speaking to Williams College students, he said: "You young gentlemen should be proud of a leader like Franklin Delano Roosevelt. Consider all the fine federal prisons he has erected to house your embezzling, bank-president fathers." To Curley, Lodge was even worse than an embezzler. He was a Brahmin.

Curley's blarney was no longer as effective as of old. There were second- and third-generation Irish voters now, and he couldn't woo their votes merely by proclaiming that his ancestors came from County Galway. Not that this approach failed in some districts!

When Father Coughlin's candidate, Thomas O'Brien, told Corkmen in South Boston that Curley preferred singing "The Isle of Capri" to "The Wearing of the Green," it may have lost him as many votes there, as it gained him in such an Italian neighborhood as East Boston; but Curley came up with a glib answer. He told the disturbed Corkmen that the composer of "The Isle of Capri" was an Irish musician. Since his audience, like himself, had no idea who the composer was, he got away with it, and all sang the Italian melody as "a tribute to a great Irish composer."

Honey Fitz took a more personal interest in the 1937 mayoral fight, when Curley opposed Maurice J. Tobin, a minor executive with a telephone company, and a onetime member of Curley's "kitchen cabinet"— that small group of aspiring politicians who had shared sandwiches and beer with Curley in the Jamaicaway house. At a Roxbury rally, Curley recounted all the favors he had done for the Tobins.

"Why, I even obtained a position—and a very good one, indeed—for Maurice Tobin's sister," he said.

"You're a liar, Curley," someone shouted. "Tobin doesn't even have a sister."

Honey Fitz's support of Tobin during this campaign was an important factor, and the background of his interest in the handsome young politico has never been told. One afternoon, Tobin met Nathan Sodekson, an old friend and North End neighbor of Fitzgerald's. "I've been trying to get Fitzie to line up for me," Tobin said as they sank on to a lounge in the lobby of the Parker House Hotel, "but he doesn't think my chances are too good. How about making a tour of the city with me, so you can make your own judgment."

After making the rounds with Tobin, Sodekson told Fitzgerald that Tobin's prospects were good. He was drawing good crowds at rallies, even on rainy nights. Honey Fitz met Tobin soon thereafter and was delighted when Tobin told him of his ambition to be another John F. Fitzgerald.

"Young man," Honey Fitz said, "I've been waiting a long time for someone to be another Fitzgerald. I'm glad to see that you have some of my qualities."

There were signs that Curley was losing his grip. Former supporters were defecting to Tobin. On his way to a rally in Pemberton Square, Curley ran into E. Mark Sullivan, an Irish Republican whom he had made his Corporation Counsel. Sensing he was for Tobin, he pulled his overcoat open, exposed a Tobin button on his lapel, and gave him a dressing down. Michael J. Ward, once a warm ally, had also lost his enthusiasm for Curley, whom he no longer considered a sincere man of the people.

"The people loved him as the sow's ear, not as the silk purse," Ward explained. "But that wasn't enough for him. He wanted to be kind of an intellectual, but he was playing the sunfield there and couldn't always see the ball." Ward added that Curley was a poor politician in some ways. "He could hurt people forever with his sarcasm, and he fought the newspapers."

Ward used tactics in this campaign that were more Curleyesque than those employed by the old maestro himself. Curley had a suite at the Parker House where he dictated some of his speeches. Ward stationed a stenographer on the fire escape, instructing her to take down every word. Curley had to make a last-minute switch one night on the radio. As he awaited his turn at the microphone, Tobin gave his speech verbatim.

At Curley rallies, Ward seated hecklers from the Tobin camp in the first two rows. Night after night, at rallies all over the city, they walked out in a "huff" when Curley attacked Tobin. One night at the Vine Street Church in Roxbury, Curley stomped in, mounted the platform and ordered everyone in the first two rows out of the hall. This time they were his own supporters!

Such tricks were on their way out by 1937, however. A candidate had to appeal to a wider radio audience, and arguments that were effective in days of cart-tail oratory, no longer could swing the votes of a serious-minded middle class who were weary of political corruption and tomfoolery. The New Deal, too, had replaced the city boss as Santa Claus.

But Honey Fitz and Curley had given the little people status and security. What the *Boston Herald* later said about Curley applied to both leaders: "In his elevation, every little person was elevated. The barber in South Boston, the North End fruit dealer, the carpenter, the waiter and the school janitor—these found Boston theirs when Mr. Curley made the city his, and they could look at a State Street banker with level eye and enjoy the agony of the Brahmins. The mighty had been humbled and the yoke of inferiority lifted from the downtrodden, and what a sensation that is!"

But with the changing times, Boston politics would never again be so brassy and colorful. Pat Kennedy died in 1929, and four years later, Martin Lomasney followed him, after a boisterous career of more than half a century in politics. In the opinion of Honey Fitz, Lomasney left no successor. "His dynamic force, his uncompromising stand for things he thought were right, his loyalty to the poor and unfortunate, had no match." While he was Mayor, Fitzgerald added, "Lomasney never asked me to do one single thing that meant money in his pocket."

Kennedy and Lomasney were gone, and Fitzgerald and Curley were going. When "Shirley Temple," as Curley called Tobin (who declined a Hollywood movie contract), defeated him, he said: "This was not a political contest for Mayor—it was a moving picture contest, and, of course, I was out-voted." Young men—Lodge and Tobin—had whipped the old master.

The *Boston Post* was credited with Curley's defeat in the mayoral fight. Its cunning use of ten words spoken many years before by Cardinal O'Connell swung the election. *Post* readers on election day morning read in a streamer over the masthead of the newspaper:

VOTERS OF BOSTON!

Cardinal O'Connell, in speaking to the Catholic Alumni Association, said, "The walls are raised against honest men in civic life." You can break down these walls by voting for an honest, clean, competent young man, Maurice Tobin, today. He will redeem the city and take it out of the hands of those who have been responsible for graft and corruption.

Election day in 1937 fell on All Souls' Day, when Catholic churches are crowded. As parishioners left church, they were given copies of the

Boston Post with the Cardinal's statement and the *Post*'s endorsement of Tobin. Few noticed where the quotation marks ended. It was as if His Eminence had endorsed Tobin.

Curley's frantic last-minute attempt to appeal to Cardinal O'Connell to correct the record was futile. The prelate refused a Curley emissary, even after the latter was kept waiting for two hours in an anteroom.

According to one story, a Curley worker called his mother to remind her to take his three sisters to the polls, adding that he was sending around a car.

"Don't bother," she said. "Coming from Mass this morning, the girls read the *Post* and there, big as life, His Eminence comes out for young Mr. Tobin. We've already voted for the lad."

With Honey Fitz still marking time, Curley tried again in 1938, this time running against Leverett Saltonstall for Governor. And again the old wizardry was missing. Curley fell into a pit he dug. When the *Boston Evening Transcript* noted that "Salty" had a Back Bay name and a South Boston face, Curley walked into the trap. "Saltonstall may have a South Boston face but he doesn't dare show it over there," he said.

On the following day, "Salty" spent the day in South Boston winning the confidence of policemen, storekeepers, bar patrons, and passersby. "If I have a South Boston face I'm proud of it," he said, "and you can be sure of one thing—it's the same face before and after the election. I'm not two-faced." The heartland of Irish Democracy was impressed by his humor and candor.

In Lawrence and Lynn, Curley promised to place more "representatives of the new races" in state offices. He told Lithuanian audiences of his vow to their hero, Heavyweight Boxing Champion Jack Sharkey (who was Lithuanian) to appoint Lithuanians to high posts.

Curley could sense that the old order was changing, and his oratory lacked its customary ringing conviction. Symbol of the new order—and a shining one—was a Harvard College student, John F. Kennedy, who was amused when Grampa Fitzgerald actively supported Curley in this contest. In a letter to his father at the London Embassy, Jack Kennedy said: "Tonight is a big night in Boston politics as the Honorable John F. Fitzgerald is making a speech for his good friend, James Michael. Politics makes strange bedfellows."

Curley lost the election, but John Gunther was wrong in concluding that "Many Bostonians had become sick of that grotesque old man." Curley, far from grotesque, was an aging charmer who would again have hurrahs. But first he lost to Maurice Tobin who, because of another expedient charter revision, was permitted to run for reelection. Old-timers smiled when Curley charged over the radio that during the morning of election day, Tobin had ordered the release of a hundred prisoners from the Deer Island jail to vote for him. Curley thanked the 116,000 Bostonians who favored him. "It cannot be construed in any sense a defeat of James Michael Curley; rather was it a defeat for the Democracy of Boston through a combination of abatement racketeers and Republican puppets, representing the forces of entrenched wealth, purchased leaders and a subservient press."

"In Boston, the Lodges own the banks," runs a Boston saying, "but the Irish control the votes." There were those who thought Mayor Tobin was a puppet of moneyed interests. A cartoon in one Boston newspaper had Tobin saying: "I never had the bankers—the bankers had me."

In 1942, both Fitzgerald and Curley were candidates for office, and the events of that year had a direct impact on the political aspirations of a young man who would one day be elected the thirty-fifth President of the United States.

CHAPTER 20

Old Memories and New Thoughts

"A rolling stone may gather no moss; but it gets polished
and molded until it rolls into the right place where, if
it's wise, it sticks and stays."
                                        —JOSEPH P. KENNEDY

H ONEY FITZ, who had been president of the Massachusetts delegation to the Electoral College in 1933, and would serve in the same
capacity in 1944, was still living at the Bellevue Hotel, a favorite
haunt of Massachusetts politicians. It was a short walk from the Athenaeum, where he spent many an hour browsing and reading, and not far
from the City Club of cherished memories and downtown spots where
he could find former associates. The entire area rekindled old memories
for him. He could recall seeing Henry Wadsworth Longfellow, Ralph
Waldo Emerson and James Russell Lowell, along with other men of
letters, in the Old Corner Book Store or at the Parker House, both near
the Bellevue.

Honey Fitz's zest for living was quickened by his interest in the ever-
changing pattern of political, social and economic life of Boston since the
long-ago, when he and Pat Kennedy had fought the Yankees in the interests of the emerging Irish Catholics of Boston. Pat Kennedy had died in
1929 at the age of seventy-one at the Deaconess Hospital in Boston, two
months after suffering a heart attack. William T. A. Fitzgerald and Judge
Joseph Corbett called on him three days before he died, and found him
still cheerful and with no thought that the end was so near. Pat, whose
wife Mary had passed away in 1923, left two daughters (Mrs. Charles
Burke and Mrs. George Connelly), besides his son, Joe. At his death, he

was president and director of the Columbia Trust and director of the Suffolk Coal Company, and the only fraternal organizations he belonged to were still the Elks and Knights of Columbus. Patrick Joseph Kennedy was not forgotten. In 1933, an elementary school in East Boston was named for him.

Honey Fitz and Pat, both sons of immigrants, had grandchildren who had achieved a social status undreamed of by them. The cycle from drab tenements to hotel suites, town houses and villas on two continents was a superficial symptom of an impressive social evolution. By the late 1930s, the Kennedys had wealth, education and enough leisure to enable them to devote themselves to public service.

Even top-drawer circles were impressed in December 1937 when President Roosevelt named Joe Kennedy Ambassador to the Court of St. James, a post which put him in the most elite society of two continents. It was the top United States diplomatic post. "You'll be the most important American in Europe," a friend told Joe on learning of the appointment. "I am simply a babe thrown into a foreign country to do the best I can," he replied.

On hearing of the appointment, Honey Fitz must have taken a turn down memory lane to a day a quarter of a century ago when Sir Thomas Lipton had said to him: "John, I think you ought to try for the ambassadorship."

"No, Sir Thomas," he had answered, "that job is too important for me. I know my limitations. I live in a peculiar community, and the post of Ambassador to England is something that I could not get and, therefore, I shall not embarrass President Wilson by being a candidate."

At that time, Honey Fitz wanted to stay in Boston, where his destiny lay. "I have big work ahead of me here. My heart is right here in this city," he said.

In London, the Kennedy children moved gracefully in the highest social circles, for protocol and hobnobbing with persons of breeding and culture were old hat for them. Even the Marquess of Hartington, heir to the Duke of Devonshire, was impressed when he met lovely Kathleen Kennedy, and the other children were just as gracious and charming.

England welcomed the new envoy as "Jolly Joe Kennedy." From the outset, he was so casual that his predecessor, Robert Bingham, would have been appalled. At his first press interview, he propped his feet on a desk. "You don't expect me to develop into a statesman overnight," he grinned. His family back home, soon to join him, were amused, and when Joe and Jack—both at Harvard—read in the papers that he had hit a hole in one on the Stoke Poges golf course, they cabled him: "Dubious about hole in one."

He refused to wear knee breeches even when he presented his credentials to King George. He admitted, however, that it was "no fun to go to one of those parties and be the only man in long pants." The staid were shocked when he told Queen Elizabeth she was "a cute trick," but the Queen herself was amused.

In the traditional speech American Ambassadors make at the Pilgrim Society dinner, which welcomes new American envoys, Kennedy said: "The Pilgrims have a more than usually understanding guest of honor tonight. You probably have never entertained a man who came closer, in his own right, to being a Pilgrim father. If any of you has ever attempted to transport a wife and nine children across the Atlantic Ocean I am sure he will understand what I mean. . . . The original Pilgrim fathers, I am sure, could not take with them on the Mayflower all of those who wanted to go. I found myself in much the same predicament. The Kennedys, therefore, are coming over in installments."

London had a warm greeting for the Kennedys. Kennedy was called "The U.S.A.'s Nine-Child Envoy," and the caption under the picture of one of his daughters in a magazine was: "Daughter of the Father of America." The ambassadors of good will were Joe, Jr., John, Rosemary, Kathleen, Eunice, Patricia, Robert, Jean, and Edward.

"His bouncing offspring make the most politically ingratiating family since Theodore Roosevelt's," Life magazine reported in the spring of 1938. "Whether or not Franklin Roosevelt thought of it beforehand, it has turned out that when he appointed Mr. Kennedy to be Ambassador to Great Britain he got eleven Ambassadors for the price of one."

King George received all the brood, and the Queen discussed babies with Mrs. Kennedy, who was described as "pretty and young looking."

The nine envoys were said to be the most handsome and charming children ever to occupy the London Embassy, and although they preferred American pancakes for breakfast and continued their family checker and backgammon tournaments, just as if they were home in Palm Beach, Hyannisport or Bronxville, they also went horseback riding on the Hyde Park bridle path (Rotton Row) in the British manner. The Ambassador tactfully commented that he was fond of Rugby football, and his son, Joe, played for Harvard when the Americans lost to the Cambridge University Rugby team, 50 to 0.

The score may not have pleased the Ambassador, whose well known slogan is, "Come in first: second place is failure," but by this time he had learned to forgive his alma mater for not always winning. In his twenty-fifth annual Harvard report he had written: "Our football teams seem to have lost their ancient power to strike terror into the hearts of the 'barbarians,' but that defect is unimportant. Of course we want to see excellence on the gridiron, but when we get licked we philosophize like the old-time football coach who when defeated solaced himself with the reflection that he was 'developing the boys' character.' "

Honey Fitz couldn't wait to visit the Kennedys at the London Embassy. On his seventy-fifth birthday anniversary, seven hundred fifty guests gave him a gala party at the Boston Chamber of Commerce. There Charles Francis Adams and he bridged the wide gap that once had separated two divergent ways of life.

"It is a pleasure to testify to the good Irish qualities that are in you, John," Adams said. "And I am glad to thank you personally for what you have done for us and the city of Boston.

"At times in the past, you, John F., have found it politically expedient to say things about my class that have sometimes hurt. You have even called us degenerate sons of splendid ancestors. Quite possibly that is true. But it takes a man of supreme gifts to tell us a thing like that without arousing rancor. Yet, it was said so pleasantly, with such good humor, that no one could take offense, or, long be angry with a man of the charm —the Irish charm—of John F. Fitzgerald. In everything you have done and in every way you could, you have tried to develop Boston and to improve our community. Even today you are sweating your heart out to bring this port back to what it was, to make it what it should be."

There is an old saying in Boston that the Brahmin ranks closed around 1820, and that nobody has been taken in since. As typical a Brahmin as any was Charles Francis Adams, the most distinguished Bostonian of his day, a lineal descendant of President John Adams. Director of some forty corporations, he had been Secretary of the Navy under President Hoover. When James Michael Curley aspired to the same Navy post under President Roosevelt, he wistfully observed: "It would have been memorable, considering their divergent backgrounds, if James Michael Curley were to hold the same Cabinet post as Charles Francis Adams."

Honey Fitz still could jibe at one of the most proper of Bostonians in Yankeeland.

"Charley," he said, lowering the microphone, "has a tough job on his hands now. He has been appointed to a committee of ten to bring the Republicans back to life. Well, I wish him luck—as Charley Adams." He added that Adams, when Mayor of Quincy, was a Democrat. Adams enjoyed his performance.

"I told Charley recently," Fitzgerald continued, "that I might go abroad pretty soon to meet the King and Queen, and Wallie and the rest of them, and asked him for some tips. You see, Charley Adams' great-grandfather and his grandfather were Ambassadors to Great Britain in times of great stress, too. Before I go, I'm going to get some pointers from him."

It was indeed a time of stress. In July 1938, the John F. Fitzgeralds returned to Boston on the *Carinthia* after touring Ireland, Scotland and England, where they were guests of the Kennedys at the Embassy. For Honey Fitz the visit was a reminder of mayoral days when, as a guest of Sir Thomas Lipton, he had moved in high places in London. However, it was not the gay, unconcerned world he remembered.

On September 19 of that year, Rose had called from the Embassy to congratulate her parents on their forty-ninth wedding anniversary. During the conversation, she said the younger Kennedy children had moved from the Embassy to Southern Ireland "in order to be away from any possible bombings in England in the event of a sudden declaration of war." Rose added that Joe, Jr., had postponed entering Harvard Law School to work at the United States Embassy in Paris under Ambassador William Bullitt.

September, 1938, was also the time of the hurricane that ripped up the coast. Mayor Maurice Tobin was away at the time, and John Kerrigan was acting Mayor. Honey Fitz came to City Hall early in the evening and remained by Kerrigan's side until three o'clock the next morning, advising his every move. Kerrigan declared a state of emergency, called in all his department heads and warned them not to spend an unauthorized penny. After two terms in City Hall, Honey Fitz knew how to deal with department heads. Honey Fitz used to drop in to see Kerrigan in later years, when he was elected Mayor, just to be sure the city machine was purring smoothly.

"He always pulled a bar of candy out of his pocket and handed it to me," Kerrigan recalls. " 'It gives you quick energy,' he would say." Mayor Kerrigan also remembers introducing City Hall workers to young Jack Kennedy in 1945.

While Honey Fitz was keeping his finger on the political pulse of Boston, his son-in-law was caught in the mesh of momentous international issues. An ambassador in *Time* magazine's definition was "a glorified reporter, a legman in a tailcoat. His main job is to interview people, get news, report accurately. To do this he must 1) have the confidence of the people he represents, 2) win the confidence of the people he is assigned to." *Time* rated Kennedy "uncommonly common-sensible, stiletto-shrewd, practical as only a former president of a small bank can be."

From the beginning, the tall, at times fiery, envoy won the respect of British officials, including Neville Chamberlain's.

"Why Franklin himself isn't as confidential with me as the Prime Minister," Kennedy told the press.

Both Kennedy and Chamberlain were shirtsleeve diplomats with the common touch. Neville was the son of Joseph Chamberlain, who in his younger days startled British conservatives by suggesting that Queen Victoria step down in favor of a republic. "Although I cannot boast of the blueness in my veins or of the fame of my forebears," Neville Chamberlain said, "I am yet prouder of being descended from those respectable tradesmen than if my ancestor had worn shining armor and carried great swords."

Chamberlain and Kennedy, however, were unlike in many ways. Kennedy thought big, while Chamberlain was accused of having "a retail mind for wholesale problems," and there were critics who felt he had done a better job as chairman of the Birmingham Town-Planning Committee than he did as Prime Minister of a great power in time of crisis. "Chamberlain had never met anybody in Birmingham who in the least resembled Adolf Hitler," sneered Alfred Duff Cooper. One cartoonist showed Chamberlain handing Mussolini a match while Il Duce was lighting a time bomb under his chair. It was said that Chamberlain would sacrifice half of the world that was not Britain's to save the British Empire.

In those parlous days, Kennedy was at first accused of sympathizing with Chamberlain's sheep-footing policy of appeasement. In October, 1938, he said in a Trafalgar Day speech: "It has long been a theory of mine that it is unproductive for both dictator and democratic countries to widen the division now existing between them by emphasizing their differences, which are self-apparent. There is simply no sense, common or otherwise, in letting these differences grow into unrelenting antagonisms. After all, we have to live together in the same world."

The *New York Post* bristled: "If this precious specimen of diplomatic expedience had been written by the British Foreign Office it could not have served better to bolster the propaganda of Prime Minister Chamberlain." The Ambassador should have listened to his wife, who told him when he was writing his speech: "Have you thought how this will sound back home? You know, dear, our ambassadors are supposed to lose all their powers of resistance when they get to London. You don't want folks to get the idea you are seeing things through English eyes."

Kennedy further showed the tenor of his thinking when he advised Hollywood associates to stop making motion pictures offensive to dictators.

Soon after Munich, however, Kennedy warned that war was imminent in 1939. One unsettling incident was the sinking of the S.S. *Athenia* after a German submarine torpedoed it. (Berlin charged that the ship, which included three hundred Americans on its passenger list of 1,418, had been sunk by a British vessel in an effort to inflame American opinion against Germany.) Kennedy cabled President Roosevelt: "All on board rescued except those killed by explosion. The Admiralty advises me survivors picked up by other ships. List of casualties later. Thank God."

Jack Kennedy was a sophomore at Harvard when his father went to the Court of St. James. During his junior year at college, he went to England for six months to serve as "a glorified office boy" in the American Embassy in London and to see whether he, as in the case of Joe, Jr., might develop an interest in the diplomatic field. This forced him to take six courses in his senior year at Harvard. "I had to work like hell," he said. "I could have coasted, but instead I went to England and then had to take that extra load."

In Berlin, Jack heard the American chargé d'affaires say Germany would go to war within a week. He reported the prediction, which came true, to his father.

His most memorable experience came when his father sent him from London to Glasgow to interview the American survivors of the *Athenia* sinking, authorizing him to announce that the U.S. *Orizaba* would return them to America, and that a neutral yacht might also be used. President Roosevelt had just announced that United States naval convoys would not be provided for returning refugees. This accounted for the angry group which confronted young Kennedy in the lounge of the Beresford Hotel in Glasgow.

"You can't trust the German Navy," one person shouted. "You can't trust the German Government." They reminded Kennedy that ninety destroyers had just been commissioned and that two years earlier the Pacific fleet had been sent to search for Amelia Earhart. (President Roosevelt had defended this action by saying the fleet was on maneuvers.)

"We are still neutral and the neutrality law still holds," Kennedy cut in, adding during the conference that it was better to be on an American ship at that time than on a British vessel, "even if it was accompanied by the whole fleet." Shouted down, he was flatly told that the survivors would definitely not leave without a convoy. That was the message Jack took to his father in London.

On September 3, 1939, Ambassador Kennedy read Chamberlain's speech declaring war two hours before it was delivered. "It's the end of the world," he said. Jack Kennedy was in the House of Commons when the Prime Minister made his speech, as his mother recalled years later.

"When Jack was seventeen, he met the late Franklin Delano Roosevelt and members of his Cabinet, and he met Winston Churchill a year later. He learned firsthand about the history of the New Deal. He was in the House of Commons the day Prime Minister Chamberlain declared war on Germany. At the Embassy he heard war issues discussed at luncheon, on the phone, and among all our friends and prominent people, like Sir Winston Churchill and Sir Anthony Eden. He had heard the issues of government discussed from the time he was a boy, and he toured Soviet Russia when he was twenty in 1937."

The nine Kennedy children returned to their home in Bronxville in relays of three, and Joe and Jack resumed their studies at Harvard. Ambassador Kennedy shuttered the American Embassy and moved to a house in the country, commuting daily in his Chrysler Imperial to confer with members of the British War Cabinet and other officials. He narrowly escaped death when a Nazi bomb fell within three hundred yards of his country house.

Meanwhile, disquieting rumors were drifting back to the White House that Kennedy had assured British conservatives that they could bank on a "safe" man in the White House after 1940. Kennedy himself was reportedly considering running for President in 1940. Writing in *Collier's* magazine in 1939, Henry Pringle said: "Yet there is slight doubt that Joe, despite the political handicaps of his religion, cherishes the hope that he may be President."

Joe Kennedy was in the public eye and was a favored Massachusetts son. He might have run had not Roosevelt decided on a third term. Asked about it, he shook his head: "I'm not a good candidate. I'm no good at going out and asking people to vote for me."

It has been noted that Kennedy had played a prominent role in the New Deal upsurge, "but was not emotionally kin to it," just as he was politically separated from most of his fellow millionaires. By the late 1930s, his disenchantment with the New Deal had set in, and by the end of that decade he and the President had drifted further apart. But when the rumor spread that he would resign, he denied it.

"I cannot forget that I now occupy a post which at this particular time involves matters so precious to the American people that no private considerations should permit my energies or interests to be diverted."

He was glum about the situation in Europe, but felt that no circumstances short of invasion should warrant America's entry into the war. The collapse of France in the spring of 1940 deepened his gloom and made him more of an isolationist than ever. When the Nazis stepped up their bombing in September of that year, Kennedy lauded the "stiff upper lip" of the British people, but doubted that England had either the leadership or resources to withstand the Nazi fury. In October, he returned to the United States and brushed aside any talk about a rift between him and the President by making a radio speech advocating Roosevelt's re-election.

At this time, the President, who was campaigning for a third term, came to Boston, and when his private train pulled into Boston's South Station he had a little reunion with an old friend. In 1953, after he had been elected United States Senator, Jack Kennedy recalled the incident.

"During the closing days of the 1940 campaign, brother Joe and I went with Grampa John F. Fitzgerald to President Roosevelt's train when it arrived in Boston. As we entered, Franklin Delano Roosevelt threw his arms out and said, 'Welcome, Dulce Adelina.' He explained that when he visited South America in the late 1930s he had been surprised to hear a band that was supposed to play the national anthem break into the strains of "Sweet Adeline."

"They told me that some years ago," the President continued, "a distinguished Bostonian traveled through their country singing "Dulce Adelina" at every stop, until finally the people were convinced the song must be America's national anthem."

"And FDR knew the Bostonian was Honey Fitz," Jack Kennedy said. "As long as the President lived, Grampa remained 'Dulce Adelina' to him. The story may not have been entirely true, and perhaps the President was seeking to make an old friend happy, but it was an insight into the enduring regard and affection with which Grampa was held by all who knew him."

During that Boston visit, President Roosevelt told a capacity crowd at Boston Garden how happy he was to "welcome back to the shores of America that Boston boy, beloved by all of Boston and a lot of other places, Ambassador to the Court of St. James, Joe Kennedy." During this speech he said: "And while I am talking to you mothers and fathers, I give you one more assurance. . . . your boys are not going to be sent into any foreign wars."

Despite this lip-service to an illustrious son, the romance between Roosevelt and Kennedy had faded by the fall of 1940. In his book, *Behind the Ballots,* Jim Farley noted that Roosevelt considered Kennedy more British than Walter Hines Page, the American envoy during the first World War, and felt that Kennedy had been taken in by the "British government people and the royal family." Farley added: "As usual, he was critical of Joe, whom he never liked." Once when Farley suggested that Kennedy might return from England to become Secretary of the Treasury, Roosevelt was against it. "I think Henry Morgenthau has tried to carry out my plans in every respect. . . . I couldn't put Joe Kennedy in his place . . . because he would want to run the Treasury in his own way, contrary to my plans and views."

Soon after the Presidential election of 1940, Honey Fitz arranged a news conference at the Ritz-Carlton Hotel in Boston at which his son-in-law was interviewed by three Boston reporters. This session, which the Ambassador had intended to be off-the-record, got him into hot water. One of the newsmen was Louis Lyons of the *Boston Globe,* later curator of the Nieman Fellows at Harvard University. According to Lyons (who took no notes during the interview, an angry Kennedy charged later), Kennedy said, among other things:

"Democracy is finished in England. . . . It's all an economic question. I told the President in the White House last Sunday, 'Don't send me fifty admirals and generals, send me a dozen real economists.' . . . It's all a question of what we do with the next six months. The whole reason for aiding England is to give us time. . . . It isn't that she's fighting for Democracy. That's the bunk. She's fighting for self-preservation, just as we will if it comes to us."

Lyons also had Kennedy saying that if the United States got into the war, we would "be left holding the bag." He planned to see William Randolph Hearst about a campaign to keep America out of the war, he added, going on to mention Sir Winston Churchill's fondness for brandy, and the King's speech impediment. He also said that Queen Elizabeth looked more housewifely than regal in her clothes. In one aside, he had this to say about Eleanor Roosevelt: She is "a wonderful woman, and marvelously helpful and full of sympathy. . . . She bothered us more on our jobs in Washington to take care of the poor little nobodies . . . than all the rest of the people down there put together. She's always sending me a note to have some little Susie Glotz to tea at the Embassy." Charles Lindbergh, who was a leader of the America First isolationist movement, he added, "is not so crazy, either."

Before returning to London, he took a holiday at his Palm Beach home, where the John F. Fitzgeralds were guests on Honey Fitz's seventy-seventh birthday anniversary. Kennedy, in his conference with President Roosevelt at the White House, sensed that his usefulness had ended, for he had become a symbol of appeasement. Late in November he resigned, explaining that as a private citizen he would pledge his efforts to keep the United States out of war.

"I do not want to see this country go to war under any conditions whatsoever unless we are attacked," he said. "England is not fighting our battle. This is not our war." In 1941, he attacked Roosevelt's interventionism, arguing that the United States would be better off for economic reasons under a barter system with a Nazi-conquered Europe than engaged in a total war on the side of Great Britain.

While he served as Ambassador, the British press lauded him for strengthening Anglo-American friendship. "Whether he comes back to us or not," said the *London Times*, "he has earned the respect due to a great American Ambassador who never for a moment mistook the country to which he was accredited for the country of his birth."

When he resigned, he brought home an air-raid siren for his Cape Cod home to summon ashore the Kennedy siblings when they were out in their boats.

In his sudden idleness—if it can be said that the agile-minded Joseph Kennedy is ever idle—he fretted.

"You know," Jack Kennedy remarked to his father's cousin, Joe Kane. "My father is on edge because he hasn't enough to do. He ought to go out and get himself a job."

FDR was not the only Chief Executive to appreciate the Kennedy talent. In 1947, President Truman appointed Joe Kennedy to a Commission on Organization of the Executive Branch of the Federal Government.

It might be noted that the Boston Irish, who had been so anti-British during World War I, were conspicuously loyal during World War II. John Gunther, in *Inside U.S.A.*, suggested that "a personal reason might have been the previous appointment of a home boy, Joe Kennedy, to the Court of St. James, and the splendid war record of his sons, though Kennedy himself was for years an isolationist."

Joe, Jr., shared his father's isolationist views. He had been taught to be an isolationist, as were the other Kennedy children, and he showed he had learned his lesson well in 1940 when he ran as a delegate to the Democratic National Convention to pledge his vote for Jim Farley for President when Roosevelt ran for a third term.

Even when FDR was nominated on the first ballot, Joe stuck with Farley. Earlier frantic third-termers had telephoned Ambassador Kennedy in London, urging him to have his son swing his vote to Roosevelt. "While Kennedy and I were never close friends," wrote Jim Farley in his autobiography, "I am happy to this day that he spurned the suggestion, saying the decision rested with his boy; and I remember that resolute young voice calling, 'James A. Farley' when the Massachusetts delegation was polled."

"I always felt," Rose Kennedy once said, "that if the older children are brought up right, the younger ones will follow their lead. It was easy for all of the children to look up to Joe Junior because he was a good scholar, a good athlete, and popular with girls as well as men in every neighborhood where we lived."

Young Joe had early set a winning pattern for his younger brothers and sisters. In June, 1933, Honey Fitz and Mrs. Fitzgerald were among family members present when Joe received the Choate trophy as the Harvard student who best combined scholarship and sportsmanship during the year at the preparatory school in Connecticut. He won the prize, based on scholarship and athletics, in competition with nine hundred other boys. That year he was also chosen one of twenty young men to take a year's trip around the world on a four-masted schooner that dropped anchor at ports on every continent.

At Harvard, Joe was a big man on campus, a congenial mixer with a ready smile and, according to one observer, with a square, open face radiating Irish charm. He was a pure extrovert, with Honey Fitz's gift of making everyone he met feel like a prince.

Joe, who missed few debutante parties, had one trying week during initiation for the Hasty Pudding Club. For that whole week, he had the same whopping haddock strapped around his waist, and in consequence was unwelcome among the debs.

He and Jack, who had teamed to win the Intercollegiate Sailboating championship off Cape Cod, had dinner often on Sunday with the Fitzgeralds at the Bellevue, and since both were majoring in government at Harvard, they enjoyed talking politics with Grampa Fitzgerald.

"Joe was six feet two and weighed 185 pounds or so," recalls Torbert Macdonald, who was Jack Kennedy's roommate at Harvard for three years. "He was a natural athlete, a good football player, varsity." He had his father's temper, which he unleashed at the proper place at the proper time. Once, in a Harvard dormitory, he leaped out of a chair and swung at a student who had made a snide reference to Honey Fitz, not knowing Joe was his grandson.

After graduating from Harvard in 1938, Joe served as private secretary under Ambassador William Bullitt at the American Embassy in Paris before entering Harvard Law School. In the summer of 1941, he enlisted at the Naval Air Station in Squantum at the age of twenty-six, just before he was to have entered his senior year at Harvard Law School. During basic training he was a Seaman Second Class. Often, when on a weekend pass, he stayed with his grandparents at the Bellevue. In May 1942, he won his wings and an ensign's commission at Jacksonville, Florida, in the presence of his father, who addressed the class. Joe was assigned to active duty with the United States fleet.

He flew heavy bomber patrols for a year in England and had completed his quota of missions when he heard of "Project Anvil," a top secret mission designed to bomb out submarine pens on the Belgian coast. These pens, invulnerable to ordinary bombing, were to be hit from the coast at water level by Joe's plane, which was loaded with explosives. At the last instant, the crew would bail out, and two other planes, by remote control, would zero the ammunition-packed plane onto the target. Before Joe and his crew had a chance to parachute into the English Channel, their plane exploded in mid-air just short of its target.

A month later, the Marquess of Hartington, Captain in the Coldstream Guards, and the son and heir of the Duke of Devonshire, was killed in infantry action in Normandy. The leader in British peerage, he would have inherited five country seats, a London town house, and the finest stables and kennels in the British Empire, and as his Duchess, Kathleen Kennedy, who had married him four months before, would have become first lady in waiting to Queen Elizabeth and Mistress of the Royal Robes. She had met William Cavendish while serving with the American Red Cross in London in 1943. In 1948, Kathleen—the Marchioness of Hartington—was herself killed when her plane crashed on the way to the Riviera. Her tragic death shocked people everywhere, and deeply grieved Honey Fitz and members of her family. In his 1947 Harvard report, Joe Kennedy included these terse notations: "My son-in-law, the Marquess of Hartington, died on September 12, 1944; and my son, Joseph P. Kennedy, Jr., died on August 12, 1944."

In 1945, Jean Kennedy christened a destroyer the *Joseph P. Kennedy, Jr.,* in honor of her brother, and Robert Kennedy, who was to become Attorney General of the United States, left a Naval Officer Training School to serve on the new destroyer as a common seaman. He had the Kennedy courage, too. In one football scrimmage at Harvard he kept playing after breaking a leg in a sideline collision with an equipment wagon.

After the war, Jack Kennedy published essays written by friends of Joe in a privately printed book titled *As We Remember Joe.* "I think," Jack Kennedy wrote in the foreword of the memorial volume, "if the Kennedy children amount to anything . . . it will be due more to Joe's behavior and his constant example than to any other factor."

Joe Senior, as his memorial to his son, set up the Joseph P. Kennedy Foundation.

Nothing came of a proposal by Michael J. Ward, chairman of the

Boston School Committee, to name a school in young Joe's honor. "It was nice seeing you the other day," Joe Kennedy wrote Ward from Hyannisport, "and all the laughs I had were certainly good for my soul. I am sending you young Jack's book about Joe. I am sure you will like it and also I want to thank you for your kind thought and consideration in deciding that at least you would like to have the School Committee name the school after him. It was a nice thought even if it never becomes possible. With my warmest personal regards, Joe."

The Kennedys were cohesive. "Long before it ever became a slogan," Joe Kennedy said, "my family and I had togetherness."

They had more than that. The family has been likened to the Rockefellers. The sons in both families were born to wealth, and in all of them was inculcated a feeling for public service, encouraged in both cases by fathers. Just as the five Rockefeller sons have, over the years, devoted time and money to public projects or government work, so have the Kennedy sons. Although younger, the Kennedys have surpassed the Rockefellers. One is President, another the head of the United States Department of Justice. When Attorney General Robert Kennedy was called the "Number Two" man in Washington, President Jack told him: "You have only one way to go—down."

Joe Senior summed it up one day when listening to a discussion of another vastly wealthy family whose fortune was as large as his, but whose members were involved in conflicting interests.

"Yes," he said, "they do have money—but no *direction*."

Togetherness and a sense of public duty and direction do not fully explain the Kennedys. Also instilled in them is an intense competitive urge and a philosophy of winning.

"Even when we were six and seven years old," said Eunice, "Daddy always entered us in public swimming races, in the different age categories so we didn't have to swim against each other. And he did the same thing with us in sailing races. And if we won, he got terribly enthusiastic. Daddy was always very competitive. The thing he always kept telling us was that coming in second was just no good. The important thing was to win—don't come in second or third—that doesn't count—but win, win, win."

"He could be pretty caustic about it when we lost," Jack Kennedy observed. If one of his children lost a sailing race, Joe Senior would tell him next time to tighten a sail that was too loose, change a faulty hull, find the cause of defeat and eliminate it.

John F. Fitzgerald, Jr., an uncle of Jack's, recalls the latter's performance in the Eastern Seaboard Boating Races off Long Island. "Each of the first two days out he finished last, but on the third day we got this wire: 'Won today. Moved masts two inches last night. Love. Jack.' He could always get quickly to the root of the problem."

"Every single kid," a friend said, "was raised to think, first, what shall I do about this problem? Second, what will Dad say about my solution of it?"

From childhood, the Kennedy children were taught skills. They all went to dancing schools. All were taught to ski, swim, play golf and tennis. And what Robert Sargent Shriver says about his brother-in-law applies to all the Kennedys:

"Jack hates to lose. He learned to play golf, and we play a lot of it now, and he hates to lose at that. He hates to lose at anything. That's the only thing Jack gets really emotional about—when he loses." "Sometimes," Eunice added, "he even gets cross." Even the Kennedy girls have been seen sobbing after losing a tennis match to their brothers. Their mutual love and loyalty never included passive acceptance of defeat.

From childhood, they were also taught to be articulate, rational, coolly analytical and forcible—to be able to harpoon a person they were arguing with with a swift retort. With a rigid family protocol that permitted the boys to speak in the order of their age, while the girls kept quiet, Joe made his children stay on their toes at the dinner table. "He used to needle," a friend recalls. "He would prod those kids, make them think fast on their feet. He would bear down on them and tell them, 'When the going gets tough, the tough get going,' and they listened and learned."

Kennedy Senior brought such distinguished men as Justice William O. Douglas to the dinner table. The conversation was always spirited and sometimes brilliant, but was never permitted to be acrimonious. Only events and ideas were discussed at table.

"Those discussions were never a formal thing," Joe Senior said. "They were informal, never organized debates." Favorite themes were significant personalities who were contemporary makers of history. "It's a natural thing to do," Kennedy said, "to talk about the people you know and the people you read about—but don't forget that I was away a great deal of the time. Their mother had a lot to do with their education. The children would be at the dinner table on a Sunday and Mrs. Kennedy would ask if they knew why the priest was wearing purple vestments instead of black that morning, and she would explain it to them."

In his absence, the children who were old enough would read the "News of the Week in Review" in *The New York Times* and test one another during a leisurely Sunday luncheon. Joe Junior took over as master of ceremonies when his father was away. It was a kind of intellectual gymnastics and made all the Kennedys nimble-witted. Knowledgeable as he was, there were times when Honey Fitz found himself beyond his depth when he visited the Kennedys.

One topic was taboo. Nobody discussed money at the Kennedy table.

Still dogging Joe's footsteps, Jack followed him to Choate School where, after a slow start, he showed a purposefulness that was commended by his father. "After long experience in sizing up people," his father wrote him, "I definitely know you have the goods and you can go a long way. Now aren't you foolish not to get all there is out of what God has given you. . . . It is very difficult to make up fundamentals that you have neglected when you were very young and that is why I am always urging you to do the best you can." Father Kennedy did not demand that Jack turn out to be "a real genius," but predicted he could be "a really worthwhile citizen with good judgment and good understanding."

A pony, a sailboat, or foreign travel was the reward for good grades. When Eddie Moore, after visiting him at Choate, reported him underweight, Jack was promised a dollar for every pound gained, scarcely a powerful inducement to a person who became a millionaire at the age of twelve. When he graduated in 1935 at the age of eighteen, chosen by classmates as the senior "most likely to succeed," he was still light for his height of six feet, but was wiry, if gaunt. Honey Fitz was pleased when friends told him his grandson Jack resembled him.

Choate could count other distinguished alumni, including Chester Bowles and Adlai Stevenson.

An attack of jaundice delayed his enrollment at Princeton, and when there was a recurrence during the Christmas holidays, he dropped out and transferred to Harvard, returning to Boston in 1936, after an absence of almost ten years.

At Harvard, Jack played golf, was backstroke on the varsity swimming team and played junior varsity football. Weighing only 150 pounds, he was too light for the varsity. "He wasn't big enough for the line and he wasn't fast enough to be a back," said Torbert Macdonald. He didn't make the first team, but he stayed on the squad as a freshman and earned his numerals. It was a matter of determination. After practice was over, he'd have me throw the ball for him and he'd practice snagging passes for an hour at a time, hundreds of passes, and he'd practice snagging them. Once he makes up his mind to do something, he does it, and nothing is going to stand in his way."

A week before the varsity swimming meet with Yale, a virus confined Kennedy to Stillman Infirmary. In an effort to regain his strength, he downed malted milks and steaks smuggled in by Macdonald, and sneaked down to the pool to practice, but he never quite made it. Richard Tregaskis of *Guadalcanal Diary* fame, whom he had edged out for a position on the team, swam in his place.

Macdonald, who is the son of a high school athletic director, remembers Jack in college as "a regular guy who never gave a hoot who had money and who didn't." And even in those days he would, like his father, often be caught without a cent in his pocket. He would suggest a top restaurant like Locke-Ober's, only to find at the end of the meal that he had no money with him. Years later a taxi driver recognized Mrs. Joseph Kennedy as a passenger. "Maybe you can pay me that $1.85 your son Jack has owed me for two months," he said. Mrs. Kennedy paid. Her husband often borrowed money from Eddie Moore or Harry Pattison, and settled at the end of the week.

Another time when Joe Kennedy was with a group delivering a million-dollar check to Richard Cardinal Cushing for a hospital building fund, he didn't have enough money in his pocket to pay for the taxi fare. Joe's mind is usually on larger things.

At Harvard, Jack lived in Winthrop House, wrote for the Harvard *Crimson,* made the Hasty Pudding-Institute of 1776, and was "punched" for the "high upper middle" Spee Club. He steered clear of the Harvard Liberal Union and the Young Democrats, but joined the St. Paul's Catholic Club.

In the summer of 1937, he and LeMoyne Billings, his roommate at Choate and Princeton, toured France, Spain, Italy, and Soviet Russia. Jack had an audience with Cardinal Pacelli and the Pope, both friends of his father, who is a Knight of Malta, Grand Knight of the Order of Pius IX, and a Knight of the Equestrian Order of Holy Sepulchre, as well as a member of the Grand Cross Order of Leopold II. While abroad, Jack saw a bullfight, climbed Mt. Vesuvius and won $1.20 playing the tables at Monte Carlo. None of the Kennedys was ever taught to lose much money in gambling.

When he was graduated from Harvard in 1940 with a *cum laude* in political science and a *magna cum laude* on his thesis, his mother and his Fitzgerald grandparents attended Commencement exercises. Ambassador Kennedy cabled him from London: "Two things I always knew about you—one that you are smart and two that you are a swell guy love dad."

He spent the summer at the London School of Economics, as brother

Joe had done before him, studying under the liberal Harold Laski, whom his father had met through Felix Frankfurter. "Dad just wanted us to be exposed to different points of view," he explained, ". . . to see what the other side has to offer." The Ambassador sent his two oldest sons around Europe on various assignments that summer, and they saw history in the making as they wrote reports which were channeled by Ambassador Kennedy to the State Department. Jack Kennedy was only twenty-three when he wrote a best-seller, *Why England Slept,* an expansion of his Harvard thesis, which earned him high honors.

His book, which analyzed England's apathy during the upbuilding of Nazi power, sold 85,000 copies in the United States and England. He turned over his English royalties to help restore bombed Plymouth, used his American profits to buy a car. He wrote the book at the suggestion of Arthur Krock of *The New York Times,* who was impressed because "it clearly stated, and ably and informatively discussed, the . . . current phase of the historic problem of self-governing peoples confronted by mighty and imperialistic autocracies."

At the London School of Economics, he hobnobbed with colonial radicals, Indian civil servants, British Laborites, and refugees from several European countries, and he found the controversial Laski stimulating. He had planned to enter Yale Law School in the fall of 1941, but went into military service instead.

He was rejected by the Army because of an ailing back resulting from a football injury. After months of strengthening exercises, he was accepted by the Navy and assigned to an Intelligence unit that published a news digest for the Navy Chief of Staff in Washington. After Pearl Harbor, with the help of his father, he received a battle assignment, a dull routine at first, since it involved protecting defense factories against bombing. In late 1942, he was transferred to a Motor Torpedo Boat Squadron, operating PT boats at Portsmouth and Newport. By early 1943, he was in the South Pacific, and in March of that year Lieutenant (junior grade) Kennedy was skippering his own PT boat in the Solomons, running a slot off Tulagi and the Russell Islands. By mid-summer, he was a cog in a vast air-sea-ground team counterattacking the Japs in the New Georgia area.

"Shafty," as his crew called him, was daring. He took so many chances, said his squadron commander, "it got so the crew didn't want to go out with him."

Torbert Macdonald, taking Jack's advice, also wound up in a PT boat squadron. "Many's the night I cussed him for it in New Guinea, too," he said.

There were nights Shafty Kennedy would remember, too.

CHAPTER 21

Waiting in the Wings

"It was involuntary. They sank my boat."

—*John F. Kennedy, when asked how he became a hero.*

Iᴎ 1942, when Henry Cabot Lodge, Jr., ran for reelection for the United States Senate, his Rooseveltian hand-picked opponent was Congressman Joseph E. Casey of Clinton, home town of Senator David I. Walsh. Casey, a clever lawyer and politician, was a good orator who during his service in the House was a triple-dyed New Dealer. Joe Kennedy, in an anti-New Deal mood, asked his cousin, Joseph Kane, a veteran politician who had been Peter Tague's secretary, whether he had any good Democrat in mind who might whip Casey.

"Well, your father-in-law isn't too busy at the moment," Kane said. "Why don't you get him to run?"

The old warhorse agreed to throw his Homburg into the ring, although he was pushing eighty. Using ghost-written speeches, he staged a radio campaign, citing rollcalls which Casey had missed and assailing him as a "rubber stamp" of the President. When Congressman Casey mentioned his knowledge of "the horrors of war," Fitzgerald supporters charged that his military duty was confined to ROTC drill on the Boston College campus.

A few days before the primaries, Kane took Kennedy to a Boston advertising agency and showed him a proposed advertising spread. "This will give Honey Fitz the nomination," Kane said.

"I agree," Kennedy said. "But can he lick Lodge?"

Kane shook his head. "No, we can't win."

"And the campaign would cost between two and three hundred thousand?"

"Right."

Joe Kennedy buttoned up his coat collar. "Isn't that nice," he said. "I don't know where you're going, but I'm going back to the Ritz."

HONEY FITZ

Two weeks before the primaries, Kane was in the Kennedy suite at the Ritz-Carlton in Boston when Congressman John W. McCormack phoned from Washington to ask Kennedy to make a speech for Casey. Kennedy refused. Twenty minutes later, according to Kane, President Roosevelt himself telephoned from Washington and made the same request. Kennedy, upset, held his hand over the mouthpiece of the phone. "What shall I say, Joe?" After a quick parley, he told the President he didn't consider it proper for him to take the stump against his father-in-law.

"I quite agree," Roosevelt said. "I've been in politics." He did not press the matter further.

Honey Fitz, showing flashes of his old militant fire, polled 80,000 votes to 108,000 for Casey, while Dan Coakley trailed with 17,000 votes.

It was, nevertheless, a setback for President Roosevelt, for the Lodge forces used tape recordings of Fitzgerald's attacks on Casey with telling effect.

"The next voice you hear will be that of a Democrat, John F. Fitzgerald," a speaker would tell the radio audience, and Honey Fitz's voice would be heard, repeating the pre-primary charges. The scars left in Democratic primaries are usually healed by election day, but Fitzgerald's attacks, along with Coakley's crisp invective against their Democratic opponent, whose chief backer was McCormack, helped Lodge, who tallied 721,239 votes to 641,072 for Casey. Roosevelt placated Casey by giving him a post with the White House secretariat.

"Although I made a lot of trouble for his candidate in the last campaign," Honey Fitz told friends who gathered at the Parker House to honor him on his eighty-first birthday anniversary, "FDR did not open his mouth." Then, referring to a birthday greeting from the President addressed to "Boston's Number One Booster," which began "Dear Honey," he added: "I am glad to get the message. After all, it is a greeting from the President of the United States."

This festive affair, arranged by Mayor Maurice Tobin and Judge Joseph Corbett, was to have been held at the Boston Garden until Honey Fitz demurred. "No, no, no," he told toastmaster Clement Norton. "It must be small and intimate. About three hundred persons, I'd say. And my dear old friend, Charley Adams, must be invited."

It was one of the happiest days in the life of the dean of Massachusetts' politicians, who could look back over a career of sixty-five years of public service. His daughter Rose, who was en route to Egypt, the Holy Land, and Jerusalem (on a previous trip she and Jessica Dragonette, the radio soprano, had been received by the Pope, who gave them an award for their Catholic charitable work), telephoned him from Paris.

At a testimonial a year before, Honey Fitz had said he was worried that his two grandsons who were away at war might say, "That old buck ought to be out here helping us instead of having a hotel birthday party." On that occasion he received the first wristwatch he ever owned, but his most prized gift had come several years earlier from young Joe and Jack Kennedy. It was a silver bonbon dish inscribed: "To Boston's best Mayor, and the next Mayor of Heaven, on his 73rd birthday, from his grandsons, Joe and Jack." Rose had flown in from Bronxville to be with her father and children at that party, which was held at the Bellevue Hotel.

The most dramatic moment at the 1944 testimonial at the Parker House came when Lieutenant John Kennedy walked into the dining room. Still drawn and wan from his bout with malaria, he had flown in from Palm Beach and barely arrived in time for the luncheon because of a storm. Honey Fitz had just rendered the old familiar tune when he turned and saw his grandson walking toward him. Honey Fitz tearfully embraced him while everyone rose and applauded.

"I haven't seen this boy for more than a year," Honey Fitz said, "and he's been through hell since that time."

Most of the guests knew the story. In the wee hours of a moonless August night in 1943, Skipper Fitzgerald was at the wheel of his torpedo boat patrolling Blackett Strait in the Solomon Islands with thirteen other PT boats. Their mission was to intercept Japanese forces that were attacking American transports supplying Allied bases. In the pitch dark, crews of two of the PT boats saw flaming high octane gasoline engulf a patch of water and concluded that "Shafty" Kennedy and his crew were lost. A Japanese destroyer, the *Amagiri,* had cut Kennedy's boat in half, slamming him onto the deck, another jar for his chronically ailing back. Two crew members were instantly killed. And, as Kennedy fell, he told himself, "This is how it feels to be killed."

Patrick H. McMahon of San Francisco, an engineer who had been below decks, crawled over the side into the blazing water and was painfully burned. Despite acute pain, Kennedy rescued him and William J. Johnson of Dorchester, Massachusetts. Stripping down to his underwear, Kennedy, with the strap of McMahon's lifejacket clamped in his teeth, towed him for five hours to an island, swimming quietly through the shark-infested and reef-studded waters off Ferguson Passage. Jack's Harvard swimming coach called it his blue ribbon performance. The eleven survivors endured a week of torture. "McMahon's a terrific guy," Kennedy recalled. "It was something which really got you, seeing old Mac lie there."

For five days, they slept and shivered through tropical rain storms, shook with fever and fought off delirium. They almost passed out after upchucking coconut milk. One night Kennedy, searching for help, was swept around the island by a current. On the fifth day, he and Ensign George Ross swam to a neighboring island, where they found food and friendly natives. Kennedy used a knife to scratch a message on a coconut shell: "Eleven alive native knows posit and reefs Nauru Island Kennedy."

The natives paddled off in a pirogue, the same kind of dugout canoe Kennedy and Ross capsized on the sixth day while trying to flag patrolling torpedo boats. Natives who brought word of a rescue mission found them bleeding from cuts on a jagged reef. Seven days after the accident, hiding under palm fronds as they lay in their boats, they were back at their base on Rendova in the Solomon Islands, where the Catholic chaplain had said a Requiem Mass in memory of the missing men.

Honey Fitz, then, was understandably moved when he saw his grandson approaching him. He also had a warm welcome for McMahon and Johnson, who came in with Kennedy.

Honey Fitz told the guests that Joe Kennedy, informed that his son was missing in action, had kept the news from his family. "I was so sure that he would be saved somehow," Kennedy said, "and that he was alive somewhere, I decided to withhold the information from Mrs. Kennedy and the others. She knew nothing about the bad news until I received the good news of the boy's rescue from the coral island."

Kohei Hanami, who commanded the destroyer that sliced the PT boat, later said: "It stuns me to think how close we came to destroying the new President of the United States, John F. Kennedy, one bleak night in the Pacific. I saw the enemy ship break in two with a tremendous roar." Hanami's ship was soon thereafter sunk by an Allied torpedo off Borneo. The seventeen survivors cabled their congratulations to Kennedy on his election as President.

Lieutenant Kennedy had refused to be sent home until he was too weak from malaria to carry on. After a back operation, he was released. In June 1943, he received the Purple Heart and the Navy and Marine Corps Medal for his "courage, endurance and excellent leadership." Asked later how he became a war hero, he said: "It was involuntary. They sank my boat." At the Parker House testimonial, Uncle Thomas A. Fitzgerald, son of Honey Fitz, teased him about driving safely all over the country as a youth, then getting "run over" while skippering a PT boat in the South Pacific.

Honey Fitz's anniversary was gay. Jack Kennedy told of an experience he had had in London with his grandfather years before. With Honey Fitz sitting beside him in a small English car, he was driving on the left side of the street near Buckingham Palace. "Following Grampa Fitzgerald's instructions, I narrowly missed having an accident and was promptly hailed by a British police officer who told me I had just missed killing the Duke of Gloucester, and that I would have to go with him to the station. Just then the officer looked over and smiled. 'Hello, John F.,' he said. And the traffic violation was immediately forgotten."

Honey Fitz beamed, delighted by another reminder that he was a celebrity everywhere he went. In Massachusetts one night, when Torbert Macdonald was driving Honey Fitz home from Hyannisport to the Bellevue, a police officer flagged him to the curb, and was about to book him for speeding when he recognized the passenger. "Why it's you, Mayor," he said, cheerily waving them on.

At the testimonial, Charles Francis Adams again reviewed his long association with Fitzgerald, noting that their fifty years of friendship had endured many differences of opinion. "I love John F. Fitzgerald," he said. At least one Brahmin and one Irishman had become genuine friends.

Schoolchildren from Roxbury and the North End serenaded Honey Fitz with songs especially written for the occasion. He was touched particularly by a tribute from pupils of the Michelangelo School in the heart of his dear old North End: "We will pattern our lives after yours and strive to imitate your love and devotion to your city, country, and God, so that, in years to come, we will be known as disciples of the truly great John F. Fitzgerald, who held service to mankind tantamount to a life of usefulness."

There was still rain in Honey Fitz's eyes when Joe Cronin, manager of the Boston Red Sox, in a tribute to the city's most vocal and eloquent Royal Rooter whose rendition of "Tessie," the fighting song of Boston baseball teams many years ago, used to thrill crowds, presented him with a baseball bat: "I'm tired of pinch-hitting," Cronin said. "You carry on."

It was a grand occasion for The Little General, who, earlier in the month, had been confined in a Dorchester hospital as a result of an attack of rheumatism. Later he spent several weeks in a hospital in Hyannisport. The engine was finally beginning to run down.

In his annual interview with reporters, he sounded off again about conservative Boston financiers who had driven the Joe Kennedys from the Bay State. Glenn Martin, he said, left Boston to go to Baltimore, where he hired a huge work force. The Fisher Brothers, "who got their start on the slope of Beacon Hill," went to Detroit for the same reason—lack of

HONEY FITZ

venture capital—as did Henry Kaiser, who went to the West Coast. (He was once with the Warren Brothers Contracting Company in Boston.)

"When the horse-and-buggy age was turning into an era of the automobile, State Street bankers bowed me down with their eyebrows for suggesting that financial backing be provided so the buggy makers of Amesbury, Boston, and Newburyport could make automobile bodies. And so the manufacturers went elsewhere."

From his Bellevue suite, he peered over downtown Boston, motioning toward a G.I. slogging through the snow. "They are coming back. Back to what? What kind of job? I want veterans in the Port Authority. I want veterans to have every chance to pitch in and restore the prestige and prosperity of their native city."

He couldn't keep up with Joe Kennedy's latest activities, he told the reporters. In 1943, Kennedy backed a Broadway show, "Another Love Story," and bought an interest in the Hialeah Race Track in Florida. Joe Kennedy might buy a race track, but he would never lose a fortune at the betting windows. One afternoon when he was at Suffolk Downs with a state senator, who limited each bet to $5, Joe Kennedy bought his few tickets at the $2 window.

Kennedy was soon to sell the Somerset Company, the liquor importing firm which gave him exclusive importing rights for Haig and Haig Scotch, Ron Rico Rum, and Gordon's Gin. That venture netted him another fortune. Over the years he had collected honors as well as money. Although his own alma mater had never seen fit to give him an honorary degree, he had received honorary doctorates from the National University of Ireland, the Universities of Edinburgh, Manchester, Liverpool, Bristol, and Cambridge, Notre Dame, and Catholic University of Washington. In 1943, Oglethorpe University, in Atlanta Georgia, which had given him an honorary Doctor of Law's degree the year before, awarded him the President's Medal. Joe Kennedy had long since arrived, and other Kennedy's were on their way.

And like Joe Kennedy, Honey Fitz couldn't wait for Jack Kennedy to get started in politics.

CHAPTER 22

Enroute to Pennsylvania Avenue

"We all like politics, but Joe seemed a natural to run for office. Obviously, you can't have a whole mess of Kennedys asking for votes. So when Joe was denied his chance, I wanted to run and was glad I could."

—JOHN FITZGERALD KENNEDY

IN his book, *I'm For Roosevelt,* written in 1936, Joe Kennedy wrote: "I have no political ambitions for myself or my children, and I put down these few thoughts about our President, conscious only of my concern as a father for the future of his family and my anxiety as a citizen that the facts about the President's philosophy be not lost in a fog of unworthy emotions."

"Woe unto the man who does not change his mind at least three times a day," said Renan, the French philosopher.

Joe Kennedy was intelligent enough to change his mind. In the August 1957 issue of *McCall's* magazine, he is thus quoted: "I got Jack into politics. I was the one. I told him Joe was dead and therefore it was his responsibility to run for Congress. He didn't want to. He felt he didn't have the ability and he still feels that way. But I told him he had to."

By 1945, Jack Kennedy was seriously considering switching from a literary to a political career, and the very person who had stymied the career of Honey Fitz gave him just the opening he needed. It was the Purple Shamrock, who in 1945 was still getting hurrahs. It was James Michael Curley.

After Curley had forced him from the 1913 mayoral race, Honey Fitz, although he would make several more bids for elective office, was through at the age of fifty. In 1945, Curley was elected Mayor of Boston for the fourth time, and his success had a direct impact on John F. Kennedy.

In 1945, Joe Kennedy, Honey Fitz and Joe Kane were mulling over the political prospects of the young Navy hero while he took a journalistic assignment. Early in 1945, he had covered the founding of the United Nations in San Francisco for the Hearst newspapers from a "GI point of view." Jack Kennedy was no pink and pearly optimist: "The world organization that will come out of San Francisco," he wrote, "will be the product of the same passions and selfishness that produced the Treaty of Versailles."

He also chronicled President Truman's role in the Potsdam conference and the significance of elections in England. For years Jack had been considering a career in journalism and literature, and his father's long association with William Randolph Hearst made it easy for him to get started with the *New York Journal-American*. Journalism was a suitable apprenticeship for an aspiring author who had already written one best-seller, and who would later write another—*Profiles in Courage*.

"In all our bull sessions, we assumed that Jack would be a writer and that I'd be a lawyer," Torbert Macdonald recalls. "If anyone had said he'd become a senator from Massachusetts and that I'd be a congressman, we would have laughed him out of the room."

Just as Honey Fitz had so often done, Jack dropped into the editorial offices of Boston newspapers, while turning his wide reading to good use by writing book reviews for the *Boston Globe*. Among books he reviewed were *More Lives Than One,* by Robert Douglas Skidmore (in November 1945) and, a short time later, Keith Wheeler's *We Are Wounded.* One morning he dropped in for a chat with Frank Buxton, editor of the *Boston Herald*. Buxton, besides being a top editor, could turn a skillful phrase and was an omniverous reader. He handed Kennedy a book titled *Lectures on the Relation Between Law and Public Opinion During The 19th Century*.

"Mr. Kennedy," he said, "why don't you write something along the lines of this A .V. Dicey book?"

Kennedy jotted down the reference.

In 1944, after a vertebra had been replaced with a metal disc in the Chelsea Naval Hospital, Kennedy summered in Hyannisport, where, one August night, two Navy chaplains brought word that his brother Joe had been killed in action over the English Channel on August 12. Until then he, like his father, had felt that Joe was the political white hope of the family, and he often voiced this thought later: "If Joe were alive," he once said, "I wouldn't be in this. I'm only trying to fill his shoes." Another time he went into more detail: "Just as I went into politics because Joe died, if anything happened to me tomorrow, Bobby would run for my seat in the Senate. And if Bobby died, our young brother Teddy would take over for him." His father later admitted that Jack "had more universal appeal" than brother Joe.

During his convalescence Jack read several books a week—some fiction, but mostly books on government and war. To improve his read:ng speed, he later took a night course in Baltimore—with some Bromo-Seltzer salesmen—according to Eric Sevareid.

Politics was in his blood, and on his many tours with Grampa Fitz-gerald and visits with Grampa Kennedy, he caught intimate glimpses of the fascinating Boston Irish version. Honey Fitz had spent hours talking to him about the political picture in the Bay State, and they were often together at the Bellevue in 1945 and 1946. One day Jack, on the way back to the hotel, lost his dog in the downtown traffic.

"Don't worry," Honey Fitz said. "I'll get the dog back for you."

After touring the downtown area in a cab in ever-widening circles, it occurred to Honey Fitz that a dog might seek a more pastoral setting. He was right. He found the dog in the Public Garden. A woman, who had it on a leash, told him she had found it roaming around a pond, and was on her way with it to the Animal Rescue League when Honey Fitz ran into her.

Honey Fitz primed his grandson for his political debut in 1946. The first thought was to have him run for Lieutenant-Governor when Paul Dever ran for Governor. Joe Kane, whose mother was a sister of Joe Kennedy's father, suggested this, but Dever, who conceded that Jack Ken-nedy was "the first Irish Brahmin," also called him "a lousy Democrat." Dever doubted that he had the common touch needed to be a winning politician in Boston's swing-the-shilleleagh brand of politics. James Michael Curley was more astute. "With those two names—Fitzgerald and Kennedy—how can he miss?"

Boston politics had changed, of course, since the days of Pat Kennedy and Honey Fitz. The Irish having routed the Yankees were being pressed by other nationalities, including Slavs, Poles, Jews—and espe-cially Italians. The new immigrants were going through the familiar up-swing pattern, moving from ditch and dock to semi-skilled jobs, and then on to better things, including college, in preparation for teaching or pro-fessional careers. They resented the treatment they received from the Irish, the former drawers of water and hewers of wood who were only one or two generations removed from the land.

HONEY FITZ

Honey Fitz had always been deft enough to give the Italians and other ethnic groups the impression that he was their great and good friend, but there are old-timers in the North End heartland of the Dearos, who remember that he, like other Irish chieftains, had tried to keep them down. Early in his career, Honey Fitz had been charged with being anti-Semitic. He was said to have been instrumental in keeping President Wilson from naming Boston's Louis D. Brandeis to his Cabinet.

Fitzgerald and his cohorts reacted to the new group just as the Yankees had reacted to the immigrant Irish. It was further noted that the Italian, French and Polish Catholics were never so warmly treated by Cardinal O'Connell as were the Catholic Irish.

By the 1920s, the loose coalition of Irish, Italians and other immigrants had fallen apart, partly because Woodrow Wilson's foreign policy had alienated immigrant groups, partly because Republican Yankees catered to Jews and Italians in an effort to curb the power of the Irish. In any event, beginning in the 1920s, the Irish had to share political power with other blocs, including Yankees. The popularity of Ely, Saltonstall, and Lodge was evidence of this.

David I. Walsh, even as far back as when he ran for Governor in 1914, had been supported by Harvard President Emeritus Charles W. Eliot, though he was running against such Proper Bostonians as Charles Sumner Bird and Augustus Peabody Gardner, son-in-law of Lodge. This triumph ended the old tradition that no Catholic could be elected Governor of Massachusetts.

Said Eliot at the time: "I cast my ballot at the recent election for Mr. Walsh. The fact he is a Roman Catholic should not interfere with my ballot. I voted for Mr. Walsh because only through him could I express my opinion. Neither do I think this changed condition in the personnel of the government is going to be influential in the future otherwise than for good. Indeed, today, this Puritanical state is said to be Roman Catholic in religion. What a marvelous change from the days of our Puritan and Pilgrim forefathers! This religious transformation, due to the change of peoples, is the greatest transformation of Puritan Massachusetts and New England."

Al Smith and the depression combined to return a powerful Democratic tide in the Bay State, and throughout the 1930s the political messiahs were Curley, Tobin, John W. McCormack (who succeeded George Holden Tinkham in Congress), and Paul Dever, all Irish. But by 1945, when Jack Kennedy became interested in politics, Boston politics was mightily affected by the feuds between the Irish and Italians, and there were other variables in the political equation, as John Gunther noted in *Inside U.S.A.:*

"Nothing could more sharply reveal the antipodal poles in Massachusetts public life than the 1946 gubernatorial race between Maurice J. Tobin, the incumbent, and Lieutenant-Governor Robert Fiske Bradford. From the point of view of background, and though the two men are good friends, this was, among much else, a straight-out struggle between the Catholic Irish and the Brahmins of Beacon Hill. Bradford won."

Bradford's progenitor, William Bradford, had filled the Governor's chair in the Pilgrim Colony of Plymouth in 1621.

Jack Kennedy had to build a personal machine to win. He had a simple explanation for his decision to run for Congress: "My brother was killed and Curley stepped out, and there it was, a matter of events, and so I ran for Congress."

Jack Kennedy was too young, some said. Rose Kennedy pointed out that her father, Honey Fitz, had been elected to the City Council when he was twenty-eight and had been one of the youngest members of Congress. "My husband was the youngest bank president in the world when we were married," she added. Honey Fitz considered the age of twenty-nine ideal for a beginning politician.

Primary elections in Boston in 1946 were still marked by neighborhood vendettas and petty bargaining among street corner Boss Tweeds who promised bloc votes for coin of the realm. Crude comedy, mudslinging and ethnic rivalries added to the confusion. The 1946 primaries in Massachusetts differed in one respect: they were held in June rather than in September so ballots could be sent overseas. Kennedy's cause was aided by the fact that school was still in session.

He set up headquarters in his suite at the Bellevue down the corridor from his grandparents' suite. The Bellevue is known in Boston as "the political nineteenth hole, hiring hall, auction block." On the floor below Honey Fitz's quarters, the Democratic State Committee maintained a suite.

Sister Eunice handled the telephone in Jack's suite, and the chief strategist was Joe Kane, the very gentleman who had masterminded the coup that unseated Congressman Fitzgerald in 1919. Kane, a back-room campaigner who knows all the tricks of Boston politics, is known among the "pros" as one of the most cynical of politicians.

"In politics," he told Kennedy, "you have no friends, only co-conspirators." (Later Jack Kennedy paraphrased this dictum: "In politics you have no friends, only allies.") During the preliminary stage of the contest, Kane was impatient with Fitzgerald's meddling. When he crashed one skull session, Jack was shocked when Kane motioned toward Honey Fitz. "Get that sonofabitch out of here!" Kane said. Joe Kennedy congratulated his son for being able to get along so harmoniously with Kane. "I didn't think you'd last three hours with him," he said.

Truth underlies the legend that Joe Kennedy's money speaks with authority in political campaigns. At a Gridiron Dinner in Washington in 1958, Jack Kennedy read a message allegedly sent from his father who was at his Riviera villa.

"I have just received the following wire from my generous daddy," Jack quipped. "It says, 'Dear Jack, don't buy a single vote more than is necessary. I'll be damned if I'm going to pay for a landslide.'"

Successful elections do cost money, of course. According to Joe Kane, Joe Kennedy was used to paying for what he got, adding that there was a resemblance between war and politics. "It takes three things to win. The first is money and the second is money and the third is money."

The Kennedy command post at the Bellevue was overrun with family members, uniformed and ununiformed veterans of the Army and Navy, prep school and college friends of the various Kennedys, obscure district leaders, old friends of Joe Kennedy's early days in East Boston and machine politicians. Brother Robert Kennedy took over wards in East Cambridge, assisted by Torbert Macdonald and LeMoyne Billings, who wondered what a Republican from Pittsburgh was doing helping a Democrat from Boston. Billings later became a Democrat.

Names that have since become well known belong to some young brain trusters, including John Droney of Cambridge, David Powers of Charlestown, William Kelly of East Boston, Timothy Reardon of Somerville and Mark Dalton and Francis X. Morrissey of Boston. One volunteer was George Taylor, who had taken care of young Joe Kennedy's wardrobe at Harvard. Although his card read "gentleman's gentleman," he was a contract tailor, not a valet, as has been alleged. To each worker, according to his ability or influence, a specific assignment was given. One young Harvardian offered to raise money for the campaign fund.

"No," Jack said. "One reason many of them are supporting me is because they think I have money."

Jack Kennedy was a long step from the old-time cigar-chomping, loud, paunchy Boston "poll." As thin as an old-fashioned riding whip, and still yellow from an attack of malaria, he was reserved and courteous, but he quickly learned under the Kane-Fitzgerald-Joe Kennedy tutelage to shake hands with, and smile at, every voter he met in the district.

"Hello," he would say, extending his hand. "My name is Jack Kennedy. I'm running for Congress."

After his friend, David Powers, arranged hundreds of house parties for him, Jack climbed creaking tenement stairs to knock on back doors and sat down in kitchens with voters from every ethnic strata. Powers rightly contended that more votes could be collected in kitchens than parlors. Jack went into alleys, barrooms, fruit stores and tiny delicatessens, and kept up a whirlwind schedule of the kind Grampa Fitzgerald had introduced to Boston.

"I never thought Jack had it in him," his father said.

A less perceptive candidate might have felt handicapped when campaigning in slums where everyone knew he was a Harvard millionaire. He had the kind of background that would have been grist to the Curley mill in sections of the district. Harvard had always been a favorite target of Irish politicians in Boston. When Republicans in the Legislature tried to tax churches, Irish Democrats added an amendment to the bill that Harvard be taxed also. In Boston, the traditionally successful politician had usually been the poor lad who rose like a kite against the Yankee wind.

At one big outing during the campaign, Kennedy, awaiting his turn to speak, heard various candidates described as worthy servants of the people who "came up the hard way." Jack, fumbling with his tie, rose to speak. "I'm the one who didn't come up the hard way," he said. The crowd loved it.

"Lincoln made fun of his face," Rowland Evans, Jr., wrote in the *Saturday Evening Post* in 1961. "Jack Kennedy's political liabilities were not homeliness, but youth, money, a powerful and controversial father, and religion. Kennedy is cool, detached and often spontaneous when making fun of his liabilities. He makes fun of himself (sometimes) and of others (often) with a flash of natural Irish wit that bubbles near the surface." His fondness for teasing, Evans added, "sharpened by the example of his quick-witted father and brightened by his mother's gentler humor, makes political fun-poking as natural for him as breathing." The "touch of blarney" Evans mentioned was a straight hand-me-down from Honey Fitz.

Kennedy's chief opponent was former Mayor Michael Neville of Cambridge, who was aided by William McMasters, Honey Fitz's publicity director in the Storrow contest. The field also included Joseph Lee, son of the member of the Good Government Association during the early mayoral days of Fitzgerald, and Catherine Falvey of Somerville, a WAC major who tried to stir the hearts of voters by wearing a resplendent white dress at rallies.

Joe Kane paid one candidate $7500 "to stay in or get out," depending on how the campaign shaped up, and when Joseph Russo, a potentially strong vote-getter (he was a veteran member of the City Council) entered the contest, Kane put in another Joseph Russo to cut into his vote. In all there were ten candidates.

Since Kennedy had no political record, the oposition attacked his respectable background. His sister, Kathleen, said one opponent, married a descendant of Oliver Cromwell, despised by every loyal son of Mayo and Galway. The Irish were reminded that the "Curse of Cromwell" referred to his ghoulish campaign in Ireland which wiped out hundreds of Irishmen in the Massacre of Drogheda, including soldiers, priests, women, and children who had already surrendered.

"It hath pleased God to bless our endeavors at Tredah," Cromwell said of the massacre.

Although Cromwell was not related to Lady Hartington, it made a good story.

Kennedy dropped into several house parties every night—another Fitzgerald tactic. It was a rough routine for Jack, who had to favor his back and at times hobble around on crutches. He mapped some campaign strategy while soaking in a hot tub.

Unknown candidates often have trouble finding suitable rallying places where crowds can be attracted. Joe Kennedy spoke to Mike Ward, "the old pro," who is known in the Bay State as the poor man's Machiavelli, for many a political conspiracy has been hatched in the kitchen and living-room of his modest duplex house in Brighton. Ward operates on the theory that "he who controls the streets of Cairo runs Egypt." "He has no equal when it comes to getting out the vote," said one Boston newspaperman, and it was significant that Jim Farley never failed to consult him when a contest was brewing in Massachusetts.

As chairman of the Boston School Committee in 1946, Ward arranged Home School Association meetings in crowded sections of the congressional district. The first was made in a junior high school in April, 1946. After his talk, Kennedy shook hands with some three hundred persons in the rear of the hall. After two more such meetings—one in East Boston High School, where he could mention his relationship to Pat Kennedy— Kennedy substituted for Ward, who had been asked to address the alumni of Brighton High School, and the Brighton High School Alumni Association became the nucleus of a youth group for Kennedy. Archbishop Cushing—later a Cardinal—introduced Kennedy at parochial school meetings, and the candidate made the usual rounds of Communion or Holy Name breakfasts, Bar Mitzvahs, and patriotic assemblies.

Kennedy campaigned as a liberal Democrat on national issues, lauding the usual run of federal aid programs and New Deal benefits, but he was also introduced to assemblies as a war hero after Joe Kennedy's private poll had shown that crowds were interested in his son's record. The introductory speaker would give highlights, but Jack Kennedy himself minimized his gallantry, telling the story of Patrick McMahon, who "was assigned to PT 109, of which I was in command."

On primary day, he went to the polls with his Fitzgerald grandparents, then went to see a movie, "A Night in Casablanca." When the votes were counted, Honey Fitz hopped onto a table and danced a jig as he led the singing of "Sweet Adeline." Kennedy had almost doubled the vote of runnerup Neville, and glamorous Catherine Falvey pulled up a lame fifth. Kennedy's vigorous campaigning won him forty-three per cent of the total vote.

After the victory celebration, Billy Sullivan, a former assistant attorney general, patted Honey Fitz on the back.

"Congratulations, John F.," he said. "Some day—who knows—young Jack here may be Governor of the Commonwealth."

"Governor?" Honey Fitz smiled. "Some day that young man will be President of the United States."

During the following days, Honey Fitz personally called hundreds of party workers, thanking them for what they "did for Jack."

Kennedy remained cool. "I was elected to the House right after the war because I was the only veteran in the race," he said later.

He invited Ted Reardon to accompany him to Washington.

"But, Jack, I don't know anything about Washington."

"Neither do I. We'll learn."

A Democratic victory in the primaries in the eleventh district is tantamount to election. Kennedy won easily in November.

When he took his seat in the House of Representatives in January, 1947, he looked younger than his twenty-nine years. After stepping out of an elevator he grinned at a colleague. "Well, how do you like that? Some people got into the elevator and asked me for the fourth floor!"

A year later, the Junior Chamber of Commerce picked John F. Kennedy as one of the nation's ten outstanding men (21-36) for his civic responsibility and his efforts in behalf of housing for veterans.

Representative Kennedy ran unopposed in 1948, and in 1950 tallied five times the combined vote of five primary opponents before winning the election easily.

In the interim, he had been involved in an incident which he feared might end his political career.

In February, 1946, soon after he took office as Mayor, Curley was sentenced by a federal court to six to eighteen months in prison after being convicted of using the mails to defraud in war contracts. He was sent to a federal penitentiary in Danbury, Connecticut. Later he spoke of himself as an alumnus of the University of Danbury.

Senator Harry Truman had been chairman of the special committee which unearthed the evidence which brought about his indictment and conviction.

"Those familiar with the Washington Merry-Go-Round," commented a Boston judge, "and with the grafters and shakedown artists who thrive there, will wonder what took Curley to Danbury. There have been few political prosecutions in America, but this indictment, conviction, and imprisonment of Curley was one. No courtier was ever led into the Tower of London on a flimsier pretext than landed Curley in Danbury. His sentence will always be a monument to the bitterness and vindictiveness of the High Priest of the New Deal. Curley wanted a Cabinet post: failing that, he wanted to be Ambassador to Rome; failing that, he said unkind things about the President, and hearing about them, the Administration went into action. Instead of a seat in the Cabinet, Curley got a cell in Danbury."

When President Roosevelt had offered to make Curley Ambassador to Poland, a wag said the President must be anti-Polish. Another quip: "Curley won't accept the post because the Polish Corridor is already paved and no contracts can be let." Soon after declining this assignment, Curley had assailed Roosevelt in harsh terms.

Curley used no end of ruses to avoid being sent to jail. In the spring of 1945, he entered the Naval Hospital, complaining that he had temporarily lost the use of one arm and one leg. He received the last rites of the Church, but was able to run for Mayor that year. When, in June, 1947, the web became tighter, he went to Washington in a wheel chair. "If he goes to jail," his physician said, "I don't think he'll last long."

During the trial. Curley tried to wring mercy from the court by pretending to be suffering from nine serious ailments, including an impending cerebral hemorrhage. His counsel, Joseph Scolponetti, admitted later that just before Curley went before the judge he had provided him with a collar two sizes too large so he would look emaciated.

Boston politicians urged President Truman to pardon Curley, and Congressman John W. McCormack drew up a petition which was signed by influential clergymen and by most political figures of any consequence in Massachusetts with the glaring exception of Senator John Kennedy, who said he favored the petition, but refused to sign it, Curley wrote in his autobiography.

Kennedy was not in favor of the petition. McCormack, on the floor of the House of Representatives, handed him the petition and asked him to sign it.

"Has anyone talked with the President or anything?" Kennedy asked.

"No," McCormack said. "If you don't want to sign it, don't sign it."

"Well, I'm not going to sign it," Kennedy said. What made his decision doubly difficult was the big following Curley had in the Bay State, especially in his old congressional district, which Kennedy was then representing. In a forty-five minute long-distance telephone conversation, Mike Ward, who had called him, warned of the political hazards of failing to sign it. Kennedy, reasoning that Curley's plea for clemency was based on failing health, had checked with the Surgeon General and was told the Mayor was in good health.

Kennedy was visibly upset after his encounter on the floor of the House with McCormack. "Well, I'm dead, now," he told Ted Reardon, when he returned to his Washington office. "I'm politically dead. Finished!"

He mentioned considerations that were involved. He had received more compelling appeals from constituents whose loved ones were in jail, and despite their pathetically sad circumstances, he had to tell them he was unable to help them. "And so," said Reardon, "he just wasn't going to sign this petition for Curley, who should have known better in the first place."

After Curley had been at Danbury for five months, President Truman —the man who in effect had sent him there—commuted his term so that he could have Thanksgiving dinner with his family. "Thanks, dear God," Curley said on hearing the news of his pardon.

Outside his Jamaicaway home, Curley was serenaded by a brass band which played "Hail to the Chief!" a tune usually reserved for the President of the United States. "I come back ten years younger," he said.

Congressman Kennedy weathered this crisis and looked forward to the next step in his political career. The trend in the Bay State was not encouraging in the late 1940s. Henry Cabot Lodge, Jr., who had beaten Curley by 142,000 votes in 1936, had been reelected six years later, and had resigned from the Senate in 1944 for combat duty before returning after the war to whip David I. Walsh. Lodge seemed solidly entrenched in the seat his grandfather had so long occupied years ago.

One encouraging trend for Massachusetts Democrats came in 1948 when Paul A. Dever was elected Governor. By this time Honey Fitz and Jack Kennedy had set 1952 as a target date, when Henry Cabot Lodge, Jr., would be seeking his third term in the U.S. Senate.

CHAPTER 23

The Elder Statesman

"The best thing I ever did is my work for Boston Harbor."

—JOHN F. FITZGERALD

HONEY FITZ was still spruce and dapper when he turned eighty. In his annual birthday communique he said: "The best thing I ever did is my work for Boston Harbor. I have just returned from a 15,000-mile cross-country trip in its interest."

Long after Honey Fitz had been out of active politics, he was still reaching for a goal set during his first term as mayor—a bigger, better, busier Boston. When, in the mid-1950s he arrived late at a dinner of the Boston Veteran Journalists Association at the Parker House, he explained that he had spent much of the day sailing around Boston Harbor, making a survey of possibilities of future growth. And he was in his mid-eighties at the time!

Since his Congressional days, he had tried to make Boston one of the top eastern seaports, as well as a more thriving manufacturing and industrial center. He clamored for new steamship lines to Boston, for better harbor facilities and modern wharves. "Our harbor ought to be used by steamers plying to every port of the world, carrying goods manufactured in New England communities," he said. He was disgusted when part of Commonwealth Pier was turned over to the State Police. "Look what they've done there," he said. "They've put in a shooting gallery."

One specific plan was a line of steamships running from Boston to Galveston, Texas. "The freight would be only one-sixth of what it is by rail, and we should be able to distribute our manufactures all through the West and Southwest cheaper than by St. Louis or Chicago. There isn't any doubt that such a line would pay, but then it would mean competition for ships running from New York to New Orleans and would be treading on the preserves of the New York money trust. So Boston holds off. Another reason why we can't get a million dollars of capital here to build these ships we need so badly is that a company promoted in Massachusetts has to be honestly promoted. The cost of the ships would have to be known and there would be no opportunity for a rake-off in the shape of bonus bonds."

Boston's first Finance Commission had cited Boston's failure to keep pace with rival cities in commerce and industry. "Boston has had more reports and studies made of his dock situation and has done less to improve conditions than most other communities." All this despite the millions that had been invested in a modern Boston pier to attract ocean commerce.

From 1810 until 1840, nearly half the commerce between the United States and China was handled by the Boston house of Bryant and Sturgis. The loss of trade with the Orient stemmed primarily from an Act of the Legislature which taxed all goods sold at auction, and since cargoes from the Far East were marketed at auction, Boston's import trade suffered, and the China trade was deflected to New York. Nevertheless, in the 1840s, according to Charles Francis Adams, Boston had the best steamship and railroad facilities on the seaboard. Then, with the establishment of selling agencies in New York by leading Boston houses, and the opening of the California trade, the commercial leadership passed to New York. The financial center of the great New England manufacturing interests, however, still remained in Boston.

When, in 1839, Boston had been selected by the Cunarders in preference to New York or other seaboard cities as the terminus for their steamship line, the reasons given were the superiority of her harbor and wharf facilities; her nearness to the lower British provinces and convenience of access from them; and the shorter distance of Boston, than any of the other ports, from Europe. Honey Fitz cited these points time and again. "The Pilgrims went ashore at Provincetown because it was the first land they saw," he said.

In an article in the *North American Review* of January, 1868, Boston's commercial shortcomings were nevertheless severely criticized and contrasted with Chicago's energetic development. Charles Francis Adams wrote: "Nature gave that city a beautiful and convenient harbor, and she placidly left Nature to take care of it. At last her citizens began to have a vague idea that the condition of their harbor was not satisfactory—that Nature had grown fickle and was neglecting her duty. By this time the mischief had gone far, and the harbor was rapidly growing unfit for vessels of heavy draught. The truth was, that Nature had made it a purely tidal harbor, owing its existence to the current of no great river, but to a system of interior reservoirs and small rivers combined. Into those great basins, which a century ago covered a water area of 8000 acres, more than seventy million tons of water once poured in each twenty-four hours through a few narrow channels, and then again quickly flowed back to the ocean, reinforced in volume by many freshwater tributaries. The rise and fall of this great volume of water had scoured out these channels, and, if undisturbed, promised forever to keep them clear. This tidal way created Boston, and the whole history of Boston has been one long record of short-sighted abuse of this first gift of Nature."

It was Congressman Fitzgerald who had set machinery in motion which culminated, during his second term as Mayor, in the establishment of the Board of Port Directors, and marked the beginning of the restoration of Boston to her old-time commercial importance. During World War I, however, the Port of Boston suffered from the readjustment of the port and transportation system to meet the demands growing out of our entry into the war. Rate discrimination in favor of other ports drew blasts from Fitzgerald. He groaned as Boston failed to keep pace with New York, Philadelphia and Baltimore, even though it was two hundred miles nearer Europe than New York and four hundred miles nearer than Philadelphia or Baltimore. Boston is also nearer South American ports than any Atlantic or Gulf port except Norfolk and Charleston.

As a result of Fitzgerald's drive, the Directors of the Port of Boston was created in 1911, whose three members supervised the administration and development of the Port. The State appropriated $9,000,000 to develop port facilities. It was a plume in Mayor Fitzgerald's war bonnet.

Over the years, various changes were made in the operation of the port until 1934, when Mayor Mansfield named Fitzgerald a member of the Port Authority to carry on his campaign. The veteran port boomer, Mansfield predicted, would "be a live wire on the board."

"Mr. Fitzgerald," he added, "is practically the father of the idea of a board of this kind and always has been deeply interested in developing the port."

An unpaid job, its chief activity was to get publicity for Boston on a world-wide scale and to get federal appropriations for such projects as dredging channels and getting better railroad and steamship rates. One aim was to eliminate the domination of the Pennsylvania Railroad over New England's transportation facilities. Wherever he was invited to speak, Honey Fitz put in a vigorous plea for his home port with the same drive that had earned him the title of "Boston Johnny" during his Congressional days.

In September, 1934, Honey Fitz postponed a trip to Palm Beach when he heard Senator Robert LaFollette's speech on the St. Lawrence treaty which was coming to a vote in the Senate. He rallied New England forces who opposed passage of the bill. It would ruin Boston, he said, for it "would wipe out millions of dollars in investments made for the past fifty years in the port of Boston. . . . Under this treaty, Lake Michigan, one of the United States' most valuable possessions, would be surrendered to British control without compensation." With his denunciation of the ratification of the Great Lakes-St. Lawrence Treaty, he was, reported a newspaper, "the hit of the day at the annual meeting of port directors from all over the United States." During his speech he paused to sing "Sweet Adeline."

Fitzgerald's grandson Jack took a broad-gauged view of the situation a generation later, when he was the first Massachusetts Senator to vote for the St. Lawrence Seaway. "And if you ask the Seaway people," Theodore Sorensen, an aide, explained, "they'll tell you that Jack's speech was the turning point for the bill. It was also the turning point between Jack as a Massachusetts senator and a national statesman."

His reason for favoring the Seaway was basic; it would benefit the whole country.

In 1940, Honey Fitz complained that New York received ninety per cent of Atlantic seaboard shipping—almost a monopoly. As a result, New York facilities were so clogged that a billion dollars worth of war supplies were ruined before they could be transhipped, he said. "At the insistence of John F. Fitzgerald," *The New York Times* noted, "Congress recommended that shipment of lease-lend and defense materials be distributed as widely as practicable among the numerous and adequate ports of the country."

In 1945, the Boston Port Authority was created and Governor Tobin made Honey Fitz one of its five members. The state appropriated another $15,000,000 for port rehabilitation. Even in these twilight years, Honey Fitz was a dynamo. Finally, when he reached the age of eighty-four, Governor Robert Bradford replaced him, whereupon Secretary of Labor Maurice Tobin and Congressman John McCormack protested, and another voice was heard in Washington.

"There were many years when his was the only voice raised in support of our seaport," said Congressman John Kennedy. "It is regrettable that in this period of great port development, the citizens of the Commonwealth are to be deprived of this experience and the vast wealth of maritime knowledge he had gathered."

Honey Fitz kept his eye on the Washington scene, where his grandson was quietly learning the ropes. "On most House roll calls," wrote Eric Sevareid in his book, *Candidates 1960,* "only a Harvard accent, a handsome face and a slightly bookish air distinguished him from scores of Democrats from the big city machines of the north." Joe Kane dropped in on him two months after Jack began his Congressional career, and was amused when his nephew asked: "Cousin Joe, is it all right to go around here without a hat?"

In 1947, when northern Democrats opposed the Taft-Hartley Law, Kennedy voted against the measure and wrote a minority report in which he said: "If repressive and vindictive labor legislation is enacted at the behest of management, a tide of leftwing reaction will develop which may well destroy our existing business system. At the same time, if labor continues to insist on special privileges and unfair advantage in its relations with management, I have grave doubts as to the future of the trade union movement." Here could be seen the germ of his interest shown later when he served on the Senate committee investigating Teamster Union racketeers.

Honey Fitz and Jack Kennedy had a brief reunion in 1947 when Jack, elected president of the Bunker Hill Court unit of the Knights of Columbus, led a goat in the ceremonial parade, in keeping with tradition.

According to Joe Kane, there had been some talk of running Jack Kennedy for Governor or United States Senator in 1948, but it was agreed that he would benefit by more seasoning in Congress. When Martin Lomasney's old lieutenant, John I. Fitzgerald, opposed Leverett Saltonstall's bid for reelection to the United States Senate, Mike Ward, who occasionally breakfasted with Honey Fitz at the Bellevue Hotel, teased him so much about how John I. was trying to pass himself off as John F., the latter finally swung his support to Saltonstall.

"What do you think of the way John I. is commercializing on your name, John?" Ward asked him one morning. "I understand that a crowd of 12,000 in Springfield last night cheered him when he sang 'Sweet Adeline.' He brought down the house. He'll lick Salty if the voters think he is you."

"That's terrible, terrible," John F. said. "I'll put out a statement that I'm not a candidate."

Congressman Kennedy met Ward at the Bellevue a few days later. "Do me a favor, Mike," he said. "Stop teasing Grampa. You may think it's a laugh, but he really gets upset."

Mike Ward also unsettled Honey Fitz when he told him an old political enemy had been made a Knight of Malta by the Pope. Honey Fitz told Ward he was the last honest mayor Boston had had.

In his last years, still looking forward, Honey Fitz found time to revisit old haunts and chat with politicians in the lobby of the Bellevue. "You don't campaign today the way we used to," he told former Lieutenant Governor Francis Kelly. "You young fellows don't know anything about politics."

"Politics are tougher today than they were in the gaslight era," Kelly said. "Modern candidates have to spend more money because they have to appeal to radio and television audiences, not merely to street-corner crowds. We also have to appeal to women voters."

"Well, what's so hard about that?" Honey Fitz said.

He was still doing favors. "Don't pay them a cent," he told Al Mello, a former prizefighter, when he got him a tavern license. It had been customary for successful applicants for liquor licenses to pay from one to three thousand dollars during the first year.

Mrs. Fitzgerald, as shy and serene as ever, still remained in the background. Nobody believed Honey Fitz when he told of the excitement one afternoon in their Bellevue suite when Mrs. Fitzgerald bid seven spades in a deal that gave every player a dream hand—thirteen cards of the same suit.

Mrs. Fitzgerald laid down her hand before the others could bid. It turned out that the new pack of cards used in the deal had been well shuffled. A contemporary statistician figured that if a hand had been dealt every minute since the Christian era began, such a perfect combination would not have occurred more than once. Honey Fitz saw that the story got into the Boston papers.

He kept up with his reading at the Athenaeum and maintained membership in several social and fraternal organizations. He was eighty-five on his Golden Wedding Anniversary, when the surviving alumni of the Eliot Grammar School he had attended more than sixty years before honored him at a party at Hotel Puritan in Boston.

Honey Fitz found the new world challenging, "and if I were starting out, this would be just my mutton." He pointed out that Goethe, Ben Franklin, and Gladstone had done some of their best work after they had passed the age of eighty.

In his early eighties, Honey Fitz was trim and bristling, with many interests. He recalled pleasant associations with every American President since Ulysses S. Grant, with whom he had shaken hands, he recalled, soon after his graduation from Boston Latin School. The greatest American President in his opinion? Franklin Delano Roosevelt, because "he was for the underdog." Next in line was Woodrow Wilson, whose "humaneness and idealism" he admired.

He still drank a glass of hot water and another of orange juice on arising—always before eight in the morning. Nor had his fondness for sweets lessened. After putting three or four heaping teaspoonfuls of sugar in his tea, he might top off a meal with a bar of chocolate and have an ice-cream soda and a piece of pastry during the afternoon. According to Clement Norton, who saw much of him during his last years, he was especially fond of pistachio ice cream.

"Fitzy met former Congressman George Holden Tinkham about twenty years ago outside the Copley-Plaza Hotel and the Congressman said, 'Come on right in with me now, John, and we'll have a cup of tea.' Tinkham's idea of a cup of tea was to order a double pot with an order of pistachio ice cream. When John F. saw the green ice cream, he asked, 'What the hell is this?' and cautiously tasted the concoction. From that moment, John F. was a confirmed addict to pistachio ice cream. As I look at John F. today in his eighties, with the energy and enthusiasm of a boy, I say to myself, 'Well, the sugar, the sweets, are energy to him,' and perhaps the most remarkable part of it all is that John F. all his life has gone in big for sweets but they have never put excess weight on him. . . . The last time I met him he wanted to race me up Park Street, on Beacon Hill, and started out to run, to prove he was not faking. . . . "

Honey Fitz was still full of advice during his final years. He would complain to the hotel manager if taxis were not immediately available at the front door, and when his daughter, Rose, and members of the family came to the hotel—usually in Mrs. Kennedy's chauffeur-driven Rolls Royce—Honey Fitz would try to have the lobby cleared of loud-talking politicians. One who particularly incensed him was a South Boston politician who used to remove his shoes, pull his hat down over his face, and take a nap on a divan in the lobby until his snores attracted the attention of a bellhop.

In connection with bellhops, there is one story—possibly untrue—that when Honey Fitz came in one night after attending the theatre, a new desk clerk asked his name, whereupon he waspishly said: "Why, Rose, of course. Rose F. Fitzgerald."

It was his annual Christmas custom to give the superintendent of service at the hotel a carton of neckties, handkerchiefs, and gloves to be distributed to the hotel employees. The superintendent of service, who used to carry Jack Kennedy in his arms up to the Fitzgerald suite, one afternoon mentioned to Honey Fitz that his wife was in the hospital. The next time he visited her ward, she was missing. Told she was "gone," he became panicky, but calmed down when he learned that his wife, thanks to a telephone call from Honey Fitz, had been transferred to a private room at no extra expense.

Honey Fitz had lost none of his nimble wit. He was at the top of the Custom House Tower one afternoon when a guide brought up a group of Dutch tourists for a panoramic view of Boston. Fitzgerald greeted them as if they were old friends. "Ladies and gentlemen," he said, "many years ago when I was burgomaster of Boston, the German people were among our best citizens." He was about to go when the embarrassed guide whispered, "Sir, they are Dutch."

Fitzgerald did not bat an eye. "But the Dutch," he said, "were my favorites."

Honey Fitz had been connected with the United States Customs in Boston, and for years had dropped into the Custom House. During the last months of his life, he suddenly lost some of his vitality, and got around less. Most of his associates had passed on, and by 1949, only Curley was left.

In that year, in his last real campaign. Curley lost to former City Clerk John B. Hynes by 31,000 votes. Hynes had fulfilled a pledge made soon after Curley had returned from the "University of Danbury." Curley, who had been met at the railroad station by cheering admirers who escorted him to his home in triumph to the blare of a brass band, had returned to his desk at City Hall where he told reporters later that day that he had done more work in five hours than Johnny Hynes had done in five months. Three months later, Curley privately apologized to Hynes, who had actually kept things in good order in the absence of "the boss." When Hynes said he might oppose him in the next election, Curley answered that he would swamp him by 125,000 votes. On his death bed, after he lapsed into a coma two days before he died, Curley was heard to whisper: "John and Dan—the two best boys I ever had in my office." "Dan," who was at his bedside, is Judge Daniel Gillen, Curley's most loyal friend, and "John" was the Mayor who defeated him.

Honey Fitz's old political enemy was seventy-four when he walked out of City Hall for the last time, having learned that his hurrahs, like Jimmy Walker's cheers, had short echoes. But there was unexpected drama even as he slowly descended the steps of City Hall. When a woman deputy sheriff tried to serve a summons on him, resulting from a suit that followed his issuance of licenses to two drive-in theatres, James Michael did not walk faster. Rather, he sprinted down four flights of stairs and outran the sheriff in a zany race to his car. She later served the summons on a servant at his Jamaica Plain home.

Honey Fitz saw in Curley's decline and fall the end of the boss era. Curley, like himself, had been the mayor of the poor, but in the new order of things, the political advantages gained from attending neighborhood wakes and socials, had dimmed. Both men had given the "little man" security, as the *Boston Herald* noted in its editorial on Curley titled "The Passing of a Prodigy." The *Herald* gave a few typical instances: "A job with the city or a contractor for the father laid off at the plant. A bed and care at the City Hospital for the exhausted mother. A warning to a hounding creditor to lay off. Or just the reassurance of a friend in power. Unless you have been poor and forlorn in a big city, you have no conception of what this means."

That was James Michael Curley, but it could have been John Francis Fitzgerald.

The *Herald* underscored the most significant change that had come over the politics of Boston: "There are a few little people left—the down-and-outers of the missions, the tuberculosis-ridden transients of the South End. But they are not many and they are growing fewer. The city has become a community as it was not in the day of Mr. Curley's prime. There is dignity and opportunity for all. There is no longer the desperate need for recognition by a mayor; there is recognition in State Street, in the Chamber of Commerce, on Beacon Hill. And the Democratic party is no longer an outcast party. It seems to offer the status and security Mr. Curley once represented."

Fitzgerald and Curley gave a needed lift to the underpossessed and the underprivileged, and together they provided Boston with an integration it had lacked when they came upon the scene.

The *Boston Traveler* pointed up the significance of Curley's last defeat. "Today," wrote Alice Burke in November, 1949, "marked the end of a florid and powerful era in American politics, as James Michael Curley, last of the big-city bosses, followed Frank Hague of Jersey City, Boss Crump of Memphis and Big Ed Kelly of Chicago, down to defeat. With the smashing of the Curley machine in Boston went the last vestige of the tight, tough-fibered and sometimes just plain tough organizations that were spawned in the chaos of swift industrial and urban growth, flourished on an open spoils system and ruled most of the nation's major municipalities for a half century."

Curley knew. "They're all gone," he said. "I'm the last of the Mohicans," and there was an aching sadness in his voice that reflected his dis-appointment. He knew the little people no longer needed him. What John F. Kennedy was to say on the passing of Curley applies with the same force to his own grandfather.

"His fabulous and fascinating career of more than half a century re-flected, in many ways, the life and growth of the city he loved. Sometimes stormy, always fascinating, and always to be remembered as an inimitable part of a memorable era."

On October 2, 1950, John Francis Fitzgerald died, and *Time* maga-zine noted the passing of "One of the most colorful figures in the history of Boston politics." At his bedside in the Bellevue suite were his wife and his two sons, John F., Jr., and Thomas A. Fitzgerald. His daughter Rose, who returned from Paris for the funeral, was executrix of his estate. His will, specifying that his wife and two sons would receive part of his estate, added: "I leave no part of my estate to any other relatives of mine, for reasons best known to myself."

Honey Fitz, who had once wistfully confided to a friend that he would like to have a statue erected to his memory in the Public Garden oppo-site that of Edward Everett Hale, would be remembered otherwise. In 1911, the Commissioner of Public Works had named a new city ferry the *John F. Fitzgerald*. There was also the "John F. Fitzgerald Society," and after his death there would be a "John F. Fitzgerald Expressway."

In 1911, when he had a life-sized bust of himself made, the *Boston Post* reported: "Paul Revere, that other famed Dearo, had nothing on Fitz, even if he could ride a horse some. But when the matter of putting the bust in Faneuil Hall came up, it was pointed out that the Art Com-mission was fussy about the adornment of the interior of the Cradle of Liberty. And if a portrait of Mrs. Julia Ward Howe couldn't get by, John, King of the Dearos, hasn't a chance on earth."

Honey Fitz enjoyed the joke.

He did not live to see his grandson upset Henry Cabot Lodge, Jr., in the 1952 senatorial race—a thrilling contest that attracted nation-wide attention. Two grandsons of two well-known grandparents would clash again in another family rematch, when, in 1960, Lodge was the Vice-Presidential candidate on the Republican ticket and Kennedy the Presi-dential candidate on the Democratic. In the 1952 senatorial contest, Curley had refused to support Kennedy, and when Lodge came to call on the Curleys, Mrs. Curley said: "I want you to know that I am not voting against Jack Kennedy. But I also want you to know that I am going to vote for Henry Cabot Lodge." Jack Kennedy found it easier to win without Curley support than did Honey Fitz.

Honey Fitz would have been pleased to know that the bigger, busier and better Boston he had spent a lifetime fighting for, was finally coming into being. In 1961, the *Boston Sunday Globe,* in noting that Boston's tide was coming in, stated: "The community is moving into an era of exciting progress, almost despite itself."

One person responsible is a vice-president of The First National Bank of Boston and president of the Boston Chamber of Commerce—Ephron Catlin—who has encouraged new growth types of industry to come to Boston. Honey Fitz would have liked Catlin, who said:

"Being half-Irish and half-Yankee and from St. Louis, I felt I owed the city something." He sounded like the old platform warrior when he commented on Boston's ancient schism: "We have to get over the idea that we are Irish, Yankees, or Italians . . . or members of various racial groups divided into opposite camps. We're all Bostonians." He said the election of President John Fitzgerald Kennedy had brought about a beneficial change that was lessening class distinctions. That observation, too, would have delighted Honey Fitz.

Ten years after the death of Honey Fitz, Senator John Kennedy visited his grandmother, Mrs. John F. Fitzgerald, then ninety-five, when he was warming up for the fight against Richard Nixon. Mrs. Fitzgerald was summering on Lighthouse Lane in Hyannis. Still remarkably erect, she said to her grandson, in a firm voice: "Don't work too hard. God bless you. I know you will win."

After the election, her son, Tom, with whom she was still living in Dorchester in 1961, remarked: "She was just as excited as the rest of us. She is very thrilled with the result and is proud of her grandson." Tom Fitzgerald, while his uncle John was in the United States Senate, worked as a uniformed toll-gate attendant on the Mystic River Bridge. How the ways of patronage had changed!

The only other surviving children of the John F. Fitzgeralds are Rose Kennedy and John F. Fitzgerald, Jr., who works for Boston Edison.

If Mrs. John F. Fitzgerald, Senior, reaches the century mark, she will receive a special scroll signed by the President of the United States.

"And I hope," she said, "that the President's signature will be John F. Kennedy."

INDEX

Index

Because of the nature of this book, John F. "Honey Fitz" Fitzgerald has not been included in the index.

327